The LAW *on* MEDICINES

Volume 1

A Comprehensive Guide

The LAW on MEDICINES

Volume 1

A Comprehensive Guide

I. H. Harrison
M Pharm, FPS

Lecturer in Clinical Pharmacy,
The Welsh School of Pharmacy,
The University of Wales Institute of Science and Technology
Cardiff, Wales

MTP PRESS LIMITED
a member of the KLUWER ACADEMIC PUBLISHERS GROUP
LANCASTER / BOSTON / THE HAGUE / DORDRECHT

Published in the UK and Europe by
MTP Press Limited
Falcon House
Lancaster, England

British Library Cataloguing in Publication Data

Harrison, I. H.
The law on medicines.
1. Medical laws and legislation—England
I. Title
344.204′41 KD3395

ISBN 0-85200-897-X v.1
ISBN 0-85200-913-5 v.2
ISBN 0-85200-912-7 v.3

Published in the USA by
MTP Press
A division of Kluwer Boston Inc
190 Old Derby Street
Hingham, MA 02043, USA

Library of Congress Cataloging-in-Publication Data

Harrison, I. H. (Ivor H.)
The law on medicines.

Includes index.
Contents: v. 1. A comprehensive guide – v. 2. Licensing and manufacture – v. 3. Distribution and selling.
1. Drugs–Law and legislation–Great Britain.
I. Title. [DNLM: 1. Legislation, Drug–Great Britain.
QV 33 FA1 H319L]
KD3460.H37 1985 344.41′04233 85–23092
ISBN 0-85200-897-X (v.1) 344.1044233
ISBN 0-85200-913-5 (v.2)
ISBN 0-85200-912-7 (v.3)

Phototypesetting by First Page Ltd. Watford, Herts.
Printed by Butler & Tanner Limited, Frome and London

Volume 1

Table of Contents

Preface vii

Foreword xi

Chronological list of statutory instruments xiii

Volumes 2 and 3 Table of Contents xxvi

1 Historical background and introduction 1

2 The administration of the Act 17

3 Medicinal products and other articles 33

4 The licensing system 45

5 Licences and certificates relating to products 65

6 Licences for activities 83

7 Controls over the sale and distribution of medicines 93

8 Wholesale sales 109

9 Retail sale of medicines for human use 115

10 Dispensing medicines 123

11 Sales, supplies and administration by exempted users 137

12 Herbal remedies 149

13 Homoeopathy and similar systems of medicine 155

14 Medicinal products for administration to animals 163

15 Medicated animal feeding stuffs 173

16 The packaging and labelling of medicines 181

17 The quality of medicinal products reaching the consumer 203

18 Promotion of sales of medicinal products 215

19 Advertisements and representations directed to practitioners 227

20 Advertisements directed to the public 235

21 Pharmacies 243

Appendix 1: Definitions of words and phrases used in the Act and subordinate legislation 257

Appendix 2: Recommended warning and advisory labels for dispensed medicines 289

Appendix 3: Code of ethics of the Pharmaceutical Society of Great Britain 295

Appendix 3B: Guide to good dispensing practice 309

Appendix 3C: Guide to the self-assessment of professional practice activites 313

Appendix 4: NHS limited list 327

Index 349

Preface

The Medicines Act 1968 together with its delegated legislation comprehensively controls the manufacture, packaging, labelling, distribution and promotion of medicines for both human and animal use in the United Kingdom. It also controls the import and export of such medicines. It replaced a patchwork of controls which evolved over a century. Since its enactment, more than 150 items of delegated legislation (orders and regulations) have been made under its provisions and about 130 are still operative. The sheer physical bulk of this mass of material causes difficulty, not only in comprehension but also in finding the detail so often required. The situation is exacerbated by the fact that some pieces of legislation have been amended several times.

My principal aim is to provide a reference book which contains all of the provisions of the Act and its various orders, regulations as amended to date. The material is arranged to facilitate the search for detail. In order to assist the reader in finding his way through this maze, Chaper 1 consists of a survey of the situation which existed before the Act came into being, together with a synopsis of the present controls. This should enable the reader to appreciate the changes which have occurred and how the system works. In Volume 1 each chapter consists of a digest of the relevant legal provisions designed to provide in simple language an understanding of the topic and the intentions behind and effects of those provisions. Such a treatment of legal matters inevitably leads to a loss of precision which can be remedied, when necessary, by reference to the original source.

Volumes 2 and 3 are separated into 'divisions' each of which deals with one topic e.g. licensing, packaging and labelling, and sales. Each division contains reprints of the relevant legislative provisions (amended to date) which can be used to amplify and verify the information given in Volume 1. The Act as reprinted takes account of the repeals and amendments made under the Statutes, Orders and Regulations which are listed at the end of this Preface.

Some orders and regulations are 'spent', that is they are no longer of importance, such as those relating to licences of right. These items have not been included.

On the other hand, some medicines are also subject to control under the Misuse of Drugs Act and Regulations. For the sake of completeness such information as is required to comply with the relevant law has been included in Volume 3.

The book is aimed chiefly at persons in the pharmaceutical industry, both within and outside the United Kingdom. It will also be of interest to health care professionals, administrators, lawyers, sociologists and those who are concerned with legal controls to improve the safety, quality and efficacy of medicines both in the developed and the developing world.

Many people have helped in the writing of this book but unfortunately it is not possible to mention them all. The following have generously given considerable help and advice on matters of detailed interpretation of various provisions of the Act and its subordinate legislation; Mr G. Appelbe LlB, MSc, FPS, Head of the Law Department of the Pharmaceutical Society of Great Britain, Mr I Basham and Miss Browning of Animal Health Division of MAFF, Mr Burgham of the Home Office, and Mr R M Saunders of the Medicines Division of the DHSS.

I am grateful to Mr P Russell MPS of the PAGB and Mrs C Kimmons of the ABPI for their help with the chapters on advertising, to Ms F Lee MPharm MPS for her help with the chapter on homoeopathy and to Mr H Carter MRCVS for his help with veterinary matters.

Several of my colleagues at the Welsh School of Pharmacy also deserve my thanks. Professor P Spencer BPharm, PhD, FPS and Professor P Parish MD, FRCGP for their enormous encouragement and support, and Dr D Luscombe, BPharm, PhD, FPS, Dr J Poston BPharm, PhD MPS and Mr P Weedle BPharm MPS for reading parts of the manuscript and making many valuable criticisms and suggestions. Mrs E Nash MLS, UWIST's Law Librarian provided invaluable assistance with the legal sources.

The manuscript was typed by a number of ladies but the bulk of the final draft was prepared by Mrs D Cotton, Miss L Goward, Mrs J Parry, Mrs J Andrews and Miss C Jim. Their care, interest and patience in what must have been a soul destroying task is very gratefully acknowledged.

My special thanks are due to Miss C Hay BPharm, Llb, MPS, Barrister, who very generously read the draft of Volume 1, made numerous helpful comments and suggested many improvements.

I am grateful to Mr D. Lewis OBE, MSc, FPS, Barrister, formerly Secretary and Registrar of the Pharmaceutical Society of Great Britain, for permission to reprint the Society's Code of Ethics, and to the Controller of Her Majesty's Stationery Office for permission to reprint the Medicines Act and the Statutory Instruments.

Mr Martin Lister, my Managing Editor, whose constant good humour, patience and care have my unbounded admiration.

Finally I would like to thank my wife for tolerating the difficulties associated with the writing of a book of this nature, for her never-failing support, and not least, for proof-reading the entire book.

The Medicines Act as reprinted contains the amendments and repeals necessitated by the following:–

The Secretary of State for Social Services Order 1968
Transfer of Functions (Wales) Order 1969
Agriculture Act 1970
Misuse of Drugs Act 1971
Local Government Act 1972
Local Government (Scotland) Act 1973
National Health Service Reorganisation Act 1973
House of Commons Disqualification Act 1975
Northern Ireland Assembly Disqualification Act 1975
National Health Service Act 1977
National Health Service (Scotland) Act 1978
Interpretation Act 1978
Customs and Excise (Management) Act 1979
Nurses, Midwives and Health Visitors Act 1979
Criminal Justice Act 1982
Animal Health and Welfare Act 1984

Cable and Broadcasting Act 1984
Dentists Act 1984
Food Act 1984
The Medicines (Retail Pharmacists – Exemption from Licensing Requirements) Order 1971 No. 1445
The Medicines (Medicines Act 1968 Amendment) Regulations 1975 No. 1169
The Medicines (Medicines Act 1968 Amendment) Regulations 1977 No. 1050
and the corresponding Northern Ireland Orders.

Note
Whilst every care has been taken in the preparation of this book, readers should be aware that only Acts of Parliament and Statutory Instruments have the force of law and that they can only be authoritatively interpreted by the courts.

The author and the publishers have endeavoured to accurately reproduce the legislation reprinted in this book but they can not be held responsible for errors or omissions which may have occurred.

The law as stated in this book is at October 1st 1985.

I. Harrison
Cardiff

Foreword

Legal control over medicines in the United Kingdom has followed a tortuous path over the centuries. Indeed the first English law to control medicines *per se* was enacted by Henry VIII in 1540, apparently because of inter-professional rivalry between physicians and apothecaries; the former accusing the latter of adulterated practice. Subsequent developments in legislation seem to have been enacted on a piecemeal basis and were largely crisis orientated in that they appeared in response to problems like adulteration, to new developments like the emergence of biological products, or to the ever-present danger of charlatans profiting from the gullible public's desire to medicate themselves to better health or virility.

Medicines are not, however, ordinary items of commerce and this fact, together with the requirements for safety, quality and efficacy, are the basic tenets underlying the incorporation of all relevant legislation into The Medicines Act 1968. This is an 'enabling Act' which lays down general policies but leaves implementation to be detailed subsequently via statutory instruments. Consequently almost two decades after its introduction, the Act has become complex, lengthy (8 parts and almost 200 statutory instruments), and with detail that is difficult to digest, assimilate and understand. There is a considerable need for a helping and expert hand to guide the enquirer through its maze of complicated legislation. Indeed the sheer physical bulk of the Act presents problems, not only in understanding the major points of legislation, but even in simply finding the relevant passages in the text.

The expert hand is provided firmly and strongly by Ivor Harrison in the three volumes that comprise this work. I hesitate to use the adjective 'monumental' since this has connotations of rigidity; I prefer to describe the book as a comprehensive, yet readable, guide to the United Kingdom law relating to medicines. That it is eminently readable is not surprising because it is written by an expert teacher who has devoted much of his academic career to teaching pharmaceutical legislation to undergraduate pharmacy students. The volumes are not, however, just undergraduate texts; they go far beyond that objective in that collectively they provide detailed information that will be of immense practical value to all (students, health-care practitioners, administrators, manufacturers, legislators) who wish to learn more about the legal controls to improve the safety, quality and efficacy of medicines. Admittedly, the book deals with United Kingdom law, but there is much within the text and discussion that is strictly relevant to the wider sphere of drug control in other nations, particularly those in the developing world.

It was some years ago that the author extracted the promise from me that I would write this Foreword; I am pleased that the time has now come – indeed it is overdue for this book is sorely needed by all who have recourse to the law on medicines.

Professor P.F. D'Arcy OBE, BPharm, PhD, DSc,
FPS, CChem, FRSC, FPSNI
Department of Pharmacy
The Queen's University of Belfast
Northern Ireland

Chronological List of Statutory Instruments made under the Medicines Acts 1968–71

Title	*S.I.No.*	*Authority*
The Medicines Commission and Committees Regulations 1970	No.746	Sched 1
The Medicines (British Pharmacopoeia Commission) Order 1970	No.1256	Sect.4
The Medicines (Committee on Safety of Medicines) Order 1970	No.1257	Sect.4
The Medicines (Veterinary Products Committee) Order 1970	No.1304	Sect.4
The Medicines (Standard Provisions for Licences and Certificates) Regulations 1971	No.972	Sect. 47(1)
The Medicines (Applications for Product Licences and Clinical Trial and Animal Test Certificates) Regulations 1971	No.973	Sect.18, 36, 129(1)
The Medicines (Applications for Manufacturer's and Wholesale Dealer's Licences) Regulations 1971	No.974	Sects.18, 129(1).
The Medicines (First Appointed Day) Order 1971	No.1153	Sect.16(1)
The Medicines (Exportation of Specified Products for Human Use) Order 1971	No.1198	Sect.49

The Medicines (Control of Substances for Manufacture) Order 1971	No.1200	Sect.105(1a)
The Medicines (Surgical Materials) Order 1971	No.1267	Sect.104(1)
The Medicines (Exportation of Specified Veterinary Products) Order 1971	No.1309	Sect.49
The Medicines (Importation of Medicinal Products for Re-exportation) Order 1971	No.1326	Sect.13(2),(3)
The Medicines (Exemption from Licences) (Food and Cosmetics) Order 1971	No.1410	Sect.15(1)
The Medicines (Retail Pharmacists - Exemptions from Licensing Requirements) Order 1971	No.1445	Sect.15(3)
The Medicines (Exemption from Licences)(Special and Transitional Cases) Order 1971	No.1450	Sects.15, 23(4)
The Medicines (Exemption from Licences) (Wholesale Dealing) Order 1972	No.640	Sect.15(1)
The Medicines Act 1968 (Commencement No.1) Order 1972	No.788	Sect.136(3)
The Medicines (Termination of Transitional Exemptions) (No.1) Order 1972	No.1198	Sects.17, 37(3)
The Medicines (Exemption from Licences) (Manufacture and Assembly Temporary Provisions) Order 1972	No.1199	Sects.15(1), 129(4)
The Medicines (Exemption from Licences) (Special Cases and Miscellaneous Provisions) Order 1972	No.1200	Sects.13(2), 15(1), 23(4), 35(8), 129(4)

The Medicines (Applications for Product Licences and Clinical Trial and Animal Test Certificates) Amendment Regulations 1972	No.1201	Sects.18, 36, 129(1)
The Medicines Act 1968 (Commencement No.2) Order 1972	No.1225	Sect.136(3)
The Medicines (Standard Provisions for Licences and Certificates) Amendment Regulations 1972	No.1226	Sect.47(1)
The Medicines (Data Sheet) Regulations 1972	No.2076	Sects.96(6), 129(1),(5)
The Medicines (Extension to Antimicrobial Substances) Order 1973	No.367	Sect.105(1b),(2)
The Medicines Act 1968 (Commencement No.3) Order 1973	No.1529	Sect.136 (3)
The Medicines (Labelling of Medicated Animal Feeding Stuffs) Regulations 1973	No.1530	Sects.85(1), 86(1), 91(2),(3)
The Medicines (Pharmacies) (Applications for Registration and Fees) Regulations 1973	No.1822	Sects.75(1),(2),76(1) (2),(4),(6)
The Medicines (Pharmacies)(Appointed Day) Order 1973	No.1849	Sect.69(3)
The Medicines Act 1968 (Commencement No.4) Order 1973	No.1851	Sect.136(3),(4)
The Medicines (Exemption from Licences) (Foods and Cosmetics) Amendment Order 1973	No.2079	Sect.15(1)
The Medicines (Exemption from Licences) (Emergency Importation) Order 1974	No.316	Sect.13(2)

The Medicines (Exemption from Licences) (Clinical Trials) Order 1974	No.498	Sects.13(2), 15(1) 35(8)a.
The Medicines (Renewal Applications for Licences and Certificates) Regulations 1974	No.832	Sects.18(1), 36(1)
The Medicines (Termination of Transitional Exemptions) (No.2) Order 1974	No.1149	Sect.17
The Medicines (Exemption from Licences)(Ingredients) Order 1974	No.1150	Sects.13(2), 15(1)
The Medicines (Standard Provisions for Licences and Certificates) Amendment Regulations 1974	No.1523	Sect.47(1)
The Medicines (Advertising of Medicinal Products) Regulations 1975	No.298	Sect.95(1)a,(6)
The Medicines (Dental Filling Substances) Order 1975	No.533	Sect.104(1)
The Medicines (Applications for Product Licences and Clinical Trial and Animal Test Certificates) Amendment Regulations 1975	No.681	Sect.18(1), 36(1)
The Medicines (Termination of Transitional Exemption) (No.3) Order 1975	No.761	Sect.17
The Medicines (Exemption from Licences) (Wholesale Dealing in Confectionery) Order 1975	No.762	Sect.15(1)
The Medicines (Committee on the Review of Medicines) Order 1975	No.1006	Sect.4(1)
The Medicines (Medicines Act 1968 Amendment) Regulations 1975	No.1169	Sect.2(2)*ECA

The Medicines (Advertising of Medicinal Products) (No.2) Regulations 1975	No.1326	Sect.95(3),(6)
The Medicines (Feeding Stuffs Additives) Order 1975	No.1349	Sect.104(1)
The Medicines (Committee on Dental and Surgical Materials) Order 1975	No.1473	Sect.4(1)
The Medicines (Child Safety) Regulations 1975	No.2000	Sects.87(1), 88(1)(2),91 (2)
The Medicines (Feeding Stuffs Limits of Variation) Order 1976	No.31	Sect.117(4),(5)
The Medicines Act 1968 (Commencment No.5) Order 1976	No.74	Sect.136(3)
The Medicines (Pharmacies)(Applications for Registration and Fees) Regulations 1976	No.667	Sects.75(1), 76(1), (2),(6)
The Medicines (Specified Articles and Substances) Order 1976	No.968	Sect.104(1)
The Medicines (Child Safety) Amendment Regulations 1976	No.1643	Sects.87(1), 88(1), (2), 91(2)
The Medicines (Labelling) Regulations 1976	No.1726	Sects.85(1)(4), 86(1), 91(2),(3)
The Medicines (Pharmacies) (Applications for Registration and Fees) Amendment (No.2) Regulation 1976	No.1961	Sect.75(1), 76(1), (2),(6)
The Medicines (Exemption from Licences) (Medicinal Tests on Animals) Order 1977	No.161	Sects.13(2),(3), 15(1),(2), 35(8a),(9)

The Medicines (Renewal Applications for Licences and Certificates) Amendment Regulations 1977	No.180	Sect.18(1)
The Medicines (Importation of Medicinal Products for Re-exportation) Amendment Order 1977	No.640	Sects.13(2),(3) 129(4)
The Medicines (Bal Jivan Chamcho Prohibition) No.2 Order 1977	No.670	Sect.62(1)(a)
The Medicines (Standard Provision for Licences and Certificates) Amendment Regulations 1977	No.675	Sect.47(1)
The Medicines (Labelling) Amendment Regulations 1977	No.996	Sects.85(1),(4) 91(2)(3)
The Medicines (Manufacturer's Undertakings for Imported Products) Regulations 1977	No.1038	Sect.19(3b)
The Medicines (Standard Provisions for Licences and Certificates) Amendment (No.2) Regulations 1977	No.1039	Sect.47(1)
The Medicines (Medicines Act 1968 Amendment) Regulations 1977	No.1050	Sect.2(2)*ECA
The Medicines (Applications for Product Licences and Clinical Trial and Animal Test Certificates) Amendment Regulations 1977	No.1051	Sect.18(1), 36(1)
The Medicines (Applications for Manufacturer's and Wholesale Dealer's Licences) Amendment Regulations 1977	No.1052	Sect.18(1)
The Medicines (Standard Provisions for Licences and Certificates) Amendment (No.3) Regulations 1977	No.1053	Sect.47(1)
The Medicines (Exemption from Licences) (Wholesale Dealing) Order 1977	No.1054	Sect.15(1)

The Medicines (Leaflets) Regulations 1977	No.1055	Sects.86(1), 91(2)
The Medicines Act 1968 (Commencement No.6) Order 1977	No.1068	Sect.136(3)
The Medicines (Certificates of Analysis) Regulations 1977	No.1399	Sects.112(9), 115(7) and Schedule 3
The Medicines (Breathing Gases) Order 1977	No.1488	Sect.130(5)c
The Medicines (Pharmacies) (Applications for Registration and Fees) Amendment (No.2) Regulations 1977	No.2077	Sects.75(1), 76(1), (2),(6)
The Medicines (Pharmacy and General Sale)(Appointed Day) Order 1977	No.2126	Sect.52
The Medicines Act 1968 (Commencement No.7) Order 1977	No.2128	Sect.136(3)(4)
The Medicines (Retail Sale or Supply of Herbal Remedies) Order 1977	No.2130	Sects.56(3), 57(1)
The Medicines (Prohibition of Non-Medicinal Antimicrobial Substances) Order 1977	No.2131	Sect.62
The Medicines (Labelling) Amendment (No.2) Regulations 1977	No.2168	Sects.85(1),(4) 91(2)(3)
The Medicines (Fluted Bottles) Regulations 1978	No.40	Sects.87(1), 91(2),(3), 129(5)
The Medicines (Labelling and Advertising to the Public) Regulations 1978	No.41	Sects.85(1), 86(1) 91(2), 95(1),(2), (3),(5),(6)

The Medicines (Labelling) (Special Transitional) Regulations 1978	No.190	Sects.85(1), 129(5)
The Medicines (Radioactive Substances) Order 1978	No.1004	Sect.104(1)
The Medicines (Committee on Radiation from Radioactive Medicinal Products) Order 1978	No.1005	Sect.4(1)
The Medicines (Administration of Radioactive Substances) Regulations 1978	No.1006	Sect.60; Sect.2(2)*ECA
The Medicines (Advertising to Medical and Dental Practitioners) Regulations 1978	No.1020	Sects.95, 129(5)
The Medicines (Fees) Regulations 1978	No.1121	Sect.1(1) (1971 Act)
The Medicines (Intra-Uterine Contraceptive Devices) (Appointed Day) Order 1978	No.1138	Sect.16(1)
The Medicines (Intra-Uterine Contraceptive Devices) (Amendment to Exemption from Licences) Order 1978	No.1139	Sects.13(2), 15(1) 23(4), 35(8), 129(4)
The Medicines (Licensing of Intra-Uterine Contraceptive Devices) (Miscellaneous Amendments) Regulations 1978	No.1140	Sects.18, 85(1),(4) 86(1),(3), 91(2),(3), 129(1)
The Medicines (Collection and Delivery Arrangements-Exemption) Order 1978	No.1421	Sect.57(1)
The Medicines (Chloroform Prohibition) Order 1979	No.382	Sect.62
The Medicines (Fees) Amendment Regulations 1979	No.899	Sect.1(1) (1971 Act)

The Medicines (Exemption from Licences)(Assembly) Order 1979	No.1114	Sect.15(1),(2)
The Medicines (Phenacetin Prohibition) Order 1979	No.1181	Sect.62
The Medicines (Committee on Dental and Surgical Materials) Amendment Order 1979	No.1535	Sects.4, 129(4)
The Medicines (Contact Lens Fluids and Other Substances) (Appointed Day) Order 1979	No.1539	Sect.16(1)
The Medicines (Contact Lens Fluids and Other Substances) (Exemption from Licences) Order 1979	No.1585	Sects.13(2), 15(1), (2), 23(4), 35(8), 129(4)
The Medicines (Contact Lens Fluids and Other Substances) (Exemption from Licences) Amendment Order 1979	No.1745	Sects.15(1),(2), 129(4)
The Medicines (Contact Lens Fluids and Other Substances) (Labelling) Regulations 1979	No.1759	Sects.85(1), 86(1), 91(2),(3), 129(5)
The Medicines (Contact Lens Fluids and Other Substances) (Advertising and Miscellaneous Amendments) Regulations 1979	No.1760	Sects.18, 36, 95, 96(6), 129(1),(5)
The Medicines (Chloroform Prohibition) Amendment Order 1980	No.263	Sects.62, 129(4)
The Medicines (Fees) Amendment Regulations 1980	No.16	Sect.1(1) (1971 Act)
The Medicines (Fees) Amendment (No.2) Regulations 1980	No.1126	Sect.1(1) (1971 Act)
The Medicines (Intra-Uterine Contraceptive Devices) (Termination of Transitional Exemption) Order 1980	No.1467	Sect.17

The Medicines (Pharmacies) (Applications for Registration and Fees) Amendment Regulations 1980	No.1806	Sects.75(1), 76(1), (2),(6)
The Medicines (Sale or Supply) (Miscellaneous Provisions) Regulations 1980	No.1923	Sects.53(4), 61, 66(1), 67(6), 129(1)
The Medicines (Pharmacy and General Sale-Exemption) Order 1980	No.1924	Sects.55(2b), 57(1), (2), 129(4)
The Medicines (Exemption from Licences)(Clinical Trials) Order 1981	No.164	Sects.15(1),(2), 35(8a),(9)
The Medicines (Data Sheet) Amendment Regulations 1981	No.1633	Sects.96(6), 129(1)
The Medicines (Contact Lens Fluids and Other Substances) (Labelling) Amendment Regulations 1981	No.1689	Sects.85(1),86(1) 91(2),(3), 129(5)
The Medicines (Contact Lens Fluids and Other Substances) (Termination of Transitional Exemptions) Order 1981	No.1690	Sect.17
The Medicines (Pharmacies) (Applications for Registration and Fees) Amendment Regulations 1981	No.1713	Sects.75(1),76(1), (2),(6)
The Medicines (Labelling) Amendment Regulations 1981	No.1791	Sects.85(1), 129(5)
The Medicines (Sale or Supply) (Miscellaneous Provisions) Amendment Regulations 1982	No.28	Sects.53(4),129(1)
The Medicines (Control of Substances for Manufacture) Order 1982	No.425	Sect.105(1)(a)
The Medicines (Stilbenes and Thyrostatic Substances Prohibition) Order 1982	No.518	Sect.62(1),(2)

The Medicines(Stilbenes and Thyrostatic Substances) Regulations 1982	No.626	Sect. 2(2)*ECA
The Medicines (Fees) Amendment Regulations 1982	No.1121	Sect.1(1) (1971 Act)
The Medicines (British Pharmacopoeia Commission) Amendment Order 1982	No.1335	Sects.4, 129(4)
The Medicines (Pharmacies) (Applications for Registration and Fees) Amendment Regulations 1982	No.1719	Sects.75(1), 76(1), (2),(6)
The Medicines (Renewal Applications for Licences and Certificates) Amendment Regulations 1982	No.1789	Sects.18(1), 36(1)
The Medicines (Products Other than Veterinary Drugs) (Prescription Only) Order 1983	No.1212	Sect.58(1),(4), 59, 129(4)
The Medicines (Medicines Act 1968 Amendment) Regulations 1983	No.1724	Sect.2(2)*ECA
The Medicines (Applications for Manufacturer's and Wholesale Dealer's Licences) Amendment Regulations 1983	No.1725	Sect.18(1)
The Medicines (Applications for Product Licences and Clinical Trial and Animal Test Certificates) Amendment Regulations 1983	No.1726	Sect.18(1)
The Medicines (Leaflets for Veterinary Drugs) Regulations 1983	No.1727	Sect.86(1)
The Medicines (Exemption from Licences) (Wholesale Dealing) Amendment Order 1983	No.1728	Sect.15(1)
The Medicines (Labelling) Amendment Regulations 1983	No.1729	Sects.85(1),(4),91(3)

The Medicines (Standard Provisions for Licences and Certificates) Amendment Regulations 1983	No.1730	Sect.47(1)
The Medicines (Fees) Amendment Regulations 1983	No.1731	Sect.1(1) (1971 Act)
The Medicines (Restriction on the Administration of Veterinary Medicinal Products) Regulations 1983	No.1732	Sect.2(2)*ECA
The Medicines (Pharmacies) (Applications for Registration and Fees) Amendment Regulations 1983	No.1787	Sects.75(1), 76(1), (2),(6)
The Medicines (Cyanogenetic Substances) Order 1984	No.187	Sect.104(1)
The Medicines (Exemption from Licences) (Importation) Order 1984	No.673	Sects.13(2),(3), 15(1),(2)
The Medicines (Products Other Than Veterinary Drugs) (Prescription Only) Amendment Order 1984	No.756	Sects.58(1),(4), 129(4)
The Medicines (Veterinary Drugs) (General Sale List) Order 1984	No.768	Sect.51
The Medicines (Products Other Than Veterinary Drugs) (General Sale List) Order 1984	No.769	Sects.51, 129(4)
The Medicines (Committee on Radiation from Radioactive Medicinal Products) (Revocation) Order 1984	No.1261	Sects.4(1),129(6)
The Medicines (Exemptions from Restrictions on the Retail Sale or Supply of Veterinary Drugs) Order 1984	No.1861	Sects.57(1),(2),(2A), 129(4)
The Medicines (Pharmacies) (Applications for Registration and Fees) Amendment Regulations 1984	No.1886	Sects.75(1), 76(1), (2),(6), 129(5)

The Medicines (Animal Feeding Stuffs) (Enforcement) Regulations 1985	No.273	Sects.117(1),(2),(3),(5A)
The Medicines (Exemptions from Restrictions on the Retail Sale or Supply of Veterinary Drugs) (Amendment) Order 1985	No.310	Sects.57(1),(2), 129(4)
The Medicines (Exemptions from Restrictions on the Retail Sale or Supply of Veterinary Drugs) (Amendment) (No.2) Order 1985	No.857	Sects.57(1),(2),(2A) 129(4)
The Medicines (Veterinary Drugs) (Prescription Only) Order 1985	No.1288	Sects.58(1),(4), 129(4)
The Medicines (Control of Substances for Manufacture) Order 1985	No.1403+	Sects.105(1a) and 129(6),(7)
The Medicines (Medicated Animal Feeding Stuffs) Regulations 1985	No.1533+	Sects.40(1),(2),(4) (5) and 129(6)
The Medicines (Control of Substances for Manufacture) (Appointed Day) Order 1985	No.1539+	Sects.16(1) and 129(6)
The Medicines (Products Other than Veterinary Drugs) (General Sales List) Amendment Order 1985	No.1540	Sects.51,129(4)

***ECA = European Communities Act 1972**
+ = not reproduced and discussed in this publication

Volumes 2 and 3

Table of Contents

VOLUME 2

Preface x
Foreword xiii
Chronological List of Statutory Instruments xv

Division 1: Administrative and Miscellaneous Matters

Medicines Act: Part I Administration of the Act 3
Schedule 1 Provisions Relating to Medicines Commission and Committees 6
The Medicines Commission and Committees Regulations 1970 7
The Medicines (British Pharmacopoeia Commission) Order 1970 as amended 10
The Medicines (Committee on Safety of Medicines) Order 1970 11
The Medicines (Veterinary Products Committee) Order 1970 12
The Medicines (Committee on the Review of Medicines Order 1975 13
The Medicines (Committee on Dental and Surgical Materials) Order 1975 as amended 13
The Medicines (Committee on Radiation from Radioactive Medicinal Products) Order 1978 14
Medicines Act: Part VIII Miscellaneous and Supplementary Provisions 15
Medicines Act 1971 47
Schedule 4 Provisions Relating to Northern Ireland 49
The Medicines (Surgical Materials) Order 1971 53
The Medicines (Dental Filling Substances) Order 1975 54
The Medicines (Feeding Stuffs Additives) Order 1975 55
The Medicines (Specified Articles and Substances) Order 1976 57
The Medicines (Radioactive Substances) Order 1978 60
The Medicines (Cyanogenetic Substances) Order 1984 61
The Medicines (Control of Substances for Manufacture) Order 1971 63
The Medicines (Control of Substances for Manufacture) Order 1982 70
The Medicines (Extension to Antimicrobial Substances) Order 1973 72
The Medicines (Breathing Gases) Order 1977 75

Division 2: Licensing Provisions

Part II Licences and Certificates Relating to Medicinal Products 79
Schedule 2 Suspension, Revocation or Variation of Licence 123

The Medicines (Standard Provisions for Licences and Certificates) Regulations 1971 (as amended) 127
Schedule 1 Part I Standard Provisions for Product Licences Including Product Licences of Right 129
Part II: Standard Provisions for Clinical Trial Certificates and Clinical Trial Certificates of Right 133
Part III: Standard Provisions for Animal Test Certificates and Animal Test Certificates of Right 134
Schedule 2 Standard Provisions for Manufacturer's Licences and Manufacturer's Licences of Right 136
Schedule 3 Standard Provisions for Wholesale Dealer's Licences Including Wholsale Dealer's Licences of Right 141
Schedule 4 Part I Standard Provisions for Manufacturer's Licences and Manufacturer's Licences of Right Relating to Vaccines 146
Schedule 4 Part II Standard Provisions for Manufacturer's Licences and Manufacturer's Licences of Right Relating to Smallpox Vaccine 147
Schedule 4 Part III Standard Provisions for Manfacturer's Licences of Right Relating to BCG Vaccine 148
Schedule 4 Part IV Standard Provisions for Manufacturer's Licences and Manufacturer's Licences of Right Relating to Toxins 149
Schedule 4 Part V Standard Provisions for Manufacturer's Licences and Manufacturer's Licences of Right Relating to Sera 149
Schedule 5 Part I Standard Provisions for Product Licences Including Product Licences of Right Relating to Medicinal Products to which Regulation 5 of these Regulations Applies 151
Schedule 5 Part II Tests for Sterility 153
Schedule 5 Part III Tests for Abnormal Toxicity 157
Schedule 5 Part IV Tests for Pyrogens 158
The Medicines (Applications for Product Licences and Clinical Trial and Animal Test Certificates) Regulations 1971 (as amended) 161
Schedule 1 Part I Particulars Required on an Application for the Grant of a Product Licence for a Medicinal Product, Manufactured or Assembled in the UK, or 165
For a substance or article not previously sold or supplied for a medicinal purpose 165
For any other medicinal product, substance or article other than those to which the succeeding parts of this schedule apply 167
Schedule 1 Part II Particulars Required on an Application for the Grant of a Product Licence an Imported Substance or Article not Previously Sold or Supplied for a Medicinal Purpose in the United Kingdom 169
Schedule 1 Part III Particulars Required on an Application for the Grant of a Product Licence to Import a Medicinal Product for Use by the Importer by being Administered to Animals or Incorporated in any Animal Feeding Stuff for a Medicinal Purpose 173
Schedule 1 Part IV Particulars Required on an Application for the Grant of a Product Licence for a Substance or Article Other

than a Medicinal Product Intended for Incorporation in Animal Feeding Stuffs for a Medicinal Purpose 176
Schedule 2 Pariculars Required on an Application for the Issue of a Clinical Trial Certificate 178
Schedule 3 Particulars Required on an Application for the Issue of an Animal Test Certificate 180
The Medicines (Applications for Manufacturer's and Wholesale Dealer's Licences) Regulations 1971 185
of a Manufacturer's Licence 186
Schedule 2 Particulars Required on an Application for the Grant of a Wholesale Dealer's Licence 188
The Medicines (Renewal Applications for Licences and Certificates) Regulations 1974 as Amended 190
The Medicines (Manufacturer's Undertakings for Imported Products) Regulations 1977 196
The Medicines (Importation of Medicinal Products for Re-exporation) Order 1971 as amended 199
Schedule Part I Medicinal Products, Articles and Substances (Other than those Specified in Part II of this Schedule) to the Importation of which Section 7(3) of the Act does not Apply 201
Schedule Part II Medicinal Products and Substances to the Importation of which Section 7(3) of the Act Continues to Apply 201
The Medicines (Exportation of Specified Products for Human Use) Order 1971 202
The Medicines (Exportation of Specified Veterinary Products) Order 1971 203
The Medicines (Exemption from Licences) (Special and Transitional Cases) Order 1971 as amended 205
The Medicines (Exemption from Licences) (Special Cases and Miscellaneous Provisions) Order 1972 as amended 208
The Medicines (Exemption from Licences) (Manufacture and Assembly Temporary Provisions) Order 1972 214
The Medicines (Exemption from Licences) (Assembly) Order 1979 216
The Medicines (Exemption from Licences) (Importation) Order 1984 218
The Medicines (Exemption from Licences) (Emergency Importation) Order 1974 223
The Medicines (Exemption from Licences) (Clinical Trials) Order 1974 224
The Medicines (Exemption from Licences) (Clinical Trials) Order 1981 228
The Medicines (Exemption from Licences) (Medicinal Tests on Animals) Order 1977 233
The Medicines (Exemption from Licences) (Wholesale Dealing) Order 1972 as amended 235
The Medicines (Exemption from Licences) (Wholesale Dealing) Order 1977 as amended 236
The Medicines (Exemption from Licences) (Wholesale Dealing in Confectionery) Order 1975 237
The Medicines (Exemption from Licences) (Foods and Cosmetics) Order 1971 239

Schedule Description of Certain Medicinal Product Foods Which are not Exempt from Licences 241
The Medicines (Exemption from Licences) (Ingredients) Order 1974 242
The Medicines (Contact Lens Fluids and Other Substances) (Exemption from Licences) Order 1979 244
The Medicines (Feeds) Regulations 1978 as amended 247
Schedule 1 Part I Capital and Annual Fees 255
Schedule 1 Part II Medicinal Products, Substances or Articles Subject to Standard Amount Capital Fees for Product Licences 259
Schedule 1 Part III Conditions Attached to Payment of Standard Amount of Capital Fees for Product Licence 259
Schedule 1 Part IV Assessment of Fees 261
Schedule 1 Part V Calculation of Turnover 262
Schedule 1 Part VI Calculation of Annual Fees 264
Schedule 1 Part VII Lesser Amounts of Fees 267
Schedule 2 Types of Medicinal Product for Which Only One Capital Fee is Payable 268
Schedule 3 Circumstances in which Fees may be Refunded, Adjusted or Set-off 269
Schedule 4 Reduction, Waiver or Refund of Fees 270

Division 3 Packaging and Labelling Provisions

Part V Containers, Packages and Identification of Medicinal Products 275
The Medicines (Child Safety) Regulations 1975 279
The Medicines (Fluted Bottles) Regulations 1978 281
The Medicines (Labelling) Regulations 1976 286
Schedule 1 Standard Particulars Required in the Labelling of Containers and Packages 310
Schedule 2 Particulars Required in the Labelling of Containers and Packages of Medicinal Products for Clinical Trials 313
Schedule 3 Particulars Required in the Labelling of Containers and Packages of Medicinal Products for Medicinal Tests on Animals 314
Schedule 4 Particulars Required in the Labelling of Containers and Packages of Medicinal Products for Incorporation in Animal Feeding Stuffs or Which are Medicated Animal Feeding Stuffs 314
Schedule 5 Words and Particulars Required in the Labelling of Containers and Packages of Medicinal Products on a General Sale List 317
Schedule 6 Words and Particulars Required in the Labelling of Containers and Packages of Medicinal Products to Which Section 52 of the Act Applies 318
The Medicines (Contact Lens Fluids and Other Substances) (Labelling) Regulations 1979 as amended 319
The Medicines (Leaflets) Regulations 1977 323
Schedule Particulars Required to be Included in Leaflets 326
The Medicines (Labelling of Medicated Animal Feedings Stuffs) Regulations 1973 327
The Medicines (Leaflets for Veterinary Drugs) Regulations 1983 331
Schedule Particulars Required to be Included in Leaflets 333

Division 4: Sales Promotion

Part VI Promotion of Sales of Medicinal Products 337
The Medicines (Data Sheet) Regulations 1972 as amended 344
Schedule 1 Part I Loose Sheet Data Sheet Requirements 352
Schedule 1 Part II Data Sheet Compendium Requirements 353
Schedule 2 Particulars Required in Data Sheets Relating to Medicinal Products for Human Use 353
Schedule 3 Particulars Required in Data Sheets Relating to Medicinal Products for Use by being Administered to Animals 355
The Medicines (Advertising of Medicinal Products) Regulations 1975 357
The Medicines (Advertising of Medicinal Products) (No.2) Regulations 1975 360
The Medicines (Advertising to Medical and Dental Practitioners) Regulations 1978 363
Schedule 1 Requirements for Advertisements 369
Schedule 2 Particulars to be Contained in, and the Form Required by, Abbreviated Advertisements 370
The Medicines (Labelling and Advertising to the Public) Regulations 1978 371
Schedule 1 Diseases in Respect of Which Advertisements are Prohibited 380
Schedule 2 Part I Infections, Degenerative and Deficiency Conditions for Which Advertisements are Restricted 380
Schedule 2 Part II 381
Schedule 2 Part III 384
Schedule 2 Part IV 386
Schedule 2 Part V Purposes for Which it is Prohibited to Advertise any Medicinal Product to the Public 386
Schedule 3 Warning and Notice Relating to Spermicidal Contraceptives 387
Schedule 4 Words and Phrases the Use of Which is Prohibited in Certain Labelled Containers and Packages and Leaflets 387
Schedule 5 Phrases and Particulars Required to be Included in Certain Labelled Containers and Packages and Leaflets 387
The Medicines (Contact Lens Fluids and other Substances) (Advertising and Miscellaneous Amendments) Regulations 1979 388
Schedule Particulars Required in Information Sheets and Data Sheets 390
Index 393

VOLUME 3

Preface viii
Foreword xi
Chronological List of Statutory Instruments xiii

Division 5: Controls over Sale, Supply and Administration of Medicines

Part III Further Provisions Relating to Dealings with Medicinal Products 3
Provisions as to Sale or Supply of Medicinal Products 3
Exemptions from Sections 52 and 53 5
Additional Provisions 7
Offences, and Provision for Disqualification 16
The Medicines (Collection and Delivery Arrangements – Exemption) Order 1978 19
The Medicines (Sale or Supply) (Miscellaneous Provisons) Regulations 1980 21
Schedule 1 Classes of Person for the Purposes of Regulation 5 27
Schedule 2 Particulars in Pharmacy Records 27
Schedule 3 Pack Sizes for Certain Veterinary Drugs Sold or Supplied by Retail 29
The Medicines (Pharmacy and General Sale-Exemption) Order 1980 31
Schedule 1 Exemptions for Certain Persons from Sections 52 and 53 36
Schedule 2 Exemption for Certain Medicinal Products of High Dilutions 45
The Medicines (Products Other Than Veterinary Drugs (General Sale List) Order 1984 50
Schedule 1 Class of Medicinal Products (Other Than Products the Subject of a Product Licence of Right) on General Sale by Virtue of Article 2(a) 52
Schedule 2 Class of Medicinal Products (the Subject of a Product Licence of Right) on General Sale by Virtue of Article 2(b) 68
Schedule 3 Classes of Medicinal Products Which are not on the General Sale List 107
The Medicines (Retail Sale or Supply of Herbal Remedies) Order 1977 108
Schedule 1 Part I Substances in Respect of Which the Exemptions Conferred by Section 56(1) and (2) do not have Effect 111
Schedule 1 Part II Substances in Respect of Which the Exemptions Conferred by Section 56(1) do not have Effect 112
Schedule 1 Part III Substances in Respect of Which the Exemptions Conferred by Section 56(2) do not have Effect 113
The Medicines (Products Other than Veterinary Drugs) (Prescription Only) Order 1983 115
Schedule 1 Descriptions and Classes of Prescription Only Medicines 124
Schedule 2 Substances not to be Contained in a Prescription Only Medicine Sold or Supplied Under the Exemption Conferred by Article 6(3) 176
Schedule 3 Exemption for Certain Persons from Section 58(2) of the Act 177
Schedule 4 Orders Revoked 185

The Misuse of Drugs Regulations 1973 as amended 187
Schedule 1 Controlled Drugs Exempted from the Prohibition on Importation, Exportation and Possession and Subject to the Requirements of Regulations 23 (CDinv) 205
Schedule 2 Controlled Drugs Subject to the Requirements of Regulations 14, 15, 16, 18, 19, 20, 21 and 24 (CD) 206
Schedule 3 Controlled Drugs Subject to Regulations 14, 15, 16 and 18, (CDnoReg) 208
Schedule 4 Controlled Drugs Subject to Regulations 14, 15, 16, 18, 19, 20 and 24 (CDlic) 209
The Misuse of Drugs (Notification of and Supply to Addicts) Regulations 1973 as amended 211
Schedule Controlled Drugs to Which these Regulations Apply 213
The Medicines (Administration of Radioactive Substances) Regulations 1978 215
The Medicines (Bal Jivan Chamcho Probition) (No.2) Order 1977 221
The Medicines (Prohibition of Non-medicinal Antimicrobial Substances) Order 1977 222
Schedule 1 Descriptions and Classes of Antimicrobial Substances to Which the Prohibition in Article 2(1) of this Order Applied 224
Schedule 2 Exceptions from the Prohibition Imposed by Article 2(1) of this Order 226
The Medicines (Chloroform Prohibition) Order 1979 as amended 228
The Medicines (Phenacetin Prohibition) Order 1979 230
The Medicines (Stilbenes and Thyrostatic Substances Prohibition) Order 1982 232

Divison 6: Controls over Sale, Supply and Administration of Veterinary Products

The Medicines (Restriction on the Administration of Veterinary Medicinal Products) Regulations 1983 237
The Medicines (Veterinary Drugs) (General Sale List) Order 1984 239
Schedule 1 Veterinary Drugs on General Sale by Virtue of Article 2 240
Schedule 2 Veterinary Drugs Which are not on the General Sale List 262
The Medicines (Veterinary Drugs) (Prescription Only) Order 1985 263
Schedule 1 Descriptions and Classes of Prescription Only Medicines 268
Schedule 2 Veterinary Drugs for Parental Administration that are not Prescription Only 317
$$$ Schedule 3 Exemption for Certain Persons from Section 58(2) of the Act 318
The Medicines (Exemptions from Restrictions on the Retail Sale or Supply of Veterinary Drugs) Order 1984 as amended 327
Schedule 1: Part A Licence of Right Veterinary Drugs 337
Schedule 1: Part B Veterinary Drugs 346
Schedule 2: Part A Licence of Right Veterinary Drugs 357
Schedule 2: Part B Veterinary Drugs 358
Schedule 3: Part A Licence of Right Veterinary Drugs 360

Schedule 3: Part B Veterinary Drugs 360
Schedule 4: Horse Wormers 362

Division 7: Quality of Medicines and Medicated Animal Feeding Stuffs

Part VIII British Pharmacopoeia and other Publications 365
Schedule 3 Sampling 370
The Medicines (Certificates of Analysis) Regulations 1977 376
Schedule Forms of Certificate of Analysis or Examination 377
The Medicines (Animal Feeding Stuffs) (Enforcement) Regulations 1985 381
Schedule 1 Part II, sections 112, 113 and 115 of the Act 1968 as Modified by Part I of this Schedule 383
Schedule 2 Manner of Taking, Dividing, Marking, Sealing and Fastening of Samples 388
Schedule 3 Methods of Analysis 401
Schedule 4 Forms of Certificate of Analysis or Examination 480
Part I Certificate of Analysis of Animal Feeding Stuff (1) 480
Part II Certificate of Analysis or Examination of Animal Feeding Stuff (1) 481
The Medicines (Feeding Stuffs of Variation) Order 1976 Schedule 483

Division 8 Pharmacies 489

Part IV Pharmacies
Persons Lawfully Conduction Retail Pharmacy Business 489
Registration of Pharmacies 493
Provisions as to Use of Certain Titles, Descriptions and Emblems 497
Disqualification, and Removal of Premises from Register 499
Supplementary Provisions 501
The Medicines (Pharmacies) (Applications for Registration and Fees) Regulations 1973 as amended 502
Extract from the Pharmacy Act 1954 Removal from and Restoration to the Register, etc. 505
Schedule 1 The Statutory Committee – Constitution 508
The Pharmaceutical Society (Statutory Committee) Order of Council 1978 509
Index 519

Chapter 1
Historical Background and Introduction

In order to understand the complexities of the Medicines Acts 1968–71, and their subordinate legislation, it is necessary to survey briefly the development of the legal control over medicines in the United Kingdom through the centuries. Such a survey shows that the law has taken a sporadic interest in medicines but, in the last few decades this interest has been sustained and continual. To some extent this has been due to the 'therapeutic explosion' and the enormous strides which have been made in understanding the action and effects of drugs and in elucidating the problems associated with their use. Currently, an emphasis on consumer protection has also contributed to the demand for stricter controls over medicines. In the past, laws have been made for the following purposes:

(a) to ensure the purity of drugs,
(b) to use them as a source of revenue,
(c) to prevent their misuse,
(d) to protect the public from charlatans and 'quacks'.

TO ENSURE THE PURITY OF DRUGS

From medieval days, there was considerable adulteration of foods and drugs. The Guilds were first given the statutory duty to maintain the purity of products sold by their members and in 1429 the Grocer's Company were empowered to inspect certain foods and drugs and to confiscate adulterated samples. There were, of course, no chemical or microscopical techniques available so testing consisted of viewing, tasting and smelling the products. The Company lost its jurisdiction over drugs in 1617.

Henry VIII enacted the first English law to control medicines *per se* (1540 Hen VIII Chap. 40). He had been persuaded by the physicians of the day that what we would regard as 'adulterated drugs' were being sold and used by apothecaries. The Act authorised the physicians to appoint four of their number each year to visit the apothecaries' shops in London to inspect their 'Wares, Drugs and Stuffs', and to destroy any which were 'defective, corrupted and not meet nor convenient to be ministered in any Medicines for the Health of Man's Body'. This Act was amended in 1727 to permit representatives of the Society of Apothecaries to accompany the physicians. These Acts were the fore-runners of a series of Acts which culminated in the Food and Drugs Act 1955. During the 19th century developments in chemistry enabled many foods and drugs to be tested chemically for evidence of adulteration and this revealed the extent of the problem. The

Adulteration of Food and Drugs Act 1872 made it obligatory for local authorities to appoint analysts and subsequently the responsibility for ensuring the quality of drugs sold to the public has been with local Food and Drug Authorities.

Unfortunately, these Acts did not specify standards for drugs nor did they specify standard methods for their analysis. This was not an oversight because proposals had been made before the Select Committee on the Bill which became the 1879 Act to incorporate section 16 of the Pharmacy Act 1868 into the Bill. This would have had the effect of legalising British Pharmacopoeial standards for compounded medicines. Neither the above Select Committee nor that which considered a similar proposal in 1894 favoured the idea. As a result it was up to each court to decide what standards to apply to a drug in a given case, with the consequence that the enforcement of the Act varied from locality to locality. This was accentuated by the fact that some local authorities enthusiastically supported their analyst and provided him with excellent facilities while others did not.

Early in the twentieth century, products derived from bacteria or from the endocrine organs of animals began to become widely used in medicine. Such products differed from other medicinal products used at the time in that they were required to be sterile (i.e. free from living micro-organisms) but could not be heat sterilised. Furthermore they had to be assayed by biological as opposed to chemical methods. The unfortunate consequences of the administration of defective batches made and used abroad prompted the establishment of a Departmental Committee to advise on measures necessary to ensure the quality and authenticity of such products. Its report (CMD 1156, 1921) resulted in the enactment of the Therapeutic Substances Act 1925. The object of this legislation was to ensure that vaccines, sera, toxins, preparations of the organic arsenical substance Salvarsan and its analogues, and preparations of digitalis, ergot, insulin, pituitary gland were manufactured under appropriate conditions and tested to ensure efficacy and quality before being sold. This was achieved by a licensing system which imposed on manufacturers and importers very strict conditions as regards manufacturing procedures, facilities, expert staff, testing and assay procedures. The licences required a product to be manufactured and tested in accordance with any regulations applicable to the product. The retail sale of such products was not controlled. Over the years other products were added to the list such as surgical ligatures and sutures, preparations of penicillin and other antibiotics, human blood and synthetic curariform products.

TO RAISE REVENUE FROM DRUGS

Fiscal duties on patent medicines were first introduced in 1783, but most of the relevant law came from the Acts of 1802, 1804 and 1812. Sellers of such medicines required a licence, and a Medicines Stamp had to be attached to each container when a medicine was sold by retail. The value of the stamp was related to the sale price of the medicine, those costing up to one shilling had to bear a stamp valued at one and a half pennies, for those costing between one shilling and two and a half shillings the duty was three pennies, and was one pound on a medicine costing more than two pounds ten shillings! Medicines on which the stamp duty had been paid were exempted from requirements relating to disclosure of composition. The stamps therefore permitted the sale of 'secret remedies'. The Medicine Stamp Acts remained on the statute book until 1941.

TO PREVENT THEIR MISUSE

As was stated in the preamble to the Arsenic Act 1851, 'whereas the unrestricted sale of arsenic facilitates the commission of crime. .....' medicinal substances have long been used for murder and suicide. In an attempt to remedy the situation the Arsenic Act 1851 put restrictions on the sale of the substance. The seller was required to (a) know the purchaser, (b) keep records of the transaction and (c) to mix the arsenic with soot or indigo to prevent its admixture with food. These provisions did not apply to sales in which the amount of arsenic sold exceeded 10 lbs! However, at that time anyone could sell arsenic, the seller needing no qualifications. This was remedied by the Pharmacy Act 1868 which contained a short list of substances to be treated as poisons and required the Pharmaceutical Society of Great Britain to prepare a list of substances, which after being approved by the Privy Council, would be controlled as poisons. The Act also restricted the retail sale of poisons (including arsenic) to what today would be called pharmacies. There was no provision for inspection of records or premises so there were no means of ensuring the effective enforcement of its provisions.

In 1903 a departmental committee which had been set up to review the list of poisons in the 1868 Act issued its report (Cmd 1442, 1903). It stated that in order to carry out its task properly, it had been necessary to consider the restrictions on the sale of poisons. Many of those who gave evidence to the committee were involved in the manufacture or sale of 'patent' or 'proprietary' medicines and were aggrieved by the High Court decision in the case of Pharmaceutical Society of Great Britain v. Piper (1893). The court had upheld the Society's view that when a proprietary medicine contained even a small amount of a poison, the medicine could only be sold from a pharmacy. The court also decided that despite common usage, the phrase 'patent medicine' meant a medicine which is the subject of letters patent. The manufacturers had believed that the phrase meant proprietary medicines and that their products were exempt from the provisions of the Act. Thus much of the evidence was hostile to the Society. Evidence was also given which suggested that a few farmers had experienced difficulty in persuading pharmacists that arsenic and nicotine had important uses in agriculture and horticulture. As a result the committee reported that a new class of seller of poisons should be created, the licensed seller.

The Poisons and Pharmacy Act 1908 created such sellers but confined their sales to arsenic and nicotine products for use in agriculture or horticulture for the destruction of insects, bacteria and fungi or for use as sheep dips or weed-killers.

In 1920, chiefly in order to comply with our international obligations under the Treaty of Versailles (one of the Peace Treaties which formally ended the First World War) the first of a series of Dangerous Drugs Acts was passed. The aim of this legislation was to control the possession and use of addictive drugs, such as cocaine and the opiates, morphine and diamorphine. The sale and dispensing of these substances were already controlled because they were classed as poisons. Furthermore, regulations made under the Defence of the Realm Act had prohibited their sale or supply to servicemen during the war except on prescription. This was the first time that it became legally necessary for a person to hold a prescription in order to be supplied with a drug. The new Act required records to be kept of sales and supplies made by pharmacists, doctors, dentists and veterinarians and also prohibited the sale or supply of these drugs to the public except on prescription. The manufacture and import and export of these drugs were similarly strictly controlled by a licensing system. Despite vociferous complaints from many members of the professions affected, the Act remained on the statute book and indeed its provisions were gradually strengthened.

The Pharmacy and Poisons Act 1933 created an Advisory Committee (the Poisons Board) to advise the Home Secretary on such matters as (i) substances to be controlled (their names being published in the Poisons List), and (ii) the various restrictions to be imposed upon some or all poisons (published as the Poisons Rules). Schedule 4 to the Rules contained a short list of substances (including the barbiturates) which would henceforth only be available to the public on prescription. For over 40 years the 1933 Act and the List and Rules provided the chief source of law relating to the sale and supply of medicines and other chemicals. However, some of the substances listed as poisons were not really toxic but were included in the List and Rules because there was no other means of controlling their distribution and use.

In 1971, a new statute, the Misuse of Drugs Act, replaced the Dangerous Drugs Acts and this statute (together with its associated Regulations and Orders) remains in force today unaffected by the Medicines Act. It is enforced by the Home Office.

When antibiotics became available in the 1940s it was thought that their use should be restricted to prevent the emergence of resistant strains of bacteria. For this reason the Penicillin Act 1947 was enacted and specified the necessary restrictions on retail distribution. These restrictions were later applied to other antibiotics as they become available. In 1956, this Act was repealed and its provisions re-enacted in a new Therapeutic Substances Act which also controlled the manufacture of the antibiotics as well as 'biologicals'. Although this Act applied to human medicines, analogous provisions relating to veterinary products appeared in the Diseases of Animals Act. The Therapeutic Substances Act 1956 and corresponding parts of the Diseases of Animals Act 1950 were repealed by the Medicines Act.

TO PROTECT THE PUBLIC FROM CHARLATANS AND 'QUACKS'

As charlatans down the ages have always known, it is easy to persuade members of the public that their health would benefit from taking particular medicines. We have already seen that a tax was payable on secret remedies but this had nothing to do with protecting the public, it was merely a method of collecting tax. In 1912 the British Medical Association began a campaign to control the sale and advertising of 'patent' or proprietary medicines and published some startling facts about their composition and efficacy. This was doubtless instrumental in causing the House of Commons to set up a Select Committee with a remit to study the situation with regard to such medicines and medical appliances, including advertisements relating thereto, and to report what amendments, if any, in the law were necessary or desirable. The Committee took evidence from 42 witnesses including nine from government departments, 11 doctors, and nine manufacturers or proprietors of proprietary medicines. Various bodies, e.g. Pharmaceutical Society of Great Britain and the British Medical Association, also gave evidence.

REPORT OF THE SELECT COMMITTEE ON PATENT MEDICINES

In its report (414, 1914), the Committee commented on the fact that no government department had any official responsibilty for, or any official knowledge of, patent medicines. The law was fragmentary and if enforced at all was administered by several departments of state.

In so far as statute law was concerned, the Pharmacy Acts 1868 and 1869 together with the Poisons and Pharmacy Act 1908, required poisons to be labelled with the word 'poison' or 'poisonous', but imposed no other restrictions on their sale. The Food and Drugs Acts 1875 and 1899 dealt with the analysis of patent medicines and drugs. The 1875 Act made it an offence to label a product falsely (section 27) but section 5 exempted foods or medicines which were the subject of a patent in force. Among other statutes which had some bearing on medicines were The Stamp Acts 1802–1875, the Merchandise Marks Act 1887, the Indecent Advertisements Act and the Larceny Act.

The departments of state involved were –

(a) The Privy Council Office which regulated to some extent the qualifications and conduct of doctors, dentists, pharmacists and midwives. It was also responsible for the issue of an Order in Council on the recommendation of the Pharmaceutical Society, to add substances to the Poisons List. In this respect the Committee noted that it had taken the Privy Council Office 18 years to respond to the Pharmaceutical Society's recommendation that a number of substances including carbolic acid (phenol) should be controlled as poisons.

(b) The Home Office had powers to deal with fraud. Few prosecutions relating to medicines had been successful mainly because it was impossible to prove that the seller had a 'guilty mind' since the seller did not know the composition of the medicine. Furthermore, the defendant was usually able to produce a witness who would state that the medicine had cured him.

(c) The Local Government Board controlled the activities of the 234 local government food and drug authorities. The Patent Office reported that up to 1912, 312 patents had been issued for medicines and medicinal preparations and were still in force. Few of these related to products of interest to the Committee because patents are only issued on proof of usefulness and novelty, and on disclosure of composition.

The Select Committee felt that the law was inadequate. The laws did not prevent fraud and proceedings against the makers or sellers of useless remedies were rare. As might be expected with statutes concerned with taxation, the Stamp Acts contained many anomalies, for example, since 1902 the Commissioners (of Inland Revenue) had required duty to be paid on medicines if the name of the AILMENT was mentioned on the label but not if the ORGAN involved was mentioned. Thus 'X's Cough Mixture' was taxed but 'Y's Chest Mixture' was not. This led to the names of a number of products being changed.

The Select Committee summarised the situation regarding legal controls over the sale and advertisement of patent medicines as follows: 'For all practical purposes British law is powerless to prevent any person from procuring any drug, or making any mixture, whether potent or without any therapeutical activity whatever (so long as it does not contain any scheduled poison), advertising it in any decent terms as a cure for any disease or ailment, recommending it by bogus testimonials and the invented opinions and facsimile signatures of fictitious physicians, and selling it under any name he chooses, on the payment of a small stamp duty, for any price he can persuade a credulous public to pay.'

Size of the Market

There was a large and rapidly growing market in the remedies as was shown by the revenue collected. The revenue from stamp duties was £327,856 in 1912; £328,318 in 1913; and £360,376 in 1914; however, it was expected to be reduced dramatically following the introduction of the National Health Insurance scheme. Many patent medicines were imported into Britain from the USA because changes in the law there prevented their sale. The annual turnover of Beechams Pills was about £360,000 (indicating that 360 million pills were sold annually!)

The Select Committee divided patent medicines into two main classes and several sub-classes, namely –

Non-secret Remedies

(a) Proprietary preparations comprising genuine drugs prepared synthetically or extracted from crude drugs. These had been made in pharmacological laboratories and tested therapeutically, for example aspirin, adrenaline.

(b) Remedies owing their value to skilful combination, e.g. emulsions of cod liver oil, mixtures of bismuth and pepsin.

(c) Non-secret drugs with secret ingredients. These comprised known drugs with disclosure of composition but containing a minute amount of a medically inert ingredient the nature of which was a trade secret. Tabloids were an example.

The Committee considered that the the only objection to the non-secret remedies might arise if it were necessary to forbid unfounded claims for curing disease.

Secret Remedies

(a) These were often simple household remedies. These had sometimes originated as doctor's prescriptions and were probably suitable for treating uncomplicated diseases but were unnecessarily expensive and were sometimes advertised for complaints they could not possibly alleviate. Apart from this they were unobjectionable.

(b) Dangerous remedies and drugs used for improper purposes such as acetanilide.

(c) Fraudulent remedies. This formed a very large class and consisted of abortifacients, alleged cures for cancer, tuberculosis, diabetes, epilepsy, etc. The Committee felt that these were 'cruel frauds' that should be prohibited under drastic penalty.

ATTEMPTS TO IMPROVE THE LAW

Despite the obvious shortcomings of the law, little was done to remedy its defects. In 1917, the Venereal Diseases Act was passed. This prohibited the sale and advertising of remedies for these diseases, and also the giving of any advice regarding their treatment or prevention except by medical practitioners. More than 20 years were to elapse before similar controls were imposed over remedies and advertisements relating to cancer (Cancer Act 1939).

In 1920 a Bill based on the recommendations of the Select Committee was introduced into the House of Lords. The Bill was intended to prohibit the advertisement and sale of medicines for the treatment or cure of various diseases. A register of proprietary medicines and their owners would be created. The Bill fell at the dissolution of the Parliament.

In 1931 a similar Bill was presented to Parliament with the aim of regulating the manufacture, sale and advertisement of proprietary medicines and proprietary surgical appliances. The manufacture of such articles would be restricted to the person who was registered as the owner of the article or someone acting on his behalf. The article itself would also have to be registered and its full composition disclosed. A specimen of an appliance would have to be supplied with the application for registration. It would be an offence to sell an unregistered article or one that did not bear a registration number.

It would also be an offence to sell or advertise for sale any medicine or appliance purporting to be a cure for deafness, rupture, or for the prevention or cure of any disease mentioned in the schedule to the Bill. Provision was made for this list of diseases to be amended in future. Advertisements and other communications relating (even indirectly) to abortifacients, or articles used in any way to cure sexual weakness, or to promote sexual virility or desire or to treat or prevent sexual excess were to be prohibited. Also to be prohibited were advertisements offering to treat, or to provide advice in connection with the prevention, treatment or relief of any ailment by correspondence. Likewise, offers to refund money paid for remedies were prohibited, as were fictitious false or misleading testimonials and recommendations made by practitioners unless the full name and qualifications of the practitioner were given. Other aspects of advertising medicines were also to be prohibited.

The Act would not have extended to Scotland or to Northern Ireland, though possibly analogous legislation could have been made. Unfortunately, the Bill never became law, and another 10 years were to elapse before some (but by no means all) of its provisions were enacted.

The Pharmacy and Medicines Act 1941 prohibited the advertisement of remedies for Bright's disease, cataract, diabetes, epilepsy, glaucoma, paralysis and tuberculosis. It also prohibited the issue of advertisements referring to products in terms calculated to lead to the use of the product in procuring the miscarriage of women. There were two aspects to the problem, firstly many of the diseases needed expert treatment and secondly most of the remedies were useless anyway. The Pharmacy and Medicines Act 1941 also required 'patent' or proprietary medicines to be labelled with details of their composition, and repealed the Medicine Stamp Acts. In addition the Food and Drugs Act prohibited the issue of false or misleading advertisements and labels relating to any food or drug.

REASONS FOR COMPREHENSIVE LEGISLATION

By the late 1950s, many of the more objectionable activities associated with the manufacture, distribution and promotion of medicines had been stopped and with such a variety of legal controls over medicines one might see little scope for, or point in, further legislation on the subject. In fact, however, the protection given to the professions and to the public was more apparent than real as many people pointed out. The legislation had been made piecemeal to remedy a particular evil and consequently, there were loopholes and anomalies. Also, the Home Office was still responsible for some Acts while the Ministry of Health was responsible for others. The enforcement of the Acts was also in a number of hands and hindered by the fact that some courts tended to treat certain offences as mere technical offences to be dealt with by a very small fine. In short, the legislation lacked cohesion.

Perhaps the greatest weakness was that no statutory or other body had to be satisfied as to the quality, efficacy or safety of a product before it was launched onto the market (biological products excepted). Most pharmaceutical companies did, in fact, spend considerable time and money on testing their potential products, especially those intended to be prescribed by practitioners before marketing them and also were quick to remove them from the market if they subsequently proved to be unsafe. When a product was found to give rise to a particular problem, steps were taken to deal with the situation, usually by placing the drug in the 4th Schedule to the Poisons Rules. This ensured that it could only be sold to practitioners or supplied to the public only on prescription.

The Pharmaceutical Society of Great Britain have long expressed the view that medicines are not ordinary articles of commerce and that legislation should provide for the control of all aspects of their manufacture, distribution and promotion. Furthermore, it has always sought to anticipate the law by advising its members not to sell certain substances to the public except on prescription even though this was not at the time a legal requirement (e.g. amphetamines).

In 1959 the Poisons Board drew attention to the need for legislation to control certain drugs and suggested that this be related specifically to medicines thus becoming the responsibility of the Ministry of Health. The Home Office and the Ministry thereupon set up an Inter-Departmental Working Party to review existing laws and collect evidence from interested parties. The report of this Working Party was not published although the Health Ministers subsequently circulated confidential memoranda outlining proposals to the professions.

Also, in 1959 the Inter-Departmental Committee on Drug Addiction (the Brain Committee) recommended that drugs affecting the central nervous system and likely to produce other ill-effects should be available only upon prescription, subject to the advice of an independent expert body. Since no such body existed this recommendation was implemented as far as possible by the Poisons Rules 1960.

In 1962, the thalidomide disaster focused attention on the lack of safeguards to prevent the marketing of a medicinal product until every precaution had been taken to ensure that it was safe and to discover any harmful side-effect it may possess. As a result the Standing Medical Advisory Committees (England, Wales and Scotland) set up a Joint Sub-Committee on Safety of Drugs with the following terms of reference:

'to advise the Minister of Health and the Secretary of State for Scotland on what measures are needed –

(1) to secure adequate pharmacological and safety testing and clinical trials of new drugs before their release for general use;

(2) to secure early detection of adverse effects arising from their release for general use; and

(3) to keep doctors informed of the experience of such drugs in clinical practice.'

The Sub-Committee which comprised six physicians and two pharmacists recommended that –

(a) manufacturers should remain responsible for the experimental laboratory testing of new drugs before they are used in clinical trials, and,

(b) an expert body be set up to review the evidence collected and offer advice on the toxicity of new drugs before they are used in clinical trials.

Subsequently, the Sub-Committee published its final report in 1963. Paragraph 6 of this report stated, 'we have interpreted our remit as requiring us to advise on measures which, firstly, will ensure that the practice of all manufacturers in the toxicity testing and clinical trial of new drugs conforms with the highest standards in this respect; secondly, will reassure the public that all possible steps are being taken to prevent the marketing of new drugs which have not been the subject of adequate safety testing and clinical trial; and thirdly, will reveal at the earliest possible time adverse reactions in humans which have not been unmasked in toxicity tests and clinical trials'.

The Sub-Committee realised that drug safety depended also on a number of other factors such as controls over sale and advertising, but felt that these matters were outside its terms of reference. In any case it was felt that legislation would be required in order to deal with such matters and a comprehensive review of the whole field would take time. A voluntary scheme was therefore suggested. This could be implemented quickly without the need for legislation and would provide a valuable if temporary safeguard.

THE VOLUNTARY SCHEME

This scheme required the Health Ministers to appoint a Committee on Safety of Drugs, with sub-committees to advise on –

(1) toxicity,

(2) clinical trials and therapeutic efficacy,

(3) adverse reactions.

In order to satisfy public opinion, it was considered that the Committee should be free from links (however tenuous) with the pharmaceutical industry.

It was envisaged that the manufacturer of a new drug would voluntarily submit details of toxicity tests to the relevant sub-committee before putting the drug on clinical trial. When the sub-committee was satisfied that the testing was adequate it would advise the parent Committee to permit the drug to be clinically tested.

The manufacturer would then arrange for the clinical trials to take place. Initially, only a small number of centres would be used to minimise the hazards and arrangements would be made so that investigators at the centres could communicate with each other. The results obtained from the clinical trials would be objectively assessed by the appropriate sub-committee. Any toxic reactions noted by the investigators during clinical trials would be immediately notified directly to the parent Committee. The Committee, after considering all the evidence would then decide whether the drug should be released for general use or whether special restrictions should be applied to it or whether further trials were necessary.

Being a voluntary scheme, there were no formal sanctions which could be applied if someone wanted to evade it but a majority of the Sub-Committee considered that the following should prove an effective deterrent –

(a) physicians should refuse to participate in clinical trials of a drug unless they had been assured that the full data on its toxicity testing had been approved by the Committee;

(b) if a drug were released for sale without the Committee's approval the facts should be drawn to the attention of all prescribers;

(c) similar action would follow if a manufacturer marketed a drug without giving the Committee an opportunity to assess the adequacy of its toxicity testing or clinical trials.

The pharmacists on the Joint Sub-Committee felt these sanctions to be too weak and too few and believed that a less scrupulous manufacturer might be tempted to take risks to secure a commercial advantage over his more conscientious rivals. Accordingly, in a note of dissent they advised the Ministers not to set up this voluntary scheme but to prepare a comprehensive statute dealing with all aspects of drugs and medicines including the supervision of toxicity testing and clinical trials.

The sub-committee on adverse drug reactions would have the task of collecting and collating reports of adverse reactions to all drugs. No machinery was laid down for this but it was expected that all practitioners would be encouraged to report suspected adverse reactions to the sub-committee.

THE COMMITTEE ON SAFETY OF DRUGS (THE DUNLOP COMMITTEE)

The government accepted the report of the Joint Sub-Committee and in June 1963 the Committee on Safety of Drugs was established under the Chairmanship of Sir Derrick Dunlop and commenced its work in January 1964. It had three sub-committees as recommended above. The sub-committees and the parent committee met monthly. The Committee published a series of annual reports which provide some idea of the success of the scheme. Each year the Committee dealt with approximately 900 applications for permission to put a product to clinical trial or to market. Some of these were not dealt with either because the Committee required additional information or because they had arrived late in the year. However, during the last 4 years of the Committee's work (1967–70) a total of 2718 decisions were given. Of the 757 applications for clinical trial, 705 were approved while of the 1961 applications for permission to market a product 1855 were approved. Many of the applications involved new drug substances.

In its report for the year 1967, the Committee mentioned that for the first time it had had to inform the Ministers about a drug which had been marketed without its agreement. Within a few days the preparation was withdrawn from the market. In 1968, a company marketed several preparations without first submitting information to the Committee. The Ministers thereupon advised hospitals, doctors and pharmacists against using any of these products. Similar action was taken by the Ministers in 1969 against another product which was distributed in the United Kingdom. These figures confirm that the industry as a whole co-operated wholeheartedly.

The Sub-Committee on Adverse Reactions devised an 'early warning system' in 1964. This consisted of yellow reply paid cards which were distributed to doctors and dentists in 1965 together with the request that practitioners would use them to report circumstances which might indicate that one of their patients was showing signs of an adverse reaction to a particular drug. Some 4000 reports of suspected adverse reactions were received that year, most of them from general practitioners. When there was sufficient evidence of an adverse reaction to a drug, its manufacturer was contacted and advised either to include a warning in the promotional literature or withdraw the product. On occasions the Committee itself issued warnings through the professional press. The Committee also issued a series of leaflets, e.g. Adverse Reactions Series No.1 Monoamine Oxidase Inhibitors. In all, the Committee received approximately 25,000 reports of suspected adverse reactions between 1964 and 1971.

The Committee also considered and commented on various other matters which relate to the safety of drugs. For instance, where new drugs were produced for 'over the counter sale' they drew the promoter's attention to claims and other statements made on the label or leaflet. The Committee was also interested in the labelling of dispensed products and was strongly in favour of N.P. labelling, i.e. that containers of dispensed products should bear the name of the medicine instead of being labelled anonymously 'The Tablets' or 'The Capsules'.

The experience gained by the Committee during its early years led it to the conclusion that there was an overlap in the interests of the Sub-Committees dealing respectively with toxicity and with clinical trials and efficacy. Accordingly, after an experimental period during which they met jointly, these two sub-committees were merged in 1968.

THE 1967 WHITE PAPER ON SAFETY AND QUALITY OF MEDICINES

In September 1967, a White Paper 'Forthcoming legislation on the Safety, Quality, and Description of Drugs and Medicines' (Cmnd 3395) was published. This set out the reasons for and the scope of the proposed legislation on medicines. It promised substantial changes or entirely new provisions where the existing law was inadequate in relation to the various aspects of safety mentioned in the report of the Joint Sub-committee. The emphasis was very much on the safety, quality, and efficacy of medicines both for human and for animal use. A licensing system was to be set up, and all new medicines would require a product licence before being marketed. Such a licence would only be issued after expert panels had examined the proposed formula, method of manufacture, quality control procedures, packaging, labelling and proposed indications to ensure that the product was of suitable quality, was safe and efficacious. Manufacturers and wholesale dealers in medicines would also require licences which would be granted only to those who had the appropriate facilities and expertise to carry out these activities correctly. Existing products would be granted licences of right as would manufacturers and wholesalers already in business. These licences would lapse after an interim period and need to be replaced by full licences. The work of the Committee on the Safety of Drugs would be put on a statutory basis.

The White Paper also recognised that medicines are not ordinary articles of commerce (see paragraphs 42 and 43) and that most of them should be sold only through pharmacies so that their sale would be monitored by a pharmacist. There would however be a class of medicines 'where the hazard to health and the risk of misuse or the need to take special precautions in handling them is small, and where wider sale would be a convenience to the purchaser' which could be sold from any shop (paragraph 49).

The legislation would replace the Therapeutic Substances Act 1956, the Pharmacy and Medicines Act 1941, and those provisions of the Pharmacy and Poisons Act 1933, the Food and Drugs Act 1955, the Radioactive Substances Act 1948, Cancer Act 1939, Venereal Diseases Act 1917 and the Diseases of Animals Act 1950 which applied to drugs and medicines but would leave unchanged the Dangerous Drugs Act. The responsibility for enforcing the Medicines Act would fall upon a group of Ministers though they would be able to delegate some of these duties.

The professions broadly agreed with the proposals though some points of detail were criticised. The industry also accepted the need for most of the proposed changes. Consequently, most of the proposals found their way into the Medicines Act which received the Royal Assent on the 25th October 1968.

Before the Act could become operative a new division (the Medicines Division) had to be created in what is now the Department of Health and Social Security. A corresponding division in the Ministry of Agriculture, Fisheries and Food (the Animal Health Division) was also created to deal with medicines for animal use. In addition, expert bodies had to be formed and given time to consider a variety of matters relating to the implementation of the Act. The Act was therefore brought into operation in stages and became fully operative on the 1st February 1978.

THE MEDICINES ACT 1968

The Act is in fact, an 'enabling Act', that is, it lays down the general policies to be followed and leaves the detailed implementation of these to be dealt with by various Ministers. The detail is made in the form of statutory instruments (Orders and Regulations) which become effective only after being laid before Parliament.

Some statutory instruments provide for transitional arrangements to followed before becoming fully operational. The Act is very lengthy and consists of eight parts. It was amended slightly by the Medicines Act 1971. The Act applies to the United Kingdom (England, Wales, Scotland, and Northern Ireland).

Almost 200 statutory instruments have been made under the Act and such a mass of detail is difficult to assimilate and understand. The account which follows has sought to emphasise the main points and for convenience, reference is made to the section number or the date and number of the statutory instrument concerned should more detail be required.

The Act makes frequent reference to safety, quality and efficacy as its chief aims and it is helpful to discuss these in relation to the various controls which have been instituted. The three criteria interlock and must be considered together.

SAFETY, QUALITY AND EFFICACY

Quality is probably the most important because when this is variable the safety and efficacy of the product become unpredictable. The quality of a medicinal product is dependent upon, among other things, the purity of each of its ingredients and the nature and quantities of the impurities present in each of them. Also of major importance is the choice of the ingredients used to convert a drug substance into a product suitable for use by a patient, and the care with which the ingredients have been mixed together. The more closely these factors can be controlled and the smaller the limits within which each is allowed to vary, the higher the quality of the product. Of equal importance is the uniformity of quality from batch to batch, and this can only be achieved by rigid adherence to the specifications of every ingredient and process used, coupled with constant quality control procedures at every stage of manufacture. In short, quality has to be built into the product, it cannot be 'tested in' at the end of the process.

The word 'safety' as used in the Act does not mean merely that the product is free from danger to the consumer as section 132 (2) makes clear:

> 'For the purposes of this Act considerations of safety, in relation to any substance or article, shall be taken to include consideration of the extent (if any) to which the substance or article –
>
> (a) if used without proper safeguards, is capable of causing danger to the health of the community, or. .. to the health of animals generally or to one or more species of animals, or
>
> (b) if administered to an animal, may be harmful to the animal or may induce disease in other animals or may leave a residue in the carcase or produce of the animal which may be harmful to human beings, or
>
> (c) may interfere with the treatment, prevention or diagnosis of the disease, or
>
> (d) may be harmful to the person administering it or (in the case of an instrument, apparatus, or appliance) the person operating it,
>
> and any reference to safety or to the interests of safety shall be construed accordingly.'

If a product of poor quality were to be permitted to be administered, safety would be affected in at least two ways. Firstly, it will probably be less efficacious than a product of superior quality, and secondly, the impurities present may themselves be dangerous. Quality is also affected by various factors other than purity and common examples are the particle size of the drug substance, and the choice of vehicle in which it is mixed for administration.

Efficacy is always related to a particular disease, condition or treatment or the diagnosis of these. It is not solely a pharmacological property and can be affected by a number of factors such as the particle size or shape of the drug substance, the excipients used, the pressures used in tabletting and of course, by variations in the purity of the ingredients. Also of importance here is the care with which the patient complies with the prescribed dosage regimen. Unfortunately, the latter while being very important is not amenable to legal control.

The three criteria differ in so far as they can be quantified. Quality is usually comparatively easy to measure especially when the ingredients of the product are chemical substances. Each of the important properties which together combine to constitute the quality of the product can also usually be scientifically determined. It must be borne in mind however, that different assay procedures often give different results, hence the need for standard assay methods laid down in official compendia. It should also be realised that official standards are usually designed for testing products at the consumer level, i.e. some months after manufacture, and therefore have wider tolerances than would be permitted in the manufacturing specification.

Safety is extremely difficult to quantify and is, in fact, arelative standard rather than an absolute one. There is no substance that if taken in sufficient quantity will not kill or injure someone. Furthermore, most drugs have been found to cause damage to a few individuals even when used in the correct dosage. Such individuals are said to be hypersensitive (or allergic) to the drug and this can seldom be predicted. Penicillin is a common example. Fortunately, the majority of adverse reactions to most drugs are either of minor significance in that they merely inconvenience the patient or are reversible (i.e. they disappear after the treatment is stopped). The assessment of safety is further complicated by the absence of reliable test methods. Animal tests often show that a substance is toxic but sometimes this is species dependent (i.e. a substance may be very toxic to cats but less toxic to dogs). It is therefore necessary to test a product on a number of species and finally commence limited trials in man. The safety of a product must also be viewed against its potential therapeutic use. Where a drug has similar therapeutic uses to a number of other drugs which are known to be safe the safety of the new drug should be clearly demonstrated before allowing it to be marketed. On the other hand, a far less safe product might be quite acceptable if it were capable of treating cancer.

Efficacy is also difficult to quantify, and experience shows that even when a diagnosis is certain, a percentage of patients treated with a given drug will fail to respond to it while some patients recover spontaneously without any treatment. However, it could be argued that a product which is not efficacious or is much less efficacious than existing products should not be marketed even though it might be 'safe', because it will be given to some patients who would benefit more from the existing products.

The Act seeks to control the safety, quality, and efficacy of products in several ways. Firstly, a product licence is required by the person responsible for its composition. To obtain such a licence the applicant must satisfy the licensing authority as to the safety etc. of the active ingredients and of the final formulation. The manufacture of the product must then be carried out by a person holding an appropriate manufacturer's licence. Such a licence is only granted to persons having the appropriate facilities and expertise to carry out the relevant processes competently. In addition the manufacturer must comply with the terms of the product licence. His premises are inspected by Ministry inspectors and samples are taken of products being manufactured to ensure that the processes are carried out properly. This system should result in the production of preparations of acceptable quality and safety. However, a product can be adversely affected by faulty storage so it is necessary to control wholesale dealers. As usual this is done by means of a licence to obtain which the dealer must show that he has the necessary facilities, both physical and in respect of record keeping, to permit drugs to be kept secure and in optimum conditions.

Deterioration can, of course, occur due to faulty storage in the retail establishment and adulteration (either accidental or deliberate) can also occur in such places. To guard against this inspectors (from the Pharmaceutical Society and from the local authority) are empowered to purchase samples of products from retail outlets and submit them for analysis. It is an offence to sell, offer for sale or possess for sale a product which does not comply with the required standard. However, there are no corresponding provisions relating to products used or issued from hospitals, doctors, dentists or veterinarians.

Since a product's activity can also be affected by its container the Act likewise permits these to be controlled. The container is also important in preventing children from gaining access to medicines and legislation provides for certain products to be packed in specified types of container.

Where despite all precautions a defective product is released for sale or a product deteriorates abnormally quickly, the affected batch can be traced rapidly and withdrawn from sale by means of the system of batch numbers which must appear on all labels including those on packing cases. In addition to this, the safety of the product is dependent upon its being used properly (e.g. in the correct dosage, and at appropriate times) so labelling provisions require that the necessary information and warnings appear on labels.

Another aspect of proper use involves advertisements and the larger question of the promotion of sales of medicinal products. The Act controls these in several ways. It prohibits advertisements relating to specified products or to specified diseases. It also controls promotional schemes aimed at practitioners by insisting that a data sheet containing a summary of all of the relevant points is issued to the practitioner before a representative discusses the product with him or before the product is advertised. Advertisements are therefore more truthful than they were and it is harder to gloss over the less desirable properties of the product. Advertisements directed at the public are also controlled, though many people believe that the controls should be tightened.

The rigid controls imposed by the Act on the manufacturers of medicines has inevitably involved the expenditure of large sums of money and this has been reflected in the price of their products. Furthermore, some manufacturers have decided to withdraw products from the market either because the demand for them did not justify the expense involved in obtaining a licence, or because it was felt that a licence for the product would not be granted. It seems that some 36,000 product licences of right were issued when the licensing control became operative. When information about them was sought on behalf of the Committee on Review of Medicines (CRM) in 1975, 10,000 of these licences were voluntarily surrendered (CRM Report 1976). While many of these products are unlamented some useful though not very popular remedies have disappeared.

Another consequence of the Act was that the DHSS had to employ a number of highly qualified experts to examine and report upon applications for licences. In the main, these experts came from the pharmaceutical industry and their transfer caused a transient shortage.

The Ministers have a duty to enforce the Act (section 108(1); 109(1); 110(1)), and are solely responsible for enforcing the licensing provisions and those which affect hospitals or the premises of practitioners. The Ministers can delegate some of their enforcement duties to local food and drug authorities and/or to the Pharmaceutical Society.

RECENT INFLUENCES ON THE DEVELOPMENT OF THE ACT

Since 1968, it has been necessary to amend the Act to cope with changing circumstances. In 1969 the Swann Report into the use of antibiotics in farm livestock was published. The report found that the practice of feeding low levels of antibiotics to farm animals posed hazards to the animals and to man. It confirmed that there was an increasing incidence of antibiotic-resistant enteric bacteria in such animals and that these were transmitted to man when he ingested their meat and other produce and also when he worked closely with such animals. Among the main recommendations of the Committee were that antibiotics used for 'feed' purposes should be limited to those economically important in livestock production but of little or no therapeutic use in man or animals; nor should they impair the efficiency of prescribed therapeutic drugs. Furthermore, the possible risk to human health resulting from the consumption of residues in animal products should be fully considered before an antibiotic be recommended for 'feed' purposes. It also recommended that 'one committee should have overall responsibility for the whole field of use of antibiotics and related substances whether in man, animals, food preservation or for other purposes.' Such a committee should be empowered to demand such information as it required. The committee recommended that the the law be changed to prevent the unprescribed use of a number of therapeutic antibiotics (e.g. tetracyclines, penicillin, tylosin) in animals. Most of these matters are now controlled by subordinate legislation made under the Medicines Act.

Further major changes were necessitated by the UK joining the European Economic Community (EEC) in 1972 and Community obligations will doubtless require more changes in the future. The EEC Directive 65/65 attempted to harmonise the laws relating to proprietary medicinal products so as to safeguard public health, without hindering the development of the pharmaceutical industry or the trade in medicinal products within the Community. Trade is hindered when different laws apply in the different countries and impose different, and sometimes even conflicting, requirements on proprietary medicines. Several sets of regulations have been made to deal with this matter.

Other EEC Directives 75/318 and 75/319 dealt respectively with the testing of proprietary medicinal products in so far as analytical, pharmacotoxicological and clinical aspects were concerned, and the qualifications of those who are responsible for ensuring that such products meet the necessary specifications ('qualified persons').

More recently, EEC Directive 81/602 on Stilbenes and Thyrostatic Substances has led to changes in the law relating to animal feeding stuffs and veterinary medicines. The EEC Directive 81/852 outlines the qualifications and experience necessary for persons to act as 'qualified persons' in respect of veterinary drugs. Furthermore, EEC Directive 83/570 has required changes to the product particulars submitted with applications for product licences. In future, the shelf life will be required to be stated for all products not merely those whose life is less than three years.

The Committee for Proprietary Medicinal Products was set up under Directive 75/319. Its function is to promote co-operation between the national registration bodies so as to prevent inconsistent decisions being given with regard to licensing. It will give an opinion relating to a product when the holder of a marketing authorisation wants to use the Committee to extend it to at least five other

Member States, or when inconsistent decisions have been made by the authorities in Member States. A Member State can also apply for an opinion where the interest of the Community is involved.

A Pharmaceutical Committee consisting of senior officials from the Member States has been set up to advise the EEC Commission on matters relating to proprietary medicines.

References

Statutes at Large, Vol 2, 1461–1601

Report of the Committee on the Control of Certain Therapeutic Substances (1921) Cmd, 1156

Report of the Departmental Committee set up to Consider Schedule A to the Pharmacy Act 1868. (1903) Cmd, 1442

Pharmaceutical Society of Great Britain v. Piper (1893) 1 Q.B. 686

Report of the Select Committee on Patent Medicines, 414 (1914)

Interim Report of the Inter-Departmental Committee on Drug Addictions (Brain Committee) (1959)

Joint Sub-Committee on Safety of Drugs. Final Report (1963)

Forthcoming Legislations on the Safety, Quality and Descriptions of Drugs and Medicines (1967) Cmd, 3395

Committee on the Review of Medicines, Annual Report for 1976, paragraph 6

Report of the Joint Committee on the Use of Antibiotics in Animal Husbandry and Veterinary Medicine (Swann Report) (1969)

Chapter 2
The Administration of the Act

The Ministers

Two groups of Ministers are responsible for the administration of the Act –

(a) 'Health Ministers', i.e. the Secretary of State for Social Services, the Secretaries of State for Scotland and for Wales, and the Department of Health and Social Services for Northern Ireland,

(b) 'Agriculture Ministers', i.e. the Minister of Agriculture, Fisheries and Food, the Secretaries of State for Scotland and for Wales and the Department of Agriculture for Northern Ireland.

'The Ministers' means all of them acting jointly.

'The appropriate Ministers' means the Health Ministers except when matters relating to veterinary drugs and the treatment of diseases in animals are involved when it means 'the Ministers' (section 1 as amended).

POWERS AND DUTIES OF MINISTERS

It would be tedious to enumerate all the powers and duties which have been given to the Ministers or to either group of Ministers by this Act. However, a brief account of the more important of them will serve to illustrate their scope.

In Part I of the Act, the Ministers appoint the chairman and members of the Medicines Commission (section 2), and may alter the Commission's powers and duties (section 5). They may also set up other expert committees (section 4), and to date six such have been created namely –

1. The British Pharmacopoeia Commission (1970/1256, amended by 1982/1335)
2. The Committee on Safety of Medicines (1970/1257)
3. The Veterinary Products Committee (1970/1304)
4. The Committee on the Review of Medicines (1975/1006)
5. The Committee on Dental and Surgical Materials (1975/1473)
6. The Committee on Radiation from Radio-active Medicinal Products (1978/1005)

The Commission and the committees must produce annual reports which the Ministers lay before Parliament (section 5). Copies of these reports may be purchased from the DHSS.

Part II of the Act deals with the licensing system. The 'licensing authority' consists of the Ministers and has powers to grant, renew, vary, suspend, or revoke licences and certificates, (section 6). There are also powers to exempt classes of persons (sections 9, 10, and 11) and products (sections 12 and 15) from the licensing provisions.

Part III of the Act empowers the Ministers to make orders to specify products which –

(1) may be sold otherwise than from pharmacies, called GSL products (section 51);

(2) may be sold only on prescription, called POMs (section 58);

(3) on safety grounds are prohibited from being sold (section 62).

The Ministers do not appear to have powers to prohibit the administration of any product or class of products but they can restrict the administration of those products which require special knowledge or skills to specially certified persons (section 60). On the occasions when it has been desirable to control administration, the Ministers have used their powers under the European Communities Act.

Section 75 in Part IV permits a Minister to prevent the registration of a premises as a pharmacy if it fails to comply with any regulations made under section 66. Such regulations have yet to be made.

In Part V various powers are available to control the packaging and labelling of medicines while comprehensive controls over the advertising of medicines can be imposed under Part VI of the Act.

In Part VII of the Act the Ministers are authorised to publish the British Pharmacopoeia, a list of 'approved names' for medicinal products and any other compendia they consider to be useful.

In Part VIII there are two very important sections (104 and 105) which enable the Ministers to extend some or all of the provisions of the Act to substances or articles which are not medicinal products within the meaning of section 130.

On the other hand, section 130(5)(c) permits the Ministers to specify by order, substances or articles which shall NOT be subject to control under the Act. The Breathing Gases Order 1977/1488 is the only example to date.

The duty of the various Ministers to secure the enforcement of the Act and its subordinate legislation is specified in sections 108, 109 and 110. Some of the enforcement functions can be delegated to the Pharmaceutical Society of Great Britain and/or the local food and drug authorities.

Since the Act was made, most of the powers and duties outlined above have been used. The Ministers, in exercising their powers and duties to make orders or regulations must do so by means of statutory instrument (section 129) and to date about 190 of them have been made and around 150 are still in force. Some have to be laid before Parliament before coming into operation, while others (e.g. those made under sections 13, 15(1), 35(2)(b), 49, 79 and 105 are made subject to annulment in pursuance of a resolution of either House. There is provision for the Orders to be varied or revoked but this does not apply to those made under sections 16(1), 17(d), 25(1), 37(3), 52 or 69(3).

Before making any such delegated (or subordinate) legislation, the Ministers are obliged to consult such organisations as they consider represent interests likely to be affected by it. In addition, before making such legislation under Parts III, V or VI of the Act, or under sections 104 or 105, they must consult the Commission or one of the expert committees. While they must take such advice into account, they are not bound to accept it. Regulations may be made so as to apply different provisions for different areas, or for different cases or circumstances and may be made subject to exceptions, limitations or conditions if necessary or expedient.

Some sections of the Act (e.g. section 108) permit the Ministers to make 'arrangements' with other bodies to participate in the enforcement of the Act. Furthermore, some sets of regulations authorise the Ministers to give 'directions' imposing restrictions upon a particular activity (such as advertising a product) as part of the conditions applicable to a licence. Such 'arrangements' and 'directions' are administrative, rather than legislative, in nature.

To cope with the multifarious effects of the Act the Medicines Division has been set up within the DHSS. The Animal Health Division has a similar role in MAFF in relation to veterinary drugs and animal feeding stuffs.

The Medicines Division

This Division of the DHSS provides professional and administrative support for the Commission and expert committees. It also carries out the functions of the licensing authority in respect of human medicines and manufacturers' and wholesale dealers' licences. It includes the staff of the medicines inspectorate and has other enforcement functions. In October 1984 the staff comprised some 50 pharmacists, 16 doctors, one dentist and four other scientists. There were also approximately 125 administrative staff.

The following brief account of the work of the Division will provide some idea of the scope and size of its task. It was collected from the Annual Reports of the Division which, until 1978, were published with the Reports of the Commission and Committee. Broadly speaking, the work can be divided into three classes.

LICENSING

The Division processes and assesses applications for product licences for consideration by the expert committees. Sometimes informal discussions between the applicant and members of the Division are necessary to clarify matters of detail.

The Division is responsible for the drafting, authorisation and issue of the licences. Being legal documents they have to be drafted with care to ensure accuracy.

In addition to dealing with applications for product licences and clinical trial certificates for new products, the Division processes licences of right which are due for renewal.

The Division also issues export certificates under section 50 of the Act. These certificates help companies to satisfy the requirements of countries to which they wish to export medicines.

The Division publishes leaflets on various topics usually, but not exclusively, relating to licensing. They are called 'MALs'. It also publishes a quarterly leaflet called 'MAIL' which contains notes about impending legislative changes and other matters of interest to licence holders.

The Division has also published the 'Guide to Good Manufacturing Practice' (sometimes called 'The Orange Guide') which is obtainable from HMSO. Although intended for manufacturers and for hospital pharmacists engaged in manufacture, it can be read with profit by any pharmacist.

LEGISLATION

The Division is involved in drafting legislation relating to medicines and also in the consultations with industry, the professions and other interests affected, which occur during the drafting stage. Some of this legislation results from our membership of the EEC and the Division is consequently involved in meetings of community committees etc., and in preparing briefs for our representatives.

INSPECTION AND ENFORCEMENT

Members of the Medicines Inspectorate visit manufacturers (both in UK and abroad) and wholesale dealers, as well as hospital manufacturing units and blood transfusion units to ensure that the provisions of the Act are being met. They may take samples of products (especially when they suspect that something may be wrong) for analysis.

In 1973, a Defect Report Centre was established to deal with reports of suspected defects in medicines received from hospitals, manufacturers and others. The Centre provides a 24 hour service. When a report is received it is investigated. The product may have to be analysed and where necessary Regional Health Authorities are notified by telephone and letter. In extreme cases, a full recall of the batch may be necessary. Some reports subsequently prove to be groundless.

The Medicines Commission

CONSTITUTION

This is specified in section 2. The Commission must consist of at least eight persons appointed by the Ministers. Each of the following activities must be represented by at least one person 'having wide and recent experience' in that activity –

(a) the practice of medicine

(b) the practice of veterinary medicine

(c) the practice of pharmacy

(d) chemistry (other than pharmaceutical chemistry)

(e) the pharmaceutical industry.

The first Medicines Commission was appointed in 1969, and consisted of a Chairman (Sir Derrick Dunlop) and 13 members. The Commission has since been enlarged to a total of 19 members comprising eight doctors, four pharmacists, three veterinarians, one dentist, one chemist, one physicist and a barrister.

The Commission is a body corporate having perpetual succession and a common seal. Its members (and members of the committees set up under section 4 of the Act) are disqualified from being members of the House of Commons, and the Commission is thus independent of political pressure and patronage.

The terms of office of members of the Commission are specified in 1970/746. Members hold office for four years but may resign by giving written notice to the Ministers. A person appointed to replace a member who has died or resigned will retire when his predecessor would have retired.

FUNCTIONS

These are specified in section 3. The chief duty of the Commission is to advise any or all of the Ministers on matters relating to the execution of the Act, or the exercise of powers under the Act or to medicinal products. This advice may be given when requested or when the Commission considers it expedient. The Commission has various other functions namely –

(1) to make recommendations regarding the number and functions of committees to be set up;

(2) to recommend to the Ministers persons qualified to serve on such committees;

(3) to review the committees and recommend any changes in number or function thought to be appropriate;

(4) to advise the licensing authority either on request or where Part II of the Act requires the Commission to be consulted. Section 21 of the Act permits an applicant for a licence or certificate to make oral or written representations to a committee or to the Commission if the Authority been advised to refuse a licence or certificate on the grounds of safety, quality or efficacy, or to grant it subject to unacceptable conditions. The Commission has similar appellate functions under Schedule 2 when the Authority has been advised to suspend, revoke or vary a licence or certificate;

(5) to consider oral or written representations against any order prohibiting the sale, supply or importation of medicinal products or medicated animal feeding stuffs (section 62);

(6) to direct the British Pharmacopoeia Commission (sections 99 and 100);

(7) to direct the preparation of any other compendia of standards or other publications giving information about substances or articles used in human or animal medicines (section 101);

(8) to undertake any functions relating to medicinal products which have not been assigned to a committee, in particular to matters relating to safety, quality, or efficacy and the study of reports of adverse reactions.

The Commission may, with the approval of the Ministers, appoint one or more committees to assist in its work. Such a committee must include at least one member of the Commission and the Chairman is appointed by the Commission (1970/746). The Commission is required to make an annual report of its work to the Ministers and each such report must be laid before Parliament.

The Report for 1972 gave some interesting statistics on applications for licences of right, approximately 55,000 were made for products for human use; 4000 for veterinary drugs; 521 for manufacturers' licences and 1589 for wholesale dealers' licences. The figures indicate the magnitude of the work involved in licensing.

The same report stated that several hospital patients had died, it was thought, as a result of the use of a contaminated batch of intravenous solution. The Secretary of State for Social Services asked the Commission to undertake an immediate review of the measures necessary to prevent microbial contamination of medicinal products. The Commission set up the 'Committee on the Prevention of Microbial Contamination of Medicinal Products' which started by investigating the problems relating to the preparation of injections. It later extended its studies into other medicinal products. The Commission published both reports of the Committee:

'Interim Report on Heat Sterilised Fluids for Parenteral Administration' HMSO 1972.

'Report on the Prevention of Microbial Contamination of Medicinal Products' HMSO 1973.

Every year, the Commission has to deal with appeals from persons aggrieved by an impending decision of the licensing authority to refuse a licence or certificate or to revoke or vary an existing one. The appeal may be made orally or in writing, the former being most common. The Commission takes a completely independent view of the problem and this is shown by the statistics for the years 1980–1983. During these years, appeals were made in respect of 83 products. In 16 cases, the Commission's advice was favourable to the applicant, in 36 cases it was unfavourable. In the 31 remaining cases, the Commission recommended a result that was broadly favourable to the applicant but contained conditions or modifications. More than half of the 83 products were contact lens fluids, and applications concerning these were dealt with in 1983.

The Commission is kept informed of relevant developments in EEC committees, and in particular receives reports and comments on the work of the Pharmaceutical Committee and the Committee on Proprietary Medicinal Products.

The Commission takes a very broad view of its responsibilities and has given advice and made recommendations on a variety of matters. For example in its Report for 1977 it recommended (para 4,), '. oral contraceptives should continue to be available on prescription only but that, when consultation with general practitioners was not acceptable or desirable, women and girls should be able to consult midwives, health visitors, nurses or pharmacists suitably trained in all aspects of family planning and that members of these professions who had been specially trained, should be authorised to prescribe oral contraceptives.'

Furthermore, (paragraph 9) 'The Commission recommended that, as the arrangements made by pharmacists in some areas for the collection and delivery of medicines were serving a useful purpose, an amending Order under section 57 of the Act should be made to provide exemption for them from the requirements of section 52 of the Act'. This was done, 1978/1421.

The Reports for the years 1978–1980 indicated that the Commission had examined the case for the strict liability for defective products, and held the view that it would cause immense difficulties for doctors and for patients and could lead to 'defensive medicine'.

In its Report for 1981, the Commission expressed concern that herbal remedies could be labelled for conditions for which advertising was prohibited in relation to orthodox medicines (para 12).

In its Report for 1983, the Commission supported the idea that all solid dose medicines should carry a unique marking, but observed that such a scheme would take a long time to implement. On the subject of experiments on living animals, the Commission emphasised the importance of continuing research into new medicines and the maintenance of the testing of safety and efficacy of existing medicines and vaccines.

The advice proffered by the Commission is not invariably accepted by the Ministers. A case in point arose in 1979 when the Commission recommended that the temporary exemption allowing 'unorthodox practitioners' to inject certain preparations into their patients should not be renewed in February 1980. The Ministers however, issued regulations which conferred on such practitioners the permanent right to inject these products (see now 1983/1212, article 9(2) and Schedule 3(III),7).

Committee on the Safety of Medicines (CSM)

This was established by the Health Ministers (1971/1257) for the following purposes –

(a) giving advice with respect to the safety, quality and efficacy in relation to human use, of any substance or article to which any provision of the Act is applicable and,

(b) promoting the collection and investigation of information relating to adverse reactions, for the purpose of enabling advice to be given.

It consists of a chairman and 19 members.

On the 1st September 1971, this committee took over the work previously done by the Committee on Safety of Drugs.

The Committee now has four sub-committees to help in the work, namely –

(1) Sub-committee on Safety, Efficacy and Adverse Reactions;

(2) Sub-committee on Biologicals;

(3) Sub-committee on Chemistry, Pharmacy and Standards;

(4) Joint Sub-committee on Adverse Reactions to Vaccines and Immunological Products.

The work of the first sub-committee is similar to that of the corresponding sub-committees of the old CSD. The sub-committee on biologicals deals with vaccines and other immunological products, blood products, hormones, antibiotics, genetically engineered products and some enzymes. The Chemistry, Pharmacy and Standards Sub-Committee examines proposed methods of manufacture, the specifications and quality control procedures for new drug substances and formulations. The Joint Sub-Committee on Adverse Reactions to Vaccines and Immunological Products has members from the CSM and the Joint Committee on Vaccination and Immunisation. It also provides advice to the CRM (see later).

The chief function of the CSM is to advise the licensing authority on applications for product licences or clinical trial certificates. The applicant must submit relevant data to the authority. This data is examined by a doctor and a pharmacist in the committee's secretariat and a detailed report prepared. The data is sent to the appropriate sub-committees for examination and they report to the main Committee. The Committee considers all the reports before deciding whether to advise the authority to grant a licence (or certificate). Sometimes the Committee feel that insufficient evidence has been provided by the applicant, in which case the deficiencies are pointed out to him. Between 1/9/71 and the end of 1983, the Committee has considered about 4200 applications for product licences, and has advised the granting of a licence in about one half of the cases, sometimes with modifications. Almost 200 applications were subsequently withdrawn by the applicants and in 140 cases the Committee advised the authority to refuse a licence. In the remaining cases the decision was deferred until additional information became available, or the applicant had been advised that the Committee would probably recommend refusal of the licence and the Committee were awaiting an appeal or further data. In the same period, almost 600 clinical trial certificates have been issued, 17 refused and 68 withdrawn.

The other important function of the CSM is to collect and investigate adverse reactions to drugs. The Committee has improved the 'Yellow Card' on which doctors and dentists are encouraged to report every suspected adverse reaction to a medicine. Each report is followed up to gain additional information which could not be included in the original report. The number of reports received annually has increased steadily since 1964. In 1983 almost 13,000 reports were received, bringing the total since 1964 to about 130,000. While there is no room for complacency, these figures have to be viewed against the number of prescriptions dispensed each year in the United Kingdom (over 400 million family practitioner NHS prescriptions in 1982). Furthermore, Griffin (1984) has reported that of the reports up to and including 1982 (117,000 approximately) there were 4658 deaths and 15,270 serious reactions. It seems therefore that over 80% of the reports refer to less serious effects.

The information derived from these reports is used in three ways. When a drug (or group of drugs) causes a number of adverse reactions, the information is published in a leaflet (Current Problems) and distributed to doctors, dentists and pharmacists. On other occasions, letters are sent to doctors giving the results of special investigations undertaken by the Sub-committee on Adverse Reactions. The Register of Adverse Reactions is also published periodically, and sent to medical schools, postgraduate medical centres and Regional and District Pharmaceutical Officers. The current edition was published in 1977 in seven volumes and includes information derived from over 40,000 reports of reactions experienced by people taking medicinal products. A working party is currently studying ways of improving the system.

The CSM has devised a new scheme for the post-marketing surveillance of drugs which will supplement the current arrangements for reporting on adverse reactions. Details of the scheme are being discussed with industry and the professions and the Committee hope to implement it shortly.

In addition to the functions outlined above, the Committee also gives advice to other expert committees and also advises the licensing authority on other matters, e.g. proposed statutory instruments, the Compendium of Licensing Requirements for the Manufacture of Biological Medicinal Products.

In 1982 it commenced a study of the issues involved in the use of drugs in the elderly. It recommended that from 1985, all applications for product licences for new substances or new formulations likely to be used in the elderly, should include clinical data obtained from studies conducted on elderly patients.

Veterinary Products Committee (VPC)

This was established by the Agriculture Ministers (1970/1304) for the following purposes –

(1) giving advice with respect to safety, quality and efficacy in relation to the veterinary use of any substance or article to which any provision of the Act is applicable, and

(2) promoting the collection and investigation of information relating to adverse reactions, for the purpose of enabling such advice to be given.

It consists of a chairman and 18 members.

The functions of the VPC are analogous to those of the CSM. It receives advice from the Joint Sub-Committee on Anti-microbial Substances, and also from its Feeding Stuffs Sub-Committee.

Like the CSM, it operates a 'yellow card' system for veterinarians and others to report suspected adverse reactions to veterinary drugs. During 1983 it received 125 such reports. Some were found to be due to errors in the manufacture of feeding stuffs and to overdosage. In some other cases products had been used in species for which the products were unlicensed.

The VPC reviews veterinary drugs having licences of right, and during 1983 reviewed intramammary products, and also Large Animal and Small Animal Immobilon and Revivon and would then review chloramphenicol products.

It receives reports from various committees dealing with EEC Directives. The UK implemented EEC Directives 81/851 and 81/852 in December 1983, by making nine new statutory instruments. The aim is to provide a common authorisation system and also harmonisation of technical standards.

British Pharmacopoeia Commission

This was established in 1970 (1970/1256) for the following purposes –

(a) the preparation of a new edition of the B.P.

(b) the preparation of amendments to the B.P. 1968 and

(c) the preparation of lists of names to be used as monograph headings in a new B.P. (Approved Names).

The original Commission completed its work in 1973 and a new, enlarged Commission was appointed to compile compendia of standards under Part VII of the Act, since it is 'the appropriate body' for that purpose. The Commission was enlarged to include experts on veterinary drugs and surgical dressings. It currently consists of a chairman and 18 members. The Commission is advised by 13 committees.

The Commission has published two Addenda (1982 and 1983) to the British Pharmacopoeia 1980, and also the British Pharmacopoeia (Veterinary), and a List of Approved Names. The latter is a useful book which not only provides an alphabetical list of approved names, but also gives advice on their pronunciation, their chemical structure, trade names (if any) and the therapeutic class. It also specifies the International Non-Proprietary Name (either Proposed or Recommended) and the United States Approved Name (U.S.A.N.) if these differ significantly from the Approved Name. It is therefore invaluable in the design of labels. During 1983 two more Supplements (Nos. 4 and 5) to 'British Approved Names' were published. The Commission also publishes a volume of Infra Red Reference Spectra.

The Commission is unique among the expert committees in that it has its own laboratory which critically examines tests proposed for inclusion in either the British Pharmacopoeia or the European Pharmacopoeia. It also devises new tests, and maintains and distributes British Pharmacopoeia Chemical Reference Samples. It has facilities to carry out a wide range of tests on substances and products, and also the small scale manufacture of liquid and semi-solid preparations. Much work has been done recently on in vitro dissolution tests for tablets and capsules especially those designed for slow or delayed release.

The Commission and its staff collaborate with the authorities responsible for the European Pharmacopoeia, and actively participate in its production.

Committee on the Review of Medicines

This was created (1975/1006) to give advice on the safety, quality and efficacy, in relation to human use, of any substance or article which was the subject of a product licence. The majority of these products had been given a product licence of right without being subjected to independent scrutiny for safety, quality or efficacy. It was therefore necessary to bring them into line with newer products. When the United Kingdom joined the European Economic Community it inherited the obligation to examine all proprietary medicinal products (except homoeopathic remedies) by 1990. Approximately 36,000 product licences of right had been issued when licensing commenced, and information about these was sought in 1976. At this stage some 10,000 such licences were voluntarily surrendered. Nowadays, the CRM also examines applications for renewal of ordinary product licences.

It consists of a Chairman and 19 members.

The review procedure was laid down by the Ministers before the Committee was set up. Very briefly it is as follows. Information and data from the companies are collected together and then considered by the Committee. The Committee then makes a provisional recommendation, normally on the drug substance. Consultation than takes place with licence holders and trade associations and comments are invited. The comments are considered and the recommendation is confirmed or modified. This represents the view of the Committee on the drug substance. The products themselves are then considered. It is clearly a lengthy process and it will be some years before the task is complete. It should be mentioned that the Committee does not evaluate every product. Some (perhaps the majority) are reviewed by the secretariat who apply the criteria developed by the Committee.

To expedite matters the Committee set up four sub-committees in 1975, each to deal with products of a particular type. The sub-committees were –

(a) Sub-committee on anti-rheumatic agents

Approximately 1250 licensed products were involved. Among the drug substances for which a recommendation was made were mefenamic acid, flufenamic acid, indomethacin, ibuprofen, colchicine, phenylbutazone, naproxen.

Some substances e.g. aspirin, paracetamol, benorylate, phenazone, and salicylamide, are both anti-rheumatic agents and analgesics, and were considered by joint meetings of this sub-committee and that dealing with analgesics.

(b) Sub-committee on Analgesics

Approximately 400 products were included in this group. Among the substances involved were dextropropoxyphene, codeine, pentazocine, phenacetin, morphine.

(c) Sub-committee on Psychotropic Agents

There were approximately 1450 products in this class and among the substances considered were imipramine, desipramine and caffeine.

(d) Sub-committee on Immunological Agents

This is the same committee as the Biologicals Sub-committee of the CSM. There were approximately 150 products in this class. Reports on three types of vaccine (Yellow Fever, BCG Vaccine (intradermal) and Dip/Tet/Per) have been considered. These groups of products were chosen because of their wide use and also because they were known to cause problems in use.

The Committee felt that it would not normally be necessary for companies to generate new data, e.g. from double-blind trials for products that had been used for some years because the experience of the members of the Committee would be sufficient to judge the value of the product. However, more information on contra-indications, warnings, and precautions was desirable. More positive statements about paediatric dosage, e.g. 'paediatric use not proven', or 'unsuitable for use in children' was also necessary.

The Committee pointed out that in the early days of licensing, some 'indications' were described in general terms but that now it is necessary to be more specific. The review would therefore remove inadequate descriptions. Advice might also be given regarding labelling and advertising where appropriate.

The CRM set up a Working Party on the Safety of Drug Usage during Pregnancy which reported in 1977. Its main recommendation was that drugs should be categorised according to the available evidence as to their safety in pregnancy. There are six such categories, namely –

(1) There is clinical or epidemiological evidence of safety of the drug in human pregnancy.

(2) There is no, or inadequate, evidence of safety of the drug in human pregnancy but it has been in wide use for many years without apparent ill consequence, animal studies having shown no hazard.

(3) There is no, or inadequate, evidence of safety of the drug in human pregnancy; it has been in wide use for many years without apparent ill consequence; there is evidence of harmful effects in pregnancy in animals.

(4) There is epidemiological or other good evidence of hazard in human pregnancy.

(5) There has been little human usage, but there has been no adverse animal evidence.

(6) There is no evidence as to the drug safety in human pregnancy nor is there evidence from animal work that it is free from hazard.

The knowledge of the category into which a particular drug falls is obviously of value to doctors when advising pregnant women about drug usage but the information must be readily accessible. It was suggested therefore, that it be included in data sheets, and perhaps even published in the form of a list under Part VII of the Act. The Committee hoped that industry would make available data which it had on drugs which have been in use for some time and also generate new data about old drugs so as to improve the data base available to the Committee. The question of providing information to the public about the use during pregnancy of non-prescription drugs was referred to the Medicines Commission.

By 1981 it became clear that the task could not be completed by 1990 using the present system. A new simplified procedure was outlined and this placed more reliance on existing legislation defining products safe enough to be on the GSL and controls over advertising to the public and less emphasis on a detailed evaluation of the product. Other products (those sold only from pharmacies) would be reviewed in smaller groups and when they were due for renewal. At the end of 1983, there remained some 11,000 products to be reviewed and this excludes some 6000 homoeopathic products which, under EEC rules, do not need to be reviewed. In August 1984 there were still some 14,000 licences of right awaiting review.

Committee on Dental and Surgical Materials (CDSM)

This was created (1975/1473) with the following terms of reference:

To give advice on safety, quality and efficacy, for human and animal use of –

(a) substances or articles to which any provision of the Medicines Act is applicable and for which neither the CSM nor the VPC is the appropriate Committee, and

(b) instruments, apparatus and appliances to which any provision of the Act is applicable, and

(c) to promote the collation and investigation of information on adverse reactions for the purpose of giving such advice.

It consists of a Chairman and 18 members.

The Committee deals with dental pharmaceuticals, dental filling substances, bone cements and tissue adhesives, absorbable surgical ligatures, sutures, etc. as defined in the Surgical Materials Order and also with intra-uterine contraceptive devices and contact lenses, contact lens blanks and contact lens fluids.

A Sub-committee on Ophthalmic Products (SCOP) has been established to advise the CDSM on the safety, quality and efficacy of contact lenses, contact lens blanks, contact lens fluids, etc. for administration to the human eye. During 1981 and 1982 almost 200 applications for product licences for contact lens fluids were received, and were given priority so as to meet the 1st July 1983 deadline for possession of licences for these products. Unfortunately, many applications could not be processed because the manufacturers had failed to provide sufficient information. As the report of the Medicines Commission for 1983 noted, many of the applications for licences for contact lens fluids were refused or granted subject to conditions.

The CDSM and SCOP liaise with the CSM and have access to advice from its various sub-committees.

Committee on Radiation from Radioactive Medicinal Products (CRRMP)

This was the latest of the expert committees and was created in 1978 (1978/1005).

Its purpose was to give advice with respect to the safety, quality and efficacy, in relation to radiation, of any substance or article for human use to which any provision of the Act is applicable.

The Committee was abolished by an Order made in 1984 (1984/1261).

Offences, Defences and Enforcement

OFFENCES

It is a general principle of English law that in order to obtain a conviction, it is necessary to prove, not only that the accused performed the guilty act (the 'actus reus'), but that he also had a guilty mind ('mens rea'), i.e. he had a guilty intention. The statutes creating such offences usually contain words such as 'maliciously', 'knowingly', 'wilfully', 'with the intention of permanently depriving...' or similar expression to define the state of mind necessary for the commission of the offence. Where a statute does not include such a phrase in the definition of an offence, the offence is said to be an 'absolute offence' or one which gives rise to strict liability.

Such offences are not uncommon in statutes such as the Medicines Act, the Foods Act or the Licensing Act which are intended to impose standards or control activities in the public interest. The reasons for this are several. In the first case, if a guilty mind is necessary, the thoughtless, the negligent and the careless are guiltless. This would defeat the purpose of the Act by ignoring the very people who would be responsible for much of the damage. Secondly, the purpose of the Act must be to ensure that the people involved do their utmost to comply with the requirements so that the products are made and dealt with so as to achieve the highest standards.

Recently, the courts have tended to take a less rigid view of the concept of strict liability, especially when it would be impossible to impute knowledge to the person charged. In Sweet v Parsley for example, Lord Reid said that "... mens rea is an essential ingredient of every offence unless some reason can be found for holding that it is not necessary." (W.L.R 1969). However, he also said that "It has long been the practice to recognise absolute offences in this class (referring to a Licensing Act case) of quasi-criminal acts, and one can safely assume that, when Parliament is passing new legislation dealing with this class of offences its silence as to mens rea means that the old practice is to apply."

The need for 'mens rea' has been discussed in at least two cases brought under the Medicines Act. In the first (Pharmaceutical Society of Great Britain v Harwood) the court held that it was an essential ingredient for a conviction relating to the dispensing of a prescription for a 'prescription only medicine' because there were some requirements that could not be known to the pharmacist. On the other hand, another court held that the unsupervised sale of a certain medicines was an absolute offence because it was clearly the intention of arliament to confine the sale of such medicines to pharmacists and persons acting under their supervision (Pharmaceutical Society of Great Britain v Logan).

It follows also that in an 'absolute offence' there may be several persons convicted for the same offence. For example, a sales assistant may actually sell the defective article, the shop manager may encourage (aid, abet, or procure) the sale, but the company itself would be held to be the seller because it is the employer of the staff and the recipient of any profits. Thus all three 'persons' could be convicted of selling the article. In most cases the enforcement authority would undoubtedly prosecute the company and may proceed against the manager too. It is unlikely that the assistant would be prosecuted unless the offence was due to his negligence or mistake. The need for such a procedure is necessary because were it otherwise, the company (who are responsible for the purchase or manufacture of the merchandise), and who would obtain the financial benefits arising from the sale of sub-standard goods could hide behind the convictions of its staff. Some offences have built-in defences which may protect the company from a malicious or careless employee. In addition, there are two defences (sections 121 and 122) which are of wider application and are discussed below.

Where an offence under the Act or regulations is committed by a body corporate and it is proved to have been committed with the connivance and consent (or due to the neglect) of an officer of the organisation, he may too be proceeded against and punished (section 124(1)). In this respect, officer includes any director, manager, secretary or anyone purporting to act in such a capacity.

Furthermore, where the body corporate is carrying on a retail pharmacy business, the word 'officer' includes the superintendent and the pharmacist in control of the premises at which the offence occurred (section 124(2)).

The offences that may be committed in relation to licensing, sale, etc. are described in the relevant chapters.

DEFENCES

The Act and regulations create numerous offences and to some of these a defence is available. There are, however, two defences which are available for a number of different offences and these are worth discussion here.

The first (section 121) applies to offences contained in sections 63, 64, 65, 85, 86, 87, 88, 89, 90, 93, 94, 95, and 96, and also contraventions of any regulations made under these sections. The sections concerned are those relating to the purity and quality of medicines sold to consumers, the labelling and packaging of such products and their advertising.

The defence is available to a person who may be charged with an offence which was due to the act or default of another person, e.g. an employee or a supplier. Section 121(1) makes it clear that under such circumstances, whether or not the first person is charged, the second may be charged and is liable to the same penalty. If both parties are charged and the first person can prove to the satisfaction of the court –

(a) that he exercised due diligence to secure compliance with the provision in question, and

(b) that the contravention was due to the act or omission of the second person,

he is entitled to be acquitted (section 121(2)).

In order to rely on the defence, the first person must give the prosecutor at least seven clear days notice (in writing) of his intention to use the defence and give such information as will identify or help to identify the true culprit (section 121(3)).

The 'Warranty' Defence

This is the second general defence. It may be used in the offences created by sections 63(b), 64, 65, 85, 86, 87, 88, and 90 and any regulations made under them (section 122(2)).

The defendant (i.e. the person charged) must prove –

(a) that he purchased the substance or article concerned in the UK as a substance or article which could lawfully be sold, supplied, offered or exposed for sale or supply, under the name, description or for the purpose for which he sold, supplied, or offered or exposed it, and with a written warranty to that effect;

(b) that at the time of the offence he had no reason to believe that it was otherwise; and

(c) that the substance or article was then in the same state as when he purchased it.

To take advantage of this defence, the defendant must send to the prosecutor at least three clear days before the hearing, a copy of the warranty, a statement that he intends to rely upon it, and the name and address of the person from whom he received it. He must also notify that person (section 122(3)). An employee of the purchaser can similarly rely upon a warranty supplied to the employer (section 122(4)). The supplier of the warranty is entitled to appear at the hearing and can give evidence (section 122(5)). For the purposes of this section, the name or description given on an invoice shall be deemed to be a written warranty that the substance or article can be lawfully dealt with under that name (section 122(6)).

It is an offence to apply a warranty or a certificate of analysis issued in respect of one substance, to a different substance (section 123(1)). It is also an offence to issue a false warranty to a purchaser (section 123(2)).

Enforcement

The individual Ministers have a duty to enforce the Act (sections 108(1); 109(1); 110(1)). Furthermore, they are solely responsible for enforcing the licensing provisions and also those which affect hospitals or the premises of practitioners.

The Ministers can delegate some of their other enforcement duties to local food and drug authorities and/or to the Pharmaceutical Society of Great Britain. With regard to the latter, people are sometimes surprised to learn that a professional body has responsibility for enforcing the provisions of certain statutes. In fact, the Society has had such a responsibility since 1868.

The Society, concurrently with the Ministers (section 108(6)) has a duty to enforce in England and Wales the provisions relating to the sale and supply of medicines other than those on the GSL (section 52), the sale, supply and administration of POMs (section 58), the regulations restricting the sale, supply or administration of medicines which can only be prescribed and used by specially certified practitioners (e.g. radioactive medicines) (section 60), and regulations restricting the sale or supply of medicines to other specified classes (section 61). The Society also has concurrent responsibility for enforcing the provisions relating to the registration of pharmacies and the restrictions on the use of certain titles (sections 77–79).

The Ministers were empowered to make arrangements (section 108(2)) with the Society or with local food and drug authorities or both, to enforce the law relating to the quality and purity of medicines offered for retail sale or supply and of their labelling, packaging and certain advertisements relating to them. The provisions affected are section 62(1)(a), section 63(b), sections 64 and 65, section 85(3),(4),(5), sections 87(2), 88(3), and 89(2) in so far as they relate to the retail sale or offer or exposure for sale or supply of medicinal products. Also the provisions of section 86(2) and (3) as they apply to leaflets supplied with such products, and the provisions of sections 93 and 94, and regulations made under section 95. Such arrangements have been made with the Pharmaceutical Society.

The Food and Drugs Authority for each area in England and Wales has a concurrent duty with the Ministers to enforce sections 53 and 54 and regulations made under section 66 in respect of premises which are neither pharmacies nor premises registered with the Pharmaceutical Society on which veterinary drugs specified in articles 3 and 4 of the Veterinary Drugs Exemption Order are sold. Presumably this refers to retailers selling GSL medicines and also the premises of herbalists. In Scotland, local authorities have analogous powers. The Pharmaceutical Society enforces these provisions in respect of pharmacies and the registered premises of sellers of veterinary drugs (1980/1923, article 2).

There are corresponding provisions for the enforcement of the sections in Scotland (section 109) but only the Procurator Fiscal may institute proceedings against offenders. In Northern Ireland, the Minister of Health and Social Services has the duty of enforcing the Act but he may delegate some of his powers to district councils, apparently, the Pharmaceutical Society of Northern Ireland has no enforcement role (section 110).

An enforcement officer may, on production of his credentials if requested, enter any premises at any reasonable time, to ascertain whether they have been used in connection with any contravention of the Act or of any regulations or orders made thereunder. He may also enter any ship, hover vehicle, aircraft, vehicle, stall or any other place for similar purposes (section 111). There is provision for the officer to obtain a warrant from a magistrate in various circumstances. The officer may take samples and take copies of any documents etc. (section 112).

References

Medicines Commission, Annual Report for 1972, paragraph

Medicines Commission, Annual Report for 1977, paragraph 4, paragraph 9.

Griffin, J. (1984). In Walker, S.R. and Goldberg, A. (eds.) *Monitoring of Adverse Drug Reactions*. (Lancaster: MTP Press)

Sweet and Parsley (1969) 2 W.L.R. at p474

Pharmaceutical Society of Great Britain v. Harwood (1981) Crim. L.R. 255

Pharmaceutical Society of Great Britain v. Logan (1982) Crim. L.R. 441

Chapter 3
Medicinal Products and Other Articles Subject to Control

MEDICINAL PRODUCT

The Medicines Act makes few, if any, references to medicines, instead it refers to 'medicinal products' which it defines thus –

'any substance or article (not being an instrument, apparatus or appliance) which is manufactured, sold, supplied, imported or exported for use wholly or mainly in either or both of the following ways, that is to say –

(a) use by being administered to one or more human beings or animals for a medicinal purpose;

(b) use, in circumstances to which this paragraph applies, as an ingredient in the preparation of a substance or article which is to be administered to one or more human beings or animals for a medicinal purpose' (section 130(1)).

There are several points worth noting in the above definition –

(1) 'substance' is defined in section 132(i), see Appendix 1;

(2) 'article' is NOT defined in the Act but there is judicial precedent indicating that it includes any corporeal or tangible object;

(3) 'wholly or mainly' but not necessarily exclusively; presumably, if a product is used mainly for a non-medicinal purpose but occasionally is used medicinally (e.g. brandy) it is not a medicinal product within the meaning of the Act; it is also possible for a product to be both a medicinal product and a food, or a medicinal product and a cosmetic;

(4) 'administered' see definition in sub-section (9) below;

(5) 'medicinal purpose' is defined below.

MEDICINAL PURPOSE

Section 130(2) defines 'medicinal purpose' as 'any one or more of the following purposes, that is to say –

(a) treating or preventing disease;

(b) diagnosing disease or ascertaining the existence, degree or extent of a physiological condition;

(c) contraception;

(d) inducing anaesthesia;

(e) otherwise preventing or interfering with the normal operation of a physiological function, whether permanently or temporarily, and whether by way of terminating, reducing or postponing, or increasing or accelerating, the operation of that function or in any other way.'

The words 'disease' and 'treating' (followed from 'treatment') are defined in Appendix 1. The phrase 'physiological function' covers a multitude of effects including perspiration; is therefore an anti-perspirant spray which is sprayed into the axillae a medicinal product? (see definition of 'cosmetic' in Appendix 1). Some anti-smoking preparations act by precipitating the protein covering the tongue and mucosa of the mouth, thus producing a nauseating taste when tobacco is smoked. Such products obviously 'interfere' with the normal operation of a physiological function and are therefore 'medicinal products'. Clearly, the phrase 'medicinal purpose' is capable of very wide interpretation.

INGREDIENTS

Substances, articles and medicinal products used as ingredients in the preparation of a medicinal product –

(a) in a pharmacy or in a hospital; or

(b) by a practitioner; or

(c) which is a herbal remedy by a herbalist, come within the scope of the definition of medicinal product due to section 130(1)(b), as amplified by subsection (3).

The words 'hospital', 'practitioner', and 'herbal remedies' are defined in section 132 (see Appendix 1).

The quality, safety and efficacy of ingredients used in the manufacture of medicines are controlled by the specifications given for them in the application for a product licence. There is therefore no need to control them under section 130.

EXCLUDED ARTICLES

Sub-section (4) excludes from the definition 'any substance or article which is manufactured for use wholly or mainly by being administered to one or more human beings or animals, where it is to be administered to them –

(a) in the course of the business of the person who has manufactured it (in this subsection referred to as 'the manufacturer'), or on behalf of the manufacturer in the course of the business of a laboratory or research establishment carried on by another person, and

(b) solely by way of a test for ascertaining what effects it has when so administered, and

(c) in circumstances where the manufacturer has no knowledge of any evidence that those effects are likely to be beneficial to those human beings, or beneficial to, or otherwise advantageous in relation to those animals, as the case may be, and which (having been so manufactured) is not sold, supplied or exported for use wholly or mainly in any way not fulfilling all the conditions specified in paragraphs (a) to (c) of this subsection.'

Thus experimental substances are excluded from the definition of 'medicinal products' unless they are to be sold, supplied or exported and one or more of the conditions is not fulfilled.

Sub-section (5) excludes from the definition –

(a) substances used in dental surgery for filling dental cavities;

(b) bandages and other surgical dressings, except medicated dressings where the medication has a curative function which is not limited to sterilising the dressing;

(c) substances and articles of such other descriptions or classes as may be specified by an order made by the Ministers, the Health Ministers or the Agriculture Ministers for the purpose of this subsection.

However, dental filling substances have been brought within the scope of most of the relevant Parts of the Act by 1975/533 and the Ministers have exercised their powers in (c) to exclude from the ranks of 'medicinal products' gases used by divers, mountaineers, etc. (Breathing Gases Order 1977/1488).

Sub-section (6) states, in effect, that once a substance or article becomes a medicinal product it shall remain a medicinal product for the purposes of this Act even if at any subsequent time it is sold, supplied, imported, or exported for use wholly or mainly in a way other than those specified in subsection (1) of this section. However, substances manufactured, sold, supplied, imported or exported as animal feeding stuffs in which medicinal products have been incorporated, are excluded from this by subsection (7), and consequently medicated animal feeding stuffs are NOT medicinal products for the purposes of this Act. Many provisions of the Act apply however to such medicated animal feeding stuffs.

In the Act and regulations, frequent reference is made to 'medicinal products of the same description'. Subsection (8) states that medicinal products are of the same description if (but only if) –

(a) they are manufactured to the same specification, and

(b) they are, or are to be, sold, supplied, imported or exported in the same pharmaceutical form, and 'description', in relation to medicinal products, shall be construed accordingly.

ADMINISTRATION OF MEDICINAL PRODUCTS

Subsection (9) defines 'administer'. It means 'administer to a human being or an animal, whether orally, by injection or by introduction into the body in any other way, or by external application whether by direct contact with the body or not; and any reference in this Act to administering a substance or article is a reference to administering it either in its existing state or after it has been dissolved or dispersed in, or diluted or mixed with, some other substance used as a vehicle.'

With reference to subsection (9) note should be taken in the meaning of 'administer' of the words 'whether by direct contact with the body or not;'.

Subsection 10 deals with false and misleading advertisements etc. and will be discussed later.

To summarise, a medicinal product is any substance or article (excluding an instrument, appliance or apparatus) which is manufactured or sold wholly or mainly for administration to humans or animals for a medicinal purpose. It also includes ingredients (whether active or not) used in the preparation of a substance to be administered for a medicinal purpose where it is to be prepared by a practitioner or in a pharmacy or a hospital or by a herbalist.

Normally, ingredients used in the manufacture of medicinal products are NOT themselves medicinal products, nor are bulk chemicals. However, various biological substances specified in the Control of Substances for Manufacture Order are to be treated as medicines and need licences when intended for use as ingredients in the manufacture of medicines.

BORDERLINE PRODUCTS

Most human and veterinary medicines are clearly 'medicinal products' but there are a number of borderline cases such as some foods, cosmetics, toilet articles and disinfectants. Most foods are only foods and if subject to legal control at all, are so controlled under the Food Act 1984 and regulations made thereunder. Likewise, most cosmetics are only cosmetics and if subject to legal control, are so controlled under regulations made under the Consumer Protection Act 1961. Such foods and cosmetics do not fall within the definition of a 'medicinal product' and the Act does not apply to them. However, it is possible for an article to be both a food and a medicinal product, or both a cosmetic and a medicinal product and such products ARE subject to control under the Act.

'Food' is defined as including 'beverages, confectionery and articles and substances used as ingredients in the preparation of food and includes any manufactured substance to which there has been added any vitamin and which is advertised (within the meaning of section 92 of the Act) as available and for sale to the general public as a dietary supplement' (1971/1410; 1980/1924). Thus 'cough lozenges' and 'throat sweets' are both foods and medicinal products, as would be 'tonic wines' and dietary supplements. The relevant order (1971/1410) merely exempts certain of these foods from licensing, it does not exempt them from other controls imposed under the Medicines Act such as labelling and advertising. There is therefore scope for confusion in the case of 'health foods', 'dietary supplements' and the like which, while labelled and advertised as foods, are often the subject of articles in popular magazines which imply a medicinal use.

The nature of any claims made on the label, wrapper or promotional material may be relevant to deciding if the purpose is mainly medicinal. It is suggested, for example, that most shampoos would be classified as toilet articles but if a particular brand is claimed to cure or prevent dandruff then it would also become a 'medicinal product'.

In order to help manufacturers, the Medicines Division have issued a booklet (MAL 8) 'A Guide to the Status of Borderline Products under the Act'. If after considering the information in the Guide, a company's lawyers are still uncertain as to the status of a product, the Division may be prepared to give an opinion on the matter.

'MEDICINAL PRODUCT' IN SUBORDINATE LEGISLATION

Usually the expression 'medicinal product' when used in a statutory instrument made under the Act has the same meaning as in the Act, for example 1977/1055. In some instruments, however, the expression has a somewhat different meaning as the relevant 'Interpretation' paragraph makes plain. For convenience these other interpretations are reproduced below together with the year and number of the relevant statutory instruments. Some of the definitions show that substances and articles specified in orders made under section 104 or 105 are included, while others exclude such substances. Furthermore, a substance may be included for one purpose while being excluded for another purpose; it is therefore necessary to read the document with care.

'medicinal product' includes, where a product licence or animal test certificate relates to any substance or article which is not a medicinal product, the substance or article to which the licence or certificate relates; (1971/972 and similar wording used in 1974/832, 1977/1038).

'medicinal product' includes articles or substances specified in orders made under section 104 or 105 of the Act which are for the time being in force and which direct that Part II of the Act shall have effect in relation to such articles or substances as that Part has effect in relation to medicinal products within the meaning of the Act; (1971/1410, 1971/1447, 1971/1450, 1972/640 and 1972/1199).

'medicinal product' shall not include substances or articles specified in orders made under section 104 or section 105(1)(b) of the Act which are for the time being in force unless such order specifically directs that this order shall have effect in relation to such substances or articles as this Order has effect in relation to medicinal products within the meaning of the Act:
(1972/1200, 1974/498 and 1977/161).

'medicinal product' includes except for the substances and fluids described in paragraph 2 of Schedule 1 to the Medicines (Specified Articles and Substances) Order 1976, articles or substances specified in orders made under section 104 or section 105 of the Act which are for the time being in force and which direct that section 96 of the Act shall have effect in relation to such articles or substances as that section has in relation to medicinal products within the meaning of the Act; (1972/2076).

'medicinal product' includes any substance or article, except for the substances and fluids described in paragraph 2 of Schedule 1 to the Medicines (Specified Articles and Substances) Order 1976, which is specified in the Medicines (Surgical Materials) Order 1971, in the Medicines (Dental Filling Substances) Order 1975 or in any other order made under section 104 or 105 of the Act subsequent to the coming into force of these regulations by virtue of which section 96 of the Act has effect in relation to medicinal products within the meaning of the Act; (1975/1326 as amended by 1979/1760).

'medicinal product' includes any substance or article for human use specified in an order made under section 104 or section 105(1)(b) of the Act which is for the time being in force and which directs that sections 31 and 35(8) and (9) shall have effect in relation to that substance or article; (1981/164).

'medicinal product' includes any article or substance in respect of which section 58 of the Act has effect by virtue of an order made under section 104 of the Act, but does not include –

(i) a medicinal product which is a veterinary drug as defined in section 132(1) of the Act or

(ii) an article or substance in respect of which section 58 has such effect where that article or substance is only for administration to animals; (1984/756).

'medicinal product' includes any article or substance specified in an order made under section 104 or section 105 of the Act which is for the time being in force and which directs that section 13(2) and (3) and section 15(1) and (2) of the Act shall have effect in relation to that article or substance, but does not include –

(i) a medicinal product which is a veterinary drug as defined in section 132(1) of the Act, or

(ii) an article or substance in respect of which section 13(2) and (3) and section 15(1) and (2) of the Act have such effect only where that article or substance is for administration to animals; (1984/673).

VETERINARY DRUG

Although the definition of medicinal product includes products for animal use, the term 'veterinary drug' is used to denote products which are designed solely for animal use (section 132).

'veterinary drug' means a medicinal product which is manufactured, sold, supplied, imported or exported for the purpose of being administered to animals, but not for the purpose of being administered to human beings; (section 132).

'veterinary medicinal product' means any medicinal product intended for animals and does not include –

(a) vaccines, toxins or serums;

(b) veterinary medicinal products based on radio-active isotopes;

(c) veterinary medicinal products not prepared in advance and intended for one particular animal or small number of animals;

(d) homoeopathic veterinary medicinal products;

(e) additives for feeding stuffs to which the provisions of Council Directive 70/524/EEC apply;

(f) medicated feeding stuffs (1983/1732).

It seems therefore that a medicinal product is something that may be used in humans and in animals, and includes most ingredients, many 'generic' (i.e. official) products, whereas veterinary drugs are intended exclusively for animals.

A veterinary medicinal product is a product which is ready for administration as distinct from an ingredient.

PROPRIETARY MEDICINAL PRODUCTS

Recently, another subdivision of medicines has been created, namely, 'proprietary' medicines.

'Proprietary medicinal product' means a ready-prepared medicinal product placed on the market in the United Kingdom under a special name and in a special pack; and for the purposes of this definition medicinal product does NOT include –

(1) vaccines, toxins, or serums,

(2) medicinal products based on human blood or blood constituents or radioactive isotopes,

(3) homoeopathic medicinal products or,

(4) additives for animal feeding stuff to which the provisions of Council Directive 70/524/EEC apply;

(section 7(7); 1977/1052; 1977/1053; 1977/1055; 1982/1729; 1983/1724; 1983/1725; 1983/1726; 1983/1727; 1983/1728; 1983/1931)

These include what are often referred to as 'patent' medicines, i.e. those sold under a registered name, and usually advertised and sold to the public. The term also includes the 'ethical' products promoted to practitioners and supplied mainly or even exclusively on prescription.

A proprietary medicinal product may now be for human or for animal use but prior to 1983, it was so defined as to exclude veterinary drugs. This point of view is supported by the fact that to differentiate between products for human and those for animal use, there is a definition for 'proprietary veterinary drug'. The need to differentiate between 'proprietary' and 'non-proprietary' products is a consequence of the EEC directives relating to the free movement of proprietary products throughout the Community. Likewise, the exclusion of vaccines, blood products, homoeopathic products, etc. is a consequence of the EEC definition.

'Proprietary veterinary drug' means a veterinary drug which is a proprietary medicinal product; (1983/1727)

'Ready-made veterinary drug' means a ready-prepared veterinary drug placed on the market in the United Kingdom in a pharmaceutical form in which it may be used without further processing, not being a drug placed on the market under a special name and in a special pack; and for the purposes of this definition 'veterinary drug' does not include –

(1) vaccines, toxins or serums,

(2) veterinary drugs based on radioactive isotopes,

(3) veterinary drugs specially prepared for administration by a veterinary surgeon or veterinary practitioner to a particular animal or herd which is under his care,

(4) homoeopathic veterinary drugs, or

(5) additives for animal feeding stuffs to which the provisions of Council Directive 70/524/EEC apply;

(section 7(7); 1982/1729; 1983/1725; 1983/1726; 1983/1727; 1983/1728; 1983/1931)

The difference between a 'proprietary veterinary drug' and a 'ready-made veterinary drug' is that the former is a proprietary product while the latter is not. A 'veterinary medicinal product' is ready-made and may be either proprietary or non-proprietary.

IMPORTED PROPRIETARY PRODUCTS

Another subdivision of medicinal products is concerned with their country of origin. In particular, special controls are imposed on products made in countries outside the EEC and in this context 'imported' means that the product has been imported from a non-EEC country.

'imported proprietary product' means a proprietary medicinal product imported other than from a member State of the European Communities; (1977/1052; 1977/1053; 1977/1056)

'imported ready-made veterinary drug' means a ready-made veterinary drug imported other than from a member State of the European Communities; (1983/1725; 1983/1731)

MEDICATED FEEDING STUFFS

These are not 'medicinal products' but many of the provisions of the Act apply to animal feeding stuffs that have been medicated. Difficulties have arisen in deciding whether a product was a 'medicinal product' or a 'medicated animal feeding stuff' but this has been resolved by an amendment to the Act made by the Animal Health and Welfare Act 1984. This enables the Agriculture Ministers to make orders specifying a description or a class of medicated feeding stuff which shall be treated as a medicinal product or which is not to be so treated (section 130(3A)).

In this context 'medicated feeding stuff' means a substance which is manufactured, sold, supplied, imported or exported for use by being fed to animals for a medicinal purpose (or for a purpose which includes that purpose) or used as an ingredient in the preparation of such a substance to be fed for such a purpose.

The 'medicament' is usually a medicinal product, but may be any other substance if its purpose is medicinal, e.g. a growth promoter.

There are several types of medicated feeding stuffs such as protein concentrates, feed supplements and premixes. A more detailed discussion of their nature and the controls over their manufacture, composition and sale is to be found in Chapter 15.

OTHER ARTICLES AND SUBSTANCES

Reference has been made above to the effect of orders made under section 104 or 105. By such orders the following products, articles and materials are to be treated as medicinal products for most (though not necessarily all) purposes of the Act.

Surgical Materials

These comprise surgical ligatures and sutures made from animal tissues, and any other absorbable ligature or suture intended for use in surgical operations on the human body, and also absorbable, absorbent or protective material intended for use in surgical operations on the human body; (1971/1267).

These products were formerly controlled under the Therapeutic Substances Act and following its repeal would have been left uncontrolled unless brought within the scope of the Medicines Act. It is essential that such items be sterile when used, so their manufacture and packaging need to be controlled and this is most conveniently done under the Medicines Act. It might also be necessary to control the sale of such materials. Their labelling and advertising is also subject to control under the Act.

Dental Filling Substances

These were brought within the scope of the Act by 1975/533. They are defined as substances used or for use in dental surgery for filling dental cavities. They are not yet subject to licensing.

Contact Lenses and Substances Used with Them

These articles and substances, and the blanks from which contact lenses are made, were brought within the scope of the Act by the Specified Articles and Substances Order 1976/968. Currently, those provisions relating to the lenses and blanks are not operable. For the purposes of the Act 'contact lens' means any thin curved shell of glass, plastic or other hard or soft material intended for use by being applied to the human eyeball.

A contact lens is intended to float on a film of tears on the eyeball. The lens is shaped to fit the cornea. There are three types of lens –

(1) Hard lenses: These are made of hydrophobic plastic and are difficult to 'wet' as well as being impervious to gases and water. They therefore

deprive the corneal tissue of oxygen and being hard, tend to irritate the eye. On the other hand, they are long lasting, cheap, less likely to cause infection, and have the best optical properties.

(2) Gas permeable lenses: These too are hydrophobic and hard, but permit the passage of oxygen and are therefore more comfortable to wear.

(3) Soft lenses: These are made of flexible plastic which is hydrophilic and porous to gases and to liquids. They are the most comfortable to wear and do not require the use of 'wetting' agents. However, they are expensive, easily damaged, and require regular cleaning because of their porous nature. Because bacteria and fungi can penetrate into the lens and damage it, they need to be sterilised frequently. They also need special 'soaking' solutions.

The contact lens user therefore needs a variety of products to keep the lens in perfect condition. The solutions are more or less specific to a particular type of lens and the use of an incorrect product can damage the lens, for example, the hydrophilic nature of the soft lens can be reversed by the use of solutions containing cationic detergents and preservatives. There is clearly a need to control their composition and for careful and complete labelling of them. Their advertising also should be controlled. These products are collectively referred to as 'contact lens substance' which is defined as any substance for use in cleaning, disinfecting, irrigating, lubricating, wetting or storing any contact lens or blank from which the contact lens is to be prepared or any fluid in which such lens or blank is soaked or rinsed or any fluid used as a barrier between such lens or blank and the human eyeball or any other substance used in connection with the use of such lens or blank; (1979/1585 and 1760). (1979/1759) is very similar.

The 'substance' referred to above is usually an aqueous solution, but some products are powders intended to be dissolved before use.

The contact lens solutions etc. have been subject to licensing since July 1983 and controls over advertising them to doctors, opticians and pharmacists were instituted in 1980. The restrictions applicable to labelling are being progressively introduced from January 1st 1985 in respect of existing products, from July 1985 in relation to supplies from wholesalers, and from January 1986 for sales from retailers.

Intra-uterine Contraceptive Devices

These too were brought under control by S.I.1976/968. They are defined as any instrument, apparatus or appliance for use by being inserted in the uterus of a human being for the purpose of contraception (1978/1138;1980/1467).

Licensing of such articles started on the 1st October 1978, and transitional exemptions relating to licensing ended on 31st October 1980. They are also subject to the labelling provisions (1978/1140).

There are five such devices commercially available, four of them comprising copper wire on a plastic carrier. All of them are POM partly because they must be fitted by someone expert in the technique and partly because special precautions are applicable to them.

Radioactive Appliances for Use in or on the Human Body

These comprise appliances and devices for interstitial, inter-cavity, or surface use (1978/1004).

They were brought under control in 1979, but are exempt from licensing under the Medicines Act though their manufacture and labelling are controlled under the Radioactive Substances Act.

Sections 60 and 67(2)(4) and Part VIII of the Medicines Act apply to them, and thus the control is over the user rather than the product.

Cyanogenetic Substances

These were brought within the ambit of the Act by 1984/187. They are exempt from licensing, but subject to controls over sales (sections 51, 52, 55(1), 57, 58, 61–67), over labels (sections 85–88), and over advertising (sections 95 and 97). They are also subject to Part VIII of the Act.

They are defined as preparations which –

(a) are presented for sale of supply under the name of, or as containing, amygdalin, laetrile or vitamin B17 or

(b) contain more than 0.1% by weight of any substance having the formula either α-Cyanobenzyl-6-O-β-D-glucopyranosyl-β-D-glucopyranoside or α-Cyano-benzyl-β-D-glucopyranosiduronic acid; (1984/187)

They are controlled because some people have advocated their use in the treatment of cancer. There is no evidence of anti-tumour effect and clinical trials in the USA have failed to show any benefit in the treatment of cancer. On the other hand, there are reports of toxicity and adverse effects especially when laetrile is taken with certain common foods. They are dangerous due to their ability to liberate hydrocyanic acid inside the body. In addition, it had been claimed that they were foods and therefore outside the scope of the Act. This Order therefore removes doubt as to their status in the UK by bringing all products intended for human consumption within the scope of the Act.

Various Antibiotics and Other Biological Products

Normally substances used as ingredients in the manufacture of various medicinal products are not regarded as medicinal products because their specifications can be strictly controlled in the product licences. The substances mentioned here are not capable of being adequately tested by chemical means, and for this reason their manufacture was controlled under the Therapeutic Substances Act. The same considerations still apply, hence they were brought within the scope of the Act to ensure that their manufacture, labelling, and all dealings therein are now subject to control.

They are subject to control under Part II of the Act, and also sections 62, 66, 67, and Parts V and VIII. A number of antibiotics and a few hormones etc. intended for use as ingredients in the manufacture of parenteral products for human use are controlled, as are oxytetracycline and tetracycline for any product for human or animal use, dextrans for parenteral use in humans (1971/1200).

Antimicrobial Substances

Most of the provisions of the Act have been extended to apply to any product (not being a medicinal product) containing any antibiotic, sulphonamide, nitrofuran or any other substance having antimicrobial properties (1973/367).

Stilbenes and Thyrostatic Substances

These substances were brought within the scope of the Act when they are sold or supplied for use as an ingredient in the manufacture of a veterinary drug or animal feeding stuff by 1982/425. When administered to animals whose produce is used as food, these substances leave residues which can have a harmful effect on human beings who consume such produce. The Order enabled the partial implementation of Council Directive 81/602.

Because they had no powers under the Medicines Act which would allow them to prohibit the administration of a product or class of products, the Ministers used their powers under the European Communities Act 1972 to make regulations prohibiting in Great Britain the administration of these substances to animals whose produce might be consumed by humans or by other animals (1982/626). The Northern Ireland Ministers made an identical order (S.R.1982/279) applicable in Northern Ireland. These orders complement 1982/518 made under the Medicines Act which prohibits the sale or supply of stilbenes or thyrostatic substances for use in the manufacture of a product for administration to animals or the sale or supply of a product or animal feeding stuff in which they have been incorporated.

The substances can be administered to animals if steps are taken to ensure that the animals will not be used in the production of food.

'stilbenes' means substances which consist wholly of any of the following (a) Benzestrol, (b) Dienoestrol (c) Hexoestrol or (d) Stilboestrol; (1982/518; 1982/626)

'thyrostatic substances' means anti-thyroid substances with a depressant effect on thyroid activity and thyroid hormone production for use by administration to animals to increase their body weight; (1982/518; 1982/626)

Feeding Stuffs Additives

Any substance or article (other than a medicinal product) which is intended to be added to an animal feeding stuff for feeding to animals or for sale, import or export, is subject to the same controls that apply to medicated animal feeding stuffs (i.e. sections 45(1)(2)(8), 46(3), 48(1)a, 90, 91, and 117(5); 1975/1349).

These are dealt with in greater detail in Chapter 15.

Chapter 4
The Licensing System

INTRODUCTION

The licensing system is the chief novel feature of the Act, and lies at the heart of all of the control over medicines. The system is designed to ensure that medicinal products (and certain other substances and articles) are of good quality, safe and efficacious and are manufactured and dealt with under optimal conditions. The system also enables batches of products to be traced and withdrawn from sale with the minimum of delay should they prove subsequently to be defective in any respect. This is achieved by a system of batch numbers and records kept by manufacturers and wholesalers. The system utilises three types of licence and two types of certificate each of which permits a person (including a 'legal person', e.g. a company) to engage in certain specified activities. It may therefore be necessary for a company to hold two or even three types of licence in certain cases. A fee is normally payable for each licence. It is an offence to engage in any of the controlled activities unless one holds the appropriate licence(s) (section 45(1)).

In order to illustrate the operation of the system, it is helpful to describe briefly the stages in the development of a new drug.

The process starts with the discovery of the new substance, either by chance, or, more likely these days, as part of a project involving the investigation of a family of compounds whose chemical structure leads one to expect a particular type of pharmacological activity. The new compounds are routinely screened for the desired activity and if this is found, a patent is filed for the substance and the development work proceeds along several lines simultaneously. The chemists determine the structure of the drug and its chemical and physical characteristics. Various possible synthetic routes are studied to find the most appropriate one. The nature and amount of impurities are determined, and assay procedures developed to detect the presence of and to measure the content of the drug in various products and in body fluids.

The drug substance (usually in the form of solution or suspension) is administered orally or by injection to animals in order to ascertain how it is metabolised and to determine its main pharmacological actions. It is also necessary to carry out preliminary studies of the drug's pharmacokinetics (i.e. the rate at which it is absorbed from the gut, and the rate at which it is broken down and excreted) in animals. The drug is administered to other animals to determine its toxicity, i.e. to see if it damages any particular tissue or organ (damage to the gonads is particularly significant). In addition, tests for mutagenicity (damage to chromosomes) are carried out using bacteria.

The object of these studies is to determine the potential drug's efficacy, safety and acceptability. Few of the potential drugs progress to the next stage because the results obtained do not warrant the expenditure of any further time or money.

All of the above work is carried out in laboratories and is not controlled under the Act because the material under test is not yet a 'medicinal product'. The same applies to the next stage which involves the administration of the experimental substance to human volunteers to ascertain whether the pharmacokinetics and pharmacological activity in man is similar to that in animals. Eventually, a stage is reached when it must be administered to patients, i.e. persons actually suffering from a disease for which the substance is likely to be useful. This stage is essential because the disease state may markedly alter the pharmacology of the substance or its pharmacokinetic properties. Before the substance can be administered to patients a 'clinical trial certificate' must be obtained. If the product is intended for use in veterinary medicine, an 'animal test certificate' must be obtained.

Before clinical trials can be arranged, the drug must be made into a form suitable for administration to a person (it must be 'formulated' into a suitable dosage form). This often involves a considerable amount of work because the dosage form must be capable of releasing the drug at the optimum site of absorption, must be stable and acceptable to the patient. The ingredients used to transform the drug into a dosage form are called the excipients. Normally, a batch of 'dummy' product (called the 'control product') is made, which is identical to the product under test except that it contains no active drug.

The purpose of the clinical trial is to ascertain the clinical worth of the drug or product, and to give reliable results it needs to be very carefully designed and carried out. Ideally, the trial should be 'double blind', i.e. neither the doctors (or dentists) nor the patients should know which of the dosage forms contains the active drug and which the placebo or control. The purpose of the trial is to confirm (or otherwise) the therapeutic potential of the drug on a small number of patients suffering from the appropriate complaint. The numbers are kept small so as to minimise the damage should the product prove to be unexpectedly dangerous. Naturally, the practitioners involved are required to keep detailed records of the patients taking part in the trial and to be alert to the possibility of adverse reactions to the drug. If the results of the clinical trials confirm the product's usefulness, then an application will be made for a product licence.

The product licence is at the centre of the system. No medicinal product can be marketed until it is the subject of such a licence. To obtain a product licence the applicant must provide a considerable amount of scientific evidence about the product's chemical, physical and pharmacological properties. This evidence is assessed by officials of the Medicines Division of the DHSS and if necessary, by panels of independent experts (the various expert committees). If found to be satisfactory the grant of a licence is recommended. Should the committees feel unable to recommend the issue of a licence they must inform the applicant and offer to hear any representation or consider any additional written information.

The licence (for which a fee is payable, see later) lays down the manufacturing and quality assurance specifications of the product, lists its therapeutic indications and contra-indications, gives details as to its packaging and labelling, method of sale, and the conditions for which it can be advertised and promoted. In short, it is the master document which contains all of the essential information about the product. The product then has to be manufactured and assembled (i.e. packed and labelled) to the specifications laid down in the licence by someone holding a manufacturer's licence for the processes involved. Such a licence is issued to persons who have satisfied the medicines inspectorate that they have the appropriate equipment and facilities and the necessary expert staff to carry out the operations detailed in the application.

Persons who wish to sell products by wholesale require a wholesale dealer's licence which is issued to persons having adequate facilities and knowledge for the correct storage and handling of medicinal products. They must also maintain adequate records of all supplies made by them.

A retail dealer does not require a licence to sell medicinal products (though such sales are controlled under Part III of the Act) unless he is 'responsible for their composition', i.e. they are made to his formula. Generally speaking, practitioners and pharmacists are exempt from the licensing provisions (sections 9 and 10).

A licensing system is ideal for controlling such a complex and technical field as the manufacture and testing of medicinal products for the following reasons –

(1) It is flexible, a person can be licensed to do one thing or many things;

(2) A licence can be tailored to meet exactly the applicant's needs;

(3) A licence can subsequently be varied to take account of major changes in the specifications of the product or of its use;

(4) A licence can be issued subject to conditions, and acceptance of the licence means acceptance of the conditions. One of the standard conditions of all licences requires the licensee to notify the authority of every change which might affect the safety, quality or efficacy of the product;

(5) If a licensee fails to comply with the terms and/or conditions of the licence, the licence can be suspended or even revoked, and while the licensing authority cannot act in an arbitrary manner, they do not have to satisfy a judge and jury of the correctness of their decision;

(6) A licence lasts for a fixed time (usually 5 years) and at its expiry it can be reviewed and renewed if desired;

(7) The licence has to be paid for and consequently the costs of the system are largely borne by the licence-holders (in fact, the fees are now set with the intention of fully covering the costs of the system).

There is, however, at least one disadvantage of the system, it is costly to the applicant not only in terms of licence fees but also in terms of the staff and time involved in producing the necessary paper work. Two economists from York University ('The costs and benefits of regulating new product development in the UK pharmaceutical industry' by Hartley and Maynard, OHE London 1982) recently estimated that the drug regulatory requirements in the United Kingdom cost the community more than M£30 per year, used 1000 staff in industry and the civil service, and delayed for about 2 years the introduction of new drugs onto the market. They also stated that a combined application for a clinical trial certificate and product licence typically exceeded 4000 pages, took 8 months to prepare and cost £35,000 at 1979 prices. A person may decide that in view of the trouble and expense involved in applying for a licence, he will not manufacture a product which is useful for a rare condition because the potential profits are too small, though there are provisions enabling him to pay a reduced capital fee (or even no capital fee). This does not, of course, reduce the cost of the research and the necessary paperwork to put the product to market. Certainly several thousand products have disappeared from the market since licensing began. It is not possible to say whether their disappearance was caused by the trouble and expense of applying for full licences or whether it was due to the difficulty of obtaining evidence of safety or efficacy.

The licensing system came into operation on the 1st September 1971 (in the Act referred to as 'the first appointed day') (see section 16). Because of the impossibility of dealing fully with applications for thousands of medicinal products and hundreds of manufacturers and wholesale dealers overnight, two temporary arrangements were made. The first involved the issue of 'licences of right' in respect of products already on the market ('licences of right' were also available to persons carrying on manufacturing or wholesale businesses). Some transitional exemptions were also made. Since both arrangements are now obsolete they will not be considered further.

In theory licences and certificates are issued (or refused) by the 'licensing authority', i.e. the Ministers. In practice, however, they are dealt with by the Medicines Division if for human use or the Animal Health Division of the MAFF if for veterinary use. It will be seen that in order to obtain a licence the applicant has to disclose details of composition, tests, manufacturing procedures and other technical matters. All of these details are expensive to obtain and are normally regarded as trade secrets and carefully guarded. In order to protect the applicant's interest in this information it is an offence (section 118) for a person having access to the information to disclose it to anyone not authorised to receive it. The penalties are really small when compared with the potential rewards but the chief protection lies in the integrity of the staff involved. So strictly is the confidentiality of information respected that the British Pharmacopoeia Commission complained in 1976 that analytical data, provided to the licensing authority in applications for product licences, was not available to that Commission. This sometimes created difficulties in drawing up a specification for a substance.

Although all applications for licences and certificates have to be made in writing, informal discussions between the applicant and the staff concerned are very often held and are normally helpful.

THE LICENSING AUTHORITY

This body consists of all of the Ministers (see definitions) though its functions can be performed by any of them or by any combination of them. The authority is responsible for the grant, renewal, variation, suspension or revocation of the various licences and certificates (section 6), and several sections of the Act deal with the ways in which these responsibilities are to be exercised.

In dealing with an application for a product licence, the authority must particularly consider the safety of the product, its efficacy for the intended purpose and its quality as indicated by its specifications. In so far as efficacy is concerned, the fact that the product is less efficacious than other products for the same purpose shall not prevent the product being licensed, unless when considering the product's safety, it is felt that the equally or more efficacious products are safer for the purpose (section 19(1),(2)). In coming to its decisions, the authority take account of advice from the Medicines Commission and the expert committees. Where the product is to be imported the authority take into account the methods, standards and conditions of manufacture and may require undertakings from the manufacturer to permit inspection of his methods and premises and to comply with any conditions imposed by the authority. In addition the manufacturer may be required to give a declaration that any requirements imposed by the law of that country have been complied with (section 19(3)).

A licence may not be refused on grounds of efficacy, safety or quality except after consultation with the appropriate Committee or the Commission (section 20(3)). Copies of each product licence are sent to the various committees giving advice on safety, quality and efficacy (section 20(4)).

In dealing with manufacturers' licences, the authority takes into account the operations to be carried out, the premises used, the equipment available and the qualifications of the persons who supervise the operations. Furthermore, the storage facilities and record keeping arrangements available are also important (section 19(5)). Very similar considerations apply to applications for wholesale dealers' licences (section 19(6)).

After considering the application, the authority may decide to grant the licence containing such provisions as they consider appropriate. Alternatively, it may decide to refuse to grant the licence (section 20(1)). The authority may NOT refuse a product licence on grounds relating to the price of the product nor may they impose conditions as to its price (section 20(2)).

Where on grounds of safety, quality or efficacy a committee considering an application feels that it may have to advise refusal or advise the grant of the licence subject to different terms, it must notify the applicant and offer to hear him or consider written representations. If he takes advantage of this the committee shall report on its findings, and send its advice and reasons for the advice to the authority for consideration in deciding on the application. Whether or not the applicant has taken advantage of the opportunity, where the committee advise refusal or the grant on unacceptable terms, the authority shall notify him of the committee's advice and its reasons for this.

The authority after considering the views of the committee then decides whether to:

(1) grant the licence as applied for, or

(2) grant the licence with modifications, or

(3) refuse the licence.

In the cases (2) and (3) the authority must notify its reasons for the decision to the applicant if he so requests (section 20(5)) and there is provision for the applicant to appeal to the Commission (section 21(4)). The authority is not obliged to follow the advice received from the expert committees but if it does not, the applicant must be notified of the reasons for not doing so.

The licensing authority also has powers to –

(1) suspend a licence for a specified time; or

(2) revoke the licence; or

(3) vary the licence (i.e. amend it in some way) (section 28(1)).

The suspension or revocation may be limited to one class of product or may apply to all products manufactured, assembled or stored at any particular premises (section 28(2)).

These powers shall only be exercised in relation to a product licence on one or more of the following grounds –

(a) the information given in the application was false or incomplete in a material particular;

(b) the provisions of the licence have been contravened by the licence holder or by the person who manufactured or assembled the product;

(c) the product as sold fails to a material extent to correspond to the characteristics by reference to which the licence was granted;

(d) the licence holder has failed to supply information relating to the product to the licensing authority;

(e) that part or all of the premises used for the manufacture, assembly or storage of the product are unsuitable;

(f) that the licence holder has not, within 2 years of the grant of the licence, notified the authority of the date on which the product was effectively on the market;

(g) that products of that description can no longer be regarded as safe or as efficacious for the purposes specified in the licence;

(h) that the specification and standards of the product can no longer be regarded as satisfactory;

(i) that the regulations relating to packaging and labelling or which impose requirements giving effect to Community obligations have not been complied with in relation to the product (section 28(3)).

(j) a licence may be terminated after being issued if it contravenes an EEC obligation. The termination is effected by a notice sent to the holder (section 24 and 1977/1050).

It has been suggested that item (d) above could be used when holders of licences of right failed to respond to a request for information made under the provisions of section 44(2) within the time specified (MAIL 40).

In relation to a manufacturer's licence or to a wholesale dealer's licence these powers of suspension or revocation may only be used where false or incomplete information was given in the application or where there has been some material change in relation to the facilities or premises. They may also be used where the licensee has contravened the provisions of his licence or failed to furnish information to the authority. Manufacturer's licences may also be suspended etc. for habitual failure to comply with the provisions of a product licence or where the manufacturer does not have the necessary facilities to properly carry out the processes authorised by his licence (section 28,(4),(5),(6)).

The authority must notify the licensee of the suspension etc. of his licence and give the reasons for it (section 29). The procedure to be followed by the authority before exercising its powers is specified in Schedule 2. Except in urgent cases, the authority must seek the advice of an expert committee or the Commission where matters of safety, quality or efficacy are concerned. If the expert committee or the Commission believes that it may have to recommend suspension etc. it must notify the licensee and offer to consider any representations he may make.

A licence may also be varied at the request of the licensee. This may be done to take account of major changes in the specifications of the product or of its therapeutic indications. The change of a company's name also requires variation of the licence but a change in ownership of the company requires a new application for a licence. Minor changes in the specifications, of assays, or methods of manufacture or of personnel, may not necessitate variation of the licence, but the authority should be informed of them. Where a specification is changed to meet the requirements of a new edition of the British Pharmacopoeia, there is no need to vary the licence (or to notify the authority) provided that the 'old' formula will not also be made. Manufacturer's licences can be varied to take account of changes in the operations or activities that may be undertaken at a particular premises. Provided that the authority is satisfied that the change will not adversely affect the safety, quality or efficacy of the product(s) concerned, the variation will be made to the licence (section 30). This enables a product to be promoted for use in a new indication.

On any matter relating to licences and certificates the decision of the licensing authority is final but an applicant may appeal to the High Court on the grounds that the decision is not within the powers of the Act or that the requirements of the Act or regulations have not been complied with (section 107). The appeal must be made within 3 months of the decision. The High Court may suspend the operation of the decision or quash it.

EXEMPTIONS FROM LICENSING

Pharmacists

No licence of any type is required for anything done by or under the supervision of a pharmacist in a registered pharmacy which consists of –

(1) preparing or dispensing a medicinal product on the prescription of a practitioner;

(2) preparing or dispensing a medicinal product to a formula provided by the purchaser for administration to himself or to somebody or some animal in his care (veterinary vaccines etc. excluded, see below under veterinarians);

(3) preparing or dispensing a medicinal product in the course of 'counter-prescribing', i.e. where the pharmacist has been asked by, or on behalf of, the patient to use his own judgment as to the treatment required and the patient is present in the pharmacy at the time;

(4) preparing a stock of products for use in (1), (2), or (3) above;

(5) preparing a stock of a medicinal product for sale from that pharmacy, provided that the product is not advertised;

(6) assembling a medicinal product for retail sale without advertisement from that pharmacy or from another forming part of the same retail pharmacy business;

(7) wholesale dealing, i.e. sales to practitioners, other pharmacists. This must not form a substantial part of the business at the pharmacy.

In the context of (5) and (6) above, 'advertised' and 'advertisement' do not include the words used on the product or its label, nor the display of the product itself, but does include the display of a showcard (section 10).

Hospitals and health centres are similarly exempt from (1), (4) and (6) above.

Pharmacist's 'Own Brand'. If a pharmacist is responsible for the composition of a product, i.e. it is his own formula, and he wants to advertise the product to the public, and perhaps arrange for its sale by other pharmacists, then the product will need a product licence. He will then have to arrange for its manufacture and assembly in accordance with the terms of the licence. If, however, the formula is one that a manufacturer makes as part of his range, and the pharmacist wants the manufacturer to pack and label it with the pharmacist's own name, then the manufacturer holds the product licence and must ask for it to be drawn in such a way as to permit the product to be assembled (i.e. packed and labelled) in the various ways required by his pharmacist customers. The pharmacist may alternatively take advantage of the facilities offered by assemblers holding a direction issued under Article 3 of the Special and Transitional Cases Order 1971. This would allow, for example, Paracetamol Tablets to be packed and labelled in such a way as to indicate that they were the product of a particular pharmacist, in that they were labelled with his name and address. If the pharmacist does not want to advertise the product and wishes to sell it only from his own pharmacies, he can buy bulk supplies of tablets and repack and label them himself at a registered pharmacy without needing a manufacturer's licence.

The criteria seem to be as follows: the preparation and sale of small amounts of products from a small number of retail outlets does not require the possession of licences. When the product is being offered to a wider public it then resembles a proprietary product and becomes subject to the same controls.

A pharmacist also needs a licence to produce a poultry vaccine and, unless prepared in accordance with a prescription from a veterinarian, for autogenous vaccines, plasma, or sera.

Medical and Dental Practitioners

A practitioner may prepare or procure the preparation or importation of a product for administration to a particular patient without requiring a licence of any kind. Furthermore, one practitioner may do any of these things at the request of another practitioner for administration to a particular patient of that practitioner (section 9).

Where a product is imported by a hospital, wholesale or retail pharmacy on behalf of a doctor or dentist for administration to a particular patient, the exemption is subject to the keeping of records, notification of the Authority, and certain other conditions (1984/673).

The exemption has been extended to permit practitioners to procure the manufacture of stocks of such products for use in their practices. The manufacture must be carried out by a person who holds a 'specials' manufacturer's licence and the practitioner may not hold more that 5 l of (unlicensed) liquid products or 2.5 kg of unlicensed solid products (1971/1450; 1972/1200). Where a practice consists of several practitioners these quantities may be multiplied by the number of practitioners.

Although each product licence specifies the indications for the use of the product, a practitioner may use it for other indications in the exercise of his professional responsibility (section 9) for the treatment of a particular patient. Clearly, when using a product for an indication not covered by the product licence, the practitioner does so at his own risk and has to accept responsibility for any harmful side-effects.

Similarly, a practitioner may use a licensed product in a clinical trial on his own initiative. However, if the product has to be specially made up or imported for the trial, the practitioner may require an official authorisation and should contact the DHSS for advice.

When a practitioner is participating in a clinical trial arranged by a pharmaceutical company, the company will hold the required certificate and communicate its terms to the participating practitioners.

Veterinarians

These are also normally exempt from the need to hold licences in relation to products specially prepared for a particular animal, herd, etc. Veterinarians can also procure the manufacture of stocks of a product of their own formula subject to the same conditions as doctors and dentists above. However, product licences are required to import products and also if the veterinarian wants to prepare the following products –

(1) vaccines specially prepared for administration to poultry, or

(2) other vaccines (except autogenous vaccines), or

(3) a serum or plasma (unless specially prepared for administration to one or more animals in the herd from which it was derived) (section 9(3)).

Midwives and Nurses

These may assemble products in the course of their professional duties without holding a manufacturer's licence (section 11).

Herbalists

A herbalist does not require any licence to prepare or assemble a herbal remedy on his own premises or to sell or 'counter-prescribe' them at the request of the customer. The premises must be capable of being closed so as to exclude the public. Furthermore, no product or manufacturer's licence is required for a remedy which is prepared only by drying, crushing, or comminuting the plant if it is sold under the name of the plant, the process involved is designated and without any written recommendation as to its use (section 12).

NHS Hospitals

No licence is required for dispensing by, or under the supervision of, a pharmacist in accordance with the prescription of a doctor or dentist. Similarly, the preparation of small amounts of stock mixtures etc. are exempt. Large scale manufacture, however, would be subject to licensing but a Health Service circular issued in 1975 stated that in view of the application of Crown exemption, it would not be necessary for hospitals under the control of health authorities to receive formal licences. Nevertheless, the health authorities have been directed by the Ministers to act as though they were subject to licensing.

The above mentioned circular controls the following activities –

(a) the manufacture or assembly of products by health authorities,

(b) direct importation of products by the health authorities,

(c) contract manufacture of products to the specification of health authorities,

(d) the introduction of a new product.

The following activities are subject to these arrangements –

(1) the preparation or assembly of products otherwise than under the supervision of a pharmacist,

(2) the preparation or assembly of a product *for sale or supply* to anyone outside the National Health Service,

(3) the preparation or assembly of a product in the pharmacy of a hospital for use in any NHS establishment which does not normally avail itself of the services of that pharmacy,

(4) the preparation of sterile products otherwise than for immediate dispensing or administration (i.e. before standard tests can be completed and not for stockholding),

(5) the preparation of 'biologicals' i.e. blood, vaccines, etc., steroids, and antibiotics (the actual chemicals),

(6) the preparation of powders, creams, ointments, liquids, or solutions (otherwise than for immediate dispensing or administration),

(7) the preparation of tablets, capsules etc. by power operated equipment,

(8) the assembly of products by automatic machinery.

In any event, the hospitals have subsequently been visited by members of the Medicines Inspectorate to ensure that the staff, procedures and facilities are of the necessary standard.

In 1984, a new policy was set out in a circular [HC(84)3]. This required health authorities to cost their manufacturing operations, and only manufacture products which were either cheaper to make than to buy, or which could not be bought. This will probably result in a reduction in the range of products manufactured in hospitals.

A more recent circular advises that manufacture should only be undertaken where it is clearly economical to do so [HC(84)C].

Private Hospitals, Nursing Homes and Clinics

These are hospitals etc. other than those belonging to the NHS or conducted by Government Departments. The person or organisation responsible for the hospital is 'conducting a business' and will require licences for any transactions not covered by an exemption.

Normally, the supply of medicines to patients in the hospital is exempt from licensing because the practitioners and pharmacists involved are exempt from licensing. However, in the following circumstances, the hospital authorities will require licences –

(a) a product licence is required if the *hospital* wishes to import a medicinal product. (N.B.: if a medical practitioner wishes to import a product for a particular patient no licence is required.)

(b) a product licence is required if the hospital specially orders a supply of a product to be manufactured. (NB: no licence is required if the product is already licensed, nor is it necessary when the supply is required for a specific prescription.)

(c) where any manufacture is done (otherwise than under the supervision of a pharmacist), a manufacturer's licence and a product licence must be held for each product.

IMPORTED PRODUCTS

Under section 7(3) of the Act, a person who wants to import a medicinal product into the UK requires a product licence for that product. Section 13(1) however exempts from this requirement the importation of a product for administration to the importer or a member of his household, and also when the product is specially imported by or to the order of a doctor or dentist for administration to a particular patient of his (the so-called 'named patient'). Furthermore, section 9(1) permits the unlicensed assembly or manufacture of an unlicensed product imported to the order of a doctor or dentist for administration to a particular patient. It should be noted that section 9(2) does not allow veterinarians to import products without a licence.

It should further be noted that if the product is subject to control under Schedules 2, 3 or 4 of the Misuse of Drugs Regulations 1973 (as amended) then an import licence from the Home Office is required.

Parallel Importation

In addition to the exemptions from licensing mentioned above, 1978/1461 was intended to permit the unlicensed importation of products not available in the UK 'for stock' ready for sale to doctors, dentists, hospitals or pharmacists, for administration to a 'named patient'. Advantage was taken of the looseness of the drafting of this Order to 'parallel import' products from abroad. These products were licensed in the United Kingdom and were readily available in the trade, but could be purchased more cheaply abroad.

The licensing authority in the UK sought to prevent these parallel imports by requiring importers to provide details of the manufacture and quality control checks done on the product abroad. One importer, De Peijper, was refused permission to import a product that was similar to a licensed product made by the same manufacturer for two reasons –

(i) he was unable to provide a complete file relating to the product's safety, quality and efficacy, which the manufacturer's authorised importer had already provided;

(ii) he could not (unlike the authorised importer) obtain reports of checks performed on each manufacturing batch.

De Peijper believed that such action hindered the free trade in pharmaceuticals and was contrary to the Treaty of Rome, and therefore took action in the Courts. Eventually, the case was heard in the Court of Justice of the European Communities which found as follows –

(a) national rules which result in imports being channelled so that some traders can effect these imports while others cannot, are prohibited by Article 30 of the EEC Treaty;

(b) while Member States can, pursuant to Article 36, decide on the level of protection they afford to the health and life of their people, and the stringency of the checks to be applied, such rules are only compatible with the Treaty if they are necessary for that protection and that such a level of protection cannot be achieved by measures which have less effect on intra-Community trade;

(c) in particular, such rules cannot be used to make administration easier, or to reduce public expenditure.

The Court held that rules which allowed a manufacturer a monopoly simply by refusing to give information were unnecessarily restrictive. 'It is only if the information or documents to be produced by the manufacturer or his . ... importer show that there are several variants of the medicinal preparation and that the differences between these variants have a therapeutic effect that there would be any justification for treating the variants as different medicinal preparations, for the purpose of authorising them to be placed on the market and as regards producing the relevant documents...'

The Commission noted the judgment of the Court and drafted for transmission to the Council a proposed Directive on parallel imports of proprietary medicinal products. Following objections raised by the Economic and Social Committee and later, the negative vote in the European Parliament, the proposal was dropped. The Commission therefore issued a Communication containing its views as to the way parallel imports should be controlled.

In the face of the judgment and the ensuing Communication, the licensing authority devised a new scheme involving the issue of a product licence (parallel importation) or [PL(PI)] which was introduced in the middle of 1984. Such licences are only issued in respect of products which can be marketed in at least one other EEC state, and are licensed for sale in the UK. For further details please see Chapter 6.

The statutory instrument 1978/1461 was revoked and replaced by the more tightly worded 1984/673. This enables the import of unlicensed products for stock for administration to a named patient provided that –

(1) the product is neither the subject of a product licence nor effectively on the market in the UK; and

(2) such products may only be sold or supplied to a doctor, dentist, hospital or to a retail pharmacist for administration to a particular patient.

Since the product is not on the UK market, it is not really a 'parallel import'. Usually a wholesaler will import the product as 'stock' ready for sale or supply to doctors, dentists, pharmacists or hospitals. The wholesaler must notify the licensing authority in writing of his intention to import the product for sale as above or as stock for sale as stated. He must also state the proprietary name of the product, the name(s) of its active constituents, the amount to be imported, and the name and address of the supplier. He must also give a written undertaking that the amount imported will not exceed that needed for 25 single administrations, or for 25 courses of treatment not exceeding 3 months, that he will notify the authority of any matter which may cast doubt on the safety of the product, and that he will not advertise (or make any representations about) the product, but will supply it only in response to bona fide unsolicited orders. He must also keep written records of the details of each importation and of the names and addresses of persons to whom he sells or supplies it together with the amounts involved. Such records and his storage premises shall be open to inspection on request.

The licensing authority may, within 28 days of acknowledging receipt of the notification above, write to the person stating that the exemption shall not apply in the case in question because either the conditions have not been complied with or there is reason to doubt the safety or quality of the product. They may also terminate the exemption on the grounds that false or incomplete information was given in respect of the notification, or because of the breach of an undertaking or condition, or because it can no longer be regarded as safe, or because the product has been granted a product licence in the UK and it is effectively on the market.

There is no corresponding exemption for the importation of veterinary drugs.

Importation for Re-exportation

No licence is required for the importation of a product which is to be re-exported in the same form and packs (section 14). Statutory instrument 1971/1326 (as amended by 1977/640) confirms that when a product, substance or article which is normally subject to licensing is imported for re-exportation in the same form and pack, no product licence is required. It also permits, without the need for a product licence, the re-assembly of the products by a person holding a manufacturer's licence provided that the importer has notified the licensing authority of the intended importation and supplied such other information as the authority required, and the authority have notified the importer in writing that he may import and reassemble the products without a product licence. The relaxation of the controls described in the last sentence do not apply to the importation of the veterinary products specified in Exportation below.

Also, section 62 enables the Ministers to prohibit the importation of products where this is considered necessary in the interests of safety, the Indian medicine Bal Jivan Chamcho is an example.

EXPORTATION

Although the Act appears to control exports of products from the UK, for most purposes the application of these controls have been postponed (section 47). There were controls over the exportation of various biologicals imposed by the Therapeutic Substances Act, and these would have ceased on that Act's repeal. Comparable restrictions have been imposed by means of statutory instruments

1971/1198 and 1309 which relate to products for human use and for animal use respectively. In the case of 1971/1198, the products concerned are antigens, antisera, antitoxins, sera, toxins and vaccines. The veterinary order applies to the same products and also to corticotrophin, heparin, hyaluronidase, insulin, plasma, and preparations of the posterior lobe of the pituitary gland, *and other medicinal products or substances derived from animals*.

Export Certificates

Some countries will only permit medicinal products (and sometimes, other substances and articles which have medicinal uses) to be imported if they are accompanied by a certificate issued by the authorities in the exporting country, certifying that the product was manufactured in premises which had been inspected, and that the product complied with all legal requirements of the exporting country. Such certificates may be issued by the licensing authority (section 50). Some countries require the certificates to be authenticated by their embassy or consulate in the UK. The requirements of the countries vary, some insist on a certificate for each product, others are content with a certificate naming several products. Furthermore, some countries require the certification of product price in the country of origin. The application for such a certificate must state the name and address of the applicant, his signature, and the name of the importing country. It must be accompanied by two copies of documents stating the name of the applicant, the number of certificates required, and the name of the product, its product licence number, the name and licence number of the manufacturer and the place of manufacture. All documents containing the phrase 'It is hereby certified' or 'We certify' must be signed and written on the company's headed notepaper, as must certificates of analysis, or those giving details of the company or its staff. The applications must be sent to the DHSS at Market Towers if for human products, or to the MAFF at Tolworth Tower if for animal products.

APPEALS AGAINST DECISIONS OF THE LICENSING AUTHORITY

Before the authority makes an adverse decision about an application for a licence or certificate, or proposes to revoke, suspend or vary such a document, the applicant (or holder) must be given an opportunity to state his case. In the case of an application for a licence or certificate, the authority can only refuse a licence after considering the advice of a section 4 committee, and such a committee will always give the applicant an opportunity of being heard by it or of sending written representations. This is done by the committee directing the secretariat to issue a 'section 21(1) notice' which also specifies the reasons for the committee's expectation that it will have to recommend refusal of the licence as applied for. The applicant can ask for further information if necessary. The applicant may elect to submit copies of written representations to the committee for consideration. Alternatively, he may request a hearing and may send several persons to represent him. The team may review the scientific evidence and may provide additional data if necessary. If it is intended to produce new written matter as well, this should be sent in advance to enable members of the committee to read it before the meeting. If the applicant will need time to produce new evidence, it is usually better to withdraw the application until it is available.

The committee then considers the evidence, and if still of the opinion that the licence should be refused or granted subject to conditions not mentioned in the application, then the licensing authority must notify him to this effect. If he so desires, the applicant may (within 28 days) request a hearing by the Medicines Commission or an opportunity to make written representations to it. The Commission considers the original application and any relevant correspondence, but does not have access to the findings and advice of the committee. It therefore considers the application afresh. The Commission reports its findings to the authority, which sends the advice and its decision to the applicant.

If the authority decision agrees with the advice of the Commission, this concludes the matter and the appropriate formal document is prepared and sent to the applicant. If the decision is adverse and contrary to the advice received from the committee or the Commission, it is possible to apply for a hearing by 'a person appointed', see below.

The appropriate committee must also be consulted when revocation, suspension or variation of a licence is contemplated (section 28(3)) because the safety, quality or efficacy of the product is in doubt. This might arise because incomplete or misleading information had been given in the application, or that the product does not correspond with the licence. On the other hand, new evidence might cast doubt on the product's safety or efficacy for the uses mentioned in the licence or its specifications might be considered to be unsatisfactory. The committee will consider the facts and if they are likely to reach a decision adverse to the licensee must notify him and offer to hear his views or consider any written material he may provide. In the event of an adverse recommendation the licensee can make use of the appeal procedures given above.

In rare cases, it may be necessary for the authority to suspend a licence or certificate immediately in the interests of safety. The suspension can last for 3 months and the committee must be informed. If necessary, the suspension may be extended for another 3 months. If the authority intend to make the suspension permanent or to revoke the licence, the committee must consider the case and will do so as stated above.

Hearing by a 'Person Appointed'

Where the authority proposes to act in a way adverse to the licence holder and contrary to the advice of a committee or the Commission, or where there is no provision for consultation with a committee (e.g. in relation to a manufacturer's licence or a wholesale dealer's licence) the person affected can within 28 days ask for a hearing or submit written representations. The latter are considered by the authority. If a hearing is requested, the authority must appoint a person who must not be an officer of the Health or Agriculture Departments to hear the case. The hearing will be in private unless the applicant requests otherwise. The applicant can state his case, giving any information he considers relevant and may, with the consent of the person appointed, call witnesses. The person appointed must ensure that the Authority have all the facts and points made by the applicant. The authority take no part in the proceedings. After the hearing, the person appointed makes his report to the Authority. This is an account of the matters raised at the hearing but does not make a recommendation. The authority considers the report and decides the issue. If the decision is adverse, the reason for it must be given.

The only step left to an aggrieved party is to appeal to the High Court (section 107) but this is only possible if he believes that the decision was not within the powers of the authority or that it had not carried out the proper procedures. If the Court finds in favour of the applicant, it may quash the decision.

FEES

To obtain a licence under Part II of the Act it is necessary to make an application and pay a fee. The collection of fees under the Medicines Act was authorised by the Medicines Act 1971. Details of the fees payable are published from time to time in regulations, the current regulations are 1978/1121 as amended to 1983/1731. At present, there are no fees payable for certificates either for clinical trials, animal tests or for the exportation of medicines.

There are two types of fee payable, namely –

(i) **Capital fee**

This is payable in order to obtain a licence and covers the cost of scrutinising the application. The scale of fee is stated in Schedule 1 to the Fees Regulations. Currently, there is no capital fee payable for manufacturers' licences nor for wholesale dealers' licences. There are two scales of fee for product licences, a standard fee, and a 'higher alternative amount'.

(ii) **Annual fee**

This is paid annually to keep the licence(s) in being.

The licensing year starts on the 1st September and ends on the 31st August (regulation 1(2)) and annual fees are payable on the 1st September of the year to which they relate (regulation 13).

The following categories of products pay the standard fee (see Schedule 1 Part II) –

(a) herbals consisting entirely of ingredients included in products on the UK market when licensing commenced;

(b) homoeopathic or related remedies sold without written recommendation as to use;

(c) allergen extracts and similar products;

(d) any substance or article used by a pharmacist, practitioner, herbalist or in a hospital as an ingredient in the preparation of medicinal products;

(e) contact lenses and fluids;

(f) intra-uterine contraceptive devices;

(g) any substance specified in the Control of Substances for Manufacture Order (antibiotics, enzymes, etc);

(h) dental filling substances;

(i) substances and articles for incorporation into animal feeding stuffs for a medicinal purpose.

Some other products, e.g. reformulations of existing products on the market before September 1971, are also eligible for payment of the standard fee under certain conditions (see Schedule 1 Part III). The existing product must either have been the subject of a product licence held by the applicant for the new licence or must have been the subject of a patent which expired at least 12 months earlier, and the patented product had been on the market continuously since before September 1971. In any event, the new product must be in the same pharmaceutical form (unless the active ingredients have been scrutinised by the CSD or under the Veterinary Products Safety Precautions Scheme), and sold or supplied in the same way as the existing product.

All other capital fees are at the higher alternative amount, though provisions exist for them to be waived or reduced in certain circumstances.

Reduction or Waiver of Fees

There are several sets of circumstances under which the Minister is empowered to reduce, waive or refund fees and these are specified in Schedule 4. If the manufacture, sale or supply of medicines of any description is (or may be) interrupted, he may make an announcement in the London Gazette, and may waive the fees for applications for licences for such products for a period not exceeding 3 months. Furthermore, he may reduce, waive or refund (either wholly or partly) –

(1) a capital fee at the higher alternative amount where the product is for use in a rare condition or that it is not to be sold; or,

(2) that its gross sales did not exceed a sum specified by the Minister for the purpose at the time of application, e.g. where the sales are small in relation to the costs of production and distribution; or

(3) where there was an existing product identical to that being applied for and that there is no need to carry out a detailed examination of the new product.

Annual Fees

Calculation of annual fees. The ways in which these fees are calculated are described in Schedule 1 Part VI. Normally, they are payable at the basic rate or the standard percentage of turnover, whichever is the greater. However, in the first year of a licence if no annual fee has been paid under these regulations, or, in the second or subsequent year the applicant is liable to pay an annual fee for the first year of a licence or has paid an equivalent amount as an advance payment in respect of an annual fee due for the renewal of an existing licence, the fee shall be the basic fee or the alternative percentage of turnover whichever is the greater.

Turnover. Annual fees are based on turnover and there are several important points to note. Firstly, turnover is based on 'manufacturer's prices', i.e. the prices charged by manufacturers to wholesalers. If a manufacturer sells direct to retailers the selling price may be reduced by a sum which represents the wholesaler's mark-up. The second point is that it is based upon the gross value of the sales of the product (or of products manufactured, or imported) for the calendar year that ended 20 months before the end of the year for which the fee is being paid. Since these fees are due on the 1st September, and cover the period to the end of the following August, it is the sales figure for the last calendar year that matter, e.g. fees due on the 1st September 1985 would be based upon the sales figures for the calendar year 1984.

The annual fees for product licences of a particular kind (i.e. either for human use or for animal use) are based on the gross value of all the licensed products of that kind sold in the *United Kingdom* during the relevant year. The value of sales of products sold as ingredients or for incorporation into animal feeding stuffs are ignored for this purpose, as are those derived from products for human use which are subject to licensing only because Article 2 (para 3) of the Foods and Cosmetics Order apply to them.

In calculating the annual fee for manufacturer's licences, turnover means the gross value of all products manufactured or assembled in the relevant year whether they were sold in the United Kingdom or elsewhere. Where the products are sold to an assembler, the value of the products as sold to the assembler forms part of the manufacturer's turnover, and the difference between that and the value as sold by the assembler forms part of the assembler's turnover. Where products are assembled under contract, the charge made for assembly forms part of the turnover of the assembler and that charge is deducted from the turnover of the manufacturer. Similarly, where the manufacturing activity consists solely of the sterilisation under contract of material manufactured by another person, the charge made for sterilisation forms part of that company's turnover, and is deducted from the other company's figures.

Lesser fees. Where a licence holder himself sells or supplies the product by retail and without advertisement, the fee is 0.5% of turnover, rounded up to the nearest £1, with a minimum fee of £10. The same provisions apply to a veterinarian who manufactures (or procures the manufacture) of products in circumstances to which section 9(3) apply.

Where the licence holder holds more than one licence of a relevant kind, and satisfies the Minister that his aggregate turnover is less than £30,000, the annual fee is 0.5% of such turnover, subject to a minimum of £10 in respect of each kind of licence.

Similarly, an annual fee at the basic rate is charged where a manufacturer's licence is limited to products to which Article 2 of the Special and Transitional Cases Order applies and manufacture consists of mixing together medicinal products and ingredients (other than active ingredients) on premises of which the licensee is the occupier and which he is able to close to exclude the public. The basic rate fee is also applicable where the manufacturing is restricted to assembly and the assembling is done by a person in the course of his business and at the request of a patient who has asked the supplier to use his judgment as to the treatment required.

Late payments. If an annual fee is not paid within 3 months of the due date, the licensee becomes liable for an additional fee by way of penalty. The penalty fee is computed by multiplying 1% of the annual fee by the number of complete months from the day after the end of the 3 months to the date it is paid. This fee is rounded down to the nearest £10, and where the annual fee is less than £10 no penalty fee is chargeable.

Where evidence of turnover has not been supplied in time for the annual fee to be calculated before the due date, the licensee can make a payment on account and this sum is deducted from the annual fee before computation of the penalty fee should such eventually be required.

No fees are payable in respect of applications made by authorities or boards set up under the NHS.

Over-payments. The Ministers have powers to refund, adjust or set-off any fee or part of a fee in the circumstances described in Schedule 3 (regulation 16). Similarly, they may waive or reduce a fee in circumstances described in Schedule 4 (regulation 18). They may suspend a licence for non-payment of any sum due, but only after having given the licensee at least 1 month's warning.

As a last resort, civil proceedings lie to recover unpaid sums due as debts due to the Crown (regulation 19). Schedule 3 deals with a variety of situations in which the applicant overpays or should receive a refund. The provisions seem to give the Minister discretion to refund the money, or to treat it as an advance payment. The Minister does not seem to be obliged to repay. The circumstances under which refunds may become due are –

(1) when an inspection fee greater than that payable under regulation 10 has been paid;

(2) where a fee has been paid at the time of application and the licence is not granted, renewed or varied;

(3) where the annual fee was based upon an estimated turnover which in the event was too large (in the event that the estimate was too small the difference becomes payable!);

(4) where a licence is revoked or expires on a date earlier than that stated in the licence, a proportion of the fee based on the actual duration of the licence will be refunded;

(5) where an application is withdrawn before it was determined, any fee or part of a fee paid may be refunded.

Offences Relating to Licensing

There are several offences that can be committed in relation to Part II of the Act. It is an offence –

(1) to contravene any provision of section 7, section 8, section 31, section 32, section 34 or section 40 (section 45(1));

(2) to possess for sale, supply or export any medicinal product or animal feeding stuff in contravention of those provisions (section 45(1));

(3) to possess any product or animal feeding stuff which a person knows or suspects to have been imported in contravention of sections 7, 31, 32 or 40 (section 45(2));

(4) for the holder of a product licence or clinical trial or animal test certificate to procure the manufacture or assembly of the product and fail to communicate to the manufacturer the provisions of the licence or certificate or to fail to inform him of a variation to those provisions within 14 days (section 45(3));

(5) for the holder of a product licence or animal test certificate to sell or supply the product to a person for incorporation into an animal feeding stuff without informing him of the appropriate provisions of the licence or certificate or of any instructions required to be communicated by the licence (section 45(4));

(6) where the provisions of the licence or certificate have been varied by the Authority, and the Authority have notified the holder that he must, within a stated time, make the variation known to affected parties, to fail to do so (section 45(5));

(7) for anyone to give false information under section 44 (section 45(6));

(8) for anyone to fail to comply with a requirement imposed upon him by a notice under section 44(2) (section 45(7)).

DEFENCES

When the holder of a licence or a certificate is charged with an offence relating to a product which was manmufactured or assembled to his order by another person, and the manufacture or assembly was not in accordance with the provisions of the licence or certificate, it shall be a defence for him to prove that:

(a) he had communicated the provisions to the other person, and,

(b) that he did not know, and could not with reasonable care have discovered that the provisions had not been complied with.

ENFORCEMENT

The premises of holders of licences and certificates are subject to inspection by inspectors from the Medicines Division. The inspectors must produce their credentials if required and are empowered to take samples (on payment or otherwise), inspect books and other documents relating to the business and make copies of any entries, and may seize any products required as evidence. They may require that containers, packages and vending machines be opened. They have similar powers to inspect homecoming ships and aircraft to prevent unauthorised importation of medicines. If it is intended to enter a private house, then either 24 hours notice must be given to the occupier or a warrant obtained from a justice of the peace.

References

B.P. Commission Annual Report for 1976, paragraph

Hartley and Maynard (1982). The costs and benefits of regulating new product development in the UK pharmaceutical industry. (London: OHE)

MAIL No. 40, p.4

Chapter 5
Licences and Certificates Relating to Products

Product Licences

PRODUCTS AFFECTED

It is now unlawful to put a medicinal product on the market unless it is the subject of a product licence. The licensing provisions also apply to numerous substances and articles which are not medicinal products within the meaning of the Act, but which have been brought within the scope of Part II of the Act by Orders made by the Ministers. Such products include –

(1) various antibiotics, enzymes, blood products, hormones, vaccines and sera when for use as ingredients in various products for administration to humans or animals; (1971/1200);

(2) certain antimicrobial substances, e.g. antibiotics, sulphonamides and nitrofurans except when they are medicinal products or for incorporation in animal feeding stuffs; (1973/367);

(3) surgical ligatures and sutures, and absorbable haemostatics used in operations on the human body (1971/1267);

(4) dental filling substances (1975/533) will become subject to licensing after a 'special day' has been appointed;

(5) contact lenses (and blanks), solutions used in connection with contact lenses, intra-uterine contraceptive devices (1976/968);

(6) animal feeding stuffs containing medicinal products (section 40) and certain feeding stuffs additives (1975/1349).

On the other hand, some medicinal products have been exempted from the licensing provisions, e.g. foods and cosmetics are only subject to licensing if curative or remedial properties are claimed for them, if they are to be promoted to doctors or dentists or meet certain other requirements (1971/1410). Similarly, herbal remedies which have not been imported and which consist only of dried, crushed or comminuted plants and which are sold without written recommendation do not need a product licence (section 12(2)). Most medicinal products are dosage forms, i.e. they are products ready for administration to a patient, but others are ingredients (whether active or merely excipients such as flavours, colours, emulsifiers) used by practitioners, pharmacists, herbalists, or in hospitals in the preparation of medicines. These ingredients are also subject to licensing, but since an exemption from licensing may be obtained, it is not usually necessary for the manufacturer to apply for product licences for each of the ingredients he wishes to market. It is necessary to notify the licensing authority that the company manufactures, imports or wholesales ingredients and which of the classes (i.e. practitioners, pharmacists, herbalists, or hospitals) it intends to supply. The authority may require additional information and may withdraw the exemption on the grounds of safety in which case the manufacturer may apply for a product licence for that product (1974/1150).

No product licence is required where a person needs a product only for administration to humans in the course of his business. This is because the person will not sell, supply or export the product. However, where such a product contains a POM, the order must be signed by a practitioner. Thus a chemical company may request a local pharmacy to prepare an antidote to a particular poison using the company's formula without the need to hold a product licence for that formula. Similarly, chiropodists, opticians and similar practitioners may request a pharmacist to prepare their own formulae for use in their practice. The pharmacist may procure the manufacture of the product from a company holding a 'specials' licence or could prepare the product himself. Such a product cannot be advertised for sale.

In effect, licensing only applies to products intended for wide distribution. This is inevitable since it would be impossible to licence every product made unless it was also intended to restrict the variety of products available to those made in large quantities. Moreover, the intention behind the Act is to protect the public generally, and not each individual.

WHO MUST HOLD THE LICENCE?

A product licence must be held by the person –

(a) who is responsible for the composition of the product; or

(b) in the case of a proprietary product, is responsible for the placing of the product on the market in the UK; or

(c) who imports the product into the UK; or

(d) who first sells or supplies it as a medicinal product (it not having been manufactured or imported as a medicinal product); or

(e) who intends to incorporate it into an animal feeding stuff.

'Proprietary product' in (b) above means a ready-prepared product placed on the UK market under a special name and in a special pack but does NOT include vaccines, toxins, serums, products based on human blood or radio-isotopes, homoeopathic products. The reason for the exclusion of these groups of products from the definition is that the phrase (and the relevant restrictions) originate in a Community obligation which is not applicable to those groups.

A person is 'responsible for the composition' of a product if, in the course of his business,

(i) he procures the manufacture of the product to his order by another person, where the order specifies, or incorporates by the reference to another document (e.g. the BP) particulars of the composition of the product whether these particulars amount to a complete specification or not, or

(ii) he manufactures the product otherwise than in pursuance of an order which fulfils the conditions specified in (i).

Some examples may help to illustrate the position. A pharmaceutical company may manufacture for sale to retail and hospital pharmacies and possibly to practitioners a range of standard mixtures, elixirs, ointments, etc. The company must hold a product licence for each such preparation. If a retail pharmacist orders from that company a mixture which is not part of the company's range the retail pharmacist might require a product licence (see later for exemptions for pharmacists).

The same pharmaceutical company purchases sugar from a refinery and intends to pack and sell it to pharmacists as 'Sucrose BP'. Since the company is the first to sell it as a medicinal product, it might require a product licence for 'Sucrose BP' but, as we have seen, there are exemptions for ingredients.

In relation to a named product, the licence authorises the holder to engage in such of the following activities as are specified in the licence –

(a) to sell, supply or export it; or

(b) procure its sale, supply or exportation; or

(c) procure its manufacture or assembly for sale, supply or export; or

(d) import it or procure its importation.

APPLICATIONS FOR PRODUCT LICENCES

The licence must be applied for by the person who, in relation to such a medicinal product, wishes to engage in any of the activities listed in (a) to (d) above. In so far as (a) is concerned, only the person who wants to put the product on the market needs the licence. Wholesalers and retailers do not need a licence for a product unless they want to put it on the market.

The licence specifies the activities it covers and also authorises the manufacture or assembly of the product by a person who holds an appropriate manufacturer's licence and acts to the order of the product licence holder or is himself the product licence holder.

The applicant for a product licence must collect a considerable amount of scientific evidence as to the nature, effects and other properties of his product. This evidence is then assessed by one or more of the expert committees who report upon it to the licensing authority. It must be understood that the expert committees do not carry out any experimental work on the product, they simply base their judgment on the evidence provided by the applicant. It is therefore essential that applicants provide full details of all experimental work carried out, both on the active constituents and on the finished product. To facilitate the work of these committees, applicants should present their evidence in the form required.

The manner in which applications must be made are specified in the Applications for Product Licences and Clinical Trial and Animals Test Certificates Regulations 1971, as amended. The Medicines Division has produced a number of useful information leaflets (called MALs) giving more detail of the information required and how it should be validated and presented. MAL 2 is particularly relevant. For convenience, a brief outline of the main requirements is given below.

All information must be given in English but a copy of any relevant document written in another language must be included. Where the relevant data about a drug substance is well documented, an abridged submission may be made. This may also be done where the active constituents comply with specifications given in official books, e.g. BP or BPC.

An application for a product licence for a product for human use must be made in writing and consists of four parts. A special form (MLA 201) is used for Part I (general matters) and Part IA(Product Particulars) and the form was revised in 1984 to facilitate the storage of the information on computer. Part IB consists of supplementary details. Multiple copies of Part I are required because each copy of each of Parts II, III, and IV are bound with Part I as a preface.

Part I

The following information must be given in MLA 201 –

(1) the name of the product (or code name if trade name undecided);

(2) the name and address of the applicant (if a company, its full legal name, registration number and address);

(3) the company's trading style if different from (2);

(4) role of proposed licensee, i.e. whether he is the person responsible for composition, or who imports it or procures its importation, or who first sells it as a medicinal product;

(5) the activities to be covered by the licence, e.g. selling, supplying, manufacturing, importing it;

(6) applicant's own reference number;

(7) details of any earlier applications (giving reference number);

(8) state whether it is to cover a product manufactured before the grant of the licences;

(9) scientific evidence, stating the number of pages in each part of (i) chemistry and pharmacy, (ii) experimental and biological studies, and (iii) clinical trials;

(10) whether the applicant consents to the disclosure of information on the standards applicable to the product or its ingredients to the British Pharmacopoeia Commission;

(11) the applicant must sign and date the application, which contains statements that the licence is for 5 years and is subject to the appropriate Standard Provisions. He must certify that the product will only be recommended for conditions specified in Product Particulars, only sold in accordance with those Particulars, that its specification and manufacture will be in accordance with the information given with the application. The signatory also confirms that no material information known to him has been omitted.

The form requires details of the Product Particulars (Part IA) which includes the following information –

(1) name of product;

(2) its pharmaceutical form and whether it is to be used as an ingredient or in a form suitable for administration to humans;

(3a) legal status;

(3b) method of retail sale;

(4) active constituents, stated in the manner in which they will be declared on labels, leaflets and advertisements. The monograph or approved name should be used if there is one;

(5) recommended indications and routes of administration;

(6) recommended dose and dosage schedule – the particulars of dosage, for adults and if applicable for children and infants by age group; if appropriate distinguish between therapeutic and prophylactic doses and between dosages for different clinical uses;

(7) manufacturer of dosage form, state name and address(es);

(8) contra-indications, precautions and warnings, to be used on labels and leaflets and in data sheets;

(9) specifications and quantities of other constituents;

(10) description of essential processes of manufacture;

(11) finished product specification;

(12) name of assembler;

(13) arrangements for storage;

(14) importer;

(15) list of other countries of registration;

(16) site and arrangements for quality control;

(17) types of containers, pack size(s), shelf life and storage conditions.

Part II: Pharmaceutical data on the dosage form

This volume contains all of the specifications for the product and for its constituents, and includes the scientific evidence which substantiates the details provided. It includes an addendum on the chemistry and pharmacy of the drug substance. The data are presented in several sections.

Finished product. This section contains the complete formula for the product, including active constituents, excipients, fillers, flavouring and colouring agents, and such items as capsule shells. The appearance of the product is described including its colour, shape, size, odour, taste, consistency, type of tablet coating, and, if a liquid, whether a solution, suspension or emulsion.

The formula states the active constituents and quantity of each in a dose unit, or for creams, lotions and similar articles as a percentage. For injections, the weight of active ingredient(s) per ml must be stated, as well as the total weight of each ingredient in the nominal volume of the container. The name used for each ingredient must be the English name used at the head of a monograph in the European Pharmacopoeia (Eur.P) or BP for constituents which are the subject of such a monograph. For constituents not included in these books, the name used is the international non-proprietary name (INN) or the British Approved Name (BAN) or both if they differ, or any other name, e.g. USAN or simple chemical name which accurately identifies the substance. A proprietary name may be used for an ingredient which is a mixture of substances. Colours must be permitted colouring matters and are identified by the appropriate EEC code number. Amounts must be stated in the metric system. Where active ingredients are present as a salt or ester the amount must also be stated in terms of the base.

If 'overage' is included, the applicant must indicate whether this is intended to cover losses during manufacture or on storage or both, and should refer to the relevant information given in other sections.

A brief description of the containers used for the product and the proposed pack sizes should be given.

If clinical evidence is being supplied with the application, the formula (set out as above) of the product used in the trial should be given unless it is identical with that given above.

The details of the manufacturing process. This forms the second section of this Part, and includes the full manufacturing formula, with the quantity of every ingredient used, including any removed during the process of manufacture. Some quantities, such as those of excipients used in coating tablets, may be given in approximate terms.

Likewise, the manufacturing process used must be fully described with details of such factors as the temperatures used in melting or sterilising the product, the particle size of active ingredients, etc. The assembling process is also described, especially where special precautions are necessary.

Quality control specifications These are required for all constituents and for the finished product. The applicant must state the specifications of every constituent and whether it is bought to a specification with a certificate of analysis or whether it will be tested by the manufacturer. The specification should indicate which tests will be carried out routinely, and those which will be checked occasionally. Where the ingredient complies with the specifications of the Eur.P, BP, BPC or any other pharmacopoeial monograph published in English (e.g. USP, USNF) a reference to the monograph will often suffice though there are circumstances where additional data will be required, for example, when a new synthetic route is used which may give rise to different impurities from those detected by the official specification. Where constituents are tested to the applicant's own specifications, full details of the specifications must be supplied. Similarly, for constituents not in official compendia, the specification and details of the analytical method must be supplied. A supplier of a constituent may send such details directly to the Authority at the request of the applicant, and this may be done especially with proprietary flavouring agents or perfumes.

Details of the in-process control must be given, stating the analytical methods and limits or criteria of acceptance. This includes any tests carried out before the analysis of the finished product, e.g. moisture content of granules before tabletting. The stages at which sampling is carried out should also be stated.

Details of the tests which are to be carried out on each batch of the product must be stated. Where products are unstable, it is necessary to differentiate between the 'Release Specification', i.e. the requirements for each batch at completion of manufacture, and the 'Check Specification', i.e. the requirements which are applicable at any time during the shelf life of the product. The tests applied should be listed together with the limits or criteria of acceptance. Where the finished product is the subject of an official monograph, a reference to the document is all that is necessary, but if additional tests or tighter limits are imposed at the time of manufacture, details must be given. A suitable identity test should also be given. Where the analytical methods used are those published in official compendia, a reference to the document will suffice, but all other methods must be described in sufficient detail to permit them to be reproduced readily if necessary. This latter is an EEC requirement (Directive 75/318).

Development pharmaceutics and biological availability. This is the subject of the fourth section and consists of an outline of the work done to determine the satisfactory nature of the proposed formulation for its intended purposes. The formulation studies performed should be described and the criteria which were applied in formulating the product should be stated.

The analytical development work, showing that the specifications and methods described in the application are adequate to ensure batch to batch uniformity, must be described and discussed. The evidence showing the validity of the methods must be given. Similarly, analytical results of different batches of the product made to the specifications given in the application must be given. The details should include the date of manufacture, the batch number and size, the place of manufacture and the results of the analytical tests. If the batches were used in clinical trials this should be mentioned.

Availability studies should normally be carried out, but if they are omitted the reasons for this must be stated.

These studies should show how the chemical, physical and biological properties of the drug, e.g. pH, solubility, particle size, crystal form, rates of absorption and excretion, have been modified or controlled to give the optimal clinical effect.

The effectiveness of the final formulation should be demonstrated by both *in vivo* and *in vitro* tests and full details of these and the results obtained should be reported. If the *in vivo* data are reported elsewhere in the application, only a brief summary is necessary here. Correlation of the results of *in vivo* and *in vitro* studies should be sought and reported and if the latter are to be used to check between batch uniformity, the rationale behind the test should be discussed.

Stability. The stability of the formulation should be shown by tests carried out on different batches of the product. These tests usually involve at least three different temperature levels and different degrees of humidity. The effect of light should also be studied. Data obtained from at least 3 months' storage under the various conditions should be reported. These tests can also demonstrate the effectiveness of the chosen container to protect the product under these conditions. Details of the analytical tests used to detect and measure deterioration of the product during storage must be given in order that their validity can be assessed. It is not only the active ingredients that may decompose on storage, the product itself may change, so checks should be carried out on such factors as the colour, taste, odour, pH, and consistency of the product after storage. The results obtained from all of this work should indicate the shelf-life of the product and also the optimal storage conditions for inclusion on labels, leaflets and data sheets.

Container. The type and material of construction of the container and its closure must be described as must any inclusions such as desiccants or cushioning pads. Where the container measures the dose (e.g. aerosols fitted with a metering device) its construction must be described in detail and evidence of accuracy of measurement is required. In the case where the nature of the container is critical to the stability of the product, the specifications of its material and construction, and also details of tests to ensure its uniformity from batch to batch should be given.

Chemistry of the Drug Substance

Where the active constituent is a new drug substance which has not been previously licensed, or where certain unusual circumstances require, an addendum to Part 2 called the 'Chemistry of the Drug Substance' must be submitted.

This contains an enormous amount of detail about the substance including its various names (BAN, INN, chemical names), descriptions of its physical form, structural and molecular formula, molecular weight. Its method of manufacture, and specifications of starting materials, the reagents and solvents used, the quality control checks to be made at each stage and the final purification stage must all be described. In addition, studies must be undertaken to detect the impurities likely to be present, and the methods used to detect, identify and quantify them must be reported.

The addendum should also contain the evidence of molecular structure and physical characteristics, tests for identity, standards of potency and purity.

Full details of stability studies on different batches of the compound must be included as must a detailed report of the analytical work done to validate the data obtained from metabolic studies.

The methods used to determine metabolic pathways and plasma levels of the drug and its metabolites should be described and the data obtained reported.

Part III: Experimental and Biological Studies

This contains details of all the tests done (both on the compound and on formulated products) to show the pharmacological properties of the product, including its kinetics, toxicology, pathology, teratology and carcinogenicity.

The pharmacological data must be obtained from a variety of animal species, such as mouse, rat, rabbit, cat, dog, monkey, and should show the action of the drug in relation to its proposed clinical use. Any other actions sought or found should also be described. The data should be classified under physiological system, e.g. central nervous system, respiratory system, and presented in species order. The aim is to obtain a pharmacological profile of the drug, and comparison with established drugs of the same therapeutic class is desirable. Any studies designed to detect interactions with excipients should also be described.

The drug's pharmacokinetics must be fully investigated and reported. The plasma levels of both the drug and of its metabolites should be determined and the methods used descibed in full. If labelled material (i.e. drug containing radio-active atoms) is used, the position of the label and the specific activity of the material must be given. These studies must be carried out on the species used in toxicological and reproduction studies. Evidence of cumulation and of enzyme induction should also be sought. Details of the distribution of the drug and of its metabolites in the organs of the body should be described, together with details as to its excretion patterns.

The toxicity of the drug should be thoroughly studied by means of single dose studies and also repeated dose studies, the latter being divided into sub-acute, intermediate and chronic or long term. These studies should be carried out using all the various routes of administration, and should involve all of the usual animal species. Every animal that dies during the tests must be autopsied and the details of the autopsy findings must be given together with a discussion of their significance and the conclusions drawn. The LD50 by each route of administration should be determined. It is necessary to include details of the analytical specification of the batch of material used in the test. Furthermore, details as to the number of animals of each species, their age and sex, diet, weight, source strain should also be given.

Studies to determine the oncogenetic (carcinogenic) and mutagenic properties of the drug must be carried out, especially when the drug is chemically similar to known carcinogens, and when the drug is likely to be taken regularly over a long period of time. Guidance on carcinogenicity testing is given in Annex 1 of MAL 2.

Evidence of effects on the foetus and neonate must be sought. As a minimum, the effect of the drug administered during embryogenesis on at least two species, one of which is not a rodent, must be presented. A fertility study on one species should be performed. Details of the desired reproduction studies are given in MAL 36.

Where the drug is to be administered by a particular route, it may be necessary to carry out special studies of its pharmacokinetics and toxicity by that route. For example, where a drug is to be administered parenterally, histopathological studies of the injection sites must be performed to detect local reactions.

Likewise, for ointments, creams and similar products, the proposed formulation should be applied topically to at least two species on both intact and damaged skin. Percutaneous absorption of the drug must be measured and its local and systemic effects studied. All ophthalmic preparations must be tested for local toxicity, in the frequency and duration of dosage used clinically.

Studies in Humans

Human pharmacological studies may be carried out but are not mandatory. If they are carried out, they must be reported if the results are relevant to the safety of the drug. In such a case, the age, sex, and weight of each volunteer must be given, together with the route, dosage, frequency and duration of dosage.

Data from clinical trials must be reported and must scientifically demonstrate the safety and efficacy of the product. The data must include a summary of all clinical trials carried out, specify the number of trials, differentiating between comparative randomised trials and single series trials, state the number of patients entering the trials and their diagnoses, the number receiving the test drug and the number withdrawn before completion of the test (the reasons for withdrawal must also be stated). Details as to dosage, its range and duration, and as to concurrent therapy must be given. The results must be summarised, together with details of the statistical methods used. ALL adverse reactions, whether major or minor, must be reported.

Information must be given in the above form for each of the proposed clinical indications. Furthermore, the results obtained from each trial must be reported in sufficient detail to permit each conclusion drawn by the investigators to be assessed. Where available, details of any data obtained from biochemical, clinical or haematological studies performed on patients participating in the trials must be given together with details of the patients involved.

Abridged Applications

Where the drug substance is the subject of a pharmacopoeial monograph (unless made by a novel synthetic route, or from a different source) or where the drug has been widely used or has been described in a previous 'new drug' application, an abridged application may be made. In such an application the Part II Addendum (Chemistry of the drug substance) and Part III, may be omitted. Part III data may be required if a new dosage level is to be used or where ingredients which are not well known are involved. Clinical trials are seldom required for pharmacopoeial substances used in normal dosages, routes, forms and for standard indications. They are not required where clinical data has previously been examined as part of a 'new drug' application for the same indications.

Proposals have been made to permit certain hydrocortisone preparations to be sold by pharmacists without a prescription. It is probable that the products concerned will be given new proprietary names and will thus need to be licensed. It will be unnecessary for a company which now makes such a product to submit a full application for the 'new' one, an abridged application will suffice.

Manual of Specifications for Ingredients and Analytical Methods

When a manufacturer uses the same excipients in several products, he can submit a manual containing their specifications. The manual may also contain details of the standard analytical methods he uses. Thereafter, he merely refers to the appropriate manual entries in his applications for product licences. This can save him considerable time and expense.

Applications for Product Licences for Herbal Remedies

The usual requirements need modification, especially those relat ing to Part II, Pharmaceutical data on the dosage form. The list of ingredients (with amounts) of the finished product must be stated as for other products. Details of all stages of the manufacturing process must be given, including milling, extraction, and the solvents used. If the herb was treated to remove infestation, e.g. with ethylene oxide, this must be stated and the process described. Where the extract has been standardised, the method used should be described.

IMPORTED PRODUCTS

The application for a product licence for an imported product is made in the usual way. The licensing authority will need to be satisfied that the methods, conditions and standards of manufacture are appropriate to yield a product of acceptable quality and safety. To this end, the applicant may be required to obtain from the manufacturer overseas one or more of the following –

(1) an undertaking to permit inspection by the Authority;

(2) an undertaking to comply with any prescribed conditions;

(3) a declaration that the product has been manufactured in accordance with the law of the manufacturing country (section 19).

The details required in the undertakings are specified in statutory instrument 1977/1038. Essentially, the manufacturer must undertake to do those things that a manufacturer in the UK would have to do under the terms of a product licence.

New administrative procedures to licence parallel imports have also been made. These arrangements have not yet been the subject of a statutory instrument, but were announced in Parliament on May 16th 1984 (Hansard 60, No.154, 157). They have been designed to meet the specific objections made about the UK arrangements and seem to be the minimum permitted under the EEC laws.

The new arrangements involve the issue of a new type of product licence, the product licence (parallel importation) PL(PI). This can be obtained for a proprietary product which –

(a) is covered by a valid and current marketing authorisation under Article 3 of EEC/65/65 by the member state from which it is to be imported, and

(b) is covered by a valid and current marketing authorisation issued by the UK.

Thus it is only possible to obtain such a licence for the import of a product from an EEC country.

Such a product must either be identical to a product having a product licence of right, or have no therapeutic difference from a product having a product licence. It must also be made by the same manufacturer or group of companies as the UK product.

It should be noted that the scheme only applies to 'proprietary products', and therefore does not cover vaccines, sera, blood products, homoeopathic preparations and the like.

To apply for such a licence, an application must be made for each product though the product may be imported from different EEC countries. Three copies of the application in English must be sent together with the fee of £150. The licence will be valid for 5 years unless one of the marketing authorisations is withdrawn. The licence will authorise the import of the product into the country and also its sale or supply. Furthermore, the licensee can procure the assembly of the product but not its manufacture. Since the licensee will be selling the product in the course of his business, he will, of course, need a wholesale dealer's licence. In addition, if he intends to repack, relabel or overlabel the product he will need to hold an 'assembler's' licence.

Each batch of product must be accompanied by batch control documents unless the authorities have verified the manufacturer's controls in one of the ways mentioned in the 'de Peijper' judgment –

(1) by taking legislative or other measures to compel the manufacturer to supply them, or

(2) obtain them from the authorities in the country of manufacture, or

(3) lay down a presumption of conformity with specifications which they might rebut after seeking verification of conformity, or

(4) allow the importer to provide proof of conformity by any means other than by documents to which he has no access.

The importer must employ a 'qualified person' to certify that each batch complies with the specifications. The licensee must keep sufficient records to facilitate batch recall if necessary.

APPLICATIONS FOR PRODUCT LICENCES FOR VETERINARY PRODUCTS

These are very similar to those for human products but there are a few important differences. It is possible to obtain a product licence for a veterinary product to allow its sale, manufacture and distribution in the UK generally or in Great Britain only, or only in Northern Ireland. Licences for products for human use are for the UK. Secondly, applications must be sent to the MAFF Medicines Unit at Weybridge using Form MLA 201(Vet).

When a substance or article is to be incorporated into an animal feeding stuff for a medicinal purpose it will need to be licensed for that purpose. Much of the pharmaceutical dosage form data normally supplied is, of course, irrelevant and is replaced by data on the feeding stuff, its nature and type, and the animals to which it will be fed and levels and methods of incorporation. Evidence of the adequacy of mixing will be required. The permitted tolerances must be stated and details given of the relevant analytical procedures. Likewise the compatibility and stabilty of the product in the feeding stuff should be clearly shown.

When a veterinary drug is only for use in cats, dogs or other animals not used in food production, the data required is similar to that needed for human medicines. Much more data is necessary for products for administration to food producing animals and of special importance is the investigation of the effects of residues in foods, and the calculation of safe withdrawal periods. The withdrawal time is the interval required between the cessation of drug treatment and slaughter to ensure that residue levels have fallen to a safe level. Similar withdrawal times are necessary for antibiotics and other drugs administered to milking cows so as to ensure that the milk is not contaminated with the drug. This is important in all drugs given to food animals but especially those intended for incorporation into animal feeding stuffs. The Scientific Committee for Animal Nutrition published Guidelines for the Assessment of Additives in Feeding stuffs, which is intended to assist in the preparation of dossiers on substances to be submitted for authorisation as additives in feeding stuffs

(Reports of the Scientific Committee for Animal Nutrition, Commission of the European Communities, Agriculture 1980).

REVIEW OF PRODUCTS

When licensing commenced in 1971, approximately 39,000 products already on the market were granted 'licences of right'. In the intervening period, many have been allowed to lapse, some have been reviewed and granted full licences, while some 16,000 remained to be reviewed in 1984 (MAIL 40). The authority has a commitment to complete the review by 1990 and licence holders have been given an idea of the date by which applications for their various products must be made. They have also been urged to consider whether each product meets present day needs and is worth licensing. Certain products, e.g. homoeopathic medicines, blood products, vaccines, sera and toxins and radiopharmaceuticals are exempt from the current review because they are outside the EC commitment.

An application for a reviewed licence must be made on MLA 201R and be supported by a pharmaceutical summary and a medical and scientific summary. In addition, the authority may require the answers to specific questions. The information required in the summaries is basically the same as for any product licence. MAL 58 contains some useful notes on the preparation of the summaries.

The authority has warned licence holders that when a notice under section 44 is sent by the authority requesting more information by a stated date, if the information is not received by that date, the authority may use its powers under section 28(3)d, to revoke or suspend the licence.

STANDARD PROVISIONS FOR PRODUCT LICENCES

The standard provisions applicable to product licences (including licences of right) are specified in Part I of Schedule 1 to the Standard Provisions for Licences and Certificates Regulations 1971/973 (as amended). Although each licence is tailored to suit a particular product, these provisions are included in all licences unless the applicant can show good reason for their omission (regulation 5(2)). A summary of the more important provisions is given below.

The licence holder must report to the licensing authority –

(1) any change in his name or address, or of any of the addresses at which the product is made or assembled;

(2) any material changes he proposes to make to the specification or composition of the product or of its constituents or methods of manufacture, assembly, quality control or storage;

(3) any information he receives which casts doubt on the continued validity of any of the data he submitted with his application;

(4) any decision to withdraw the product from sale, supply or exportation, and give his reasons for doing so.

He shall keep records –

(1) of reports of adverse reactions associated with the product;

(2) of his arrangements for procuring the sale, supply, manufacture, assembly or importation of the product, and for obtaining raw materials and for the quality assurance of both raw materials and finished product;

(3) which will facilitate the recall from sale etc. of the product.

These records must be kept available for inspection by authorised persons who may make copies or extracts from them if necessary. They may not be destroyed within 5 years of the date of release of the batch without the consent of the licensing authority.

If the authority informs the licensee that a batch of product is not up to specification or fails to conform with the provisions of the Act or regulations made under it, and instructs him to withhold it from sale etc., he shall do so for a period (not exceeding 6 weeks) specified by the authority.

The licence holder may also be required not to issue or consent to the issue of advertisements containing particulars as to the uses, nature or effects of the product or warnings concerning it, which do not correspond with the particulars or warnings given in the licence, the application for the licence or a notice sent to the authority at least 6 weeks before the advertisement was issued. He may also be required to supply particulars of advertisements relating to the product, including its content and form and the medium by which it is issued. He shall comply as soon as possible with any written direction of the authority which requires him to withdraw or modify any advertisement.

Where the product has been imported and the authority have required an undertaking to be given by its manufacturer, the licence holder shall ensure that it was manufactured or assembled in the premises and under the conditions specified in the undertaking.

When, subsequent to the renewal of a licence of right, these regulations have been amended, the licence holder must within 3 months, apply for his licence to be varied to incorporate the new provisions.

The licensee shall use the most up to date methods of quality control where these provide a greater degree of security. This does not apply to products for administration to human beings nor to veterinary drugs which are vaccines etc., radio-isotopes or homoeopathic preparations.

Additional standard provisions (see Schedule 5 to the Regulations) apply to products specified in the Control of Substances for Manufacture Order 1971, e.g. various antibiotics used as ingredients in parenteral preparations for human use, various hormones and enzymes used as ingredients in medicinal products for human or animal use. The additional provisions are very detailed but the following are noteworthy. The licence holder shall keep samples of each batch of material for a period which extends to 6 months after the expiry date of the batch and submit some of the sample to the authority if requested. Detailed protocols of the tests applied to the batch must also be supplied if requested.

New Standard Direction on Reporting Adverse Reactions to Medicines

Early in 1984, it was stated (MAL 39) that both the Division and the CSM considered that the situation regarding the reporting of adverse reactions by the industry required revision. It was admitted that the legal requirements, though clear, were difficult to find because they were scattered throughout a number of statutory instruments and in Standard Directions and Special Directions. Basically, a company must report all adverse reactions associated with new products, and serious effects associated with other products. These reports should be made within 1 month of receipt. The work of the CSM in assessing these reports was hindered by the lack of a standard format for the reports, and by the large number of 'preliminary reports' which took a long time to assess because they had to be followed up to obtain sufficient data to make a proper assessment. In addition, many reports are of minor, well-known reactions.

A new Standard Direction became operative on the 1st November 1984 and replaced the corresponding Standard and Special Directions on all existing licences. New guidance was issued in relation to it. It seems that a change will be necessary to bring the Clinical Trial Exemption scheme into line with that for Clinical Trial certificates.

The decision as to what should be reported and when, is a medical judgment and should therefore be made by the medical director or other medically qualified senior manager of the company, but the advice was to report when in doubt and as soon as possible. The report of the suspected reaction should contain the following data –

(a) name or identifying code of patient;

(b) reporting doctor's name and address;

(c) name(s) of drug(s) the patient was taking;

(d) details of the reaction.

The doctor (or dentist) should confirm the report in writing to the company, and if the report has been made verbally, the company should ask for written substantiation before reporting the reaction to the Licensing Authority. They should not await the outcome of the reaction before reporting.

RENEWAL APPLICATIONS

Normally, a product licence is valid for 5 years after which an application may be made for its renewal. Such applications are governed by the Renewal Applications for Licences and Certificates Regulations 1974/832 as amended. The requirements are that all applications must be made in writing, on the appropriate form (MLA 231 for product licences), and be signed by or on behalf of the applicant. It must contain the particulars specified in the relevant schedule to the Regulations.

Among the particulars required are those relating to the applicant such as the licensee's name and address, those relating to the licence or certificate including any variation or notification applicable thereto, and any material change in any of the matters given in the original application for the licence or certificate.

In relation to an application for the renewal of a licence or certificate relating to a product, the particulars required are similar to those supplied for the original licence. Details of its specification and pharmaceutical form, qualitative and quantitative particulars of all ingredients, as to its manufacture and that of its active constituents, the quality control procedures and tests to ensure purity, potency and stability, must be given. Also particulars as to its packaging and labelling, methods of administration and dosage must be specified.

Clinical Trial Certificates

A clinical trial is a trial to determine whether a specified drug is of use in a specified condition. It follows that a clinical trial certificate is needed to test the drug against a particular condition and a different trial (and therefore a different certificate) is required to hold trials of the drug against another disease. Most trials are carried out by companies during the development of a drug and are designed to elicit the information required for an application for a product licence. A few are organised and carried out by doctors (or dentists) seeking to compare the effects of different treatments on a particular disorder. Most such trials involve the use of licensed products for indications covered by the licence, and thus present no problems. Occasionally, a doctor will want to try a drug for a new indication, or in a dose (or by a route) different from that for which it is licensed, and for this he will need a clinical trial certificate.

The clinical trial process is divided into four phases. In phase 1 the aim is to ascertain the drug's therapeutic potential by obtaining data on safety and efficacy. The work consists of early pharmacological studies carried out on healthy volunteers or a few patients who can be closely monitored. The dosage schedule is restricted and detailed studies of the pharmacodynamics and pharmacokinetics are carried out to ascertain the dose–response curve for the drug, to determine the safe dose, and to ascertain the nature and severity of adverse reactions. Once satisfied as to the safety of single doses, the effects of chronic dosing is studied. Naturally, the volunteers are carefully monitored both clinically and in the laboratory. If this work has to be carried out in patients a clinical trial certificate must first be obtained. No such certificate is required where the volunteers are normal. If the results obtained during the phase 1 trial and those obtained more or less simultaneously from long term toxicity tests on animals, are satisfactory, then phase 2 trials commence.

These involve studies using different dosage ranges, open clinical trials to determine and characterise efficacy, and also to provide evidence of short term safety, acceptability and tolerance. If the results are still encouraging, the study proceeds to a full clinical trial. In order to do this a clinical trial certificate is essential. In addition, the hospital ethical committee must also be consulted and give its approval to the trial. Normally, this phase is carried out in several locations each being the responsibility of a named physician. One of the difficulties encountered here is the variation between the several physicians' views of what is happening. If all is still satisfactory, phase 3 trials are carried out.

In these, the aim is to show the efficacy of the product as compared with a placebo (or control product), or with a drug of known efficacy in the disease. The opportunity is also taken to look for possible interactions with other commonly prescribed drugs. At this stage, the results of long term studies on animals (e.g. life span studies on mice or rats) seeking evidence of carcinogenicity, become available. In addition, pharmaceutical studies, e.g. stability and bioavailability from various dosage forms, will be nearing completion. When all the available information has been assessed, the decision is taken to apply for a product licence or not. If this is granted, the product may be licensed for use in hospitals only, or may be subject to some other limitation. During this period, often called phase 4, the drug is administered to a much larger population than before and incidence of adverse drug reactions is monitored and the patient acceptability of the product assessed.

The original procedures for applying for a clinical trial certificate for a new drug were costly and time-consuming. In 1981 an attempt was made to facilitate the process by allowing companies to apply for an exemption from the need to hold a clinical trial certificate in certain circumstances. Although the same information has to be supplied whether one is applying for a certificate or for an exemption, in the latter case there is no examination of the data by the CSM and hence can only be used when the data available show that there are no major problems involved. The process is therefore more rapid.

Unless the drug is a vaccine, serum or plasma, a clinical trial certificate is not required when testing a product covered by a product licence so long as it is used in accordance with the licence, and is in the same pharmaceutical form (even if made without identifying marks or in a different colour). Similarly, placebos and control products are exempt under certain conditions.

WHO NEEDS THESE CERTIFICATES?

The person who arranged the trial normally requires the certificate, and this is usually the product licence holder.

APPLICATIONS FOR THESE CERTIFICATES

As usual the data supplied must be legible, the pages serially numbered, bound or stapled together on A4 paper. Parts II and III must be separately bound each with a copy of Part I included. The information required is similar, though necessarily less complete, to that required for a product licence. For complete details of the documentation required see 'Guidance Notes on Applications for Clinical Trials Certificates and Clinical Trial Exemptions' recently published by the DHSS.

STANDARD PROVISIONS RELATING TO CLINICAL TRIAL CERTIFICATES

These are contained in Part II of Schedule 1 to the Regulations.

The licence holder shall keep samples of each batch of material for a period which extends to 6 months after the expiry date of the batch and submit some of the sample to the authority if requested. Detailed protocols of the tests applied to the batch must also be supplied if requested.

The certificate holder must report any change in his name or address and any information which casts doubt on the validity of the data submitted with the application. Similarly, a decision to discontinue the trial must be reported together with the reasons for the discontinuation.

The trial must be carried out in accordance with the outline contained in the application, and the products shall only be administered by (or under the direction of) the doctor or dentist approved by the authority. It is possible to obtain the Authority's approval of changes in the trial. When a doctor or dentist ceases to participate in the trial this fact, and the reasons for the cessation, shall be reported to the authority.

Before the product is administered, the certificate holder shall communicate the provisions of the certificate to every doctor or dentist participating in the trial.

EXEMPTIONS FOR DOCTORS AND DENTISTS

If a doctor or dentist carries out a clinical trial of his own design using a product he has imported or had manufactured specially for the purpose and administers it to his own patients he is automatically exempt from the need to hold a clinical trial certificate. He does not need to notify the licensing authority nor seek its approval to carry out such a trial, nor will he need a product licence for the product if it was imported or manufactured for a particular patient (MAL31). If, however, the product was imported, or sold exclusively for the trial, or is sold in accordance with the licensing requirements then the doctor must inform the licensing authority. The authority may direct that the trial is exempt from the need of a certificate. Alternatively, the exemption may be refused. Since this decision may be made on the basis of confidential information, the reason for refusal may not be given. In applying for the exemption, the practitioner must state the name of the product, the proposed use, and the name and address of the supplier using special forms (MLA 161 for imported products, MLA 162 for others).

A doctor or dentist is also automatically exempt from the need to hold a clinical trial certificate when organising the trial of a licensed product that has been obtained through the normal trade channels provided that it is to be used strictly in accordance with the terms of the licence (i.e. it is used in the dosage and for the indications stated in the licence). If, however, a different route is to be used, or some other change made, then the approval of the licensing authority must be obtained (SI 1974/498). Approval must also be obtained if the product is to be changed in any way, for example, tablets being made without the usual distinguishing marks, or being differently coloured. The product may be packed and labelled in a way different from usual, so that neither the patient nor the doctor or nurse are able to distinguish between the active drug and the control, but all warnings normally used on the labels must be notified to the attention of the person who is to administer the product.

Animal Test Certificates

Broadly analogous provisions relate to animal test certificates (see Schedule 1, Part III to the Regulations). Where the test involves a product or substance intended for incorporation into an animal feeding stuff for a medicinal purpose, details must be given as to the type and nature of the feeding stuff, the method of incorporation, known compatibilities and incompatibilities, its stability in the feed, inclusion rates, and methods of analysis and limits of tolerances. Furthermore, the species of animals for which it is intended to be fed must be given. Data should be included as to the possible hazards to wild life, insects, birds, fish, livestock and the soil. Possible hazards to man both as a consumer of the produce of the animal and as a worker involved with animals must be given together with any precautions to be taken in the use of the feeding stuff.

If a veterinarian in private practice wants to import a product to determine its effect on animals, or if he wants to buy such a product from a company in the UK but the company does not want to apply for an animal test certificate, then the veterinarian will generally need to hold one.

If the product was manufactured in the UK and all of the conditions specified below are met, the veterinarian will be exempt from the need to hold the certificate –

(a) he has notified the Authority giving the name of the product, the intended use, and the name and address of the supplier using form MLA 162(vet);

(b) the test was not arranged by the manufacturer or supplier (unless he is one of the veterinarians);

(c) the product is sold exclusively for the test or is in accordance with the product licence;

(d) the test does not involve the administration of vaccines, sera, or plasma. The Authority may, within 21 days of receipt of the notification, direct that the test is not exempt and may refuse to give reasons for the decision. It helps the Authority if the notification is accompanied by a form MLA 163(vet) completed by the manufacturer.

If the exemption is refused, or if the conditions for exemption are not met, the veterinarian may apply for an animal test certificate in the usual way.

References

MAIL **40**, p.1

Hansard, **60**, No. 154, p. 157

Chapter 6
Licences for Activities

Manufacturer's Licence

INTRODUCTION

Any person who, in the course of his business, manufactures or assembles a medicinal product must hold a manufacturer's licence (section 8). The licence normally entitles him to manufacture (or assemble) only a product which is licensed. However, a 'special manufacturer's licence' can be obtained which permits the manufacture of unlicensed products to the order of pharmacists and practitioners (1971/1450). It is also possible to obtain a manufacturer's licence which is limited to assembly, i.e. packing and filling, or re-labelling.

APPLICATIONS FOR A LICENCE

The manner in which an application must be made is specified in the Applications for Manufacturer's and Wholesale Dealer's Licences Regulations 1971 as amended. MALs 5, 14, 18, 23 also contain valuable information relevant to the application. The following is a brief summary of the main points.

An application for a manufacturer's licence should be made in writing (1971/974) and contain the following particulars –

(1) name and address of the applicant;

(2) period for which the licence is required (if less than 5 years);

(3) activities to be covered by the licence;

  (a) either manufacture or assembly or both;

  (b) where manufacture, a statement of the operations to be carried out and the products involved;

  (c) the category of manufacturing operation (see below);

  (d) where assembly is undertaken, a description of the operations involved, e.g. labelling only or 'filling and packing';

(4) a description of the products concerned and whether they are for human use, animal use, as ingredients or for incorporation into feeding stuffs;

(5) the address(es) of all premises at which any manufacturing or assembling operations are carried out, and where ingredients or products are stored;

(6) description of the facilities available at each premises and the transport facilities between various premises;

(7) a brief description of the operations carried out at each premises and of the equipment available (e.g. blenders, autoclaves) and their make and capacity;

(8) details of any other operations carried out by the applicant at or near any of the premises (to assess the possibility of contamination);

(9) names, addresses and qualifications of key personnel, e.g. production manager at each premises, the quality controller. An indication of the quality controller's authority to reject unsatisfactory batches must also be given;

(10) if animals or tissue culture is involved, the names, addresses and qualifications of the persons in charge of them;

(11) an outline of the facilities available for identifying and storing ingredients and materials before, during and after manufacture;

(12) details of the arrangements made for keeping production records including 'master' and 'batch' records;

(13) details of the quality control procedures and arrangements made for keeping reference standards.

In respect of (3c) above, there are five categories of manufacturing operation, namely –

(1) Manufacture of 'biologicals', e.g. vaccines, blood products, hormones, enzymes.

(2) Manufacture of sterile products, e.g. powder or solution ampoules, eye preparations, some powders.

(3) Manufacture of unit dose forms, e.g. tablets, lozenges, capsules, pessaries, suppositories.

(4) Manufacture of multi-dose liquids, pastes or solids, e.g. mixtures, lotions, creams, gels, ointments.

(5) Manufacture of medicated dressings, e.g. lint, tulle, medicated plasters.

Each category excludes those which precede it, hence insulin injection would be category 1.

Six copies of the application should be sent to the licensing authority.

INSPECTION OF THE PREMISES AND FACILITIES

Before the application for the licence is determined, inspectors from the Medicines Division visit the premises. They inspect the premises, facilities, and equipment, interview the personnel, and may take samples of products for analysis. They report to the licensing authority on the visit and the authority takes this report into consideration when deciding whether a licence should be granted.

A licence may be refused if the authority are not satisfied that the premises, equipment, facilities, personnel or record keeping facilities are of a sufficiently high standard. When it seems likely that a licence will be refused, the applicant is notified and the deficiencies of his operation are stated. He thus has an opportunity to remedy the defects.

'QUALIFIED PERSON'

It is a Community obligation that manufacturers and certain distributors, e.g. wholesalers and importers, of medicinal products must employ or have at their disposal the services of a 'qualified person'. The qualifications and experience of such a person must satisfy the provisions of Articles 23 and 24 of the Second Council Directive (75/319) in respect of human medicines or Article 31 of Directive 81/851 for veterinary products. A person who is a member of the Pharmaceutical Society or of the Royal Society of Chemistry, or the Institute of Biology, satisfies these provisions as respects formal qualifications if he is regarded by the body of which he is a member as so satisfying those provisions. He must also have at least 2 years post-graduate experience in the testing of medicines or animal feeding stuffs. Clearly, a person may be 'qualified' in respect of human medicines or of animal medicines or of animal feeding stuffs or of any combination of these. The licensing authority may recognise other professional bodies for the same purposes.

The licensing authority also have power to notify the licensee (in writing) that they are not satisfied as to the qualifications, experience or professional integrity of a person and such a person cannot act as a 'qualified person' until such notification has been withdrawn. Both the licensee and the person are entitled to make representations to the authority before such a notification is made. A company may appoint more than one 'qualified person' and there are obvious advantages in so doing.

The duties of the qualified person are –

(a) to ensure that each batch of the medicinal product to which the licence relates has been manufactured or assembled and checked in compliance with the provisions of the Act and regulations made thereunder, and the provisions of the licences which relates to it.

(b) to certify in a register or other record, whether each production batch of the medicinal product satisfies the requirements set out in (a) above, and

(c) to ensure that such register or other record is regularly maintained, and that the appropriate entries are made as soon as practicable after each such batch has been manufactured.

The licence holder shall at all times provide and maintain such staff, premises, equipment and facilities as will enable the qualified person who is at his disposal to carry out the said functions.

The provisions of this paragraph shall not apply in relation to medicinal products (or veterinary drugs) consisting of vaccines, toxins or sera, medicinal products based on human blood constituents, radioactive isotopes or homoeopathic products. They do not apply to additives for animal feeding stuffs to which the provisions Directive 70/524 applies.

Furthermore, the provisions of this paragraph do not apply where the licence relates to manufacturing activity which –

(a) is limited to medicinal products to which Article 2 of the Medicines (Exemption from Licences (Special and Transitional Cases) Order 1971 as amended applies, and consists solely of mixing together medicinal products and ingredients, other than active ingredients, on premises of which the licence holder is the occupier and which he is able to close so as to exclude the public, or

(b) is limited to assembly only, where all the products to be assembled are for sale or supply in the course of a business and are supplied, without any recommendation, for the purpose of administration to a particular person after the licence holder has been requested by or on behalf of that person, and in that person's presence, to use his judgment as to the treatment required.

(c) is limited to assembly only, where all the products to be assembled are for sale or supply in the course of a business and are supplied, without any recommendation, for the purpose of administration to a particular animal or herd after the licence holder has been requested by the owner of that animal or herd to use his judgment as to the treatment required.

GUIDE TO GOOD MANUFACTURING PRACTICE

This guide (often referred to as the 'Orange Guide') is published by the Health and Agriculture Departments. It has no legal status, neither does it purport to explain or interpret the Act or any of its regulations. It does however complement these by defining the principles necessary for the production of high quality pharmaceuticals and by outlining procedures designed to achieve this. The third edition (1983) is more comprehensive than its predecessors and must be essential reading for all engaged in the manufacture and distribution of medicines. It is divided into 18 sections grouped into three parts.

Section 1 is concerned with quality and explains the differences in meaning between 'quality assurance', 'quality control' and 'good manufacturing practice' and also discusses their inter-relationship. The objectives of quality assurance are laid down and so are the requirements of good manufacturing practice. The steps necessary to achieve quality control are also specified. Section 2 deals with personnel and training. It emphasises the need for all levels of staff to receive adequate training not only in the specific tasks in which they will be involved, but also in the wider issues of good manufacturing practice. The point is made that cleaning and maintenance staff should be made fully aware of the importance of these principles and their implications for such staff. The training programme should be written down and approved both by the person responsible for production and by the person responsible for quality control. Also of importance, is the fact that the production manager and the person responsible for quality control should be different persons and that neither should be responsible to the other. Their responsibilities and the limits of their respective authority should be clearly defined. High standards of hygiene should be observed throughout the plant.

The principles and importance of documentation in the prevention of errors is explained in Section 3. Advice is given on the design of records, and on the types of information that should be recorded, e.g. specifications of starting materials, of packaging materials, of intermediates and bulk products and of the finished product. The record should ensure that all materials are sampled and tested and should be signed by the person responsible for quality control. The type of data required in the Master Formula and Method and in the Master Packaging Instruction is also specified. The information required in batch manufacturing, packaging and distribution records is also specified. A record of all complaints relating to a product or its packaging should also be kept.

The location, design and construction of both the premises and of the equipment used in manufacturing are described in Section 4. Where possible the fabric of the building and the materials used in the construction of equipment should be chosen to facilitate cleaning and the avoidance of the emission of dust. It is also important to prevent contamination of products with dust, fumes,etc. from neighbouring factories. The building should be so designed that the risk of mix-up or contamination is minimised. Animal houses should be isolated from the manufacturing area. Access to manufacturing areas should be restricted to authorised personnel. The requirements of the storage areas are also described. Advice on the manufacturing process is given in Section 5, and the need for labelling throughout the entire process is emphasised. The precautions to be taken in using re-worked or recovered material are described in Section 6, while the complaints procedure which includes a recall system are discussed in Section 7. Section 8 lays down principles of good control laboratory practice.

Part 2 (Sections 9 to 13) deals with the manufacture and control of particular types of products, e.g. sterile products, dry products (such as tablets, capsules), liquids, creams and ointments, medical gases, and radiopharmaceuticals.

Part 3 deals with contract manufacture, analysis or services, with veterinary medicines, homoeopathic products,and electronic data processing. It also contains a section on good pharmaceutical wholesaling practice. There are five appendices which contain valuable advice on the control of cross-contamination, on certificates of analysis, the assurance of the identity of starting materials,and the avoidance of labelling errors. Appendix 1 contains the basic environmental standards for the manufacture of sterile products.

A number of terms used in the Guide including 'batch', 'bulk product', 'finished product' and 'quarantine' are defined in a glossary at the end of the Guide.

ASSEMBLER'S LICENCE

In the majority of cases, the assembler is packing and labelling a licensed product. It is a condition of his licence that he complies with the requirements for containers and labels specified in that product licence. There are various ways in which an assembler may be involved. He may be responsible for the product's composition or he may import it, in which case he must also hold the product licence. Alternatively, the product licence holder may manufacture the product and send it to the assembler for packing and labelling. In this case the relevant terms of the product licence must be made known to the assembler.

Another possibility is that the assembler wishes to buy a licensed product manufactured by someone else, and pack and label it for various retail pharmacists as though it were their own brands. To do this, the assembler must apply to the licensing authority for a 'direction' under Article 3(1) of the Special and Transitional Cases Order 1971. To obtain this direction he must notify the authority of his intention to offer this service, give details (including product licence numbers) of the products involved, send specimen labels for each product, and show how he will keep records of the names and addresses of the pharmacists who use his service. The direction authorises him to use the name and address of a retail pharmacist on the label of the product as though that pharmacist were the manufacturer. The details on the label must be consistent with the product licence in so far as indications, dosage, contra-indications and warnings are concerned. The assembler must keep a copy of the labels used for the various pharmacists and for the different products.

STANDARD PROVISIONS FOR MANUFACTURER'S LICENCES

These are contained in Schedule 2 to Standard Provisions For Licences and Certificates Regulations 1971 as amended.

The licensee is required to –

(1) provide and maintain suitable staff, premises, equipment and other facilities necessary for the operations covered by his licence and the product licences concerned and also for handling, storing and distributing the products so as to avoid deterioration of the products;

(2) carry out the manufacturing, assembling and storing operations only at premises specified in the licence;

(3) carry out all operations in such a way as to ensure that the products conform with the standards of strength, purity and quality specified in the product licence;

(4) give prior notice to the licensing authority of any changes he proposes to make to his premises, facilities or to the staff named in his licence;

(5) keep available for inspection for at least 5 years from the date of manufacture, durable records of all the details of the operations carried out on every batch of material manufactured or assembled so that containers in which the product is sold or supplied can be identified;

(6) keep records to facilitate the withdrawal from sale etc. of products to which the licence relates;

(7) withhold from distribution at the request of the authority (for a period specified but not exceeding 6 weeks) any batch of product which does not conform to the specifications;

(8) either provide the necessary facilities and staff to carry out quality assurance tests as required by the licence or arrange for other approved persons to do so;

(9) ensure that the containers of the product are correctly labelled so as to comply with the product licence;

(10) permit his premises to be inspected and provide any documents or samples requested by the inspectors.

(11) have at his disposal at all times a 'qualified person'.

Additional standard provisions apply to manufacturer's licences relating to vaccines and these are detailed in Schedule 4 to the Regulations. Briefly, they require that each premises where products are made or tested be under the control of a person approved by the Authority. Separate premises, or separate parts of the premises shall be used for cell cultures for vaccine production, for viral vaccines, and for vaccines made from micro-organisms or detoxified microbial toxins. In addition, only the personnel necessary for each activity may have access to the separate parts of the premises. Precautions shall be taken to prevent contamination of the material with transmissible agents. Any animals used in the process shall be quarantined before use, shall be isolated in additional separate premises, and only persons actually involved in the work or in maintaining the premises shall have access to those premises. A special room capable of being disinfected shall be set aside for inoculating the animals, and for collecting the material used in the production of the vaccine. In addition to the usual records, the fullest details of the origin, properties and characteristics of the cell cultures used in the production of vaccine shall be kept for 5 years.

Additional standard provisions apply to the production of smallpox vaccine (Part II of Schedule 4) and to BCG vaccine (Part III of Schedule 4). Analogous provisions apply to licences for the production of toxins (Part IV of Schedule 4) and of sera (Part V of Schedule 4).

PHARMACISTS

While pharmacists in general and hospital practice are usually exempt from the need to hold manufacturer's licences when engaging in small scale manufacture, they would be well advised to follow the principles laid down in the Guide to

Good Manufacturing Practice. The Council of the Society issued an analogous guide, the Guide to Good Dispensing Practice, see Appendix 3. Many of the points raised, e.g. cleanliness and suitability of the room, equipment, staff and the final containers, are so integral a part of the pharmacists' training as to require no repetition here. A few other points, however, are less well-known and deserve mention.

For every product which is made in bulk for stock (i.e. in a quantity larger than that normally required to fill an individual prescription) there should be a 'master record'. This may be on a card or page in a book, and should state –

(1) the name of the product;

(2) the name of each ingredient;

(3) the amount of each ingredient in a dose;

(4) the total amount of each ingredient used in preparing a batch of the product;

(5) the number and capacity of each container to be filled from that batch (this applies more to 'own remedies' than to stocks used for dispensing);

(6) the method for making the preparation;

(7) a specimen label ('own remedies') or the usual dose volume.

In addition, at the time of manufacture of a batch, a 'batch working document' should be completed in the following form –

Name of product...

No. of items of product prepared ....

Date of preparation...

Batch identification mark ....

Raw material	Supplier	Date received	B.No.	Amount weighed or measured	Checked by:

In order to complete the third column, pharmacists should mark every container of 'raw materials' with the date of receipt. This also, of course, enables stock to be rotated correctly.

The 'batch working document' should be kept for at least 2 years.

There is no legal requirement for a pharmacist to subject his products to a full analytical test but should this be felt to be necessary because of the size of the batch, samples may be sent to the Society's laboratories in Edinburgh.

COMPOUNDERS OF MEDICATED ANIMAL FEEDING STUFFS

At present compounders of medicated animal feeding stuffs do not require a licence. There are proposals that they should be registered, possibly with the Pharmaceutical Society of Great Britain or with the Department of Agriculture for Northern Ireland and legislation to give legal effect to this is imminent.

Wholesale Dealer's Licence

Such a licence is required for wholesale dealing (see definition) in medicinal products made by other persons, including those manufactured to the order of the wholesaler. It should be realised that it is possible to engage in 'wholesaling' without ever having physical possession of the products, but a licence is still necessary. A wholesale dealer's licence is also required by anyone who sells or offers to sell by wholesale or who distributes other than by sale any proprietary medicinal product.

A manufacturer who holds a product licence for a product but does NOT himself manufacture it, requires a wholesale dealer's licence to sell the product to the trade unless he does not at any time have possession of the product. The sale by the actual manufacturer to the product licence holder is not regarded as 'wholesale'. Furthermore (1972/640), a licence is not required for the sale or offer for sale by wholesale in either of the following cases –

(1) where the sale is by the product licence holder (even if the product licence holder assembled the product); or

(2) where the sale is by the assembler of the product and the assembly was to the order of the product licence holder.

In either case, the product must have been kept on premises at which it was manufactured or assembled until the sale.

Distributors (other than sellers) of proprietary products which have been imported from non-EEC states, must hold a wholesale dealer's licence (1977/1050). Such persons (and wholesalers who import medicinal products from non-EEC sources) must have the services of a 'qualified person' at his disposal. As before, the licence holder must provide that person with the necessary facilities and staff. It is the duty of the 'qualified person' to ensure that each production batch of the imported proprietary product has been thoroughly analysed and that its quality satisfies the requirements of the product licence. He must certify this in a register which must be properly maintained and readily available for inspection. (N.B.: if there is written evidence that the batch had been shown to satisfy the requirements on entry into another Community country before being imported into the UK, there is no need to analyse it in the UK. It is only the wholesaler who first receives the imported product who needs to have the product analysed.

APPLICATIONS FOR WHOLESALE DEALERS' LICENCES

The applicant must submit six copies of the application stating –

(1) his name and address;

(2) period for which the licence is required (if less than 5 years);

(3) activities to be included, e.g. whether dealing

  (a) in many kinds of medicinal products (and indicating if herbal remedies are included),

  (b) dealing only in GSL products,

  (c) dealing only in herbals,

  (d) in any other case give details of classes of products;

(4) use of the products, i.e. whether for human or animal use, whether for use as ingredients in human or animals products or for incorporation into animal feeding stuffs;

(5) details of the premises and equipment available (all premises used for storage or distribution to be listed), and the classes of products to be stored or distributed at each address. Where special storage conditions etc. are necessary for certain products, these products should be mentioned;

(6) the arrangements for keeping records etc. to ensure proper turn-over of stocks.

STANDARD PROVISIONS FOR WHOLESALE DEALERS' LICENCES

These require the licensee to –

(a) provide and maintain the necessary staff, premises, facilities and equipment to prevent the deterioration of the products he distributes, and only use premises which have been approved by the Authority for the purpose;

(b) provide any information required by the Authority concerning the type and quantity of products stored, handled or distributed;

(c) inform the Authority of any structural changes proposed for the approved premises;

(d) keep documents relating to transactions so as to facilitate the recall from distribution of any products;

(e) permit his premises, records and stock to be inspected, and copies of records and samples of products to be taken by the inspector;

(f) distribute only medicinal products which are licensed and in accordance with the product licence (there are certain exceptions to this);

(g) to withhold from distribution for up to 6 weeks any batch of product which the authority has informed the licensee does not conform to the required specifications;

(h) where proprietary products have been imported from non-EEC states, the dealer must have at his disposal a 'qualified person'.

EXEMPTIONS FROM WHOLESALE DEALERS' LICENCES

There are certain exemptions from the need to hold a such a licence. Persons lawfully conducting a retail pharmacy business do not require such a licence if the 'wholesale' side of their business constitutes only a small part of that business (section 10(6)).

The sale of a product by the person who manufactured it is specifically excluded from being a 'wholesale' sale, section 131(1). A statutory instrument (1972/640) seems to put a product licence holder in an analogous position by exempting him from the need to hold a wholesale dealer's licence in order to sell or offer for sale his product by wholesale, provided that until such sale, the product is kept on authorised premises used by the person who manufactured the product or who assembled it. Similarly, provided that he complies with the same conditions, the person who assembled the product to the order of the product licence holder may sell the product by wholesale without such a licence.

No wholesale dealer's licence is required if the only medicinal products sold by a wholesaler are in the form of medicated confectionery products which are on the GSL and provided that –

(a) the product licence for the confectionery permits it to be sold by wholesale by persons exempt from the need to hold a licence; and

(b) the product is not sold with written claims of curative or remedial properties other than in relation to the relief of coughs, colds and nasal congestion; (1975/762).

Thus persons in business primarily as food or confectionery wholesalers do not need a wholesale dealer's licence if the only medicines they sell are 'cough sweets' and similar products.

There are also exemptions for import agents who import proprietary medicinal products or ready-made veterinary drugs or persons who act as carriers (1977/1054).

Chapter 7
Controls Over the Sale and Distribution of Medicines

INTRODUCTION

We have seen that strenuous efforts have been made to ensure that medicinal products are safe, efficacious and of good quality when manufactured. The benefits of all of this would be lost if there were no, or inadequate, controls over their subsequent distribution. Thus, section 61 enables the Ministers to make regulations to restrict the sale of medicines by manufacturers and wholesalers to specified classes of purchasers. These regulations have been made (1980/1923 regulation 5 and Schedule 1) and form the first step in the control of the distribution chain.

The 15th century physician Paracelsus remarked that the difference between a poison and a medicine is merely a matter of dose. While this is equally true today, we now recognise that there are additional ways in which modern medicines can be dangerous. Some react with foods and lose activity, while others react with foods and become very toxic. Many medicines, safe enough in themselves, become very dangerous when taken with other drugs, including alcohol. Not all of these interactions are necessarily lethal, but many of them are the cause of a significant degree of morbidity. Furthermore, by interrupting therapy, some interactions needlessly prolong treatment and others are responsible for 'treatment failures'. It is therefore a truism to state that in the interests of safety, the Act should confine the retail sale of medicines to pharmacies. This would enable the public to receive appropriate advice at the time of purchase and also help to ensure that medicines are used correctly and for bona fide medicinal purposes. It is also in the public interest because pharmacists are subject to a professional code which is in many ways superior to the law in the protection it provides to the public. Several pharmacists have been struck off the register for selling medicines perfectly lawfully but unprofessionally. Restriction of the number of retail outlets would also contribute to the enforcement of the Act. On the other hand, rigid adherence to this principle would cause inconvenience to the public, hence the wider availability of GSL products.

Although the majority of medicinal products are obtained by the public from shops, some are supplied directly to their patients by doctors, dentists and veterinarians. Furthermore, various other paramedical personnel such as chiropodists, opticians, nurses, and midwives need to be able to supply medicines specific to their professions to their patients (see Chapter 11 for details). Employers are often required by law to provide first aid facilities and some go further and provide occupational health schemes. Children in school may be provided with dental treatment aimed at the prevention of caries. It is therefore necessary to make special provision for these activities and to exempt the persons involved from some or all of the restrictions that would normally operate in the sale or supply of medicines.

The framework of the restrictions over the administration, sale and sellers of medicines is contained in Part III of the Act and for these purposes medicines have been divided into THREE main classes, namely –

(1) General Sale List (GSL); section 51 authorised the compilation of a list of medicines which, 'with reasonable safety' may be sold otherwise than under the supervision of a pharmacist. Section 53 specified the conditions which must be observed by sellers (other than pharmacists) of these medicines, and the GSL Order lists the products and contains some other conditions. GSL products may even be sold from automatic machines in accordance with section 54. While many GSL products may, perhaps, be safe, some are obsolete and their efficacy is questionable.

(2) Section 52 required all other medicines to be sold by 'persons lawfully conducting a retail pharmacy business'. Such persons may only sell these medicines from registered pharmacies and each sale must be by or under the supervision of a pharmacist. There is no list of these products, but some of them are subject to additional restrictions, mentioned in (3) below.

The requirements to be complied with in order to become a 'person lawfully ..... business' and the procedure involved in registering a pharmacy are described in detail in Chapter 21.

(3) Section 58 authorised the preparation of a list of medicines which may only be sold or supplied to the public on the prescription of a practitioner (Prescription Only Medicines, POMs). The lists and various other matters relating to these medicines are published in the Prescription Only Medicines Orders.

EXEMPTIONS

The above is a summary of the general position with regard to the sale and supply of medicines to the public but there are certain exemptions to it. Section 55 exempts practitioners (i.e. doctors, dentists, and veterinarians) from the restrictions imposed by sections 52 and 53 when they sell or supply medicines to their patients. The same section exempts nurses and also midwives from such restrictions but only to the extent specified in regulations (1980/1924 as amended). Herbalists are similarly exempt from sections 52 and 53 under certain circumstances (section 56) and while many herbal substances are included in the GSL a statutory instrument (1977/2130) specifies those which may only be sold by herbalists or pharmacists. The Ministers have power to modify or extend the exemptions and have used them, e.g. Pharmacy and General Sale-Exemption Orders.

OTHER PROVISIONS OF PART III

Part III also contains provisions relating to new products (section 59), mainly making them POM for a period of 5 years from first licensing unless there is existing evidence of safety. It would not enable medicines to be placed on limited release, e.g. use in hospitals only for a period, but presumably the product licence could contain such a condition. Restrictions may also be imposed on the sellers, users and prescribers of other products (section 60). The Ministers have powers to prohibit the sale, supply, and importation of products in the interests of safety and have used these on several occasions (section 62), see under Prohibition Orders below. This power is seldom used and only after consultation with an expert committee or the Commission. There is no power under the Medicines Act to prohibit the *administration* of any product.

Three sections, 63–5 inclusive, deal with the adulteration of medicines and their quality and purity when sold or supplied to the consumer. These are dealt with in detail in Chapter 19.

CONTROLS OVER ADMINISTRATION OF MEDICINES

The administration of medicines is also controlled. No controls have been instituted over GSLs or [P] medicines, but POMs can only be administered to human beings by doctors or dentists, or persons acting in accordance with the directions of a doctor or dentist. Similarly, the administration to animals of veterinary drugs which are POM is restricted to veterinarians or persons acting in accordance with the directions of a veterinarian (section 58(2)b). Again there is provision for the Ministers by order to exempt from these controls, persons or products specified in the Order. Such an exemption has been made in respect of a number of injectable products to permit their administration by anybody in an emergency for the purpose of saving life (1983/1212, article 5). The products concerned are –

Adrenaline Injection BP
Atropine Sulphate Injection
Chlorpheniramine Injection
Cobalt Edetate Injection
Dextrose Injection Strong BPC
Diphenhydramine Injection
Hydrocortisone Injection
Mepyramine Injection
Promethazine Hydrochloride Injection
Snake Venom Antiserum
Sodium Nitrite Injection
Sodium Thiosulphate Injection
Sterile Pralidoxime

Article 7 of the same order also lifted the restrictions on the administration to human beings of non-parenteral POMs. The result is that, in respect of human beings, only the parenteral administration of a POM (other than one controlled under the Misuse of Drugs Act) is now restricted to practitioners and persons acting under their instructions.

Furthermore, when necessary in the interests of safety, and where specialised knowledge or skills are required, additional restrictions may be imposed on the practitioners who may administer, prescribe or be supplied with certain medicines (section 60); such restrictions have been imposed in respect of radioactive medicines (1978/1006).

The administration of veterinary drugs to animals is controlled, but farmers and certain other persons can administer those POMs which are PML to animals otherwise than under the direction of a veterinarian (1983/1213 article 6 and Schedule 3(3)). With the exception of a product made especially for the animal or one which is also similarly specified in the regulations, it is an offence to administer an unlicensed veterinary medicinal product to an animal (1983/1732). Exception is also made for administration for the purposes of tests and clinical trials.

CLASSIFICATION OF MEDICINES

Products on the General Sale List

There are two General Sale List Orders 1984, one for human medicines (1984/769) and one for veterinary drugs (1984/768). They are reproduced in Volume 3. The Schedules to the Orders list the products and drugs which can be sold by any shopkeeper. It was formerly the practice to publish the names and product licence numbers of GSL products, but this has ceased and the new Orders contain only lists of substances. The 'human' order has one Schedule which lists the substances which are GSL in fully licensed products, and another Schedule lists substances which are GSL in products having a licence of right. The veterinary drugs order does not differentiate between the two types of licences.

In both orders, Schedule 1 is divided into Table A, in which the substances may be used either for internal or external use, and Table B consisting of substances which are GSL only when used in products for external use. In both Tables there are limitations as to dose, pharmaceutical form, route of administration or strength for certain substances, and some of these vary with the type and intended use of the product.

Schedule 2 of the 'human' order similarly consists of two Tables A and B and are comparable to those in Schedule 1. This Schedule however applies to the ingredients of products which were granted a licence of right for human use and which are composed only of such ingredients. Again some substances are subject to limitations as to strength, form or route, or to use, or to maximum recommended dose (or maximum recommended daily dose) or to two or more of these. For example, a product having a licence of right and containing acetic acid would have to contain not more than 7.5% of acetic acid if for internal use or 15% if for external use, in order to be GSL. Products containing aloin are subject to the restriction that they are labelled to show a maximum dose of 20 mg. If a product is labelled to show a larger dose, it is [P]. There is a separate list of ingredients for external use. These lists will shorten as products are granted full licences or are removed from the market.

Schedule 3 to the 'human' list specifies classes of products which, regardless of composition, *cannot* be GSL. These are products advertised, sold or recommended for use as anthelmintics (worm killers), eyedrops, eye ointments, and injections. A similar list is contained in Schedule 2 to the veterinary drugs order but anthelmintics containing dichlorophen, diethylcarbamazine, and several salts of piperazine are GSL, while preparations for the internal treatment of ringworm are excluded from being GSL.

In addition to the substances mentioned respectively in Tables A and B of the two Schedules, excipients and alcoholic or aqueous extracts, spirits, syrups, or liquid suspensions of the different substances are also permitted as ingredients in GSL products. In products having a licence of right, haemoglobin and certain specified parts of animals are also permitted (see Schedule 2, paragraph 1(5),(6),(7)), as are substances of vegetable origin used as a food (see Schedule 2, paragraph 1(8)). The veterinary order contains a similar list which includes grit in veterinary drugs for birds.

There is no longer a special list of GSL products cleared for sale from automatic machines, all such products may now be sold from machines (see article 3).

Although, by the application of the criteria described above, a product may seem to be GSL, it may, nevertheless be [P]. This may arise in one of the following ways –

(a) because regulations made under section 53(4) impose restrictive conditions upon it, e.g. pack sizes for products containing aloxiprin, aspirin, paracetamol or salicylamide; (see below for details)

(b) the product licence itself renders the product [P]. It is open to the licence holder to restrict on marketing grounds the distribution of his products to pharmacies or even to hospitals.

When products containing either aspirin or any of the other substances mentioned in (a) above are sold or offered or exposed for sale by retail elsewhere than at a pharmacy, the container may not contain more than 30 effervescent tablets, or 25 non-effervescent tablets, or if the product is presented as granules or powder, not more than 10 sachets (1980/1923, article 8). The same article imposes limits over the pack sizes of some veterinary drugs; these are given in Table 1.

Table 1
Pack size limits for certain veterinary drugs when GSL

Substance contained in the veterinary drug	Number of dosage units or weight or volume of substance per container or package
Aminonitrothiazole	100 ml of solution or 50 capsules
Aspirin	25 tablets or 25 sachets of powder
Bromhexine Hydrochloride	20 g
Paracetamol	25 tablets
Phenylephrine Hydrochloride	15 ml
Potassium Chlorate	30 ml

A product which is labelled with directions for use in certain indications which are prohibited from public display by the Labelling and Advertising to Public Regulations might cause problems for a retailer ignorant of the prohibitions on advertising. For this reason, the Division 'permit' the product to be labelled [P] when as a matter of strict law, it is GSL. Such a product cannot, of course, be displayed in pharmacies.

An unofficial list of GSL products together with their PL numbers has been published by the DHSS and made available to distributors.

Pharmacy Medicines [P]

There is no list of these medicines. Some are [P] because one or more of their ingredients is present in a concentration greater than that specified in the GSL or because the product fails to meet other criteria (e.g. maximum dose or maximum daily dose) laid down in the GSL. Other products are [P] because they are exempt from the POM provisions on the grounds of concentration, dose, use or route of administration. Other products are [P] because their ingredients are not mentioned in either the GSL or the POM lists, e.g. promethazine. Furthermore, a product made in a pharmacy is [P] even if all its ingredients are GSL.

Moreover, as stated above, a manufacturer can request in his application for a product licence that the product be classed as [P] when its use, composition, etc. would permit it to be GSL. Similarly, it is open to a manufacturer to request that a product be classified as POM when its composition would normally make it [P].

For these reasons it is not always easy to determine the legal class of a given product from a consideration of its composition or intended use. Wholesalers and retailers are therefore obliged to rely on the manufacturer to comply with the legal requirement to label the product correctly by including the [P] symbol when appropriate.

Prescription Only Medicines (POMs)

There are two Prescription Only Orders which are amended periodically, one applies only to veterinary drugs (1985/1288) while the other applies to medicines which may be administered to humans or to animals (The Products Other Than Veterinary Drugs (Prescription Only) Order 1983/1212). The latter is a lengthy document. Part 1 of Schedule 1 to the Order consists of a list of about 1200 substances. The list in the Veterinary Drugs Order is similar but not identical, there being substances which appear in one list but not the other. These, and such of their preparations as are not specifically exempted, comprise the majority of POM products. Preparations may be exempted from POM if the entry for the substance in Schedule 1 sets a maximum dose (MD) or a maximum daily dose (MDD) and the preparation is labelled to recommend a dose not exceeding this. Other preparations are exempt when they contain less than a stated maximum strength (MS). Sometimes the entry excludes a particular type of product, e.g. dequalinium chloride, throat lozenges or pastilles containing not more than 0.25 mg or paints for external use containing not more than 1% are exempt from POM. Chloroquine phosphate is exempt from POM in antimalarial preparations. The list contains most of the therapeutically useful antibiotics and sulphonamides (except tyrothricin), all of the psychoactive drugs, most hormones, most alkaloids, and all the major drugs used in cardiovascular disease or in the promotion of diuresis. All parenteral products (except insulin injections) are POM, even water for injections! Local anaesthetics are POM when included in ophthalmic preparations but are exempt in other pharmaceutical forms, for example, creams ointments and lozenges and for other purposes.

Also included in the POM, but not listed in Schedule 1 are all of the drugs controlled under the Misuse of Drugs Act 1971. In order to assist the reader, the Misuse of Drugs Regulations have been reprinted in Volume 3.

Part 2 of Schedule 1 to the POM Order does mention six of the controlled drugs and specifies limits below which they are exempt from control as POMs. The Misuse of Drugs Regulations also exempts them from control when in preparations containing less than certain specified amounts or concentrations. Unfortunately, different limits are set in the two documents. In the Misuse of Drugs legislation for example, preparations containing less than 0.2% anhydrous morphine are exempt from control unless the morphine can be readily recovered (in practice if other ingredients are present recovery would be difficult). In the POM Order however, the limit is 0.02% in liquid preparations or 0.04% in solid preparations, in either case the maximum dose being 3 mg. The MoDA limits are internationally agreed. The result is that some products which have been free from control for years are now available on prescription only. It is worth mentioning here that the Veterinary Drugs (POM) Order does not contain a corresponding list of strengths below which controlled drugs are exempt from POM. A given preparation may therefore be POM if for animal treatment, but [P] when for human use.

One wonders why it is necessary to have lower domestic limits, especially at a time when there are plentiful supplies of illicitly imported narcotics available to addicts. Furthermore, were the POM limits to be raised to those of the MoDA, the products would still be [P] medicines and their sale would still be restricted to pharmacies. A pharmacist making irresponsible sales of such products would be subject to the Code of Ethics and, as has happened in the past, removed from the register.

Part 3 of Schedule 1 consists of eight named proprietary products.

Schedule 2 names those products which cannot be supplied in an emergency at the request of a patient. Most of them are barbiturates and consequently now also controlled under the Misuse of Drugs Regulations. There is a specific exemption for phenobarbitone which can be so supplied to an epileptic.

Persons authorised to possess and prescribe controlled drugs. The Misuse of Drugs Act makes it an offence to possess, manufacture, trade in or have any dealings with 'controlled drugs'. The Misuse of Drugs Regulations authorise certain persons to engage in specified activities in relation to these drugs in so far as is necessary for the practice of their profession. Other people, e.g. manufacturers, can be licensed to produce a drug or to carry out some other activity.

The regulations authorise all fully registered doctors, dentists and veterinarians to prescribe, administer, sell or supply to their patients, any of the controlled drugs specified in Schedules 1, 2, or 3 to the regulations. Likewise, all pharmacists working in hospitals, health centres or in pharmacies are authorised to sell or supply such drugs to persons authorised to possess them. Certain other classes of persons may be authorised to possess or supply the drugs under strictly defined conditions, and the appropriate details will be discussed in Chapters 8–14.

SPIRITS

Several types of spirits are used for medicinal purposes and also in making medicines. All spirits are subject to legal controls which are mainly concerned with preventing tax avoidance and contraventions of these controls can lead to heavy fines. Basically, there are two types of spirits, those suitable for internal consumption, and those which have been rendered unsuitable for drinking (called 'methylated' or 'denatured' spirits).

Ethanol

This is suitable for internal use and is available in various forms including absolute alcohol, rectified spirits (S.V.R.) and of course, as wines, beers and the like.

A retailer who wishes to sell ethanol in any form requires a Justices' Licence. A pharmacist who wishes to sell only absolute alcohol or rectified spirits to doctors, hospitals, other pharmacists, or to scientific establishments can obtain a Justices Licence quite easily if he gives the court an undertaking to confine his sales to those spirits and classes of purchasers. If, however, he also wishes to sell wines, spirits, beers, etc. he may have to prove that there is a local need for an additional retail outlet for such products.

A Justices' Licence is not required for the sale or dispensing of medicines containing ethanol.

Ethanol is subject to a spirit duty when it is purchased. When it is used in the making of medicines (or for certain other 'recognised' articles), most of the duty paid by the retailer may be reclaimed. In order to make such a claim the retailer must keep detailed records in a Spirits Book of purchases and amounts used, and make application for a refund on the appropriate form (Ex 224). Few general practice pharmacists use sufficient ethanol to make the work involved in claiming refunds worthwhile, especially in view of the fact that the ethanol is mainly dispensed on NHS prescriptions. They prefer to endorse the NHS prescription with the amount of ethanol used and the words 'rebate not claimed', whereupon the prescription is priced on the basis of the cost of the ethanol including duty.

Ethanol is not listed in either the GSL or in the POM lists, therefore it is [P]. However, it is seldom used as such in medicines because of its cost.

Denatured or Methylated Spirits

There are several of these available for a variety of purposes. Much of the law applicable to these spirits is contained in the Methylated Spirits Regulations 1983 No.252. The Commissioners of Customs and Excise periodically issue Notices giving further information. Notice No. 474 is particularly relevant.

Mineralised methylated spirits. This is the only form that can be sold to members of the general public. No special authority is required for its purchase whether from a methylator, a wholesaler or a retailer. It is made by mixing 90 volumes of spirits with 9.5 volumes of wood naphtha and 0.5 volumes of pyridine. To this is added mineral naphtha and a purple dye. The only restriction on its sale in England and Wales is that it cannot be sold between 10 pm on Saturday night and 8 am on Monday morning. In Scotland it can only be sold by pharmacists or licensed sellers and a record of the sale must be kept, but again not between the times stated.

Industrial methylated spirits, IMS. This contains 95 volumes of spirits and 5 volumes of wood naphtha. Only persons who hold an authority to receive industrial methylated spirits may obtain them. A general practice pharmacist can apply on form Ex 225 to the Commissioners of Customs and Excise for authority to receive IMS for one or more of the following purposes –

(a) making for sale any of the articles listed in Appendix A to Notice 474;

(b) for dispensing any product (including IMS itself) for medical or veterinary purposes on the prescription or order of a doctor, dentist, veterinarian, nurse or chiropodist;

(c) making any article approved by the Commissioners;

(d) for sale as IMS in quantities not exceeding 20 l to other authorised users.

The pharmacist may also sell up to 3 l of IMS to a 'medical practitioners' which in the Methylated Spirits Regulations means 'doctors, dentists, nurses, chiropodists, veterinary surgeons and other persons entitled by law to provide medical or veterinary services in the United Kingdom;' (regulation 2). The medical practitioner must provide the supplier with a signed order for the spirits.

The pharmacist obtains the spirits from an authorised methylator if he buys quantities exceeding 20 l at a time, or from a wholesaler or other retailer in smaller amounts. He must provide his supplier with a letter stating that –

(a) he is authorised to receive industrial methylated spirits,

(b) a certificate of authority has been issued to him,

(c) quoting the number of the certificate, and

(d) the period of time for which this statement is intended to apply.

A specimen letter containing these points is sent by the Customs and Excise office to persons authorised to receive IMS.

All stocks of IMS must be kept under lock and key, in containers which are labelled to show their contents and the words 'Not to be Taken' or 'For external use only'. The spirits may only be used for the purposes stated in the application. It is an offence to purify or recover or re-distil the spirits without the prior permission of the Customs and Excise officer.

The use of IMS is restricted to those purposes for which the Commissioners have authorised the pharmacist to receive the spirits. It follows therefore that he cannot use it to prepare products to the formulae of customers (except on prescription or orders of 'medical practitioners') or to make products of his own formulation unless such formulae have been approved by the Commissioners. The fact that industrial methylated spirits is included in Schedule 1A to the GSL does NOT negate the restrictions imposed under the Methylated Spirits Regulations.

Denatured ethanol. There are three of these, namely denatured ethanol 'B', 'Q', or 'S' (DEB) (DEQ) or (DES). They consist of 98 parts of ethanol denatured with 2 parts of *n*-propanol and either Bitrex, Quassin or sucrose octa-acetate. They are used in the manufacture of those perfumes, toilet articles or pharmaceuticals where IMS has been shown to be unsuitable. They too are only obtainable by persons who hold an authority to purchase them.

PROHIBITION ORDERS

Generally speaking, the intention behind these orders is to prohibit the sale, supply and importation of products containing certain hazardous substances. Sometimes, however, the restrictions fall short of a total prohibition. It is an offence (section 67(3)) to possess a product which one knows or reasonably suspects to have been sold, supplied or imported in contravention of a prohibition order.

There have been five of these Orders, one of which was amended. In the case of Bal Jivan Chamcho (a proprietary product of Indian origin intended for administration to children), the product was found to contain unacceptably high concentrations of lead, so the prohibition is complete and the substance may only lawfully be sold to sampling officers, analysts and various officers engaged in enforcement duties (1977/670).

In the cases of chloroform, phenacetin and the various anti-microbial substances, certain sales are permitted. For example, a preparation containing chloroform (or phenacetin) which is prepared by or at the request of a doctor or dentist for administration to a particular patient may be sold or supplied, by the practitioner or by a pharmacist, hospital or health centre. Likewise phenacetin and chloroform and their preparations may be sold to practitioners, pharmacies, hospitals and the like for use as ingredients in the preparation of medicines for sale. The sale or supply of preparations containing phenacetin or chloroform for export is also permitted.

Other exemptions applicable to chloroform are –

(1) to doctors, dentists or hospitals for use in anaesthesia, also to persons who buy chloroform to sell to hospitals and practitioners for that purpose;

(2) products containing not more than 0.5% chloroform (either w/w or v/v);

(3) products for use solely in dental surgery;

(4) products to be applied to the external surface (excluding mouth and teeth, and the mucous membranes) of the body;

(5) veterinary drugs (1979/382 as amended by 1980/263).

Another exemption applicable to phenacetin relates to products for external use which consist of or contain a solution of hydrogen peroxide where the latter contains not more than 0.1% of phenacetin as a stabiliser.

Both chloroform and phenacetin are also subject to control under the POM Order. In the latter, preparations for internal use in human beings containing more than 5% chloroform are POM, as are all preparations for the internal treatment of animals. All preparations containing more than 0.1% phenacetin are POM whether for internal or external use and whether for human or animal treatment.

The restrictions on the non-medicinal use of antimicrobial substances are necessary to fill a gap caused by the repeal of the Therapeutic Substances Act. The controls over medicinal products and medicated animal feeding stuffs containing the antibiotics (and other substances described in the Order) imposed by the POM Order does not prevent their sale for alleged 'non-medicinal purposes'. It was therefore necessary to fill this gap by prohibiting their sale for non-medicinal purposes and this was done by 1973/367. There are exemptions permitting their sale to universities and other institutions of higher education or research, to enforcement officers, sampling officers, analysts, to veterinarians and to persons lawfully conducting a retail pharmacy business, to holders of manufacturers' licences, and to wholesalers.

There are special exemptions which permit the sale of –

(1) Sulphanilamide – when in the form of sulphaquinoxaline it is

(a) contained in a product for destroying rats and mice and the product contains not more than 0.5% sulphaquinoxaline and also contains warfarin or its sodium or triethanolamine derivative; or

(b) sold for use in the manufacture of such a product.

(2) Sulphanilamide – when in the form of methyl-4-aminobenzene sulphonyl-carbonate it is,

(a) contained in a herbicide for sale for agricultural, horticultural or forestry purposes or for use in or near water or on uncultivated land; or

(b) sold for use in the manufacture of such a product.

(3) Griseofulvin

(a) when contained in a fungicide sold for horticultural purposes and rendered so unpalatable as to prevent its consumption by human beings, or

(b) when sold for use in the manufacture of such fungicides.

(4) Streptomycins

(a) when contained in a fungicide for horticultural purposes and the product is rendered so unpalatable as to prevent its consumption by human beings; or

(b) when sold for use in the manufacture of such fungicides.

There is a prohibition on the sale and supply of stilbenes and thyrostatic substances for use in fattening cattle etc. (1982/626). For further details please see Chapter 15.

ADDITIONAL RESTRICTIONS ON PRACTITIONERS IN CERTAIN CASES

Section 60 of the Act enables the Ministers to restrict the prescribing and administration of medicines to specially certified practitioners.

Radioactive Products for Human Use

Regulations have been made (1978/1006) applying such restrictions to radioactive products for human use. Any doctor or dentist who wishes to prescribe or use such products must apply to the Ministers in writing for a certificate and give the following details –

(a) his name, address, qualifications and relevant experience, the post he holds (or will hold) and in which he will use the products;

(b) the radioactive medicinal products he proposes to administer or have administered;

(c) details of the equipment, facilities and staff available to him; and

(d) any other relevant information.

If the Ministers are satisfied as to his knowledge, experience and competence, and as to the facilities, equipment and staff at his disposal, they may grant him a certificate. This will specify the products he can use and may specify the purposes for which he may use them. If they have any doubt as to his suitability, they may refer the case to the Administration of Radioactive Substances Advisory Committee, which is composed of persons having wide and recent experience relating to the administration of such substances and related radiological and scientific safety matters.

A certificate is valid for 5 years or for a shorter period if this is specified therein. It can be renewed by informing the Ministers in writing of any changes in the matters mentioned in the original application.

Restrictions on Prescribing for Addicts

The prescribing and administration of heroin, cocaine and dipipanone to *addicts* is similarly restricted to licensed doctors unless the drug is required to treat organic disease or injury (Notification and Supply to Addicts Regulations). The majority of such licences have been issued to doctors working in the Drug Treatment Centres attached to hospitals although some have been granted to doctors in private practice. These licences are issued by the Home Office under the Misuse of Drugs Act.

MEANING OF 'WHOLESALE' AND 'RETAIL' SALE

These are defined in section 131 –

(1) In this Act any reference to selling anything by way of wholesale dealing is a reference to selling it to a person as being a person who buys it for one or

more of the purposes specified in subsection (2) of this section, except that it does not include any such sale by the person who manufactured it.

(2) The purposes referred to in the preceding subsection, in relation to a person to whom anything is sold, are the purpose of –

(a) selling or supplying it, or

(b) administering it or causing it to be administered to one or more human beings,

in the course of business carried on by that person.'

This definition is broader than that given in the poisons legislation. The word 'business' is defined in section 132 so as to include a professional practice, therefore sales by a retail pharmacist of medicinal products to a medical or dental practitioner for use in his practice are wholesale transactions but if the practitioner purchases the medicine for the use of his family or himself then the sale is a retail sale. Similarly, a sale by a retail pharmacist to a chiropodist, nurse, optician or physiotherapist for use in their respective professions would be a wholesale transaction.

The definition gives rise to some anomalies and potential problems. For example, the sale of a product to a veterinarian for re-sale or supply to a farmer or pet-owner is a wholesale transaction as one would expect since it is analogous to the sale to a doctor for issue to his patients. However, the sale of the same product to a veterinarian who intended to *administer* it to an animal in the course of the veterinarian's practice, would seem not to constitute a 'wholesale' sale because of the inclusion of the words 'human beings' in (b) above. Likewise, the sale of medicines to a farmer, a zoo-keeper or other person who owns the animal for 'business' purposes is also not wholesale for the same reason. This viewpoint is in line with that expressed in MAL 51 (paragraph 1) where such sales are described as 'retail'. This should be contrasted with the sale to the farmer of a poison (e.g. a weed-killer) for use on his farm. The Poisons Rules would treat such a sale as wholesale (because it is for use in his business).

The potential problem that arises from the fact that a sale to a veterinarian might be either retail or wholesale depending upon the circumstances is as follows. If it is wholesale, the seller must either hold a wholesale dealer's licence or be the manufacturer of the product or a retail pharmacist. Such a seller is subject to control under the Act. If, on the other hand, the sale is retail, then the seller is free from all control because of the exemption specified in 1980/1924 Schedule 1, Part I, paragraph 9. There does not appear to be any compelling reason to treat sales to veterinarians any differently from sales to medical or dental practitioners so perhaps the time has come to reconsider the wording of section 131(2)(b), and the necessity for the exemption mentioned above. Certainly, there is disquiet in many areas about the ease with which potent and dangerous substances can be obtained illicitly by farmers and others.

It sometimes happens that one manufacturing company make, pack and label a product for another company. Since the first company is 'the person who manufactured it' the sale of the product to the second company (or to anyone else) is not a wholesale transaction, (see sub-section 1). However, all sales of the product by the second company to hospitals, wholesalers, retailers and practitioners are wholesale transactions.

According to sub-section 3 below, any sale which is not wholesale is a retail transaction. Evidently then, the sale of a medicine by its manufacturer is a retail sale but the trade would regard it as wholesale. What though is the sale of a product made (manufactured?) by a pharmacist to the formula of a doctor for use in his practice, or a member of the public? The sale to the doctor would (apart from the proviso relating to manufacture) be wholesale, whereas that to the member of the public for his own use would be retail. If the inclusion of the words 'except. person who manufactured it' was intended to relieve the manufacturer of the need to hold a wholesale dealer's licence, it might be preferable in the interests of clarity to make an exemption order to that effect and repeal the words at the end of sub-section 1.

'(3) In this Act any reference to selling by retail, or to retail sale is a reference to selling a substance or article to a person as being a person who buys it otherwise than for a purpose specified in subsection (2) of this section.

(4) In this Act any reference to supplying anything in circumstances corresponding to retail sale is a reference to supplying it, otherwise than by way of sale, to a person as being a person who receives it for a purpose other than that of –

(a) selling or supplying it, or

(b) administering it or causing it to be administered to one or more human beings,

in the course of a business carried on by that person.

(5) For the purpose of this section the provision of services by or on behalf of the Minister of Health, the Secretary of State or the Ministry of Health and Social Services for Northern Ireland under the National Health Service Acts 1946–73 the National Health Service (Scotland) Acts 1947–72 or the Health and Personal Social Services (Northern Ireland) Order 1972 shall be treated as the carrying on of a business by that Minister, the Secretary of State or that Ministry, as the case may be.'

The supply of a product to a patient on a prescription (whether 'private' or NHS) would amount to a 'supply in circumstances corresponding to retail sale' in subsection 4 above. This corrects the situation which followed a court's refusal to convict a pharmacist for an offence under the Food and Drugs Act, after he had supplied a defective product on a NHS prescription.

Since the service provided by or on behalf of the Health Ministers under the various NHS Acts is to be treated as the carrying on of a business by the appropriate Minister, sales to state owned hospitals, health centres and clinics are wholesale.

The provision of medicines by first aiders to persons requiring treatment is another example of 'supply in circumstances...sale', though it might also involve 'administration'. A spectator at a sporting event is stung on the neck by a wasp. He seeks relief at the first aid tent. Here the first aider applies a soothing cream to the swollen area (this is 'administration') and gives the man a cup of tea and two paracetamol tablets (this is the 'supply') for the headache. Since no charge is made, the service cannot amount to a sale. Incidently, such supplies made by certificated nursing members or certificated first aiders who are members of the St John's Ambulance or the Red Cross and similar bodies of GSL and [P] medicines are authorised by 1980/1924. It would seem however that the bodies seldom take advantage of this.

Offer or Exposure for Sale, and Possession for Sale

A number of regulations and sections make reference to one or more of these phrases and it might be helpful to explain the difference between them. Contrary to popular belief, the display of goods in shops and shopwindows, does not, in English law, constitute an offer to sell on the part of the shopkeeper. Several legal cases based on the law of contract have been decided on the basis that the shopkeeper invites the public to offer to buy the goods, and that this offer can be accepted or rejected by the seller (lawyers refer to the display or advertisement as an 'invitation to treat'). The situation is not changed even if the retailer or advertiser uses the word 'offer'. The same legal principle has been invoked when shopkeepers or even members of the public advertise items for sale, and because of the nature of the goods there is some breach of the criminal law. Some examples may be helpful. Boots had converted one of their shops to self-service and placed the cash desk in such a position that a pharmacist could see what was being bought and could prevent the sale if necessary. At the time, many medicines were Part I poisons and could only be sold by or under the supervision of a pharmacist. The Pharmaceutical Society prosecuted Boots, it being alleged that the sale took place when the customer removed the medicine from a shelf and put it in the basket provided by the store. Consequently, the sale occurred before the pharmacist could intervene. The defendants argued that the display of products on the shelves amounted to an 'invitation to treat' and that the sale actually occurred when the customer's offer to buy was accepted at the cash desk after the pharmacist had approved it. The court held that the display was an offer to treat, and that the sale occurred at the cash desk (Pharmaceutical Society of Great Britain v. Boots). This decision and the reasoning behind it was subsequently upheld in the Court of Appeal.

In Fisher v. Bell, 1961, a retailer displayed 'flick knives' in his shop window. He was prosecuted under the Restriction of Offensive Weapons Act 1959 for 'offering for sale' these knives. The High Court held that he was not guilty because though the knives may have been 'exposed for sale' they were not 'offered for sale' in view of the 'invitation to treat' principle of the ordinary law of contract. Likewise when a man advertised for sale a pair of bramble finches, a bird which is protected by law. It was successfully pleaded on his behalf that the law prohibited the offer for sale of the birds, but that an advertisement did not constitute such an offer (Partridge v. Crittenden 1968). Subsequent cases have been decided on similar grounds. The phrase 'offer for sale' therefore has a legal meaning different from the ordinary colloquial meaning.

'Exposure for sale' has a wider meaning than 'offer for sale', and is free from legal overtones. It does not seem to embrace 'advertise', but seems to imply that one must have possession of the article. On the other hand, an article may be in one's 'possession for sale' without necessarily being 'exposed for sale'. Clearly, if the aims of the Act are to be attained, it is important to draft its provisions with care so as to cover every eventuality.

Where and When a Sale Occurs

In contract law, a sale takes place where and when the offer to buy is accepted by the offeree (i.e. the person to whom the offer is made) unless the parties expressly agree otherwise. Therefore, in the absence of any conditions imposed by either of the parties and accepted by the other before the agreement was reached, the buyer of an article in a shop obtains the property in the article when the seller accepts his offer to buy. This is true whether or not the seller has the article in stock, though in such a case the intending buyer may withdraw his offer. It is also true that the property passes whether or not the buyer has paid for the article, though the seller can, of course, make payment a condition of delivery. All of this means that in the most common case, a sale takes place in a shop when the buyer offers to buy, the seller accepts the offer, the buyer pays the price, and the seller hands over the article. It also means that the sale would be complete even if the seller agreed to invoice the buyer at the end of the month, or the buyer paid his account quarterly. Likewise, sales may be made by telephone, by post, by Prestel, by Telex or by any other means, and in each case the sale occurs where the seller accepts the offer to buy, i.e. at the seller's premises.

A consequence of this is that retail sales (with the exception of certain veterinary drugs) can only occur at 'premises', a retailer cannot canvass for orders door to door. Wholesale transactions are not similarly affected, hence the representatives of manufacturers and of wholesalers can solicit orders from retailers and practitioners.

Another consequence is that mail order sales are lawful. If the product is on the GSL and so long as the orders are received and dispatched from a 'premises-...public'. In the case of [P] medicines the orders must be received and dispatched from a registered pharmacy and the packing etc. supervised by a pharmacist. However, the Code of Ethics of the Pharmaceutical Society of Great Britain has reservations about this method of sale (see Chapter 9 for more detail).

References

Fisher v. Bell (1961), 2 Q.B. 394

Partridge v. Crittenden (1968), 2 All E.R.421

Pharmaceutical Society of Great Britain v. Boots Cash Chemists (Southern) Ltd. (1952), 2 All E.R. 456

Chapter 8
Wholesale Sales

INTRODUCTION

It is important to control the wholesale trade in medicines for several reasons. Firstly, the benefits obtained by manufacturing medicines to the highest standards of purity and quality would soon be lost were they subsequently stored under inappropriate conditions or for excessively long periods by the wholesaler. Such sellers therefore require knowledge of the properties of the products they sell and of their optimum storage conditions, as well as the facilities necessary to provide such conditions. Furthermore, it is imperative that a system exists which facilitates the recall of faulty batches, hence the need for some list of wholesalers and the use of batch numbers on packages of the products and also the maintenance of adequate records of purchases and sales by the wholesaler. Secondly, it is pointless restricting the retail distribution of most medicines to pharmacies, if wholesalers are able to supply any retailer with [P] or POMs. Thus a strictly controlled distribution chain is necessary.

We have seen in Chapter 6 that most wholesale dealers require a wholesale dealer's licence and also the conditions with which they must comply in order to obtain such a licence. These restrictions are unnecessary for persons lawfully conducting a retail pharmacy business because they have the necessary facilities and knowledge. Consequently, they have been exempted from the need to hold a wholesale dealer's licence provided that such sales do not comprise a substantial part of their business. The intention was to allow retail pharmacists to sell small amounts of medicines to practitioners, opticians, nurses and similar classes of professional users. This was beneficial to all parties because such users seldom require large stocks of products and wholesalers would find the maintenance of such small accounts more trouble than they were worth.

It is now necessary to examine the controls over the distribution chain in some detail. Regulations made under Part III confine the sale of pharmacy [P] and of prescription only medicines [POM] by product licence holders, manufacturers and wholesalers, to the following classes –

(a) practitioners;

(b) persons lawfully conducting a retail pharmacy business;

(c) persons carrying on the business of a hospital or health centre;

(d) holders of wholesale dealer's licences, or persons who are exempt from holding a licence under the Act or by section 48;

(e) Ministers of the Crown and government departments (1980/1923 regulation 5 and Schedule 1).

This would, of course, control the majority of such sales, but there is provision for such medicines to be sold to persons who are permitted to sell, supply or administer them in the course of their employment. These people and the products involved are listed in Schedule 4 to the Prescription Only Order (1980/1923, regulation 5(2)). Examples of such people are midwives, ophthalmic opticians, and sellers of homoeopathic remedies. Ophthalmic opticians can also buy some other ophthalmic products listed in regulation 5(2)(c), e.g. oxyphenbutazone, amethocaine hydrochloride, framycetin sulphate. Almost invariably, such persons would buy their medicines from retail pharmacies rather than directly from manufacturers or via wholesalers.

When sales are made by manufacturers or by wholesale dealers, records are kept of the transaction usually in the form of copies of the invoice or delivery note. Similarly, when retail pharmacists make such sales the regulations require a record of it to be kept (see below). In addition, where the drugs are controlled under Schedule 2 to the Misuse of Drugs Regulations, a record of every sale must be kept in the seller's register and of the purchase in the buyer's register. In the case of products controlled under Schedule 1 to the regulations, it is sufficient to keep the invoice for 2 years.

The restrictions on who may be supplied by manufacturers, wholesalers, etc. and the requirement to keep records of such sales combine to ensure that non-GSL medicinal products are not supplied to retailers who are not allowed to sell them and thus facilitates the enforcement of section 52.

The restrictions, if any, imposed upon sales to the various classes of professional user are given below. The restrictions imposed upon the use of the products by the various classes of purchaser are described in Chapter 11.

SALES TO PRACTITIONERS

A practitioner may purchase any medicine he requires for his practice. Although it is not a legal necessity to do so (except for products controlled under the Misuse of Drugs Act), most practitioners issue a signed order (or requisition) for the product and this is very helpful to the pharmacist. The only restrictions as to products that practitioners may purchase are –

(1) only specially certified medical or dental practitioners may buy radioactive medicinal products, there is no corresponding requirement that veterinarians need certification;

(2) products included in Schedule 4 to the Misuse of Drugs Regulations may only be sold to specially licensed purchasers.

In both cases, there are very few suppliers of these products and this also facilitates their control.

All fully registered doctors, dentists and veterinarians are authorised to purchase, administer, possess, supply, etc. products controlled under Schedules 1, 2, or 3 to the Misuse of Drugs Regulations (regulations 7, 8, 9, and 10). This authority may be withdrawn from an individual by the Home Secretary and such an individual cannot be supplied with those drugs (sections 12 and 13 of the Misuse of Drugs Act).

MIDWIVES

Midwives employed in the domiciliary service are authorised to supply or administer certain products to their patients. They usually obtain these drugs directly from NHS sources, though both the medicines legislation and that relating to controlled drugs permit her to buy them.

Under the Misuse of Drugs Regulations, regulation 11 authorises midwives employed in the domiciliary service to obtain, possess and administer the drug on their own authority to their patients under the following conditions –

(1) she must notify the local supervising authority of her intention to practise;

(2) she must obtain the drug on a midwife's supply order signed by the appropriate medical officer (this bears her name and occupation, the amount to be obtained and the purpose for which it is required);

(3) she must surrender any stocks no longer required by her, to that medical officer;

(4) she must keep a book in which she records the date, the name and address of the person from whom she obtained the drug, and the form and amount of drug obtained;

(5) she must also record in that book the name and address of each patient to whom she administered the drug together with the amount administered and the form in which it was administered (regulation 21).

The pharmacist from whom the midwife obtains her supply must keep the midwife's supply order for 2 years, and record the sale or supply in his controlled drugs register (regulation 19).

OPHTHALMIC OPTICIANS

These can buy certain products (excluding controlled drugs) for application to their patients, and for sale to their patients in an emergency. They can also buy certain products for use in their practices. They must provide a signed order.

NATUROPATHS, OSTEOPATHS, ACUPUNCTURISTS

These are allowed to administer by injection any product which is a POM only because it is in parenteral form. In other words, they may inject substances which are normally P or GSL, such as local anaesthetics. This privilege is restricted to such persons who were before the 11th February 1982 customarily administering such products by injection (Schedule 3(3), paragraph 7 to the POM Order).

PERSONS CONCERNED WITH TESTING THE QUALITY OF MEDICINES

There are several different groups of people involved here but basically the same controls apply to them all so it is convenient to deal with them together. The groups comprise public analysts appointed under the Food Act, sampling officers similarly appointed or appointed under Schedule 3 to the Medicines Act, inspectors employed by the enforcement authority, agricultural analysts, and persons engaged in the drug testing scheme under the NHS Acts. Inspectors employed by the Pharmaceutical Society of Great Britain are involved in some of these activities and have the same powers.

Any person included in one of the classes specified above can purchase any medicine on presentation of an order signed by himself. The order must specify his status and the amount of medicine required and the purchase is only in connection with his statutory functions (1980/1924, Schedule 1(1), paragraphs 5 and 6).

With the exception of agricultural analysts, the same groups are authorised by the Misuse of Drugs Regulations (regulations 8, 9 and 10) to possess and supply controlled drugs to anyone who may lawfully possess them.

OWNERS AND MASTERS OF SHIPS

These are entitled to purchase any medicines required for the treatment of persons on the ship (1980/1924, Schedule 1(2), paragraph 8).

They may also purchase drugs controlled under Schedules 2 or 3 to the Misuse of Drugs Regulations if the ship does not carry a doctor as part of her complement (regulations 8, 9 and 14).

MANAGERS OF OFFSHORE INSTALLATIONS

These are not specifically mentioned in the medicines legislation. The Misuse of Drugs Regulations permits them to possess and supply drugs controlled under Schedules 2 and 3 to the regulations. They can obtain such drugs by issuing a written requisition in the usual form.

PERSONS IN CHARGE OF SCIENTIFIC OR EDUCATIONAL LABORATORIES

It is perhaps questionable whether the sale for use in such laboratories is 'wholesale' within the meaning of the Act since the medicine will rarely, if ever, be administered to a human being in the course of the business of the institution and it will not be sold. Whether the institution can be said to 'supply' the medicine to its workers or students, in the course of the institute's business is likewise open to debate. However, it is convenient to deal with sales to such institutions here.

A university or other institution concerned with higher education or with research can buy any medicine for the purposes of that education or research. The sale or supply is subject to the issue of an order signed by the principal or by the head of department in charge of the research. The order must state the name of the institution, the purpose for which the medicine is required and the amount required (1980/1924, Schedule 1(1), paragraph 4).

If the medicine is also controlled under the Misuse of Drugs Regulations, the position becomes slightly more complicated unless the drug is controlled only under Schedule 1 to the regulations (i.e. it is CDinv). Drugs subject to full control under the regulations (i.e. CD) can only be supplied to a person in charge of an educational or research laboratory attached to a university, a university college, a hospital maintained out of public funds or by a charity or by voluntary subscriptions, or any institution specifically approved for the purpose by the Home Secretary (regulation 8). The same institutions can also buy drugs controlled under Schedule 3 to the regulations (CD no register). Furthermore, the latter drugs can also be purchased and used by persons in charge of any laboratory concerned with education or research (regulation 9). In addition, certain Schedule 3 drugs can be sold to persons in charge of any laboratory if the drug is required for use as a buffer in chemical analysis (regulation 9(ff)).

PHARMACY RECORDS

When a person lawfully conducting a retail pharmacy business sells a POM by wholesale he must record the details in a register kept for that purpose. In practice, the prescription book is used. The particulars required for wholesale sales are –

(a) the date of the sale;

(b) the name, quantity, pharmaceutical form and strength of the medicine sold;

(c) the name and address, trade, business or profession of the person to whom it was sold; and

(d) the purpose for which it was sold.

The record shall be made on the day of the sale or if that is not reasonably practicable, on the next day.

Strictly speaking, no records are required when –

(1) a record of the sale is made in the controlled drugs register; or

(2) the order or invoice relating to the sale or a copy thereof is retained by the person lawfully conducting the retail pharmacy business who makes the sale, or

(3) in Scotland, the sale or supply is to a doctor and is in compliance with the arrangements made under the NHS which permit a doctor to obtain drugs or appliances which he is required or entitled to supply under his terms of service, or

(4) in Northern Ireland, the sale or supply is to a doctor and in response to an order for a stock of medicinal products which are drugs and appliances to be supplied by the doctor for immediate administration or in other similar cases.

Nevertheless, most pharmacists do make an entry in the prescription book because they regard it as good pharmaceutical practice. It is also useful for VAT purposes.

All registers, orders and invoices shall be kept for a period of 2 years from the date of the last entry or of the transaction.

RECORDS OF CONTROLLED DRUGS

The following classes of persons are authorised to possess, supply, use or administer controlled drugs in certain circumstances –

(1) practitioners;

(2) the matron or acting matron of a hospital or nursing home;

(3) the person in charge of a laboratory concerned with scientific education or research;

(4) the owner or master of a ship that does not carry a doctor as part of her complement;

(5) the master of a foreign ship in port in Great Britain;

(6) the manager of an offshore installation.

They obtain these drugs either from the manufacturers, from wholesalers, or from pharmacies. The documentation involved in the transaction is specified in regulation 14 of the Misuse of Drugs Regulations 1973. In every case, the purchaser must supply the seller with a written requisition which states:

(a) his name, address and profession or occupation;

(b) the amount of drug required and the purpose for which it is required;

(c) the requisition must be signed by him;

(d) any other information required for special users (see below).

Where the requisition is furnished by the matron or acting matron of a hospital or nursing home, it must be signed by a doctor or dentist employed at the hospital or home.

Where the requisition is supplied by the master of a foreign ship, it must contain a statement signed by the proper officer of the port health authority, that the quantity is necessary for the equipment of the ship.

If the purchaser does not collect the drug personally from the seller, he must provide the person who will collect it on his behalf with a written document empowering the seller to hand the drug to the bearer.

The seller may only supply the drug if he is satisfied that the signature of the purchaser is genuine and that he is engaged in the profession or occupation stated.

The requisition, and the bearer's note if any, must be kept by the seller for 2 years from the date of the sale (regulation 22).

Whenever a drug in Schedule 2 to the Misuse of Drugs Regulations is sold, a record of the sale must be made in a special register kept for the purpose. The details relating to these registers are given in Chapter 10.

Chapter 9
Retail Sale of Medicines for Human Use

RETAIL OUTLETS

The Act and several pieces of subordinate legislation applicable to the sale and supply of medicines refer to 'premises which can be closed so as to exclude the public' (see, for example section 53). The context in which the phrase is used often connotes a 'shop' but this specific word has been avoided possibly because it had caused problems in earlier legislation. 'Shop' was used in the Pharmacy and Medicines Act 1941 to describe premises at which medicines could be sold. That Act defined the word in the same way as the Shops Act 1912, namely, as 'including any premises where any retail trade or business is carried on'. The Pharmaceutical Society of Great Britain had the duty of enforcing the 1941 Act and brought numerous prosecutions against stallholders and others. Sometimes there was lengthy argument as to what constituted a shop. In Summers v. Roberts (1943), a case involving the sale of medicines from a stall, the court held that the word 'shop' did not include a stall in an uncovered part of a market. In this case, the stall was a board resting on trestles and was only used by the stallholder for the sale of medicines on 2 days a week. The case went to the High Court on appeal, and part of the judgment given there by the Lord Chief Justice seemed to imply that the Court had been influenced by the lack of a permanent structure and also by the fact that the business only operated on 2 days a week. In Stone v. Boreham (1958), a man was prosecuted for selling a packet of tea from a van on a Sunday contrary to the Shops Act. It was held by the magistrates and later by the High Court that a mobile van did not constitute a shop.

In Greenwood v. Whelan (1966) it was finally decided by the High Court that a stall was a 'place not being a shop' despite the fact that the trader in question occupied the same site 5 days a week, that the site was clearly marked, and that the stall was a tubular steel structure fitted with an awning, equipped with electric light and bearing a sign giving the stallholder's name. The Lord Chief Justice stated that a retail trade could be carried on in three ways, from a shop, from a place other than a shop (such as a stall) or from no fixed place such as a van or barrow.

The word 'premises' means a building or a part of a building and the land attached to it. This clearly includes a shop and also includes a private residence. Thus the word is also appropriate to describe the consulting rooms used in the practice of a practitioner, chiropodist, optician and similar persons and this is advantageous because it covers supplies made from such rooms.

The view that the Act recognises a difference between a 'premises' and a 'stall' is reinforced by the wording of section 111(2)(b) '.......... any stall or place other than premises........'. Furthermore, in respect of the sales by agricultural merchants and saddlers of those veterinary drugs which are specified in the Veterinary Drugs Exemption Order, the word 'premises' specifically includes 'a stall of a permanent nature situated at a market or agricultural showground'. There are, however, two qualifying factors to be mentioned with this. Firstly, the registering authority is empowered to refuse to register premises which are unsatisfactory because they lack essential facilities or are insecure. Secondly, the relevant Codes of Practice make it plain that the 'premises' cannot be part of a residence. The fact that it was considered necessary to state that permanent stalls at a market etc. would be regarded as 'premises' for the purpose of the Exemption Order lends support to the belief that this would not otherwise have been the case. It also removes a possible ambiguity.

Some people considered that the Society (who had the legal duty to enforce the 1941 Act) were being excessively legalistic in pursuing the stallholders but there was a very good reason for the Society's concern. Persons who lack a permanent place of business cannot be monitored properly to ensure that they sell only what they are entitled to sell and that the products are correctly stored etc. Clearly, it is in the public interest that the Act be properly enforced and this implies some permanency in the place of business.

From the enforcement point of view, shops are easy to inspect since they have to be open to the public. Private residences on the other hand are very difficult to inspect. In fact, the enforcement authorities would only want to inspect the latter when there was reason to suspect that unlawful acts were being committed therein. In such an event, the authority could apply to the justices for a search warrant (section 111(4) and (5)).

MEDICINES ON THE GENERAL SALE LIST

Any retailer can sell GSL medicines both for human and for animal use from his shop. Veterinary GSL products and foods and cosmetics which are medicinal products may also be sold from vans.

There is good reason for the requirement that the sale of GSL medicines by most retailers be in unopened containers. Such retailers lack the necessary knowledge and facilities to correctly identify medicines and there is an obvious need to prevent them from selling medicines in 'broken bulk'. It is also dangerous to allow untrained persons to repack and relabel medicines, because of the possibility of adulteration, and of mistakes as to the identity of the product. This is recognised by the Act which requires such activities to be subject to an 'assembler's' licence, unless carried out by a pharmacist or certain other professionals. The same considerations apply to the requirement that products sold by such retailers be packed and labelled for sale elsewhere than at the place of sale.

The Ministers may precribe additional conditions to be fulfilled by persons selling GSL products (section 53). Among these are the restrictions on pack size mentioned in Chapter 7.

AUTOMATIC MACHINES

Until the coming into operation of Part III of the Medicines Act, only those medicines which did not contain poisons could be sold from automatic machines. The intention was to allow certain GSL products to be sold by such methods and to have a list of such products. The Medicines (Products Other Than Veterinary

Drugs) (General Sale List) Order 1984 has abolished the special list and now enables any GSL product to be sold from a machine (article 3). There is, however, no corresponding provision in the Veterinary Drugs (General Sale List) Order 1984.

Regulations require that automatic machines must be situated in premises which the occupier can close to exclude the public (1980/1923, regulation 4). This would seem to prevent access to the machines when the premises were closed, and to a large extent defeats the object of such machines except in hotels, railway station buffets and similar places.

SALE OF MEDICINES FROM PHARMACIES

As mentioned in Chapter 7, the Act was intented to confine the sale of medicines to pharmacies because they are not ordinary articles of commerce. Modern medicines are potent and complex substances and the public need the advice of a pharmacist to ensure that the remedy is appropriate for the complaint and compatible with the life-style of the patient. Furthermore, the pharmacist is best able to advise as to dosage regimens that maximise the benefits of the medicine while minimising its side-effects. All of these advantages are secured by requiring that sales of pharmacy medicines take place under the supervision of a pharmacist.

Supervision

'Supervision' is neither defined in the Act nor in any of the relevant statutory instruments. It was not defined in the Pharmacy and Poisons Act 1933, which required that Part I poisons (and consequently the majority of medicines) be sold only under the supervision of a pharmacist. It has, however, received judicial attention in the High Court (Roberts v. Littlewoods Mail Order Stores Ltd 1943) where it was held to mean that the pharmacist must be aware that the sale was taking place and that he was in a position to intervene in the sale if he considered it necessary. Thus, he should be able to see and hear what is taking place at the counter and be able to talk to the purchaser. In many pharmacies, there is a bell on the counter which enables the sales assistant to attract the pharmacist's attention when such products are requested. It is also the reason for the fact that in many pharmacies the dispensing area is elevated above the normal floor level of the shop, and for the proximity of the medicines counter to the dispensary.

It was held in a recent case (PSGB v. Logan 1981) that the requirement of supervision was one of strict liability and that 'mens rea' is not a necessary ingredient for a conviction for unsupervised sales.

Self-service Sales Methods

The Society's dislike of self-service sales methods applied to medicines is partly rooted in the concept of supervision. However, many retailers do use such methods to sell GSL medicines and the Ministers are apparently content with this for they have never sought to prevent it by imposing conditions under section 53 to prevent it. In view of this, it might seem inequitable to pharmacists that the Society insist that pharmacists should not use such methods. Nevertheless, the Code (guidance note 1.H) makes plain the profession's dislike of the practice by repeating paragraph 5.4 of the Guide to Self Assessment. This requires [P] medicines to be displayed in such a way as to be inaccessible to the public and states that other medicines 'should not be displayed on self-selection where there is a possibility that they may be obtained without the intervention of a pharmacist or other trained person.'

It was because the Society felt that self-service methods were inappropriate to the sale of medicines, and also the 'supervision' requirement, that a prosecution was brought against Boots in 1952. The prosecution failed because the Court found that the sale occurred at the checkout where a pharmacist was in a position to see and hear what was being sold.

It is now accepted by the profession that self-service methods are not really appropriate for selling medicines. In addition, the fact that it is easier to steal goods offered for sale by this method and that certain normally innocuous products can be dangerous if taken in large amounts, make the use of the method professionally indefensible.

General Sale List Products

The sale of GSL products need not be supervised by a pharmacist, unless they are in packs larger than those permitted for general sale. If the product needs to be repacked or relabelled, then this must be done under the supervision of a pharmacist.

Pharmacy Medicines

These may be sold (under the supervision of a pharmacist) to anyone in any quantity that the pharmacist considers appropriate, unless they are POM. There are no other legal constraints upon the pharmacist, but he is, of course, subject to ethical constraints which are designed to protect the public (see article 1 of the Code of Ethics and the relevant guidance notes). Over the years, the Society and its Statutory Committee have built up an excellent reputation for protecting the public against (the very rare) pharmacist who sold medicines in inappropriate quantities, or for non-medical purposes even when such sales have been perfectly lawful.

The pharmacist can repack or relabel products if he considers it appropriate, and can make up his own formulae (see Chapter 11).

There is no need in law to keep a record of the sale of pharmacy medicines. Nevertheless, article V.B of the Code requires the pharmacist to keep a record of those extemporaneous preparations made on his advice.

PML Sales via Pharmacies

There are two groups of veterinary products which are classed as PML (pharmacy and merchants list). One group are products which would normally be POM but which are exempt from the restrictions under certain circumstances. The other group are normally [P] medicines. Both groups can be sold by certain agricultural merchants, and the conditions to be fulfilled by such sellers and the drugs concerned are discussed in Chapter 14. Here, the restrictions as they apply to pharmacists are discussed.

A PML medicine is packed and labelled for sale by its manufacturer. The pharmacist is bound by the Code of Ethics (IIIB) to comply with the Codes applicable to agricultural merchants and saddlers. The sale of a PML medicine is subject to the same controls as apply to [P] medicines, especially supervision. Unlike the agricultural merchant, the pharmacist can sell to pet-owners as well as to farmers and other business users. Those PML products which are injectable or would otherwise be POM can, however, only be sold to farmers etc. Also, he can prepare products which are [P] for sale to pet-owners, farmers and any other purchaser, either to the customer's formula or to the pharmacist's own formula.

The pharmacist must record the following particulars in respect to the sale of every PML drug –

(a) the date on which the veterinary drug was sold;

(b) the name, quantity and, except where it is apparent from the name, the pharmaceutical form and strength of the veterinary drug sold; and

(c) the name and address of the person to whom it was sold.

There is no need to keep such a record if a written order for the product has been received or an invoice given and the particulars are given thereon, and the order or a copy of the invoice has been kept.

These records must be kept for 2 years from the date of the sale.

PRESCRIPTION ONLY MEDICINES

These can only be sold or supplied on the prescription of a practitioner. Most of them may be supplied without a prescription in an emergency at the request of a doctor, and many can similarly be supplied at the request of the patient. The details as to such supplies are stated in Chapter 10.

ETHICAL CONTROLS OVER SALES OF MEDICINES

There is very little statute law relating to the sales of medicines by pharmacists. However, the Code of Ethics does impose upon the pharmacist the professional obligation to observe a number of requirements, and is very strictly enforced. Some people believe that statute law is better able to protect the public than are the activities of professional bodies who sometimes appear to be biassed towards their members. Such a person is recommended to examine the record of the Pharmaceutical Society of Great Britain in enforcing laws relating to poisons and medicines (going back to 1868) and of its Statutory Committee in enforcing and improving professional standards. Those who have studied the records have been impressed both with the thoroughness of the enforcement and also with its impartiality.

Article 1 of the Code of Ethics and especially its accompanying notes contain a considerable amount of information relevant to the sale and dispensing of medicines by pharmacists. It mentions the importance of buying only from reputable suppliers and the need to ensure that products of doubtful quality or safety are not stocked. The pharmacist is required to keep up to date with current developments so as to be able to re-evaluate each product when necessary. He must ensure that patients understand how to use their medication most effectively, and particularly that blind, disabled or persons with language difficulties can use their products safely. In this context, the concurrent use of other medication is very relevant, as is the patient's lifestyle.

The pharmacist should discourage or control the excessive or unnecessary purchase of medicines. This is, of course, contrary to normal business practice. It is very gratifying to learn that non-pharmaceutical researchers (e.g. the

Consumer's Association, the Price Commission) have consistently found that the overwhelming majority of pharmacists do, in fact, behave very professionally.

Many people are unaware of the fact that some medicines (even some on the GSL) can be, and are, abused especially by the young. Some of medicines in common use for treating trivial ailments can give rise to hallucinations and other desirable (?) effects when consumed by the bottleful and particularly when combined with alcohol or other drugs. It is the duty of the general practice pharmacist to be mindful of this and to report to the local drug squad (or to his local Drugs Advisory Committee) any suspicious increase in demand for a product, especially when the purchasers are teenagers or young adults. The pharmacist also has a professional duty to control the sale of medicines which are likely to give rise to or support drug dependence.

The Code recognises that pharmacists sell poisons and other substances for use in various domestic purposes and hobbies. It expects the pharmacist to apply the same caution and care in such sales. The sale of chemicals to children should always be refused unless the parents are present and have been warned of the dangers of the substance. Very great care should be taken in the sale of oxidising or reducing agents and similar substances which might be used to make explosives or fireworks.

Perhaps it is worth observing that since the Code represents the profession's collective view as to desirable conduct, those who ignore its requirements must be prepared to justify their actions. Furthermore, failure to observe the Code might be interpreted as evidence of professional negligence should someone suffer damage as a consequence of that failure.

STORAGE

Although the Act empowers the Ministers to make regulations controlling the storage and safekeeping of medicinal products (section 66(1)) in pharmacies, such powers have not yet been used.

Insofar as veterinary medicines are concerned, the Sale or Supply (Miscellaneous Provisions) Regulations require those PML veterinary drugs stored retail premises, to be stored in a part of the premises separate from that to which the public are permitted access (regulation 3). In addition, they must be stored in conditions which comply with storage instructions printed on the labels or leaflets applicable to those products. The Pharmaceutical Society of Great Britain and the Department of Health and Social Services for Northern Ireland may refuse to register premises of agricultural merchants and saddlers if the premises do not meet the requirements, or remove the premises from the register if products are stored under inappropriate conditions (1984/1861 regulations 3 and 5).

The Misuse of Drugs (Safe Custody) Regulations impose detailed requirements upon pharmacists who store controlled drugs in a pharmacy or health centre. In relation to the cabinet, these regulations specify the materials of construction, the type of lock, of hinge and the maximum permissible gap between door and frame. In addition, the methods used to secure the cabinet to the wall or floor are also specified. The safe custody regulations do not apply to the storage of products which are CDinv, to non-parenteral liquid preparations of amphetamines and certain other drugs, or to the barbiturates. These regulations also apply to various nursing homes. They do not apply to practitioners or to hospitals but the latter have facilities which provide comparable security.

Although there are no statutory provisions controlling the storage of medicines in pharmacies, the Society's Code of Ethics does include such provisions. Some of these are couched in general terms such as as the premises being clean, adequately lit and ventilated and providing protection against pests, the elements and theft. One specific recommendation is that a pharmacy should be equipped with a refrigerator capable of storing products within a selected temperature range from 0 to 10°C. The efficiency of the refrigerator should be checked at regular intervals (Guide to Good Dispensing Practice, Part 2(vii).

References

Summers v. Roberts, 1943, 2 All E.R. 757; 1943, 60 TLR 102; *Pharm. J.*, 1943, 151, p.214

Stone v. Boreham, 1958, 2 All E.R. 715

Greenwood v. Whelan, 1967, All E.R.757

Roberts v. Littlewoods Mail Order Stores Ltd., 1943, All E.R.271

Pharmaceutical Society of Great Britain v. Logan, 1981, Crim. L.R., 444

Pharmaceutical Society of Great Britain v. Boots Cash Chemists (Southern) Ltd., 1952, 2 All E.R.456

Chapter 10
Dispensing Medicines

INTRODUCTION

To a pharmacist, the word 'dispensing' has traditionally meant 'the supply of a medicine on and in accordance with the prescription of a doctor, dentist or veterinarian'. It did not necessarily include the actual preparation of the product to a formula written by the prescriber. The mixing together of the ingredients to prepare the medicine was known as 'compounding', but the word 'preparation' is now preferred. Neither the Act nor any of the orders or regulations made under Part III of the Act define 'dispensing' but a definition is given in the Labelling Regulations 1976/1726, namely –

'Dispensed medicinal product means –

(1) a medicinal product prepared or dispensed by a practitioner or prepared or dispensed in accordance with a prescription given by a practitioner, or

(2) a medicinal product for use by being administered to human beings where that medicinal product has been sold or supplied by a doctor or dentist for administration to a particular patient of his and that doctor or dentist sells or supplies that medicinal product to that patient or to a person under whose care that patient is, or

(3) a medicinal product for use by being administered to animals where that medicinal product has been sold or supplied by a veterinary surgeon or veterinary practitioner for administration to a particular animal or herd which is under the care of that veterinary surgeon or veterinary practitioner, to a person having the possession or control of that animal or herd, or

(4) a medicinal product prepared or dispensed in a registered pharmacy by or under the supervision of a pharmacist in the circumstances set out in sections lO(3) or lO(4)(a) of the Act, or

(5) a medicinal product where the person selling or supplying the medicinal product sells or supplies it for administration to a particular person after being requested by or on behalf of that person and in that person's presence to use his own judgment as to the treatment required.'

It seems, therefore, that dispensing now includes the sale or supply by a practitioner to his patient, the supply by a pharmacist on the prescription of a practitioner, or the 'counter-prescribing' by a pharmacist of a product for a patient and the preparation of a product to the formula of a customer. It also includes the preparation by a herbalist of a herbal remedy for a particular patient who has asked the herbalist to 'counter-prescribe' for him.

In the section dealing with dispensing procedures in the Society's Guide to the Self Assessment of Professional Practice Activities, dispensing 'includes all of the activities which occur from the pharmacist's initial scrutiny of a prescription to the collection of the dispensed medicine by the patient or agent' (4.1).

PRESCRIPTIONS

Neither the Act nor any of the regulations define the word 'prescription' so recourse is made to the dictionary which states that a prescription is the physician's (usually written) direction for the composition and use of a medicine. In the UK it also includes the directions of dentists and of veterinarians, and the three classes will be referred to as 'practitioners' or 'prescribers'. Since the public can obtain GSL and [P] medicines without the need of a prescription, no requirements have been laid down for such prescriptions under the Act. The POM Order lays down conditions for POMs and additional requirements apply to those POMs that are also controlled under Schedules 2, 3 or 4 to the Misuse of Drugs Regulations. For the purposes of the Misuse of Drugs Regulations, 'prescription' means a prescription issued by a doctor for the medical treatment of a single individual, by a dentist for the dental treatment of a single individual, or by a veterinarian for the treatment of animals (regulation 2).

The NHS Regulations require doctors and dentists to write prescriptions for all medicines, reagents and appliances they prescribe for their patients, even when the prescriber administers the drug himself or dispenses it himself. All NHS prescriptions must be written on the appropriate form (FP 10 for doctors and a distinctive yellow form FP 14 for dentists in England and Wales) and be signed in ink by the prescriber with his forename or initials and his surname. A separate form must be used for each patient unless a 'bulk' prescription is used. The NHS Regulations permit a 'bulk' prescription to be issued by a doctor who is responsible for the treatment of a minimum of ten persons living in a school or institution in which at least 20 persons normally reside. According to the NHS Regulations, such a prescription may only be issued for a preparation included in the current edition of the BNF but not for a controlled drug or a product 'in the former Schedule IVA of the Poisons Rules 1972'. In fact, a bulk prescription for any POM is invalid because such a prescription must bear the name and address of the patient. The Secretary of State may notify doctors and chemists of additional preparations that may be ordered on bulk prescriptions (see paragraph 37 of Part I to Schedule 1 to the NHS Regulations).

Private prescriptions are usually written on the prescriber's headed notepaper. The prescription is the property of the patient and should be returned to him after dispensing. A prescription for a POM must be retained by the pharmacist unless it may be repeated. A prescription for a controlled drug can never be repeated, nor may it be returned to the patient.

Prescriptions for POMs

When a patient requires a product that is POM then he will need a prescription which conforms to the following requirements. It must –

(a) be in indelible writing (a carbon copy is permissible for NHS prescriptions other than for controlled drugs);

(b) be signed in ink by the practitioner;

(c) be dated by him;

(d) bear the address of the practitioner;

(e) contain particulars indicating the profession of the practitioner;

(f) bear the name and address of the patient, and his age if less than 12 years;

(g) if for an animal, bear the name and address of the person to whom the medicine is to be delivered, and a declaration by the veterinarian that the POM is required for an animal under his care.

The prescription must be dispensed within 6 months of the date on the prescription unless it is repeatable when it must be dispensed the first time within the 6 months.

A repeatable prescription is one which contains a direction that it may be dispensed a stated number of times. If it is marked 'Repeat' or 'To be repeated' and the number of times is omitted, then it may be dispensed only twice (i.e. it may only be repeated once) unless it is for an oral contraceptive when it may be dispensed six times before the end of the 6 month period.

The date is that on which the prescription was signed by the practitioner, but the NHS regulations permit prescriptions to be pre-dated by practitioners.

Prescription Only Medicines that are also Controlled Drugs

Where a product is POM and also controlled under Schedule 2, 3 or 4 of the Misuse of Drugs Regulations, then several modifications to the above are necessary to make forgeries and alterations more easily detectable. The practitioner must sign the prescription with his usual signature, date it, and, in his own handwriting, state –

(a) the patient's name and address;

(b) the name of the medicine, its form, and strength if there is more than one;

(c) the amount required in both words and figures; and

(d) the dose to be taken.

Thus, the tendency for doctors to use computers to write their prescriptions, while welcome from a communication point of view, is of no use when applied to prescriptions for controlled drugs. There is a specific exemption from the handwriting requirement for certain named doctors. These are mainly employed in centres treating drug addicts and usually have a rubber stamp which prints the body of the prescription leaving spaces in which the doctor inserts the number of dosage units prescribed and the number to be supplied on each day. The prescription is of an unusual type in that it is intended that the drug be supplied in instalments. The doctors in such treatment centres use a special prescription form (HP10 Add), and the prescriptions are sent by the centre directly to the general practice pharmacy at which the addict has elected to collect his supply. The object of this is to prevent the addict from altering or from selling the prescription. These arrangements for supplying addicts with drugs are not embodied in any regulations, but are purely administrative.

Table 1 CD inv preparations

All of these are preparations which contain not more than the specified amount or strength of one or more of the following drugs. A product which does not fall within the strength or dose stated is a fully controlled drug (CD).

Cocaine (not more than 0.1%) and morphine whether as such or in the form of opium (not more than 0.2%), provided in either case that the drug cannot be recovered by readily applicable means or in a yield that would constitute a risk to health. This would preclude simple aqueous solutions of either drug and therefore injections.

Codeine, dihydrocodeine, ethylmorphine, nicocodine, nicodicodine, norcodeine, pholcodine, or their salts containing not more than 100 mg per dosage unit or not more than 2.5% in undivided preparations. All parenteral products of these substances are CD.

Currently, there are no products containing ethylmorphine, nicocodine or nicodicodine on the market in the UK. All tablets containing either codeine or dihydrocodeine contain less than 100 mg of the base and are therefore CD inv. Likewise syrups, linctuses, mixtures and other undivided preparations of either codeine or pholcodine contain less than 2.5%.

Diphenoxylate in preparations containing not more than 2.5 mg per dosage unit and containing atropine sulphate equivalent to at least 1% of the dose of diphenoxylate. Lomotil is the only example currently on the UK market.

Most of these preparations are classed as [P] but some, such as DF118 Tablets, Paramol Tablets and Lomotil are POM.

In all cases above, the amount or strength refers to the base, the actual amount of salt will, of course, be greater.

Also included in the list are products containing difenoxin and those containing propiram but there is no such product currently marketed in the UK.

Dover's Powder, a preparation containing 10% of opium powder and 10% of powdered ipecacuanha is also CD inv.

Table 2 List of controlled drugs commonly available in UK

Amphetamine	
*Cocaine	
*Codeine	
Dexamphetamine	
Dextromoramide	'Palfium'
*Dextropropoxyphene	
Diamorphine	
Diethylpropion	'Apisate', 'Tenuate'
*Dihydrocodeine	
Dipipanone	'Diconal'
Fentanyl	'Sublimaze', 'Thalamonal'
Levorphanol	'Dromoran'
Methadone	'Physeptone'
Methylphenobarbitone	
*Morphine	
*Opium, whether raw, prepared or medicinal	
Oxycodone	
Pethidine	
Phenazocine	'Narphen'
*Pholcodine	
Piritramide	'Diplidor'

*These substances, their salts etc. and their parenteral products are 'CD'. Most of their other preparations are CD inv.

Table 3 List of CD no reg preparations currently available in UK

Diethylpropion	'Apisate', 'Tenuate Dospan'
Any 5,5 disubstituted barbituric acid, examples –	
Amylobarbitone	'Amytal'
Butobarbitone	'Soneryl'
Pentobarbitone	'Nembutal'
Phenobarbitone	
Quinalbarbitone	'Seconal'

Table 4 List of CD lic drugs (there are no licensed medicinal products containing any of these)

Bufotenine Cannabinol
Cannabinol derivatives
Cannabis
Cannabis resin
Coca leaf
Concentrate of poppy straw
Eticyclidine
Lysergamide
Lysergide and other *N*-alkyl derivatives of lysergamide
Mescaline
Psilocin
Raw opium
Rolicyclidine
Tenocyclidine
4-Bromo-2,5-dimethoxy-α-methylphenethylamine
N,N-Diethyltryptamine
N,N-Dimethyltryptamine
2,5-Dimethoxy-α,4-dimethylphenethylamine.

WHAT MAY BE PRESCRIBED

The only products that cannot be prescribed by any doctor, dentist or veterinarian are those specified in Schedule 4 to the Misuse of Drugs Regulations (reproduced in Table 4 above), and medicinal products that are radioactive substances. However, in both cases an individual prescriber can apply for a licence to use, supply or prescribe named products. Section 58(1) enabled the Ministers to make an order specifying classes or descriptions of medicinal products which should be restricted to supply on prescription only, and could have classified them so that some were restricted to doctors, others perhaps to dentists and others to veterinarians. In the event two Orders were made (Products Other Than Veterinary Drugs (Prescription Only) Order, and the Veterinary Drugs (Prescription Only) Order. The first enabled all such practitioners to use any of these products, but the second restricts to veterinarians the prescribing and use of the drugs specified therein. Consequently, unlike the situation in many other countries, prescribers in the UK have (for all practical purposes) the utmost freedom to prescribe whatever they consider best for their patients.

NHS Limited List

The NHS however, has always limited dentists to preparations listed in the Dental Practitioners' Formulary. Despite vigorous opposition from the industry and from the medical and pharmaceutical professions, the Secretary of State for Social Services has amended the NHS General Medical and Pharmaceutical Services Regulations 1974 to limit the freedom of choice of doctors to prescribe under the NHS. Since April 1st 1985, the terms of service for doctors prevent them from prescribing a 'scheduled drug', and the pharmacist's terms of service prevent him from dispensing such a drug. There are two parts to the Schedule, Part A contains about 1700 entries and these items cannot be supplied on FP 10 forms. Part B contains one drug (Clobazam) which can be prescribed on FP 10s for the treatment of just one condition, epilepsy. These lists are reproduced in Appendix 4.

Drugs specified in the limited list fall into the following categories –

(a) antacids,

(b) laxatives,

(c) analgesics used for mild to moderate pain,

(d) cough and cold remedies including cough suppressants, expectorants, demulcents, mucolytics, nasal decongestants, and inhalations,

(e) bitters and tonics,

(f) vitamins,

(g) benzodiazepines, tranquillisers and sedatives.

For each of the categories specified above, there is a selection of products which remain prescribable on FP 10s, some of them are 'official' preparations but many are 'ethical', i.e. proprietary products.

Examination of the list of scheduled products reveals a number of interesting points. First of all, 197 products are unidentifiable except to the licensing authority and the holders of the product licences. It seems that they are products made for distribution through health clubs, health clinics and sometimes for sale in supermarkets under the name of the company. The next point is that many of the products listed have seldom if ever been prescribed on FP 10s. They comprise products advertised to the public for the treatment of trivial ailments and available from a variety of outlets, in other words, they are typical 'patent' medicines. Although there was no prohibition on their prescription under the NHS, the DHSS and the medical profession had a tacit understanding that such products would not be prescribed. This meant that when a doctor did prescribe one of them, the pharmacist would dispense it in the usual way and be paid for so doing. When the prescription had been priced, the family practitioner committee would be notified and request the doctor to justify the product. If he could not give a satisfactory explanation, the price of the product could be deducted from his remuneration.

The majority of the benzodiazepines are listed under their proprietary names and many of these are for a small number of substances, e.g. 23 products contained diazepam in various forms and strengths. Another 53 benzodiazepine preparations appear in the list, but 19 preparations are still available. The result is that doctors may only prescribe the benzodiazepines by using their generic names, and some benzodiazepines are not prescribable at all on FP 10.

Some of the 'scheduled drugs' were included in the list of 'borderline' products in the Drug Tariff. Such products are foods, cosmetics or toilet articles which have some remedial or beneficial action, and were prescribable under the NHS for certain well-defined complaints. The prescriber has to endorse the prescription 'ACBS' to indicate that he is prescribing the product for a complaint for which the Advisory Committee on Borderline Substances has given approval. There are still some borderline substances prescribable on FP10s.

DISPENSING

Doctors, dentists and veterinarians are entitled under the Medicines Act to dispense medicines for their patients. This entitlement is personal to the practitioner and cannot be delegated to unqualified staff. Pharmacists are similarly entitled to dispense medicines and also to supervise dispensing carried out by unqualified staff. In fact, few doctors and dentists dispense medicines except in an emergency. Some doctors have a contract with the local family practitioner committee to dispense medicines for patients who live more than a mile from a pharmacy. Most veterinarians dispense their own medicines.

The NHS Regulations require the dispensing of all NHS prescriptions in a pharmacy to be carried out by, or under the supervision of, a pharmacist. The pharmacist is expected to supply 'with reasonable promptness' any of the drugs, listed drugs, and listed appliances, written on a prescription form by a doctor or dentist (regulation 2). The Code of Ethics requirespharmacists to supervise the dispensing of all prescriptions and this includes all steps between the interpretation of the prescription to the handing of it to the patient or his representative.

The Code requires a pharmacist to supply exactly what the prescriber ordered except where it is necessary to protect the patient (I,D,iv). Provision is made for substitution under certain circumstances in hospitals (see later) or with the prescriber's consent (I,D,ii). Furthermore, in an emergency, substitution may also be permissible. Where a pharmacist is uncertain as to the prescriber's intentions, or believes that the patient could be harmed by the product prescribed, he should make every effort to contact the prescriber. If the prescriber confirms that he wants the potentially dangerous product dispensed, the pharmacist may refuse to dispense it, but, before doing so, must carefully balance the potential harm resulting from the supply against the harm that may result from not dispensing it. If the prescriber cannot be contacted the pharmacist must use his professional skill and judgment to decide what would be best for the patient (I,D,iv).

The pharmacist is also expected to comply with the Guide to Good Dispensing Practice. This is analogous to the Guide to Good Mnaufacturing Practice observed by manufacturers. The premises in which dispensing is carried out should be clean, free from pests and other animals, well lit and ventilated. There should be adequate room for the work to be performed efficiently. The processing of materials for non-medicinal use should not be carried out in the dispensary. There should be an adequate range of suitable equipment to carry out the various dispensing operations including a refrigerator whose efficiency should be checked periodically. Only containers which meet the appropriate specifications should be used to pack dispensed products.

A very high standard of cleanliness is required both in regard to the room and its facilities and also in regard to the staff. Smoking, and the preparation and eating of food and drink should not be permitted in the dispensary.

The materials used for dispensing should be purchased only from reputable suppliers, should be carefully examined and properly stored before use. Any stock the quality of which is suspect should be safely destroyed or returned to the manufacturer.

The dispensary should be equipped with an adequate supply of up to date reference books.

LABELLING

The legal requirements relating to the labelling of dispensed products are discussed in Chapter 16. The warning and cautionary labels recommended for use by the Pharmaceutical Society of Great Britain are specified in Appendix 3. The Council of the Society have recommended that, in the interests of safety and clarity, all labels should be typed or mechanically produced. It is also a matter of professional conduct, that every effort should be made to ensure that all patients understand how the medicine should be used most effectively.

EMERGENCY SUPPLIES OF POMS

The emergence of a class of medicines which could only be supplied to the public on prescription is a relatively recent innovation in the UK. The size of this class has, however, grown rapidly. Its existence has caused problems to patients, who, for one reason or another, are unable to obtain a prescription before their existing supply has run out. Most pharmacists have tried to help such patients in an emergency even when it meant breaking the law and such conduct has always been regarded by the profession as tolerable if not laudable. Although some pharmacists have been prosecuted for making illegal sales of such drugs, the circumstances usually indicated that the seller's motivation was profit rather than to a genuine desire to help someone. The POM Order overcame the difficulty by permitting two types of emergency supply and laid down the conditions to be fulfilled in each case (article 6).

The POM Order permits pharmacists to make emergency supplies of most, but not all, POMs under TWO different sets of circumstances, namely –

(a) at the request of a DOCTOR, or
(b) at the request of a PATIENT.

In each set of circumstances, the pharmacist must comply with specified conditions.

Conditions for a Lawful Supply at the Request of a Doctor

(1) The pharmacist must be satisfied that some emergency prevents the doctor from providing a prescription immediately.

(2) The doctor has undertaken to furnish a prescription within 72 hours.

(3) The medicine is sold or supplied in accordance with the directions of the doctor, and no repeats are allowed until the prescription has been received.

(4) The medicine does not contain any 'controlled drug' other than a CD inv POM.

(5) The details of the sale or supply are recorded in the prescription book (see below).

Conditions for the Lawful Supply at the Request of the Patient

(1) The pharmacist must interview the patient and satisfy himself that –

(a) the product is needed immediately and that a prescription cannot be obtained without undue delay,

(b) the treatment has been previously been prescribed for the patient by a doctor,

(c) the dose is appropriate.

(2) Only sufficient medicine for FIVE DAYS treatment is sold or supplied except where the product is –

(a) an ointment or cream, or a preparation for the relief of asthma packed in an aerosol container, when the smallest pack the pharmacist HAS AVAILABLE, may be supplied;

(b) an oral contraceptive , a full cycle, may be supplied;

(c) an oral liquid antibiotic preparation, the smallest quantity that will provide a full course of treatment may be supplied.

(3) The POM product is neither a controlled drug, i.e. CD, CD no reg, CD lic; nor included in Schedule 2 to the POM Order (except Phenobarbitone and Phenobarbitone Sodium for an epileptic).

(4) The product is labelled with –

(a) date,

(b) name, quantity, form, and strength of the product,

(c) the name of the patient,

(d) the words 'Emergency Supply',

(e) the name and address of the pharmacy.

(5) The appropriate details are entered in the prescription book.

The Council of the Society have offered some advice and guidance as to what constitutes an 'emergency' (see *Pharm. J.*, 1978 p.133). According to a leading article in the *Pharmaceutical Journal* 1979(a) the existence of the rules has been alleged to cause problems for pharmacists some of whom are said to be afraid to use them in case they make a mistake and supply drugs to someone who has deceived them. Others are said to ignore some or all of the conditions. The Council regards the procedure as a valuable opportunity whereby pharmacists may provide a better service to the public, and laid down guidelines. There are eight of these –

(1) The pharmacist should identify the patient through documentary evidence or personal knowledge.

(2) The doctor who previously prescribed the drug should preferably be identified and contacted if possible.

(3) The question should be asked of the patient as to whether the doctor has stopped the treatment.

(4) The pharmacist should consider the medical consequences, if any, of NOT supplying the product.

(5) Inquiries should be made as to whether any other medicine is being taken at the same time to check any drug interactions.

(6) An emergency supply should not be made if the item requested had been prescribed previously more than 6 months prior to the request. Exceptions may be made in the case of those illnesses which occur infrequently, for example, hay fever, asthma attack, or migraine.

(7) Consideration should be given to supplying less than 5 days' quantity if this is justified in the circumstances.

(8) Labelling should be clear and legible and there should be some suitable indication of emergency supply entries in the prescription book.

These guidelines have been criticised as being 'inhibiting and restrictive' (*Pharm. J.*, 1979(b)).

While pharmacists will no doubt take note of this guidance it should be stressed that the law requires the pharmacist concerned to be satisfied that an emergency exists and affords him an opportunity to exercise his professional discretion to benefit his patient. Furthermore, article ID iii of the guidance notes to the Code require the pharmacist to do his utmost to help people requiring medicines in an emergency. The author is convinced that the overwhelming majority of pharmacists will use this discretion wisely to the advantage of the public whenever the occasion demands whether or not all eight criteria are fulfilled.

COLLECTION AND DELIVERY SERVICE

A pharmacist may organise a collection and delivery service for prescriptions. The prescriptions are left by patients at particular addresses for collection by the pharmacist. They are then taken to a pharmacy, dispensed in the usual way, and the medicine delivered to the original collection point, though where appropriate, the pharmacist may decide to deliver them to the patient personally. Such a scheme is authorised by 1978/1421.

During the organisation of such a scheme, the pharmacist is advised to contact the local inspector of the Pharmaceutical Society.

COUNTER-PRESCRIBING OR RESPONSE TO SYMPTOMS DESCRIBED

The Act permits a pharmacist to supply a remedy to a person who is present in the pharmacy and who asks the pharmacist to use his own judgment as to the treatment required. Pharmacists frequently refer to this activity as 'counter-prescribing', but a more modern and perhaps accurate description is 'response to symptoms described'. The pharmacist may respond by merely selling a ready packed and labelled proprietary or non-proprietary product and he could do this whether or not the patient was present. If, however, the patient is present the pharmacist may prepare a remedy specially for the patient, or he may re-pack a proprietary or a non-proprietary product and label it with directions for use and the patient's name. Alternatively, he may supply a quantity of a product of his own making which he keeps in stock for such a complaint.

There are some statutory constraints on the pharmacist's choice of suitable product. He cannot, of course, supply a POM in these circumstances. Likewise, if the signs and symptoms described by the patient indicate that he is, or might be, suffering from venereal disease or from cancer, then the pharmacist must refer him to a doctor. There are no other statutory restrictions but there are numerous ethical and common law points to be considered.

The pharmacist should obtain sufficient information from the patient to enable him to be satisfied that the condition can safely be dealt with in the pharmacy. In this context, the history of the symptoms, their frequency and extent are important. The person should be asked questions designed to reveal the existence of a serious pathology and particularly whether he is currently receiving medical treatment. Patients who are, or were recently, receiving treatment from their doctors should be referred back unless the new symptoms are clearly unconnected with the disease or its treatment.

It is frequently the case that the patient does not need any medication and when this is so, this should be explained. Various persons who have conducted surveys into the advice that pharmacists give in response to symptoms described, have commented favourably (some with considerable surprise) on the fact that pharmacists often advise against taking medication although this is clearly not in their economic interests. For example, the Price Commission Report (page 44) stated 'As a professional the pharmacist is consulted by the public and research (Jones 1976) indicates that the consultation rate of pharmacists is twice that of doctors. The return to the pharmacist for the time so expended is perhaps disproportionately low. Indeed, such consultation often involves dissuasion from purchase. However, while consultation may be commercially incongruous it is professionally vital. Were such advice not so freely given undoubtedly the public would suffer and an additional burden would be placed on the NHS.'

The pharmacist must ensure that he takes all the care necessary to avoid harm to his patient, i.e. he tries to foresee all the consequences that would follow from the various courses of action open to him. This is to avoid possible allegations of professional negligence. Also of importance in this respect is the quantity of medicine supplied. It should be sufficient to do its work but not so much that the patient is taking it long after he should have been better, normally 5 days supply would seem to be appropriate. In addition, the patient should be instructed to seek medical advice if the symptoms worsen or persist after a stated period.

PHARMACY RECORDS

Records of NHS presriptions are not required to be kept, unless the drug is a controlled drug, when the details must be recorded in the controlled drugs register (see below).

The law does not require records of [P] or GSL medicines dispensed on private prescriptions to be recorded, but the majority of pharmacists keep such records. The Guide to Good Dispensing Practice states that such records should be kept (see paragraph 5 vi). These records are also useful for VAT purposes when the prescriptions are for human use. Hence, the law requires private prescriptions for POMs to be recorded (unless the prescription is for oral contraceptives). It is also permissible to omit the entry in the prescription book if the transaction is recorded in the controlled drugs register. If the sale or supply is to a person employed or engaged in connection with a scheme for testing the quality and checking the amount of drugs and appliances supplied under the NHS no record need be kept in the prescription book.

The records are made in the Prescription Book on the day of the transaction or if that is not reasonably practicable, on the next day. Where the sale or supply is an emergency supply at the doctor's undertaking to furnish a prescription, the particulars specified in paragraphs (e) and (f) below may be entered on the day that the prescription relating to that sale or supply is received.

The prescription book must be kept for at least 2 years after the last entry therein, and all private prescriptions, copies of orders, invoices and other supporting documents must be kept for at least 2 years.

Prescriptions and Emergency Supplies at Doctor's Request

The following details are required –

(a) the date on which the medicine was sold or supplied;

(b) the name, quantity and, except where it is apparent from the name, the pharmaceutical form and strength of the medicine sold or supplied;

(c) the name and address of the prescriber;

(d) the name and address of the person for whom or for whose animal, as the case may be, the medicine was prescribed;

(e) the date on the prescription; and

(f) in relation to the emergency supply of the medicine under the date on which the prescription relating to that supply is received.

Where the sale or supply is the second or subsequent sale or supply in pursuance of a repeatable prescription the details required are either a full entry as above or the date of the subsequent supply and a reference to the original entry in the register.

Record of Emergency Supply at Patient's Request

The details to be recorded are –

(a) the date on which the medicine was sold or supplied;

(b) the name, quantity and, except where it is apparent from the name, the pharmaceutical form and strength of the medicine sold or supplied;

(c) the name and address of the person requiring the medicine; and

(d) the nature of the emergency.

CONTROLLED DRUGS RECORDS

The Misuse of Drugs Regulations, Schedule 5, specifies the form in which records of all controlled drugs obtained and supplied by a person must be kept.

DISPENSING IN HOSPITALS

Dispensing in NHS Hospitals

Patients being treated in NHS hospitals are supplied with medicines in either or both of two ways. In most hospitals, each ward holds a stock of the most commonly used products (including controlled drugs if necessary), and nurses administer these drugs to patients according to directions written by a doctor on the patient's treatment sheet or similar document. When a patient requires a product that is not held as a stock item, the product is dispensed for that patient in the hospital pharmacy and is administered by the nurse as before. In the majority of hospitals the treatment sheet is used not merely to prescribe the products but also as a record of the administration of each dose, the nurse being required to initial the appropriate 'box' on the sheet. Despite the exemption granted to nurses in NHS and charitable hospitals by the Misuse of Drugs Regulations (regulation 19(3)(b)) each ward and department of a NHS hospital keeps a register of all amounts of each drug obtained and supplied. A page is used to record receipts and supplies of a particular strength of a stated product and a running balance is kept of the stock. The sister obtains her supplies from the hospital pharmacy using a special duplicating book. For security reasons, administration of a dose of a controlled drug is usually witnessed by another nurse and both initial the treatment sheet.

Stock supplies are sent from the pharmacy in response to written orders from the sister or nurse in charge of the ward. This might happen on a daily basis or perhaps on alternate days. A record of these supplies is kept at the pharmacy and the ward sister usually has a copy too.

When a patient is being discharged from hospital, a prescription is written for his 'take home medication' and this is dispensed especially for him. Likewise, most out-patients are given prescriptions which are dispensed in the hospital pharmacy.

None of these prescriptions needs to comply with the requirements for POM prescriptions (article 10) nor need they comply with the controlled drug requirements (if applicable) provided that they are written on the normal forms used for that hospital and signed and dated by a doctor or dentist employed therein. Occasionally, a hospital suspends its out-patient dispensing service and prescribers are required to write prescriptions on special NHS forms (similar to the normal F.P.10) for dispensing in pharmacies in the community. Such prescriptions must, of course, comply with the normal requirements.

In all but the smallest hospitals, the pharmacy is under the control of a pharmacist, and all dispensing is done under the supervision of a pharmacist. All drugs used within the hospital are ordered by the pharmacist and are stored within the department until issued for use. Records are kept of supplies.

In order to avoid the stocking of a multiplicity of products having the same or similar effects and to achieve economy in the supply of medicines, most hospitals have set up a 'Pharmacy and Therapeutics Committee'. Such committees typically consist of the principal pharmacist and a doctor representing each of the major specialties at that hospital. This committee draws up a list of the most useful products in each therapeutic class, and these will be stocked. Prescriptions for a drug not listed will be filled by supplying the representative of that class unless the prescriber indicates that this should not be done and states the reason for this. Likewise, prescribing is usually in terms of 'generic names', i.e. the official names, thus enabling the pharmacist to stock only one brand of each drug. The supply of a generic product when a named proprietary product is prescribed is called 'substitution' and is normally regarded as unethical under the Code, as well as being actionable by the owner of the proprietary product. In the situation outlined above, substitution is neither unethical nor actionable. In some hospitals, the list is printed as a hospital formulary, and a copy is issued to every prescriber, nurse and pharmacist employed there.

In many of the larger NHS hospitals, some products are manufactured in bulk and other products are 'assembled'. Although such activities would normally require a manufacturer's licence, the application of 'Crown privilege' is claimed to obviate this. In any event, although no formal licences have been issued, all hospital departments at which such activities are carried out have been inspected by the Medicines Inspectorate and comply with the same standards as are applied to commercial operators.

Dispensing in Hospitals Maintained by Charities

Broadly speaking, these are very similar to the NHS hospitals. They are not allowed to 'manufacture' unless the hospital holds a manufacturer's licence, but medicines can of course be made for individual patients by or under the supervision of a pharmacist. Similarly, stocks of such products may also be made.

Dispensing in Private Hospitals

A pharmacist employed at such a hospital has all of his ordinary professional privileges and can dispense medicines for the patients and for stock. The hospital must hold a licence for each controlled drug it holds in stock. Such a licence currently costs £70.

Private hospitals are subject to inspection by the District Pharmaceutical Officer.

References

Pharm. J., 1978, 2, 133

Pharm. J., 1979(a), 1, 301

Pharm. J., 1979(b), 1, 303

Jones, RVH, 1976, *J. Roy. Coll. Gen. Practit.*, 26, 410-13

Price Commission. 'Prices, Costs and Margins in the Production and Distribution of Proprietary Non-ethical Medicines. HMSO, 1978, Cmd 469, p. 44

Chapter 11
Sales, Supplies and Administration by Exempted Users

INTRODUCTION

If the sale and supply of medicines were confined to pharmacies and other shopkeepers, considerable hardship would be caused to the public. Furthermore, many health care professionals and certain other classes of person would be severely hindered in their work if they could not sell or supply medicines to their patients or clients. Some also need to be able to administer certain products to their patients. To take account of these difficulties, various modifications to the general case have been made.

HEALTH CARE PROFESSIONALS

The restrictions imposed by sections 52 and 53 do not apply to any of the undermentioned classes in so far as the use, sale or supply of the specified medicinal products are concerned (section 55; 1980/1924, article 5 and Schedule 1). The usual practical effect of the exemptions is to free the professional person from the necessity of selling the products from shops or registered premises and in unopened containers. In the case of chiropodists and opticians the exemption is conditional.

It also exempts the person concerned from the requirement of employing a pharmacist to supervise the sale of [P] medicines. This is reasonable because the health professional has knowledge of the properties and dangers of the products he uses, and can thus be relied upon to supply them safely. Furthermore, he is professionally liable for his actions. There is no provision permitting him to delegate the sale, supply or administration to his employees.

The members of certain registering bodies are permitted to 'assemble' products without holding a manufacturer's licence. In this context, 'assemble' means relabelling and does not include repacking the product in another container (1979/1114, article 2).

Doctors and Dentists

No restrictions apply to the sale, supply or administration of medicines by doctors or dentists when treating their patients. If the treatment requires the use of radioactive products, then the practitioner must hold the appropriate certificate for the device in question. Doctors and dentists are generally authorised to possess, supply, prescribe, and administer controlled drugs to their patients (MoD Regulations, regulations 7, 8, 9, 10), but this authority can be removed by the Home Secretary either for contraventions of the law or for irresponsible prescribing (MoDA sections 12 and 13).

These practitioners may also prepare and assemble products and sell, supply or dispense them for their patients. The wording of section 55 requires them to perform these activities personally there being no mention of 'supervision'. It is noteworthy that three doctors were recently found guilty of professional misconduct 'for delegating the work of a registered doctor to people without the appropriate knowledge and skill'. They had allowed their receptionists to insert the details on pre-signed blank prescriptions (*Pharm. J.*, 1984). Clearly, the analogous situation in which the receptionist counts out tablets and labels the containers would also fall within the same form of words.

As mentioned previously, doctors and dentists do not require licences to make or prepare products for administration to their patients nor for importing a product for administration to a named patient.

Veterinarians

Veterinarians do not require licences to prepare and assemble products except for poultry vaccines. Veterinarians do require a product licence in order to import a product; there is no veterinary equivalent of 'the named patient' exemption available to doctors and dentists.

Veterinarians may sell, offer for sale or supply any medicinal product whether or not it is included in the veterinary orders. Such a sale, however, must be 'for administration by him or to an animal or herd under his care' (section 55). In addition, they may issue prescriptions for products including POMs and controlled drugs but again only for administration to animals 'under his care' (section 58), and the prescription must bear a statement to that effect. There is no statutory definition of the term 'under his care' but the Royal College and the British Veterinary Association have issued a joint statement on the matter and this has been reprinted in Appendix 7 of the Guide to Professional Conduct issued by the Royal College of Veterinary Surgeons 1984.

The statement was made in relation to POM and PML products used in animal husbandry and veterinary medicine and pointed out that the lack of a statutory definition was due to the difficulty of drafting one which would apply with precision to every possible case and circumstance. The Royal College has found it necessary for ethical and professional purposes to attempt a definition. In effect, for professional purposes, an animal or herd would be considered to be under a veterinarian's care if the following conditions were met –

'(a) the veterinary surgeon should have been given the responsibility for the health of the animal or herd in question by the owner or his agent;

(b) the care of the animal or herd by the veterinary surgeon should be real and not merely nominal; and

(c) in amplification of (b) above, although circumstances will vary enormously, the veterinary surgeon must at least –

   (i) either have seen the animal or herd for the purposes of diagnosis or prescription and immediately prior thereto; or

   (ii) have visited the farm or other premises on which the animal or herd is kept sufficiently often and recently enough to have acquired from personal knowledge and inspection, an accurate picture of the current health state on that farm sufficient to enable him to make a diagnosis or prescribe for the animal or herd in question.'

The agriculture departments have indicated that they accept this interpretation and are prepared to so advise any other interested party that seeks guidance on the matter. Two Scottish courts have dealt with cases involving consideration of the term and neither of the presiding Sheriffs dissented from the interpretation.

Where an animal or herd is attended both by a local practitioner and by a consultant veterinarian, each must inform the other of the products he is supplying or administering, and there should be regular discussions between them.

Several veterinarians have been convicted of selling products to owners of animals that the veterinarian has never examined or seen. At the subsequent disciplinary hearings, the registrations of two veterinarians were suspended and the name of the third was removed from the Register.

The Guide contains a considerable amount of valuable information and advice regarding the use of antimicrobial products in veterinary practice and animal husbandry. Advice is also given on the use of prostaglandins, on controlled drugs and on the supply and use of products for use in dart guns. The need to keep detailed records of the supply and use of these drugs is also emphasised. Appendix 8 of the Guide contains information on the use of drugs in racehorses and greyhounds and lists those classes of drugs which are prohibited by the Jockey Club. The prescribing and administration of drugs to racehorses and greyhounds, and also to show animals is discussed in Paragraph 13.3 of the Guide.

State Registered Chiropodists

These are persons who are registered in the register established and maintained under section 2(1) of the Professions Supplementary to Medicine Act 1960 by the Chiropodists Board. They may sell or supply or offer or expose for sale or supply in the course of their practice (1980/1924, Schedule 1, Part II, paragraph 1) any of the following products in unopened labelled containers as received from their suppliers –

(1) Any GSL product for external use on human beings;

(2) Any of the following pharmacy medicines for external use –

(a) potassium permanganate crystals or solution;

(b) ointment of heparinoid and hyaluronidase; and

(c) products containing, as their only active ingredients, any of the following substances, at a strength not exceeding that specified –

9.0%	Borotannic complex
10.0%	Buclosamide
3.0%	Chlorquinaldol
1.0%	Clotrimazole
10.0%	Crotamiton
5.0%	Diamthazole Hydrochloride
1.0%	Econazole Nitrate
1.0%	Fenticlor
10.0%	Glutaraldehyde
0.4%	Hydrargaphen
2.0%	Mepyramine Maleate
2.0%	Miconazole Nitrate

2.0% Phenoxypropan-2-ol.
20.0% Podophyllum Resin
10.0% Polynoxylin
70.0% Pyrogallol
70.0% Salicylic Acid
0.1% Thiomersal.

Those registered chiropodists who hold a certificate of competence in the use of analgesics issued by the Chiropodists Board can administer *parenterally* a POM which contains as sole active ingredient the following local analgesics –

Bupivacaine Hydrochloride
Lignocaine Hydrochloride
Mepivacaine Hydrochloride
Prilocaine Hydrochloride

It should be noted that the chiropodists cannot use the injections that contain adrenaline which is perhaps unfortunate.

Midwives

A registered midwife may, in the course of her professional practice, sell or supply (but not offer for sale) –

(a) any GSL or [P] medicine (1980/1924, article 4);

(b) any of the following POMs (1983/1212, Schedule 3(1), paragraph 4) –

Chloral Hydrate
Dichloralphenazone
Ergometrine Maleate (except in parenteral form)
Pentazocine Hydrochloride
Triclofos Sodium

She may also in the course of her professional practice, administer parenterally any of the following POMs (1983/1212 Schedule 3(3), paragraph 2) –

Ergometrine Maleate
Levallorphan Tartrate
Naloxone Hydrochloride
Oxytocins, natural or synthetic
Pentazocine Lactate
Pethidine
Pethidine Hydrochloride
Phytomenadione

and, but only when attending on a woman in childbirth,

Lignocaine
Lignocaine Hydrochloride
Promazine Hydrochloride

The Pethidine and Pethidine Hydrochloride mentioned above are drugs controlled under the Misuse of Drugs Act, consequently, their possession, administration, supply and use are therefore strictly controlled. A special procedure has been laid down enabling the midwife to buy the drugs (see Chapter 8). Regulation 11 of the Misuse of Drugs Regulations permits the midwife to administer the pethidine to her patient. She must record the name and address of each patient to whom she administers the drug, the amount and the form in which it was administered (regulation 21).

Nurses

Nurses employed in NHS hospitals are authorised to administer or supply any product to a patient in accordance with the written directions of a doctor or dentist employed at that hospital. They can obtain the products only from the hospital pharmacy.

The Misuse of Drugs Regulations authorise the sister or acting sister (an expression which includes a male nurse occupying a similar position) in charge of a ward, theatre or department to obtain on a requisition controlled drugs for use on her ward (regulation 14(6)). The sister keeps a copy of the requisition (which was signed by the pharmacist who supplied the drug) and the pharmacist keeps the original. In fact, a special requisition book is issued by the DHSS and contains provision for the signature of the person who carries the drug from the pharmacy to the ward.

The sister can administer or supply such drugs to the patients on her ward in accordance with the directions of a doctor or dentist. Although regulation 19(3) specifically exempts her from the need to keep records of the drugs administered, all hospitals follow the recommendations of the Aitken Report (1958) and insist that such records be kept. Likewise, the sister may herself destroy drugs that are no longer required (regulation 24), but she would be better advised to do so in the presence of a pharmacist, and many hospitals actually lay down a procedure for this.

Nurses employed in factories etc.. Those nurses employed at places of work have been given a group authority under the Misuse of Drugs Regulations to possess any drug specified in Schedule 2 to the Regulations. The authority is subject to the following conditions –

(1) the drug may only be administered to persons injured or taken ill at that place of work;

(2) the drug must have been supplied to the nurse by the authorised medical officer of the place of work, and in a quantity considered necessary by the medical officer;

(3) the drug shall be kept in a locked receptacle of which every key shall be in the possession of the nurse;

(4) the nurse shall record in a register every amount administered;

(5) the drug and the register shall be produced by that nurse for inspection by any constable or other person authorised in writing by the Secretary of State;

(6) any loss or theft of the drug shall be immediately reported to the police, and to the Chief Inspector, Drugs Branch.

Nurses and certificated first-aid persons employed at mines. These have been authorised by the Home Secretary to possess any drug specified in Schedule 2 to the regulations and to supply or offer to supply any drug specified in Schedules 1 or 2 in the following circumstances –

(a) the nurse may only supply or offer to supply the drug for immediate emergency administration to persons injured at the mine;

(b) the nurse or first-aider may only possess those drugs supplied by a doctor and in the amount the doctor considered reasonably necessary for the purpose;

(c) the authority to possess does not extend to any purpose other than for immediate emergency administration to a person injured at the mine.

The drug must (except when required for use) be kept in a locked receptacle at the mine and every key must be in the possession of the nurse or other authorised person, the mine manager or a person authorised by him. It must be produced for inspection on request by a constable or person authorised in writing by the Home Secretary. If a drug is lost or stolen the facts must be reported immediately to the police and in writing to the Chief Inspector Drugs Branch at the Home Office. The nurse must keep a controlled drugs register and enter therein full details of all Schedule 2 drugs received and supplied.

These group authorities are recognised by the POM Order (Schedule 3(3), paragraph 3).

Registered Ophthalmic Opticians

These are persons who are registered in either of the registers of ophthalmic opticians established and maintained under section 2(a) of the Opticians Act 1958. They can buy certain products from a pharmacy for use in their practices (1983/1212, Schedule 3(1), paragraph 5). They must provide a signed order.

They can also 'prescribe' the same eye products for their patients (1983/1212, Schedule 3(1), paragraph 6).

In emergencies, they can also sell or supply these products in the course of their professional practice directly to their patients (1980/1924, Schedule 1(1), paragraph 2). The products concerned are –

(a) all products on the GSL, all pharmacy medicines, any POMs not for parenteral use which are specified in (b) or (c) below;

(b) products that are eyedrops or eye ointments and which are POM only because they contain Mafenide Propionate or not more than 30% Sulphacetamide Sodium, or Sulphafurazole Diethanolamine equivalent to not more than 4% Sulphafurazole;

(c) are POM products only because they contain any of the following substances –

Atropine Sulphate
Bethanechol Chloride
Carbachol
Cyclopentolate Hydrochloride
Homatropine Hydrobromide
Hyoscine Hydrobromide
Naphazoline Hydrochloride
Naphazoline Nitrate
Neostigmine Methylsulphate
Physostigmine Salicylate
Physostigmine Sulphate
Pilocarpine Hydrochloride
Pilocarpine Nitrate
Tropicamide

Among the products described in (a) above which ophthalmic opticians may use or sell or supply in an emergency to their patients are eyedrops containing Adrenaline (Acid Tartrate or Hydrochloride) and Ephedrine Hydrochloride which are exempt from POM when used externally (e.g. in eye preparations). In addition there are eye preparations which are only [P], e.g. Antazoline,

Diphenhydramine, Phenylephrine, Zinc Sulphate, Xylometazoline. No eyedrops and no eye ointments are GSL (see 1984/769, Schedule 3).

An ophthalmic optician may purchase eye ointments containing Oxyphenbutazone, and also any POM which is POM only because it contains one or more of the following –

Amethocaine Hydrochloride
Framycetin Sulphate
Lignocaine Hydrochloride
Oxybuprocaine Hydrochloride
Proxymetacaine Hydrochloride
Thymoxamine Hydrochloride

(See 1980/1923, article 5(2)c.)

Acupuncturists, Naturopaths, Osteopaths

Such persons can administer parenteral products which are POM solely because they are for parenteral use, if they were customarily doing so on the 11th February 1982, but only if asked by a patient to use his own judgment as to the treatment required. Examples of parenteral products that can be used by such healers are local analgesics (1983/1212, Schedule 3(3), paragraph 7).

Schemes for the Prevention of Dental Caries

There are two such schemes, one (the pre-school dental scheme) for under-fives, and the other for older children (school dental scheme). Both schemes must be supervised by a doctor or dentist. The persons running the school or a health authority may supply pharmacy medicines containing sodium fluoride for the use of children whose parents have previously consented to the supply. In the pre-school scheme the supply must be made by a registered or enrolled nurse (1980/1924, Schedule 1(2), paragraphs 10, 11).

OTHER SPECIAL USERS

Owner or Master of a Ship not Carrying a Doctor

The owner or master of a ship that does not carry a doctor as part of her complement can supply any medicinal product necessary for the treatment of persons on board his ship (1980/1924, Schedule 1(2), paragraph 8).

Furthermore, he may supply (or administer parenterally) any POM necessary for the treatment of anyone on the ship (1983/1212, Schedule 3(2) and (3) and article 4). This includes any controlled drug specified in the relevant parts of the Merchant Shipping Acts, though the Misuse of Drugs Regulations actually states that the owner may only supply a controlled drug to a member of his crew (regulations 8(5)a and 9(5)a). This would seem to imply that such a drug could not lawfully be supplied to the survivors from another vessel, but it would be a mean-spirited individual who would attempt to prosecute in such a case.

The master may obtain any medicine necessary for the treatment of persons on the ship (1980/1923, article 5(2)). A requisition is necessary for controlled drugs (see Chapter 8 for details). He must record each supply by making an entry in the ship's logbook, or, if the ship is not required to carry a logbook, by means of a signed report (regulation 21(1)).

The Operator or Commander of an Aircraft

The operator (i.e. the person for the time being having the management of the aircraft) or commander of an aircraft has analogous powers to supply any medicine (other than one for parenteral use) which has been supplied for use on the aircraft in response to an order written by a doctor. Such medicines can only be used when necessary for the immediate treatment of sick or injured persons on the aircraft (1980/1924, Schedule 1(2), paragraph 12).

He can also supply or administer POMs to persons needing immediate treatment. He uses the medicines in accordance with instructions which have been previously written by a doctor. The aircraft is supplied with medicines on a written order signed by a doctor (1983/1212, Schedule 3(2), paragraph 6; Schedule 3(3), paragraph 6).

Offshore Installation Manager

Under the Misuse of Drugs Regulations, such a person is entitled to possess and supply drugs controlled under Schedules 2 or 3 to anyone on the installation (regulations 8(5)(b), 9(5)(b), and 10) whether or not the person supplied is employed thereon. The manager must record the supply in the installation's log-book (regulation 21(2)).

This group of persons is not specifically mentioned in the medicines legislation, but is presumably included among those who are required by law to provide medical treatment for employees.

Persons Required by Law to Provide Medical Treatment of their Employees

They may supply those POMs and pharmacy medicines specified in the enactment and any GSL products.

The supply shall be to enable them to comply with the enactment and subject to the conditions and circumstances specified therein (1980/1924, Schedule 1, Part II, paragraph 7).

Royal National Lifeboat Institution and Certificated First Aiders

These can supply any medicinal product necessary for the treatment of sick or injured persons.

The Home Secretary has issued a group authority to coxswains, motor mechanics and crew members of the Royal National Lifeboat Institution under regulations 8(3) and 10(3) of the Misuse of Drugs Regulations 1973. This enables them to possess any drug specified in Schedule 2, and to supply or offer to supply any drug in Schedules 1 or 2 to anyone who may lawfully possess that drug. The authorisation is limited to possession and supply in the course of their service or employment and in the following circumstances –

(a) the supply or offer to supply is only for immediate administration to sick or injured persons at sea by a certificated first-aid crew member;

(b) the coxswain or motor mechanic may only possess those drugs supplied to him by the honorary medical adviser to that lifeboat station;

(c) the certificated first-aid crew member may only possess a drug if it is required for immediate administration to a sick or injured person and has been supplied to him by the coxswain or motor mechanic.

A 'certificated first-aid crew member' is a person serving in a lifeboat of the Institution who possesses a first-aid qualification approved by the Institution and who has been individually certified in writing by the honorary medical adviser to that station, as competent to administer drugs specified in Schedules 1 and 2.

The drug in a person's possession must be kept in a locked receptacle, every key of which must be in the possession of the coxswain or motor mechanic. The drug must be produced for inspection when required by a constable or any other authorised person. If any drug is lost or stolen, the facts must be reported immediately to the police and in writing to the Chief Inspector, Drugs Branch of the Home Office. A controlled drugs register must be kept and full details of all drugs obtained and supplied must be entered in it.

First-aiders and Nursing Members of Certain Voluntary Bodies

The bodies concerned include the British Red Cross Society, St.John Ambulance Association and Brigade, St.Andrew Ambulance Association and the Order of Malta Ambulance Corps. Certificated first-aid and certificated nursing members of these organisations
are entitled to supply all pharmacy medicines and all products on a general sale list, so far as is necessary for the treatment of sick or injured persons.

Persons Licensed Under Regulation 5 of the Misuse of Drugs Regulations 1973 or Regulation 5 of the Misuse of Drugs (Northern Ireland) Regulations 1974 to Supply a Controlled Drug

These persons are manufacturers of controlled drugs and medicines containing them. The Home Office licence has enabled them to manufacture, sell, supply and possess these drugs and products lawfully under the Misuse of Drugs legislation. These products are either POM or [P] medicines under the Medicines Act and consequently the manufacturer needs to be able to sell or supply lawfully under that Act. Such authority is granted subject to the conditions and in such circumstances as are specified in the Home Office licence by 1980/1924, Schedule 1(II), paragraph 6.

Persons Operating an Occupational Health Scheme

An 'occupational health scheme' means a scheme in which a person, in the course of a business carried on by him, provides facilities for his employees for the treatment or prevention of disease. Such a person may supply any pharmacy medicine, any GSL product and any POM supplied in response to a written order signed by a doctor or a nurse.

The supply shall only be in the course of the health scheme, and the person supplying or administering the product shall be a doctor or a nurse. Where the product is a POM the supply shall be in accordance with the written instructions of the doctor as to the circumstances in which it is to be used (1980/1924, Schedule 1(2), paragraph 9; 1983/1212, Schedules 3(2), paragraph 5, and 3(3), paragraph 5).

The person operating the scheme obtains the products by means of a written order signed either by a registered nurse or a doctor.

Manufacturers of Product for the Treatment of the Hair or Scalp

The manufacturer must hold a manufacturer's licence which permits the manufacture of the product. The licence must also contain a provision that enables the manufacturer to use his own judgment as to the treatment required and make the product at the request of the patient and in his presence (1980/1924, Schedule 1(1), paragraph 3). The products shall be for external use only and are either GSL or contain only the following pharmacy medicines –

not more than 5.0% of Boric Acid;
Isopropyl Myristate or Lauryl Sulphate;
not more than 0.004% Oestrogens;
not more than 1.0% of Resorcinol;
not more than 3.0% of Salicylic Acid;
not more than 0.2% of Sodium Pyrithione or Zinc Pyrithione.

Persons Selling to Veterinarians

Can sell all medicinal products and no conditions are applicable (1980/19224, Schedule 1, Part I, paragraph 9).

Sales to British Standards Institution

All medicinal products can be sold or supplied in response to a written order signed on behalf of the Institution and stating the status of the signatory. The order shall state the amount of the medicinal product required, and that the product is required only for the purpose of testing containers of medicinal products or determining the standards for such containers (1980/1924, Schedule 1(1), paragraph 10).

Product Licence Holders and Manufacturer's Licence Holders

May sell the products covered by their licences –

(a) to a pharmacist,

(b) so as to enable him to prepare an entry relating to the medicinal product in question in a tablet or capsule identification guide or similar publication, and

(c) of no greater quantity than is reasonably necessary for that purpose (1980/1924, Schedule 1(1), paragraph 11).

Universities and Other Institutions Concerned with Higher Education or Research

These can buy and use any medicine whether POM, [P] or GSL provided that the product is required for education or research. There is a difference between universities and hospitals on the one hand, and other educational or research institutes on the other in respect of controlled drugs. The former can use drugs subject to full control while the latter can only use those which are CD no register. When an institution requires access to fully controlled drugs, it may seek the approval of the Home Secretary for the purpose.

Persons Supplying First Aid Equipment for Liferafts and Air–Sea Rescue Launches

Persons who manufacture or service liferafts intended to be carried on aircraft, or who provide such liferafts or who have a contract with the Crown for the manufacture, service or repair of aircraft or air–sea rescue launches, have been issued with a group authority to possess and supply certain controlled drugs.

The authority enables them to supply or offer to supply any drug in Schedule 1 or 2 to the Misuse of Drugs Regulations 1973 when the drug is contained in a first-aid kit. The supply or offer may only be made to a person who may lawfully possess the drug.

The authorised person must keep a controlled drugs register in the usual form, and must enter therein details of all drugs in Schedule 2 obtained and supplied by him. This register (and any drug in his possession) must be produced on request of a constable or any person authorised in writing by the Home Secretary.

The authority also enables him to possess the drugs in Schedule 2. All such drugs must be kept in a locked receptacle (unless contained in a first-aid kit) which can only be opened by him. The first-aid kits must similarly be stored in a locked part of the premises constructed and maintained so as to prevent unauthorised access to the drug. The person must immediately report to the police any lost or stolen drugs and also notify the Chief Inspector Drugs Branch in writing.

References

Pharm. J., 1984, 2, 677

Aitken Report 1958, Report of the Joint Committee on 'Control of Dangerous Drugs and Poisons in Hospitals'

Chapter 12
Herbal Remedies

INTRODUCTION

These have a long history and most of the naturally occurring medicines used today originated as herbal remedies. Their use declined during the 'therapeutic explosion' in which numerous sulphonamides, tranquillisers, and other classes of drugs were synthesised. Currently they (and other 'alternative regimes') are undergoing a resurgence in popularity. Many people feel that, being 'natural' they are superior to synthetics, and certainly many of them do not give rise to the side-effects that frequently accompany the use of the pure active constituents.

In theory, herbal remedies are subject to the same controls as other medicines but provision was made to exempt them from some restrictions in certain circumstances. Section 12 exempts some of them from licensing. Section 56 exempts sellers of certain herbal remedies from the restrictions imposed by sections 52 and 53 but these exemptions have been modified and limited by the Herbal Remedies Order 1977. The position is further complicated by the fact that although some herbalists have studied and obtained qualifications in the subject, others have not and at present there is nothing to prevent anyone from calling himself a herbalist.

For the sake of simplicity, sellers of herbal remedies by retail can be divided into three classes –

(a) shop-keepers, e.g. 'health food' shops, supermarkets, grocers;

(b) herbalists, i.e. persons who make and sell herbal remedies to persons who seek their advice;

(c) pharmacists.

MEANING OF 'HERBAL REMEDY'

In the Act 'herbal remedy' means a medicinal product consisting of a substance produced by subjecting a plant or plants to drying, crushing or any other process, or of a mixture whose sole ingredients are two or more substances so produced, or of a mixture whose sole ingredients are one or more substances so produced and water or some other inert substance; (section 132).

Thus they appear in a variety of forms. At the one extreme, the remedy may simply be the dried leaves, stems, etc. of a plant which might be crudely broken or crushed, senna pods would be a common example. Such a remedy would probably be used by soaking it in water and drinking the infusion or decoction. At the other extreme, herbal remedies may be tablets or capsules containing the powdered drug or an extract thereof. Volatile oils distilled from various leaves and liquid extracts and tinctures made by percolating the drug with alcohol are also common ingredients of herbal remedies.

LICENSING

Like all other medicinal products, herbal remedies are subject to licensing, but two types of herbals are exempt from this under the terms of section 12, namely –

1. A herbal remedy made or packed on the premises of a herbalist, when the product is sold or supplied to a patient who has asked the herbalist to use his judgment as to the treatment required (i.e. the herbalist has 'counter-prescribed' the product) (section 12(1)). These are often called 'herbal practitioner's remedies'.
2. Products made ONLY by drying, crushing or comminuting (i.e. breaking up) plants and which is labelled with the name of the plant and the process but not with any other name. Such a product must not contain any written recommendations to its use as a remedy (section 12(2)). These are not available as tablets, capsules, extracts.

It follows therefore, that herbal products made, packed and intended for a wide distribution and labelled with indications for use must be licensed.

CONTROL OVER SALES

Whoever sells them must do so from a shop or other premises that can be closed so as to exclude the public, unless they are for veterinary use. Although a few herbalists still collect and dry etc. their own plants, most herbalists and all other retailers buy pre-packed herbal remedies from specialist manufacturers.

Ordinary Shopkeepers

Any shopkeeper can sell a herbal product which is a dried and crushed or comminuted plant provided that the plant is not mentioned either in Table 1 or Table 2 and the product bears no written recommendation. Such shopkeepers can also sell GSL herbals. The products must have been prepared, packed and labelled elsewhere than where sold, and the retailer may only sell them in unopened containers.

Herbalists

These are usually persons who have studied the subject and many of them are members or fellows of the National Institute of Medical Herbalists. They normally have premises at which they make and sell herbal remedies to persons who seek their advice. To take full advantage of his position, the herbalist must notify the enforcement authority in writing of his name and business address, and state that he sells herbal remedies to which Article 2 of the Herbal Remedies Order applies, i.e. those specified in Table 2 provided that the product is labelled to show a strength or dose not exceeding that shown in the Table (article 3). A herbalist holding a manufacturer's licence in respect of a remedy need not notify the enforcement authority.

Herbalists can, of course, sell those products which can be sold by any shopkeeper. In addition, a herbalist can sell the same herbs in the form of tablets, pills or mixed with water.

A herbalist may prepare unlicensed herbal remedies for his patients in the same way as a pharmacist may 'counter-prescribe', i.e. he can mix together (herbal) products to produce a preparation he believes to be suitable for a patient present in his shop who has asked the herbalist to use his own knowledge as to the treatment required (article 3(4)). To do this, he must have notified the enforcement authority that he carries out this activity. The authority may require him to specify the herbal remedies that he sells or supplies in such circumstances (article 3(5)).

He may also supply unopened containers of herbal remedies he has purchased without holding a licence.

A herbalist will require a licence to –

(1) Repack or re-label a product he has bought for re-sale. For this purpose he will need a manufacturer's licence (assembly) and he will either need to comply with the original product licence or with an Article 3 direction (see Chapter 4, page 9 and Chapter 6, page 6).

(2) Alter the composition of a product (a manufacturer's licence) and if he is responsible for the composition of the final product he will need a product licence too.

Where the herbalist wishes to mix together herbal products made by someone else for 'counter-prescribing' and these products are not products which can only be sold from a pharmacy and they are not advertised, he may apply for a manufacturer's licence under the provisions of article 2 of the Special and Transitional Cases Order. This obviates the need to hold separate product licences for these products. Special application forms (MAL 24A and MAL 24B) are available respectively for manufacturer's licences authorising mixture and assembly or assembly only.

Pharmacists

These can sell any herbal remedy without restriction. They do not require licences to prepare or pack such products.

LABELLING AND ADVERTISING

Where a herbal remedy is licensed for use for any of the indications, diseases or disorders specified in Schedule 2 to the Labelling and Advertising to the Public Regulations it may be labelled with directions for use in the prevention or treatment of any of those conditions if –

(1) the label on the container and any package of the product and any leaflet supplied with it contains the phrase 'A herbal remedy for . ...'.

(2) similarly, the product must also be labelled

'Warning: If you think you have [ ] consult a registered medical practitioner before taking this product. If you are already receiving medical treatment, tell your doctor that you are also taking this product.'

The warning must be enclosed in a rectangle containing no other matter of any kind.

In 1 and 2 above, the name of the disease for the treatment of which the herbal remedy is sold must be inserted into the phrase and in the warning after the words 'If you think you have'. For the words 'this product' in paragraph 2 the name of the product may be substituted, but no other words may be substituted.

Among the diseases, complaints and purposes specified in Schedule 2 are infections, diseases of the heart, kidneys, lungs, menstrual disorders and psychiatric conditions. These are, of course, potentially serious conditions the advertising of remedies for which is normally prohibited. No reference may be made to the diseases mentioned in Schedule 1 to the regulations (cancer, tuberculosis and the like). Furthermore, no mention may be made of any of the diseases specified in Schedule 4, e.g. amenorrhoea, angina, atherosclerosis, erysipelas, gallstones, multiple sclerosis, osteoarthritis, phlebitis, thrombosis, or ulcers (except in the phrase aphthous ulcer or mouth ulcer) unless it is required to explain contra-indications or precautions.

Table 1 Herbal remedies containing one or more of these substances are pharmacy medicines [P]

Common name	Botanical source
Areca	*Areca catechu*
Canadian Hemp	*Apocynum cannabinum*
Catha	*Catha edulis*
Chenopodium	*Chenopodium ambrosioides var anthelminticum*
Crotalaria fulva	*Crotalaria berberoana*
Crotalaria spect.	*Crotalaria spectabilis*
Cucurbita	*Cucurbita maxima*
Duboisia	*Duboisia myoporoides*
	Duboisia leichardtii
Elaterium	*Ecballium elaterium*
Embelia	*Embelia ribes*
	Embelia robusta
Erysimum	*Erysimum canescens*
Holarrhena	*Holarrhena antidysenterica*
Kamala	*Mallotus philippinensis*
Kousso	*Brayera anthelmintica*
Male Fern	*Dryopteris filix-mas*
Mistletoe Berry	*Viscum album*
Poison Ivy	*Rhus radicans*
Pomegranate Bark	*Punica granatum*
Santonica	*Artemisia cina*
Savin	*Juniperus sabina*
Scopolia	*Scopolia carniolica*
	Scopolia japonica
Stavesacre Seeds	*Delphinium staphisagria*
Strophanthus	*Strophanthus kombe*
	Strophanthus courmonti
	Strophanthus nicholsoni
	Strophanthus gratus
	Strophanthus emini
	Strophanthus sarmentosus
	Strophanthus hispidus
Slippery Elm Bark	*Ulmus fulva*
(whole or unpowdered)	*Ulmus rubra*
Yohimbe Bark	*Pausinystalia yohimbe*

Table 2 Herbal remedies containing one or more of these substances are pharmacy medicines, but may be sold by herbalists if the remedy contains less than the stated maximum dose or percentage

Substance			
Common name	Botanical source	Maximum dose and maximum daily dose	Percentage
Aconite	*Aconitum napellus* *Aconitum stoerkianum* *Aconitum uncinatum var japonicum* *Aconitum deinorrhizum* *Aconitum balfourii* *Aconitum chasmanthum* *Aconitum spicatum* *Aconitum lycoctonum*		
Adonis vernalis	*Adonis vernalis*	100 mg(MD) 300 mg(MDD)	
Belladonna herb	*Atropa belladonna* *Atropa acuminata*	50 mg(MD) 150 mg(MDD)	
Belladonna root	*Atropa belladonna* *Atropa acuminata*	30 mg(MD) 90 mg(MDD)	
Celandine	*Chelidonium majus*	2 g (MD) 6 g (MDD)	
Cinchona bark	*Cinchona calisaya* *Cinchona ledgerana* *Cinchona officinalis* *Cinchona succirubra* *Cinchona micrantha*	250 mg(MD) 750 mg(MDD)	
Colchicum corm	*Colchicum autumnale*	100 mg(MD) 300 mg(MDD)	
Conium leaf	*Conium maculatum*		7.0%
Conium fruits	*Conium maculatum*		7.0%
Convallaria	*Convallaria majalis*	150 mg(MD) 450 mg(MDD)	
Ephedra	*Ephedra sinica* *Ephedra equisetina* *Ephedra distachya* *Ephedra intermedia* *Ephedra gerardiana*	600 mg(MD) 1800 mg(MDD)	

Gelsemium	*Gelsemium sempervirens*	25mg (MD) 75 mg(MDD)	
Hyoscyamus	*Hyoscyamus niger* *Hyoscyamus albus* *Hyoscyamus muticus*	100 mg(MD) 300 mg(MDD)	
Jaborandi	*Pilocarpus jaborandi* *Pilocarpus microphyllus*		5.0%
Lobelia	*Lobelia inflata*	200 mg(MD) 600 mg(MDD)	
Poison Oak	*Rhus toxicodendron*		10.0%
Quebracho	*Aspidosperma quebracho-blanco*	50 mg(MD) 150 mg(MDD)	
Ragwort	*Senecio jacobaea*		10.0%
Stramonium	*Datura stramonium* *Datura innoxia*	50 mg(MD) 150 mg(MDD)	

Chapter 13
Homoeopathy and Similar Systems of Medicine

INTRODUCTION

Homoeopathy is a system of therapeutics which is based on the principle that 'like cures like', i.e. a medicinal product which will produce the symptoms of a given disease when administered to human beings, is used to treat persons suffering from that disease. A characteristic of homoeopathy is the concentration of the medicinal product used, this is usually very low, e.g. one in a million or even lower. Another characteristic of homoeopathic and related therapies is that they are not specific to a disease but are chosen to meet the specific requirements of a particular patient, the disease and other factors. This calls into question the real value of proprietary brands of homoeopathic remedies. For this reason, the Council of the Pharmaceutical Society of Great Britain believes that pharmacists should not make them available by self-selection.

Homoeopathy makes most use of herbal products or relatively simple inorganic minerals. An extract or tincture of the herbal material (called the mother tincture) is first prepared, and this is serially diluted usually with a dilute alcohol solution either one in ten or more commonly one in a hundred, several times. The 'potency' of the resulting product is stated in terms of the number of dilutions and whether each was one in ten (referred to as x) or one in a hundred (referred to as c). Thus a potency of 3x means that the mother tincture was diluted one in ten three times (in other words it now contains one part of the mother tincture in a thousand parts of product). A 6c product has been diluted six times each time being diluted one in a hundred, so that it now contains one part in a million million! An important feature in the making of these dilutions is vigorous shaking between each dilution, this is called 'succussion'. Products made from insoluble substances are prepared by the method of trituration, i.e. carefully mixed with a solid inert diluent such as lactose. The mother tincture or the first dilution of the drug is called the 'unit preparation', and this term is throughout the Act and its subordinate legislation. The final product is almost invariably administered orally in the form of powders, granules, or tablets though there are a few topical preparations, e.g. arnica ointment. Homoeopaths do not use parenteral products, though some similar systems do, e.g. anthroposophy.

'Unit preparation' means a preparation, including a mother tincture, prepared by a process of solution, extraction or trituration with a view to being diluted tenfold or one hundredfold, either once or repeatedly, in an inert diluent, and then used either in this diluted form or, where applicable, by impregnating tablets, granules, powders or other inert substances for the purpose of being administered to human beings; (1983/1212; 1980/1924).

Biochemic Remedies

A similar system using only certain inorganic salts found in living cells was developed by Dr W H Schuessler in the last century. This is called the 'biochemic' system. The remedies consist of one or more of 12 tissue salts all used in homoeopathic concentrations.

Anthroposophic Remedies

Anthroposophy was founded by Rudolph Steiner and views man as being composed of a body, a soul and a spirit. Illness is regarded as a disturbance of the three elements, and treatment is therefore based on restoring the balance. Anthroposophic medicine can only be studied by medically qualified persons and takes a minimum of 3 years. Most practitioners learn the skills and techniques in Germany.

The treatments are based on plants and relatively simple minerals. The doses used are tiny, very similar to homoeopathic potencies.

Bach Remedies

This is a range of remedies made from flowers many of which are included in Table 3 below. The stock solutions sold to the public are about 3x but when diluted as instructed the patient takes a dose approximating to 6x. There is no instruction relating to 'succussion'.

LICENSING

Like all medicines, homoeopathic, biochemic, etc. remedies are subject to licensing when made up for sale otherwise than on a prescription or 'counter-prescribed' by a homoeopath or a pharmacist. They are also classified as GSL or [P] according to what is present and the concentration. It is indicative of the difference in outlook between allopathic (i.e. conventional) medicine and homoeopathy that the weakest preparations in terms of concentration are regarded as 'safest' by the expert committees but regarded as the most potent by homoeopaths!

The details of the restrictions upon, and the exemptions applicable to, various prescribers and sellers of homoeopathic remedies are contained in the Pharmacy and General Sale – Exemption Order (1980/1924 as amended) article 6 and Schedule 2, and in the Products other than Veterinary Drugs (Prescription Only) Order (1983/1212 as amended), article 8.

PRACTITIONERS AND SELLERS

Many homoeopathic practitioners are fully qualified medical practitioners who use homoeopathic remedies routinely or even exclusively. Such practitioners have, of course, all the rights and privileges of medical practitioners under the Act and can make, use, prescribe and administer any product to their patients without needing a licence under the Act. Some veterinarians use homoeopathic remedies and have analogous rights and privileges.

Other homoeopaths are not registered medical practitioners. They can sell, offer or expose for sale, and can 'counter-prescribe' certain homoeopathic remedies in the course of their practice. The products may be made by them but more usually are purchased from specialist suppliers. Some pharmacists sell homoeopathic remedies and a small number have been trained to dispense homoeopathic prescriptions. Homoeopaths can sell and supply any of the following products and are exempt from the provisions of section 52 (i.e. they can sell etc. from premises which are not registered pharmacies, etc.) and from section 53 (i.e. they are not restricted to selling unopened packs of products which have been packed and labelled elsewhere) so long as the products are neither for injection nor controlled drugs (as stated above, injections are not used, and only the only controlled drug used in homoeopathy is opium and that is used in 'potency', i.e. in concentrations that are neither POM nor CD) and the purchaser is present and has asked the homoeopath to use his own judgment as to the treatment required –

1. unit preparations diluted to at least (6x)(even if the drug is POM);
2. unit preparations of any product in Table 1 below, diluted to at least (3x);
3. any substance in column 1 of Table A of Schedule 3 to the GSL or in Table 3 below, where the unit preparation has been diluted to at least one in ten (1x);
4. any substance for external use listed in column 1 of Table B of Schedule 3 of the GSL Order or in Table 4 below, where the unit preparation has been diluted at least one in ten (1x).

(N.B. the GSL Order mentioned in 3 and 4 above was 1980 Order as amended, and the substances concerned were ingredients of products having licences of right. In the 1984 Order these substances are listed in column 1 of Table A or Table B of Schedule 2.)

Lastly, some homoeopathic remedies can be sold in unopened containers as received from the manufacturer or wholesaler, from any shop, i.e. they are GSL. Such products must not be for parenteral use nor contain controlled drugs. The remedies are –

1. any substance (including POMs) where the unit preparation is diluted to at least one in a million million (6c);
2. any substance in Table 2 where the unit preparation is diluted to at least one in a million (6x);
3. any of the products in 3 and 4 above.

LABELLING AND ADVERTISING

When these medicines are sold to the public otherwise than on prescription or when 'counter-prescribed' by a pharmacist or homoeopath, the usual labelling requirements apply (for details see Chapter 15). In addition, remedies labelled (or containing a leaflet) for the prevention or treatment of any of the diseases mentioned in column 1 of Parts I–IV of Schedule 2 to the Labelling and Advertising to the Public Regulations, or for any purpose mentioned in Part V thereof must be labelled –

'a homoeopathic remedy for ....' or
'a biochemic remedy for...' or
'an anthroposophic remedy for. ....'.

and the name of the disease for which it is sold must be stated.

Furthermore, a label stating –

'Warning: If you think you have .... consult a registered medical practitioner before taking this product. If you are already receiving medical treatment, tell your doctor that you are also taking this product.'
must be applied to the product (1978/41, regulation 9 and Schedule 5).

Only homoeopathic remedies diluted to at least 6x may be sold for such purposes. The label or leaflet of a 3x product could not mention any of the above diseases or purposes.

Table 1 Dilutions of unit preparations diluted to at least one part in a thousand (3x)

Agaricus muscarius
Ailanthus glandulosa
Apocynum cannabinum
Aurum iodatum
Belladonna
Bismuth Subgallate
Bryonia alba dioica
Calcium Fluoride
Cantharis
Cerium oxalicum
Chelidonium majus
Chenopodium oil
Cina
Colocynthis
Convallaria majalis
Gelsemium sempervirens
Hyoscyamus niger
Lycopodium
Manganese acetate
Ranunculus bulbosus
Terebinthinae oleum

Table 2 Dilutions of unit preparations diluted to at least one part in a million (6x)

Adonis vernalis	Balsamum copaivae
Agaricus bulbosus	Balsamum peruvianum
Agaricus muscarius	Barium Citrate
Agnus castus	Barium Sulphate
Ailanthus glandulosa	Bismuth Metal
Alum	Bismuth Subgallate
Amethyst	Bismuth Subnitrate
Ammonium Iodide	Boletus laricis
Amygdalae amarae	Bovista
Apatite	Cade Oil
Apocynum androsaemifolium	Calcium Fluoride
Apocynum cannabinum	Cantharis
Argentite	Carduus marianus
Argentum Chloride	Cedar Wood Oil
Argentum Iodide	Cerium Oxalicum
Arnica	Chalcocite
Artemisia cina	Chalcopyrite
Aspidium filix-mas	Chelidonium majus
Aspidium anthelmintica	Chenopodium Oil
Aurum Sulphide	Colocynthis

Convallaria majalis
Copper Silicate, Nat.
Crotalus horridus
Cucurbita
Cucumis melo
Datura stramonium
Derris
Diamond
Ephedra vulgaris
Ferric Acetate
Ferrous Iodide
Ferrous Oxalate
Ferrous Sulphide
Formic Acid
Gall
Gelsemium sempervirens
Gneiss
Granatum (Pomegranate Bark)
Hamamelis virginiana
Hepar Sulfuris
Hyoscyamus niger
Iris florentine
Jaborandi
Juniperus sabina
Kaolinite
Lachmanthus tinctoria
Lapis Albus
Lycopodium
Magnesium
Magnesium Acetate
Magnesium Chloride
Magnetite
Manganese Acetate
Nicotiana tabacum
Nicotiana tabacum oil
Oleander
Opuntia vulgaris
Oxalic Acid
Petroleum
Phellandrum aquaticum
Pix Liquida
Platinum
Platinum Chloride
Potassium Hydroxide
Potassium Silicate
Pyrethrum
Pyrolusite
Ranunculus acris
Ranunculus bulbosus
Ranunculus flammula
Ranunculus repens
Ranunculus sceleratus
Rhodium Oxynitrate
Rhododendron chrysanthemum
Rhus toxicodendron
Salicylic Acid
Scrophularia Aquatica
Sodium Aluminium Chloride
Sodium Auro-chloride
Sodium Hypochlorite
Sodium Nitrate
Squill
Stannum Metal
Staphisagria
Sulphur Iodide
Tamus communis
Tannic Acid
Terebinthinae Oleum
Theridion
Thuja occidentalis
Topaz
Uric Acid
Zinc Hypophosphite
Zinc Isovalerate

Table 3 Dilutions of unit preparations diluted to at least one part in ten (1x)

Abies excelsa
Abies nigra
Abies nobilis
Acalypha indica
Agate
Alisma plantago Aq.
Alstonia scholaris
Aluminium
Amber (Succinum)
Amber grisea
Ammonium Phosphate
Angostura vera
Anthoxanthum
Apis mellifera
Aqua Marina
Aqua Mellis
Aralia racemosa
Aranea diadema
Arum maculatum
Arum triphyllum
Asarum
Asperula odorata
Astacus fluviatilis
Auric Chloride
Badiaga
Beech (fagus sylvestris)
Bellis perennis
Berberis aquifolium
Borago officinalis
Butyric Acid

Calcium Metal
Calcium Chloride
Calcium Oxide
Calcium Sulphate
Castoreum
Ceanothus americanus
Cedron
Cerato (Ceratostigma Willmottiana)
Cherry Plum (Prunus cerasifera)
Chestnut, Red and Sweet
Cholesterinum
Chrysolite
Cistus canadensis
Clematis erecta
Conchae vera
Conchiolinum
Corallium Rubrum
Crab Apple
Crocus sativus
Erbium
Erigeron Canadense
Fuligo
Genista tinctoria
Geum urbanum
Glycogen
Gnaphalium leontopodium
Gold
Gorse (Ulex europocus)
Graphites
Gratiola officinalis
Gymnocladus (American Coffee Tree)
Haematoxylon campechianum
Hecla Lava (Ash from Mount Hecla)
Hedeoma pulegioides
Hedera helix
Heliotrope
Heracleum spondylium
Herniaria
Hornbeam (Carpinus betulus)
Iberis amara
Impatiens
Iris germanica
Iris pseudacorus
Jacaranda procera
Jatropha curcas
Juncus communis
Justicia adhatoda
Lamium album
Laurus nobilis oil
Laurocerasus
Ledum Palustre
Lillium tigrinum
Lonicera caprifolium
Lysimachia vulgaris
Magnesium Phosphate
Magnesite
Magnolia
Marum verum
Melilotus officinalis
Menispermum canadense
Mephitis putorius
Mercurialis perennis
Mimulus (Mimullis guttatus)
Moschus
Myrica gale
Myrtus communis
Ocimum basilicum
Olive
Oxalis acetosella
Pangamic Acid
Paullinia cupana
Penthorum sedoides
Pollen (mixed)
Polygonatum multiflorum
Polygonum aviculare
Polypodium vulgare
Primula vulgaris
Prunella vulgaris
Ptelea trifoliata
Ratanhia
Robinia pseudoacacia
Rubia tinctorium
Rumex acetosella
Sal Marina
Sarcolactic Acid
Sarracenia purpurea
Scleranthus (Scleranthus annuus)
Silica
Silphium laciniatum
Sodium Benzoate
Spongia marina
Star of Bethlehem (Ornithogalum umbellatum)
Ulmus campestris
Vine
Walnut (Juglerus regia)
Water Violet (Hottonia palustris)
Wild Oat
Wild Rose

Table 4 Dilutions of unit preparations diluted to at least one part in ten (1x) for external use

Adonis vernalis	Gelsemium sempervirens
Agaricus bulbosus	Gneiss
Agaricus muscarius	Hamamelis virginiana
Agnus castus	Hepar Sulfuris
Ailanthus glandulosa	Hyoscyamus niger
Alum	Iris florentine
Amethyst	Jaborandi
Ammonium Iodide	Juniperus sabina
Amygdalae amarae	Kaolinite
Apatite	Lachmanthus tinctoria
Apocynum androsaemifolium	Lapis Albus
Apocynum cannabinum	Lycopodium
Argentite	Magnesium
Argentum Chloride	Magnesium Acetate
Argentum Iodide	Magnesium Chloride
Artemisia cina	Magnetite
Aspidium filix-mas	Manganese Acetate
Aspidium anthelmintica	Nicotiana tabacum
Aurum sulphide	Nicotiana tabacum oil
Balsamum copaivae	Oleander
Balsamum peruvianum	Opuntia vulgaris
Barium Citrate	Oxalic Acid
Barium Sulphate	Petroleum
Bismuth Metal	Phellandrium aquaticum
Bismuth Subgallate	Pix Liquida
Bismuth Subnitrate	Platinum
Boletus laricis	Platinum Chloride
Bovista	Potassium Hydroxide
Cade Oil	Potassium Silicate
Calcium Fluoride	Pyrethrum
Carduus marianus	Pyrolusite
Cedar Wood Oil	Ranuculus acris
Cerium Oxalicum	Ranunculus bulbosus
Chalcocite	Ranunculus flammula
Chalcopyrite	Ranunculus repens
Chelidonium majus	Ranunculus sceleratus
Chenopodium Oil	Rhodium Oxynitrate
Colocynthis	Rhododendron chrysanthemum
Convallaria majalis	Rhus toxicodendron
Copper Silicate, Nat.	Salicylic Acid
Crotalus horridus	Scrophularia aquatica
Cucurbita	Sodium Aluminium Chloride
Cucumis melo	Sodium Auro-chloride
Datura stramonium	Sodium Hypochlorite
Derris	Sodium Nitrate
Diamond	Squill
Ephedra vulgaris	Stannum Metal
Ferric Acetate	Sulphur Iodide
Ferrous Iodide	Tannic Acid
Ferrous Oxalate	Terebinthinae Oleum
Ferrous Sulphide	Topaz
Formic Acid	Uric Acid
Gall	Zinc Hypophosphite
	Zinc Isovalerate

Chapter 14
Medicinal Products for Administration to Animals

INTRODUCTION

The health and welfare of animals is very important to human beings for two chief reasons. Firstly, many animals are vectors in the transmission of human disease, secondly we consume the produce and meat of other species and therefore we need to ensure that it is wholesome. In the UK a large proportion of the population keep at least one pet and many people have more. These must be kept free from disease for social as well as for psychological reasons. Animals therefore constitute a very sizeable market when the number of pets, farm animals, animals in zoos and safari parks are totalled together and this has encouraged the growth of the veterinary product industry. The advent of 'factory farming' has also stimulated the growth of the industry, and the multiplication of distribution outlets.

The word 'animal' as defined in the Act includes all members of the animal kingdom, but some controls over veterinary products and animal feeding stuffs apply only to such articles for administration to animals used as a source of food (the so-called economic animals). An example of the latter is 1982/626 in which 'animals' means domestic animals of the bovine species, swine, sheep, goats, solipeds and poultry, and wild animals of these species and wild ruminants which have been raised on a holding. The reason for the difference in definition in the statutory instrument cited is to ensure that human consumers of the produce are not harmed by residues of hormones and anti-hormones present in the food. This is one of several reasons for distinguishing between pets on the one hand and farm animals on the other. Medicines are given to all animals when they are ill, and individual treatment is often necessary to combat or prevent disease. Among the additional reasons for administering medicines to farm animals are improving or accelerating growth in the animal, anaesthesia, capture or restraint of the animal, synchronisation of oestrus in a herd or flock, chemical sterilisation, euthanasia, and to increase human acceptance of the produce of the animal.

Formerly, animals were treated with medicines that had been intended for human use, the dose being adjusted usually in terms of body weight. Human dosage forms such as tablets, creams and ointments are still used in veterinary practice, especially for administration to pets.

Specialised dosage forms are constantly being developed for use in agriculture. Some of the latter are designed for rapid treatment of individual animals with a pre-determined dose of the drug. These include pastes which are administered orally by means of a syringe or gun into the animal's mouth. The consistency of the paste ensures that most of the dose is swallowed. Drenches are liquid products and may be suspensions, emulsions or simple solutions to be administered orally by means of a tube. Boluses are solid objects intended to remain in the rumen or reticulum for prolonged periods, e.g. a year, slowly releasing the active drug or drugs. Some are used to provide 'trace' elements such as cobalt, copper or selenium where the pasture is deficient in these. There are also teat dips intended to kill bacteria on cows' teats and so help to prevent mastitis. Some of these dips are also formulated to keep the skin in good condition. Intramammary injections are also used to treat mastitis and these are of two types. One type is intended for use in lactating animals and is therefore made to disperse readily and be excreted rapidly in the milk. The second type is a prolonged release form for use in non-lactating animals. Sprays of various sorts are used to kill parasites living on the animal's skin and sometimes to repel flies and other pests.

Economic animals are seldom treated individually because if one animal has an infectious disease it rapidly spreads to the others and this is especially true in 'intensive' farming where animals are kept in close proximity to one another. Even when animals graze naturally, a deficiency disease due to some soil inadequacy will similarly affect them all. It is difficult and time consuming to dose each of perhaps 50–100 animals individually, and consequently methods have been devised to dose them all at once. This is usually achieved by medicating their feed or water especially when the dosage is not very critical. If the disease is one which causes animals to stop feeding then medication of the water is important because most sick animals will drink. Medication of the food therefore tends to be used prophylactically. The dosage forms applied to foods are top dressings consisting of powders or granules and they have the disadvantage that dosage is variable which is another reason for using them only prophylactically. Other forms intended for the mass medication of a herd include 'licks', i.e. blocks of material which can be licked by the animals. Many diseases are caused by parasites which are transmitted by flies, ticks and other insects. The regular dipping of the animals at the appropriate times of the year does much to reduce the incidence of these diseases.

When medicinal products are administered to a farm animal, it may be necessary to identify the animal to prevent its produce being consumed by man. The time required for the product to disappear from the milk, eggs or meat of the animal will clearly vary with the drug and the species. As an example, when a cow is treated with antibiotics for mastitis, her milk should be discarded for 3 days after treatment stops. It is preferable, where possible, to use drugs which are not absorbed by the animal, and which cannot get into the produce.

From the point of view of the Medicines Act, there are two different types of product to control, these being animal medicines and medicated animal feeding stuffs. This chapter is devoted to the former while the latter is dealt with in Chapter 15.

Veterinary drugs are subject to the same types of control as those for human use although sometimes there are differences in detail. The controls over licensing and the purposes for which licences are required are identical with those for human use and have been dealt with in Chapters 4–6. Similarly, their sale and supply both on and off prescription by pharmacists and veterinarians have been described in Chapters 9–11, and their labelling and advertising in Chapters 16 and 18 respectively.

The purpose of this chapter is to describe the restrictions on the sale of such products by dealers in agricultural supplies, and also certain other specialised persons, e.g. those carrying on a poultry vaccination service.

Mention has already been made of the class of veterinary drugs called 'PML' (Pharmacy and Merchant List) products. These are specified in the Schedules to the Exemptions from the Restrictions on Retail Sale Order (called 'The Veterinary Drugs Exemption Order') and comprise feed additives, medicated feeding stuffs and medicines which contain substances which would other-wise be [P] or POM. The purpose of the Order was to facilitate their purchase by farmers by enabling agricultural merchants to sell them. These cannot be sold from vans (1984/1861, article 3(2)(c)).

There has long been disquiet about certain aspects of the trade in veterinary medicines and in animal feeding stuffs. Indeed, the original report on the subject by the Medicines Commission (1973) recommended that after a 3 year period, all such products should be brought under the control of the pharmacist. In the mean time in an effort to improve the trade, merchants were required to apply for their names and the addresses of the premises from which they operate, to be listed with the Pharmaceutical Society of Great Britain. In 1981 there were about 1800 names on the list of merchants covering some 3000 premises. Many of the premises did not come up to the necessary standards. It seems that of the 1800 names, only about 500 were genuine merchants, the others operated from their homes (*Pharm. J.*, 1982). The economic benefits that can accrue to a farmer who uses growth promoters (especially the antibiotics, sex hormones and anabolic steroids) encourage excessive use of such products. This can be dangerous to the ultimate consumer of the meat or milk from that animal. It is therefore necessary to control the availability of such drugs, e.g. by making them prescription only, but this is only effective if the products are controlled from source. This implies a limitation on the outlets and the keeping of records. The point had, of course, been foreseen by the administrators and professions involved, and a system devised to deal with it but the system was open to criticism. That there was considerable room for improvement was shown by some court cases. In one, a newsagent was fined £1000 for unlawful supplies of veterinary products not on the GSL. In fact they were antibiotics and one is entitled to ask how and from where he was able to obtain such products (*Pharm.J.*, 1982).

The Veterinary Products Committee proposed that there should be pharmacist supervision of all supplies of products on the merchant's list. It also recommended that some PML should be reclassified as POM. The recommendation was that the list should continue for up to 5 years, but that thereafter each merchant should employ a pharmacist to supervise sales as in a pharmacy. The ABPI supported the view that animal medicines should be sold only by pharmacists because it was the only way to guarantee that products that had been correctly made, were subsequently dealt with in conditions which were appropriate (*Pharm.J.*, 1982).

The distribution of antibiotics used either therapeutically or prophylactically in animals is usually from a manufacturer via his salesmen directly to a veterinarian and then either to the farmer for administration or administration is done directly by the veterinarian. Some veterinarians employ salesmen to help with the distribution. The supplier (whether veterinarian, salesman or pharmacist) has a duty to ensure that the farmer knows how and when to use it and especially to comply with withdrawal periods. Labelling is also important in this respect.

LEGAL CLASSIFICATION OF VETERINARY MEDICINES

As with human medicines, there are three basic classes, namely –

(a) GSL medicines;

(b) [P] medicines;

(c) POM medicines.

The GSL products can be sold in unopened containers by any retailer including supermarkets, pet shops and the like. They can even be sold from vans, since the 'premises' provisions do not apply to them (section 53(2)(b)). Most of these products are intended for cats, dogs, cage birds, fish and other domestic pets.

The [P] medicines (and the PML products) can be sold by pharmacists. There are no restrictions as to original packs for [P] drugs, but the sale of both classes must be supervised by a pharmacist. The PML products must be in the form, for the purpose and of the strength specified in the Veterinary Drugs Exemption Order. Pharmacists can, of course, sell those which are [P] in other forms and for other purposes. Pharmacists can also make up medicines containing GSL and [P] medicines of their own design or to the order of the owner of an animal.

The classification reflects not only the relative dangers of the drugs but also the differing levels of knowledge of the buyers. It is presumed that persons who keep animals for business purposes, e.g. farmers, zoos, racehorse breeders, have a considerable knowledge and interest in their animals and can therefore be relied upon to use medicines responsibly. It follows that such people should have easier access to the products. Unfortunately, some of these people abuse their privileges and cause harm to the animal and perhaps the public.

The POM products are, for the most part, only available from veterinarians or on prescriptions issued by a veterinarian. We have seen in Chapter 11 that a veterinarian may only supply these drugs for use in 'animals under his care'.

OTHER SELLERS OF VETERINARY MEDICINES

Recently, the controls over agricultural dealers etc. have been tightened in an attempt to prevent the abuses mentioned above. The Animal Health and Welfare Act 1984, inter alia, amended the Medicines Act so as to require the registration of sellers of veterinary products. Some of the new requirements are to be found in the Exemptions from Restrictions on the Retail Sale and Supply of Veterinary Drugs Order 1984 (referred to as the Veterinary Drugs Exemption Order), which revoked all the previous Orders bearing that name. The registers are kept by the Pharmaceutical Society of Great Britain in so far as Great Britain is concerned, and the Department of Health and Social Services for Northern Ireland for that province. The registers are published annually (article 3(7)).

The new Order affects neither the sale of veterinary drugs on the GSL nor the sale or supply of other veterinary drugs by pharmacists or veterinarians, though both classes will be required to comply with the Code of Practice. It applies to three types of sellers, (article 3(1)) namely –

(a) the holder of a product licence;

(b) a 'specially authorised person';

(c) a person carrying on a 'qualifying business', i.e. a business in respect of which more than one half of the total sales for its last accounting period was derived from the retail sale of agricultural requisites. 'Agricultural requisites' are defined as things used in the cultivation of the soil or in the keeping of animals for the production of food or as game and equipment used in or for the collection of produce from animals kept for the production of food and things used for the maintenance of such equipment, and includes any protective clothing but does not include any other kind of human apparel (article 2).

The 'specially authorised person' means in relation to a veterinary drug either –

(i) a person specially authorised, by virtue of a direction of the licensing authority under article 3(1) of the Medicines (Exemptions from Licences) (Special and Transitional Cases) Order 1971, to assemble that drug otherwise than in accordance with a manufacturer's licence, or

(ii) a person specially authorised by the product licence in respect of that drug to sell the drug under the alternative product name specified in the licence (article 2).

Thus, a product licence holder or a specially authorised person can sell by retail only those drugs for which they have a licence or are authorised. If the products are on the GSL there is no restriction on their sale but the Order permits the sale of certain products not on the veterinary GSL. Likewise, the agricultural merchant could sell any veterinary drug on the GSL without complying with any of the requirements specified below, but if he wishes to sell PML drugs and feeding stuffs he will have to comply with the requirements of the Order.

PRODUCTS AFFECTED

These are veterinary drugs which are either the subject of a product licence of right but which are not GSL because they contain one or more of the substances specified in column 2 of Part A of Schedule 1 to the Order or they are specified in Part B of Schedule 1 (article 3). Those in Part A of Schedule 1 may only be sold in the pharmaceutical form stated and in containers labelled to show a daily dose not greater than that specified for the drug, in a strength not greater than that specified and in compliance with any other restrictions. Drugs in Part 1B are in the form which have been cleared for sale by agricultural merchants. The veterinary drugs specified in Schedule 4 (horse wormers) may also be sold by the various classes for a period of 3 years from the 1st January 1985.

The veterinary drugs specified in Schedules 2 and 3 may only be sold for incorporation into animal feeding stuffs. The drugs in Schedule 2 are normally [P] products while those in Schedule 3 are normally POM.

SALES OF VETERINARY DRUGS BY AGRICULTURAL MERCHANTS

The merchant must carry on a 'qualifying business' and every address at which he carries on the business must be registered as described above. In order to become and to remain registered, he must complete an application form (a specimen of which is published in the Code) and pay a fee (£50 per year per premises). The merchant is required by law to comply with the 'Code of Practice for Selling or Supplying Veterinary Drugs' published by the Ministry of Agriculture, Fisheries and Food. He must also nominate a person to be responsible for all matters relating to the storage, sale or supply of the PML products on each of the premises.

Premises

The agricultural merchant must register his business with the Pharmaceutical Society of Great Britain if in Great Britain, or with the Department of Health and Social Services for Northern Ireland if in that province. The application form requires details to be given of the name and address of every set of premises at which the business is carried on, together with the name of the nominated person in control. For the purposes of agricultural merchants, 'premises' includes a building or a market stall of a permanent nature at a market or agricultural showground. Every such premises must be capable of being closed so as to exclude the public (article 3(2)).

The Code contains a number of desirable features of such premises. For example, the premises must be adequately lit, heated, and ventilated, etc. so as to ensure compliance with the needs of the Shops Acts, and of the Health and Safety at Work etc. Act. They should be secure so as to deter theft. The premises used for sale, supply or storage of the drugs must not be any residential part of a dwelling house (Code 2.1).

There is provision for registration to be refused if the premises are not considered to be suitable (article 3(13)) or if the merchant or the nominated person fails to observe the Code or stores or sells products under unsuitable conditions (article 3(15)). Similarly, a person's name may be removed from the register (de-registered) for failing to comply with the law and Code. In all cases, the merchant can appeal against the decision to refuse registration or to de-register. The appeal is made to the Minister of Agriculture, Fisheries and Food if the merchant is in business in Great Britain or to the Department of Agriculture for Northern Ireland if in that province.

Personnel

Only persons approved and listed by the Animal Health Trade Associations Group (AHTAG) are eligible for nomination to be in charge of a registered premises. Such a person must be 'reasonably available' at the premises and ensure that the provisions of the law and of the Code are obeyed. When the nominated person is absent from the premises, his place should be taken by an alternative person from the AHTAG list of eligible persons. In order to be eligible for nomination, a person must have a knowledge of the composition, storage, use, purchase and sale of animal medicines. Pharmacists and veterinarians are eligible. Other persons are eligible if they produce evidence that they have either –

(a) at least 3 years practical experience between 1st January 1978 and the 1st January 1985 in the sale and supply of animal medicines; or

(b) successfully completed a course of instruction and examination recognised by AHTAG.

An applicant for listing must make written application to the Secretary of AHTAG giving his full name and address, the postal address of the premises, the name and address of the business and the details of his qualifications or experience. Persons on the list must notify AHTAG of any change in these particulars.

The nominated person should ensure that all staff are familiar with the provisions of the Code, have adequate product knowledge and are given regular training in matters connected with veterinary products.

Sale or Supply

The products may only be sold in the original, unopened containers, as packed by the manufacturer or assembler, and from the registered premises.
Sales may only be made to persons known by the seller to keep animals as part of his business (not as pets) (article 3(2)d). The products cannot be sold by 'self-service' methods.

In respect of a PML product the seller must record –

(1) date of sale,

(2) name and amount, and if necessary the form and strength of the drug sold,

(3) name and address of the purchaser.

If a written order was received or an invoice given, no record need be kept. The record, order or invoice must be kept for 2 years (1980/1923, article 7).

Storage

The products must be stored in a part of the premises separate from that to which the public have access (article 3(3)). In addition any storage conditions mentioned on labels or leaflets must be complied with, and particular care is required in relation to vaccines and sera where the maintenance of a narrow temperature range is very important. The Code suggests (5.5) that the temperatures of places in which vaccines and sera are stored should be recorded daily, preferably by means of a chart. Good stock control procedures are also important to ensure that stock is correctly rotated.

Enforcement

Inspectors from the appropriate registering bodies are entitled to enter any premises at any reasonable time to ascertain whether the provisions of the law and of the Code are being observed. They have all the rights and duties of enforcement officers described in Chapter 2 and it is an offence to wilfully obstruct them.

SALES OF HORSE WORMERS BY SADDLERS

For a period of 3 years from the 1st January 1985, a person carrying on a saddlery business may sell those horse wormers specified in Schedule 4 to the Veterinary Drugs Exemption Order (called The Saddlers' List) provided that he complies with the necessary conditions. A saddlery business is one in respect of which more than half of the total sales for its last accounting period was derived from the retail sale of saddlery requisites – (commonly known as 'tack') (article 5(17)). 'Saddlery requisites' means equipment used in the keeping of horses or ponies and things used for the maintenance of such equipment and includes any human apparel used in the keeping of horses or ponies (article 5(17)).

Registration of Premises

The saddler must register every premises from which he carries on his business either with the Pharmaceutical Society of Great Britain or with the Department of Health and Social Services for Northern Ireland as appropriate and pay a fee of £5 for each year for each premises (article 5(5),(10)).

Registration may be refused if the fee is not paid or if the applicant fails to give an undertaking to comply with the Code (article 5(11)). Registration may also be refused if the premises are considered to be unsuitable in some respect (article 5(12)) but only with the approval of the Minister or of the Department of

Agriculture. Similarly, the registering bodies may refuse to register or may remove from the register the name of a person who fails to observe the provisions of the Code or who sells or stores products under unsuitable conditions (article 5(14)) but again this may only occur with the approval of the Minister or of the Department of Agriculture for Northern Ireland. The word 'premises' includes a permanent stall at a market or agricultural showground (article 5(16)) as well as a shop which is occupied by the seller and which can be closed so as to exclude the public. The Code prevents the use of any residential part of a dwelling house being used for the sale, supply or storage of horse wormers.

A specimen form of application for registration of a saddlery business is included in the Code. The exact address of every set of premises at which the business is carried on must be given, together with the name of the nominated person in control. The application form contains a declaration that the person carrying on the business agrees to comply with the Code of Practice for Saddlers Selling or Supplying Horse Wormers.

The Code specifies a number of desirable features for the premises some of which are required under the Shops Acts, or Health and Safety at Work etc. Act.

Personnel

The nominated person in each premises is responsible for all matters relating to horse wormers. He must be either a pharmacist, a veterinarian, have successfully completed an AHTAG course or have had at least 1 year's practical training. It is his duty to ensure that the requirements of the law and of the Code are met. He should be reasonably available at the premises and when he is absent, an alternative person eligible for nomination should take his place.

The nominated person must ensure that all staff are thoroughly familiar with the requirements of the Code and have adequate product knowledge.

Sale or Supply

The drug must be sold in the original container as packed and labelled by the manufacturer or assembler. It should bear the PML mark and all the other labelling details. Products with damaged or defaced labels should not be sold. The sale must take place on the registered premises but the saddler can deliver products ordered from the premises. The products must not be exposed for sale by self-service methods. The saddler can sell these products to anyone he knows or reasonably believes to have charge of horses or ponies and is no longer restricted to sales for business use (i.e. he is not limited to selling them only to riding stables and people who keep horses as part of their business).

A record of the sale must be kept for 2 years. This may take the form of an order, an invoice or an entry in a book. It must specify the date of the sale, the name, quantity, form and strength of the product, and the name and address of the purchaser.

Storage

The products must be stored in a part of the premises to which the public are not permitted access. The storage conditions, i.e. as regards temperature, light, etc. stated on the label must be complied with, and these products must be kept separate from food, drink and animal feeding stuffs.

Enforcement

An inspector from the appropriate registering body has the right to enter any registered premises at any reasonable time to ascertain whether the provisions of the law and of the Code are beng observed. He has all of the rights and duties of enforcement officers described in Chapter 2.

SALES TO BULK MANUFACTURERS OF ANIMAL FEEDING STUFFS

Certain drugs specified in Schedules 2 (these are normally [P] products) and 3 (these are normally POM products) of the Veterinary Drugs Exemption Order can be sold or supplied by retail by a 'bulk supplier' or by a 'specially authorised person'. These drugs may be sold only for incorporation into animal feeding stuffs and to a person known to the seller to be carrying on a business in which animal feeding stuffs are made for sale.

POULTRY VACCINATION SERVICES

In this context 'poultry' means domestic fowls, turkeys, geese, ducks, guinea-fowls, pigeons, pheasants, and partridges. There are a few companies who provide this service, but most large scale poultry farmers now have an 'in house' service. Obviously, the vaccinating company needs to be exempt from the restrictions of sections 52 and 53 in respect to premises etc. This is achieved by the Pharmacy and General Sale Order 1980/1924 article 5 and Schedule 1. The company also needs to be exempt from the 'prescription only' requirements that apply to most parenteral products, and this is granted by the POM Order in respect of the poultry vaccines specified in paragraph 10 of Schedule 1A and paragraph 11 of Schedule 1B to the Veterinary Drugs Exemption Order 1984.

Persons providing a poultry vaccination service may sell poultry vaccines only to persons who keep poultry in the course of their business, either as his sole business activity or as a substantial part of his business activities (1980/1922, 1980/1924 (Schedule 1, paragraph 6).

The person carrying on the vaccination service obtains the vaccines on a signed order stating name and the amount of the poultry vaccine required (POM Order, Schedule 3(1), paragraph 7).

References

Report on the Retail Sale of Certain Veterinary Medicines to Farmers; Medicines Commission, 1973

Pharm. J., 1982, i, 559

Pharm. J., 1982, i, 189

Pharm. J., 1982, i, 559

Chapter 15
Medicated Animal Feeding Stuffs

INTRODUCTION

Animal feeding stuffs are nutritive products made and sold for consumption by animals. The Medicines Act (as amended by the Animal Health and Welfare Act 1984) defines animal feeding stuff as 'any substance which is intended for use either by being fed to one or more animals or as an ingredient in the preparation of such a substance, not being in either case a medicinal product' (section 132). When used in various statutory instruments, the term is intended to include such articles as feed supplements, protein concentrates and complete feeds (1973/1530; 1976/30; 1976/1726; and 1985/273) and these terms are defined (see Appendix 1). The quality and purity of animal feeding stuffs intended for consumption by farm animals (but not animals not used in the production of food) are controlled under Part IV of the Agriculture Act 1970.

Sometimes, animal feeding stuffs are medicated by the incorporation of a 'feed additive'. This may be a medicinal product, e.g. an anthelmintic, antibiotic or coccidiostat. Alternatively, some substance or article which is not a 'medicinal product' may be incorporated for a medicinal purpose, for example to promote growth or as a contraceptive. Either way, the resulting product is a medicated animal feeding stuff and thereby comes within the scope of the Medicines Act. Some additives are used in very small concentrations (e.g. parts per million, i.e. ppm) and to facilitate the proper mixing of such small amounts, the substance is added in the form of a 'premix', which is a product consisting of the active substance mixed with a suitable diluent. The premix may be licensed as a medicinal product, or alternatively, the active constituent may be licensed, in which case the premix becomes a feeding stuff. The sale, supply, import, export and possession for sale or supply of such products are subject to control under the Medicines Act (notably sections 40, 85, 86, and 90) and delegated legislation made thereunder. The provisions relating to exports have not yet been brought into effect.

Although the provisions apply to persons acting 'in the course of their business', only a few of the controls currently apply to a farmer, dog-breeder or other owner who mixes his own medicated animal feeding stuffs. Certain prohibitions apply universally, such as the prohibition of the inclusion of stilbenes or thyrostatic substances into feeding stuffs of animals used for food production. There are also restrictions on the use of antibiotics in such animals. As was pointed out in the 'Swann Report' these provisions are necessary to protect the health of persons who will consume the produce, and also other animals and contraventions of the law should not be regarded as mere technical offences.

TYPES OF ANIMAL FEEDING STUFFS

There are several types of animal feeding stuffs and the chief means of distinguishing between them seems to relate to the proportion of the product which is added to a feed. For example, a 'complete feeding stuff' means a substance or a mixture of substances designed for feeding to animals without further mixing with other feeding stuffs (1973/1530; 1976/30; 1976/1726; 1985/273), in other words it is fed to animals as it is, without further dilution. A 'feed supplement' on the other hand is a substance or a mixture of substances designed for further mixing before feeding to animals at an inclusion rate of less than 5% with other animal feeding stuffs (1973/1530; 1976/30; 1976/1726; 1985/273), while a 'protein concentrate' means a substance or a mixture of substances designed for further mixing before feeding to animals at an inclusion rate of 5% or more with other animal feeding stuffs. An 'animal feeding stuff' includes a complete feeding stuff, a feed supplement and a protein concentrate (1973/1530; 1976/30; 1976/1726; 1985/273) and seems to be an 'umbrella' term for them all. 'Medicated' when use in relation to an animal feeding stuff, feed supplement or protein concentrate, means having a medicinal product incorporated therein; (1973/1530; 1976/1726). 'Medicated' can also mean having a substance incorporated into it for a medicinal purpose.

A feed supplement is usually intended to supply predetermined proportions of vitamins, minerals, trace elements and perhaps other non-nutrient additives or special ingredients. They are normally available to farmers and to feeding stuffs manufacturers. Protein concentrates do contain protein rich ingredients such as fish meal, soya and the like, as well as vitamins, trace elements, etc. Some are intended to be mixed with cereals, silage or grass to balance the feed.

MANUFACTURE OF ANIMAL FEEDING STUFFS

By Farmers, Dog Breeders and Similar Animal Owners

These persons can make their own feeding stuffs for consumption by their animals. In addition, they can medicate such feeding stuffs. The substances used to 'medicate' the feed may be –

(a) a medicine on the GSL;

(b) a medicine which is [P] and which has been purchased from a pharmacy;

(c) a medicine on the PML, i.e. one listed in Schedules 1, 2 or 3 of the Veterinary Drugs Exemption Order, purchased from an agricultural merchant or a pharmacy;

(d) some other 'feed additive'.

The farmer must comply with the provisions of the product licence if the additive is a medicinal product, i.e. he should follow the directions provided by the manufacturer. Currently, there are enforcement difficulties which should be reduced when the new regulations are brought into force.

With regard to the owners of other animals, there is little need to control their activities since there is not the same incentive to use growth promoters and the like, and the consequences to human beings would be far less serious. Moreover, such owners have less opportunity to purchase the necessary additives.

By Co-operatives

These are usually owned by groups of farmers and normally have an identity in law separate from the individuals who own the company. They are subject to the same controls as commercial companies, but again are not so easy to 'police' as the latter. They too will have to register and comply with the code of practice.

By Commercial Companies

For the most part these are reputable companies that have done much to improve the standards and economics of animal husbandry. Their existence is known as is the location of their premises, so they are relatively easy to 'police'. For these reasons the new regulations will have little practical effect upon them, in fact, the other compounders will have to reach their standards.

The companies (or compounders) obtain the necessary veterinary medicinal products by retail from bulk suppliers. The sale is 'retail' because the compounder is the final purchaser of the medicinal product, what he sells is a medicated animal feeding stuff.

Normally, section 52 restricts the retail sale of medicinal products to pharmacists, but the Veterinary Drugs Exemption Order permits the retail sale of those veterinary medicinal products that are additives to compounders of animal feeding stuffs or to wholesalers.

CONTROLS OVER THE MEDICATION OF FEEDING STUFFS

Generally speaking, only a medicinal product whose product licence (or an animal test certificate) contains provisions permitting its inclusion in animal feeding stuffs may be so included, and then only in accordance with the terms of the licence or certificate. A veterinarian may of course issue a prescription calling for the inclusion of any medicinal product into the feeding stuff for an animal or herd under his care. It is unlawful to sell etc. a medicated animal feeding stuff which does not comply with these requirements.

The actual incorporation of medicinal additives into animal feeding stuffs is controlled by section 40 of the Act.

LABELLING AND PACKAGING OF ANIMAL FEEDING STUFFS

Labelling is controlled by a special set of regulations, and false and misleading labels and leaflets by section 90(2). The labelling controls do not apply to farm mixed feed but the incorporation provisions do. Ministers may prohibit, by order, the sale etc. of medicated animal feeding stuffs of a particular type (e.g. those containing stilbenes).

The Act required regulations to be made to ensure that such feeding stuffs are correctly described and readily identifiable, that appropriate warnings and instructions are given and that false or misleading information is not given (sections 85, 86 and 90). It is an offence to give false or misleading information about a medicated animal feeding stuff, either on a label or other document, or in an advertisement, or orally by means of a representation. In this context, false or misleading means falsely describing the product or misleading as to its nature or quality, in relation to its composition, uses and effects, or its safety.

The Labelling of Medicated Animal Feeding Stuffs Regulations 1973 specifies the detailed control. Every container or package in which a medicated animal feeding stuff is sold, must be labelled (regulation 4) with –

(a) its name or a description of its nature;

(b) the name of its manufacturer or seller;

(c) its batch reference number;

(d) if it is a medicated feed supplement or medicated protein concentrate, a statement to that effect (unless it is being sold to a manufacturer of medicated animal feeding stuffs);

(e) the proprietary name of any medicinal product incorporated in the feeding stuff and the appropriate non-proprietary name or other name by which the active ingredient can be identified and the number of the product licence (if any) authorising the incorporation;

(f) the common chemical name of any substance, other than a medicinal product, incorporated in the feed for a medicinal purpose and the number of the product licence (if any) authorising the incorporation;

(g) the medicinal purpose for which the product or substance was added and the species and categories within species, of animals to which it should be fed;

(h) the quantity (in parts by weight or as a proportion) of each active ingredient present;

(i) instructions as to the rate and the permissible daily level of active ingredients to be fed (where this is stated in the product licence), and in the case of medicated feed supplements or medicated protein concentrates, the inclusion rates with other feeding stuffs and the level of active ingredient to be present in the complete feed;

(j) a statement that it must be incorporated in an animal feeding stuff either in accordance with the product licence or with a veterinary prescription (this does not apply to a complete feeding stuff);

(k) any instructions relating to safety, storage, contra- indications, withdrawal periods and the like;

(l) an expiry date for the active ingredient, if this is before the expiry date of the feeding stuff;

(m) where the container is too small to permit the inclusion of all of the particulars on the label, those omitted shall be contained in a leaflet which shall accompany the feeding stuff;

(n) any other information required by the product licence relating to the feeding stuff or the active ingredient(s).

Where a feeding stuff is medicated in accordance with a veterinary prescription or the directions of the purchaser, (otherwise than in accordance with an animal test certificate), it must be labelled with the particulars specified in (a), (h), (i), (k), and (n) above, together with a reference number of the prescription or order in question.

Where the feeding stuff has been medicated in accordance with an animal test certificate, it shall be labelled with the full particulars except for (g) and instead of (e) and (f) the number of the test certificate. If desired, the name of the product may be omitted and the code number of the certificate used instead.

Sometimes, animal feeding stuffs are delivered in bulk rather than packed in containers. This is lawful (regulation 6) provided that the particulars that would be given on a label are given on a leaflet supplied with each delivery.

The particulars required on a label or leaflet shall be printed legibly in letters and figures not less than 1.5 mm high and on a contrasting ground and those relating to rate of incorporation and to safety shall be prominently displayed (regulation 7). It is an offence to alter, remove or render illegible the label of a product which is in a person's possession for sale but a label can be amended if necessary to comply with regulations (regulation 8).

Nothing in these regulations applies to transparent wrappers or to crates, packing cases and the like used to transport labelled containers and packages of feeding stuffs, or to paper bags in which labelled containers may be supplied. If the feeding stuff is for export, it may be labelled with the particulars required by the importing country (regulation 9).

The labelling regulations do not, of course, apply to a farmer or other owner who medicates food for his stock.

SALE OF ANIMAL FEEDING STUFFS

Animal feeding stuffs, whether medicated or not, or sold mainly by the compounders and by agricultural merchants and co-operatives.

QUALITY AND TESTING OF ANIMAL FEEDING STUFFS

Due to the physical nature of the feeding stuffs, to the quantities in which they are medicated and also to the low levels of medicament normally required (perhaps 5% or less), it is difficult to achieve a uniform mix. For this reason, the Ministers have used their powers under section 117 to make regulations specifying the permissible levels of variation for additives in feeding stuffs.

ENFORCEMENT OF STANDARDS AND OTHER PROVISIONS

The provisions relating to the enforcement of the Act and its subordinate legislation applicable to medicated animal feeding stuffs is specified in sections 108–115 and 117, but some of these required modification to make the wording correct. The modifications were contained in the Animal Feeding Stuffs (Enforcement) Regulations 1985. The appropriately modified sections 112, 113 and 115 are reprinted in the Enforcement Regulations at the end of this volume. These regulations are very extensive and contain details as to the taking of samples of medicated animal feeding stuffs, and of their division, marking, sealing and disposal (Schedule 2). Schedule 3 comprises the bulk of the regulations and consists of the methods of analysis to be employed for 24 commonly used substances, and on the preparation of the sample for analysis.

The Minister of Agriculture and the Secretaries of State for Scotland and for Wales and the Department of Agriculture for Northern Ireland are primarily responsible for enforcing the provisions of section 40 and also the Labelling Regulations, and provisions under 90(2) and any under 62(1)(b). However, county councils and the Pharmaceutical Society of Great Britain have a concurrent power to enforce most of the provisions. Only the Departments have the power to visit veterinarian's premises or veterinary hospitals. All of the enforcing bodies employ 'inspectors'.

A person authorised in writing by an enforcement authority has, on production of his credentials if requested, the right to inspect any substance or article which appears to be an animal feeding stuff, a container, package, label or leaflet used or to be used in connection with an animal feeding stuff. He may also take a sample of such a material. In addition, he may require a person carrying on a business which consists of or includes the manufacture, assembly, sale or supply of such feeding stuffs, or one of his employees to open any container or package or to produce any book or document relating to the business which is in his possession or control and may copy any entry in any such book or document. He has the right to seize any article, substance, book or document he reasonably believes to be evidence of any offence committed under the Act but must inform the person from whom it was seized. He has similar rights in respect of persons applying for a licence or certificate under Part II of the Act.

The person who was informed of the seizure of any article or substance may, at the time or at any time within the next 21 days, request the inspector to either set aside a sample of it or treat it as a sample whichever the inspector considers appropriate. The inspector shall divide the sample into three parts if this is reasonably practicable and send one to an agricultural analyst for analysis or examination.

Any purchaser of an animal feeding stuff is entitled to have an inspector take a sample of it and send it for analysis on payment of the fee fixed by the enforcement authority. The purchaser, the person from whom he bought it, and any other person against whom a cause for action may lie in respect of the sale, may require the inspector to send one part to the Government Chemist for analysis or examination, and that person is entitled to a copy of his certificate of analysis.

Where it is intended to prosecute someone for an offence, the prosecutor is entitled to a copy of the Government Chemist's certificate. The prosecutor shall send with the summons a copy of the agricultural analyst's report and that of the Government Chemist. If there is no Government Chemist's report (because no one has requested one), the prosecutor shall send a copy of the agricultural analyst's certificate and a notice of intended prosecution to the person charged at least 14 days before the hearing. The person charged may, within the 14 days, pay the fee and request that a sample be sent to the Government Chemist. The proceedings will then be stayed until the Government Chemist's report is available. If the prosecution is not brought, the fee is repaid to the person. In any event, the court may order a sample to be examined by the Government Chemist if this has not already been done.

OFFENCES

There are numerous offences that can be committed in relation to medicated animal feeding stuffs. They can conveniently be considered in groups.

(1) Those connected with licensing, e.g. the sale, supply or possession for sale or supply of unlicensed products; the importation of unlicensed products.

(2) Those connected with labelling, e.g. products which are incompletely or incorrectly labelled or which have damaged or defaced labels. It is an offence to damage or deface a label. It is an offence to sell, supply or possess for sale or supply a medicated animal feeding stuff which contravenes the

regulations relating to labels (section 85(3)) or give with or possess for so supplying with, such a product a leaflet which contravenes any regulations (section 86 (2)).

Section 90(2) makes it an offence to sell, supply or possess for sale any medicated animal feeding stuff in a labelled container or package which falsely describes the composition of the feeding stuff or is likely to mislead as to its nature or quality or as to its uses or effects, or to issue or have in his possession for issue a leaflet which does the same.

(3) Those related to the quality or nature of the feeding stuff.

A company and two of its directors were fined a total of £5,850 after pleading guilty to 13 charges under the Medicines Act. Seven charges related to labelling offences and concerned deficiencies in the information provided, e.g. safety instructions, inclusion rates, name of the active ingredient. The other six charges involved the use of a substance in a way not covered by its product licence, the incorporation of an antibiotic which was not licensed for inclusion, and the use of an ingredient in a way that the inclusion rate in the final feeding stuff did not accord with that prescribed by the licence. It was claimed that the Company had difficulty obtaining the necessary information from some firms, and that the detail required on labels was excessive (*Pharm.J., 1979*).

FUTURE DEVELOPMENTS

Recently, the Animal Health and Welfare Act amended the provisions of the Medicines Act relating to animal feeding stuffs. Section 40 was re-worded and sections 41 and 42 were repealed. The change is intended to improve the control over the medication of feeding stuffs and also to comply with recent amendments to EEC 70/544. The new section 40 enables the Agriculture Ministers to make regulations to prohibit the incorporation by a person in the course of his business of any medicinal product into an animal feeding stuff unless –

(1) the incorporation is in accordance with a product licence or animal test certificate;

(2) it is incorporated in accordance with the 'written directions' of a veterinarian and these directions comply with the regulations;

(3) the compounder is registered for the purposes of the regulations either with the Pharmaceutical Society of Great Britain or with the Northern Ireland enforcement authority.

If a person who is not the holder of a licence or certificate incorporates a medicinal product into an animal feeding stuff in the reasonable belief that he is doing so in accordance with a licence or certificate held by another person, condition (1) above shall be deemed to be satisfied.

The new regulations will apply to farm made feeding stuffs as well as those made commercially. It is probable that all compounders of animal feeding stuffs (including farmers) will be required to register and to comply with a code of practice. These regulations are expected to be made during 1985 and should help to deter farmers from mixing otherwise than in accordance with product licences. Tighter controls over the sale and supply of additives, e.g. antibiotics and hormones, are also of value in this respect.

Regulations may also be made to prohibit the sale, offer for sale, supply or export in the course of a business of any animal feeding stuff in which a medicinal product has been incorporated, or the import of such a feeding stuff except under conditions analogous to those mentioned above. The regulations may require the registration of persons (on payment of a fee) either with the Pharmaceutical Society of Great Britain or with the Northern Ireland enforcement authority. The fee shall take into account the costs of enforcing the regulations and by other persons (e.g.AHTAG) for the purpose of maintaining or improving standards among those carrying on the commercial activities relating to medicated animal feeding stuffs. In this section, reference to the incorporation of a medicinal product into an animal feeding stuff shall not include a reference to incorporation in the course of making a medicinal product but does include the incorporation of any substance for a medicinal purpose, or the incorporation of a substance in which a medicinal product has been incorporated.

Reference

Pharm. J., 1979, i, 487

Chapter 16
The Packaging and Labelling of Medicines

INTRODUCTION

Part V of the Act specifies the types of controls to be imposed over the packaging and labelling of medicines. The controls are intended to enhance the safety of medicinal products by ensuring that they are correctly described, readily identifiable, and bear appropriate warnings and instructions and that false or misleading information is not given with them, (section 85(2)).

For these purposes, the Ministers may make regulations to control –

(i) The labelling of containers and packages (section 85(1)),

(ii) The display of distinctive marks on containers and packages (section 85(1)),

(iii) Leaflets supplied with medicinal products (section 86(1)),

(iv) The colour, shape and distinctive marks to be displayed on the products (section 88(1)).

For the same purposes, and also for preserving the quality of the product, regulations may be made to control –

(v) The containers in which the products are enclosed (section 87(1)).

Regulations may also be made to control the information displayed on automatic machines used for the sale of medicinal products (section 89(1)).

Analogous provisions relate to medicated animal feeding stuffs (section 90) and are described fully in Chapter 15.

It is important to realise that both containers and packages need to be labelled and that sometimes different requirements apply.

Fifteen sets of regulations have been made under Part V of the Act viz –

Child Safety Regulations 1975/2000 as amended by 1976/1643

Labelling of Medicated Animal Feeding Stuffs Regulations 1973/1530

Labelling Regulations 1976/1726 as amended by 1977/996, 1977/2168, 1978/41, 1981/1791, 1983/1729

Contact Lens Fluids and Other Substances (Labelling) Regulations 1979/1759 as amended by 1981/1689

Leaflets Regulations 1977/1055

Leaflets for Veterinary Drugs Regulations 1983/1727

Fluted Bottles Regulations 1978/40

The Labelling (Amendment)(Special Transitional) Regulations 1978/190 were of transient application and are now spent.

The controls apply to substances and articles which have been brought within the scope of the Act by orders made under sections 104 or 105. However, some of the regulations made under this Part do not apply to all such substances and articles, e.g. dental filling substances and contact lenses, are not controlled by the Labelling Regulations. On the other hand, intra-uterine contraceptive devices and contact lens solutions are subject to these regulations.

Containers

The container in which a medicinal product is packed has a number of important functions. First of all, it holds the product and provides mechanical protection for it and also carries the label. Secondly, it provides protection against moisture and gases in the air. If the container is made from actinic glass or plastic, or is opaque, it will also protect the product from light. These are very important considerations because many drugs such as vitamins are damaged or even destroyed by oxygen, dampness and by light. Ribbed or fluted bottles have long been used to help the blind or visually handicapped distinguish poisons or liquid products for external use from those intended to be swallowed.

Recently, containers have been given an additional function, namely to protect children from the dangers of ingesting the often brightly coloured and attractive tablets, capsules and similar solid dosage forms, and several types of 'child resistant containers' have been developed. Some of these are special caps or lids which require a certain amount of manual dexterity to remove. One, the 'Clic-Lok' has to be pressed down while being turned anti-clockwise in order to unscrew it. If it is turned without being pressed down, it makes a loud clicking noise which is intended to alert an adult to the fact that 'junior' is playing with the medicines. Another type requires the lid to be turned so that two arrows one on the lid and the other on the bottle are in line before the lid can be removed. Another type of 'child resistant container' is the foil or 'blister' or 'unit' or 'strip' pack although it was originally introduced for other reasons.

In ordinary usage, the words 'container' and 'package' are used more or less synonymously, but in the Medicines Act and its delegated legislation they have different meanings. The definitions of 'container', 'package', 'labelling' and 'leaflet' should be carefully studied.

Essentially, the difference between a container and a package is that the container is that which immediately encloses the product or products provided that the container is not going to be administered. An ordinary gelatin capsule or a cachet intended to be swallowed is not a container, whereas the capsule shell of a powder intended to be propelled into the nose or lungs is a container since it remains behind in the inhaler after its contents have been released. A package on the other hand encloses one or more containers. Clearly, one package may be enclosed within another package *ad infinitum*. Other containers include the paper used to contain individually-wrapped powders or the sachets used to hold quantities of mouthwash powder or shampoo.

A 'strip pack' (also sometimes called a 'unit pack') consists of a series of containers, and special provision is made for labelling these containers.

The choice of container is clearly an important matter both in terms of effectiveness for the purpose, and also on aesthetic grounds. An additional factor is the material of construction of the container since this will be in intimate contact with the product. Some types of glass impart alkalinity to a solution and this might alter the pH of the solution to an extent that adversely affects the product. Some injection solutions are therefore packed in ampoules made from 'alkali-free' glass. In the same way, some plastics 'leak' chemicals into products packed in them or allow vapours and fumes to pass in or out of the container. Obviously, the container should be made of materials that do not affect the product.

The Act and regulations do not contain much detail relating to containers. However, it will be recalled that the application for a product licence must describe the type and material of construction of the container to be used for the product. This obviously permits a more appropriate form of control than would be possible by trying to draft regulations to cover all the eventualities. Moreover, the British Pharmacopoeia contains standards for the glass to be used in the manufacture of ampoules and other containers for injectable preparations (Appendix XVIIIB) and for containers for Water for Injections (Appendix XVIIIC). It also contains *guidance* (not mandatory requirements unless invoked in the Monographs) for plastic containers for pharmaceutical products (Appendix XIX). Such standards and guidelines are obviously observed by the manufacturers of containers for use in retail and hospital pharmacies and the pharmacists who purchase and use them.

It is an offence under the Act to sell, supply or possess for sale or supply a product which is NOT enclosed in a container when sold, supplied etc (section 85(4)) or whose labelling and/or packaging does not comply with the appropriate regulations (section 85(3)).

CHILD SAFETY REGULATIONS

With certain exceptions, the sale or supply of medicinal products for human use containing aspirin or paracetamol in dosage unit form of tablets (except effervescent tablets containing not more than 25% of aspirin or paracetamol), capsules, pills, lozenges, pastilles, cachets or suppositories is prohibited unless packed in child resistant containers. Such containers may be of one of three types

(a) An opaque or dark tinted 'strip pack', resistant to opening by children, in which the dosage units are separately enclosed;

(b) Opaque or dark tinted reclosable containers which comply with British Standard 5321 as amended by AMD 2077;

(c) Containers having child resistant qualities and which are required by a product licence granted after 1/1/76 to be used for the sale or supply of the product in question.

Where the product is for administration exclusively to children, then unless the container is of type (c) above, the container (or package in the case type (a)) shall not contain more than 25 dosage units.

The above restrictions do NOT apply to –

(i) Products assembled in packs not intended for retail sale;

(ii) Products for export;

(iii) Products sold or supplied by or under the supervision of a pharmacist on registered premises and either on a practitioner's prescription or at the request of an adult who specifically requests the use of an ordinary container;

(iv) Sales or supplies by doctors or dentists to their patients;

(v) Sales or supplies by hospitals or health centres for administration in accordance with the directions of a doctor or dentist.

In addition, all such dosage forms must be white.

Child Resistant Containers

Notwithstanding (iii) above, the Council of the Pharmaceutical Society of Great Britain and other interested parties proposed a voluntary scheme whereby all solid dose products of aspirin and paracetamol would be so packed unless the patient requested otherwise. The scheme was embodied in a Council Statement, [Pharm.J. 1982] and has since been extended all solid dosage forms for oral use but, as before, ordinary containers can be used at the patient's request and for the elderly and handicapped. Furthermore, there is no need to repack products when the manufacturer's container gives superior protection e.g. aluminium tubes for lozenges. The widespread use of child resistant containers has certainly reduced the incidence of child-poisoning with drugs but has caused problems for the elderly, the arthritic, and other handicapped persons some of whom fail to replace the lid once they have gained access to the contents. This is not only more dangerous to any children who are present, but can also lead to accelerated decomposition of the product. Obviously, the only real protection for children is to store medicines out of their reach. In its Report for 1980 the Medicines Commission stated that it was impressed by Dr Goulding's view that 'the extent and severity of child poisoning by medicines had been widely overstated in some quarters and that action to improve packaging could have little effect on total child poisoning cases since the prime cause was carelessness by adults' [Medicines Commission Report for 1980, paragraph 4.6].

The following containers comply with the relevant BSI standards –

'Clic-loc' made by United Closures and Plastics Ltd, these caps fit standard screw necks of tablet bottles.

'Snap-safe' containers and special caps made by Cope Allman Plastics Ltd. The arrow on the closure must be lined up with that on the container before the lid can be removed.

'Securisafe' containers and special caps made by Johnsen & Jorgensen. These too rely on the alignment of arrows. The company also produce TRaCeR caps (Tamper Resistant and Child Resistant). They can only be opened by tearing off a security strip which seals the cap to the container, and the cap can then only be removed by aligning the arrows.

Discussions are taking place to revise the British Standard and to draft an International Standard. It is intended that the new tests will use fewer children, will also involve the use of elderly persons (to ensure that they can open the containers). In addition, they should markedly reduce the cost in terms of time and money of obtaining marketing approval in the countries of the world. The existing containers mentioned above will meet the new standards.

FLUTED BOTTLES

Regulations require that liquid products for external use which contain certain specified substances be packed in fluted bottles so as to be recognisable by touch. There are exemptions for ear and eye preparations packed in plastic containers and also for products packed in bottles larger than 1.14 L. Similarly, products for export, scientific education or research are exempt.

The wording of the regulations seems to be capable of two interpretations. Regulation 2 states '.... the sale or supply of liquid medicinal products for external use containing or consisting of any substance set out in the Schedule to these regulations shall be prohibited unless such products are contained in a bottle the outer surface of which is fluted vertically with ribs or grooves recognisable by touch.' This may be interpreted as prohibiting the packing of such a product in any container other than a bottle i.e. making it an offence to pack such a product in a tube or canister. On the other hand, the phrase may be interpreted as permitting products to be packed in any type of container, but requiring bottles to be fluted. Since the regulations replace the corresponding provisions of the Poisons Rules, it is generally accepted that the second interpretation is correct because the Poisons Rules did not require canisters etc to be ribbed.

Although the regulations only apply to products containing one of the specified substances, general practice and hospital pharmacists will no doubt prefer to follow the advice given by the Council of the Society and continue to pack all products for external use in fluted bottles. Exceptions are made for a product which is sterile or already in a distinctive pack. The recommendation was that under normal circumstances coloured ribbed glass bottles be used for the following preparations (*Pharm. J.*, 1982) –

> APPLICATIONS; COLLODIONS; EAR DROPS; ENEMAS; EYE DROPS; EYE LOTIONS; GARGLES; INHALATIONS; LINIMENTS; LOTIONS; MOUTHWASHES; NASAL DROPS; PAINTS; SOLUTIONS FOR EXTERNAL USE; SPRAYS.

Labels and Leaflets

INTRODUCTION

The labelling requirements are contained in the Labelling Regulations and apply to all medicinal products including Controlled Drugs. The only additional requirement imposed by the Misuse of Drugs Regulations is that preparations not in unit dose form should be labelled with the amount of the preparation in the container and the *percentage* of each controlled drug present. This is not necessary when the product is a dispensed medicine (regulation 18). Special regulations apply to the various solutions (and to powders for the preparation of such solutions) intended for use with contact lenses (The Contact Lens Fluids and Other Substances (Labelling) Regulations 1979 as amended). The Leaflets Regulations control the content of any leaflet supplied with a proprietary medicinal product other than one which merely contains instructions as to how to use the product such as those supplied with inhalers.

The labelling requirements apply to medicinal products which are sold, supplied, imported or in a person's possession for sale or supply in the UK. They also apply to articles and substances specified in the Control of Substances for Manufacture Order 1971, the Surgical Materials Order 1971 or in paragraph 3 of Schedule 1 to the Specified Articles and Substances Order 1978 (intra-uterine contraceptive devices), as well as to certain medicinal products exempted from the licensing provisions (e.g. foods and cosmetics). They do not, however, apply to dental filling substances nor to contact lenses.

It is suggested that stock mixtures and other products in the course of preparation or assembly would not be considered as 'in a person's possession for sale or supply' and are thus not covered by the regulations.

Modified requirements apply to products for clinical trial, medicinal tests on animals, import or export, or for incorporation into animal feeding stuffs.

It is an offence to sell, supply etc a product which has a label or contains a leaflet which falsely describes the product or is likely to mislead as to its nature, quality, uses or effects (section 85(5), 86(3)).

It should be remembered that the provisions of a product licence or of a certificate may modify the standard labelling requirements applicable to a product, and that all labels must be consistent with such a licence or certificate (regulation 16).

GENERAL PROVISIONS

These are contained in regulations 17 and 18 and apply to ALL labels. The provisions are –

(a) All labels must be indelible;

(b) All particulars must be legible and clear so as to be easily read by intending purchasers and users;

(c) The label must be on the body of the container, or inside it if the container is transparent (N.B. the batch number of lozenges and pastilles may be shown on a separate sheet inside the container);

(d) All particulars (except numerals) shall be in English, though other languages may also be used in addition, (a product known in the U.K. under a foreign name may be labelled with that name). Also, botanical names may be used for herbal remedies or their ingredients provided that it is a monograph name in the Eur.P., B.P., B.P.C etc.,

(e) Where a product contains a single active ingredient whose non-proprietary name is required on the label, ('aspirin' is an example) it must be prominently displayed;

(f) Products containing aspirin or paracetamol must refer to these by name in the appropriate quantitative particulars;

(g) No label or leaflet may refer, directly or indirectly, to the Act, its regulations or to the Commission or any of the Committees unless such a reference is required by the Act, regulations or a licence,

(h) Every container and every package immediately enclosing the container, of a medicinal product for retail sale must be labelled 'keep out of the reach of children' or similar phrase. Exemptions apply to –

    (i) Toothpastes on the GSL,

    (ii) Foods and cosmetics exempt from licensing;

    (iii) Small containers and 'strip packs' BUT the PACKAGE must bear the warning;

    (iv) Confectionery which is GSL and recommended only for coughs, colds or nasal congestion;

(i) Every container and package of a product intended solely for veterinary use (unless the product is for use in a medicinal test on animals) and every leaflet (except a data sheet) referring to it, must be labelled 'For Animal Treatment Only' (N.B. the words may be omitted if the container is very small).

The Labelling Regulations do not apply to a package which is transparent or cut away so that the particulars on the label of the container are clearly visible. The regulations do not apply to packing cases, crates and the like used only for delivery, but where such a crate contains only packages of a single product, it must be labelled with the batch number, expiry date (if any) and storage conditions. Finally, there is no need to label either the wrapping paper and bags used when the products are sold by retail, the package of a dispensed product or the container and immediate package of a product intended for export.

LABELLING OF PRODUCTS FOR SALE

The detailed controls are specified in regulations 5, 8, 10 and schedule 1. Normally, all containers and all packages which immediately enclose a container of medicinal products must be labelled with the particulars specified below (often referred to as the 'standard particulars'). However, some of the particulars may be omitted if the product licence or clinical trial or animal test certificate so permits.

1. (a) The name of the product (i.e. either the 'non- proprietary name' or a proprietary name).

   (b) Its pharmaceutical form (where the container is enclosed in a package this need only appear on the package.)

   (c) The 'appropriate quantitative particulars' in a conspicuous position. Where both active ingredients and non-active ingredients (e.g. excipients) are stated, the label shall distinguish between them. Where the quantities stated are those used in the preparation of the product that fact must be stated. It is no longer permissible to state the strengths of oral preparations (except for pastilles and lozenges) as percentages.

   (d) Where in 1(a) or 1(c) above the product or an ingredient is identified by a monograph name in a specified publication or in a foreign or international compendium of standards (or by an abbreviation of it or by an approved synonym in the European Pharmacopoeia), the publication and, unless it is the current edition, the edition must be specified.

   (e) Furthermore, where such a name, abbreviation or synyonym is different from the International Non-Proprietary Name (if any) the latter followed by the letters INN must also be used.

2. The quantity of product in the container (or for 'strip- packs' in the package), expressed as weight, volume, capacity or number of dosage units.

3. Directions for use (and for veterinary products the purpose for which it is to be used). The directions may be omitted if a leaflet is enclosed in the package and both the container and package are labelled to refer to the leaflet. A phrase to the effect that the product is to be used in accordance with the directions of a practitioner will suffice on containers not intended for retail sale and also on products which are POM.

4. Any contra-indications, warnings or precautions required to be stated by the product licence.

5. For a veterinary product any restrictions imposed upon its use by the product licence, or if it is a proprietary medicinal product or a ready made veterinary drug, the withdrawal period.

6. Any special handling or storage requirements.

7. If the product should be used within 3 years, its expiry date. This requirement was drafted to comply with Directive 65/65 EEC which was amended by 83/570 so as to require all products to be marked with an expiry date in plain language. The Labelling Regulations will be amended during 1985 to give effect to the change, and it is probable that the new provisions will apply to all new licence applications. Existing products will have to comply by January 1st 1990.

8. The name and address of the product licence holder (or of the general practice pharmacist who assembled it for sale or supply.) In the case of a product assembled under an Article 3 direction (i.e. a direction which allows the product licence holder to pack and label the product with the name and address of the retailer) the name and address of the retailer.

9. Product licence number (if any), preceded by letters PL or other acceptable abbreviation. The number consists of two groups each of four digits. The first group identifies the holder of the licence and any digit which is 0 and not preceded by another digit may be omitted. The licence number may be replaced by the number of the relevant direction if the product was assembled under an Article 3 direction.

10. Batch number of manufacturer, preceded by the letters BN or LOT (the letters can be omitted from small containers and from the crimp of collapsible tubes.)

11. Manufacturer's licence number, preceded by the letters ML (if the manufacturer or assembler has no licence, his name and address). The ML may be omitted if the manufacturer holds the product licence and in certain other cases.

11A. In the case of a veterinary drug which is a proprietary medicinal product or a ready made veterinary drug, the name and address of the product licence holder is used instead of the PL and ML numbers.

12. Any other information required by the product licence (or by a direction if the product is exempt from licensing) to be stated in the label.

13. A veterinary drug which is a proprietary medicinal product or a ready made veterinary drug must be labelled with the species of animal for which it is intended and the route of administration.

Sometimes practical difficulties arise in complying with the above, consequently the requirements have been modified in the cases described below.

Small Containers

These comprise ampoules and other containers with a nominal volume not exceeding 10 ml. When enclosed in a package which is labelled with all the particulars 1 to 12 inclusive, the container need only be labelled with 1(a), (c), (d), (e), 2, 7, 10 and 12 above together with the route of administration unless the latter is obvious. Ampoules must always be labelled with the route of administration (regulation 5(3)).

Unit Packs, 'Bubble' Packs

When the container is a wrapper or a 'bubble' pack etc., and is enclosed in a package which is labelled with all of the particulars 1 to 12 inclusive, the container must be labelled with 1(a), (d), (e), and 12. However, 12 may be omitted if the container is so small as to render it impracticable, and if the container is a capsule etc intended to be broken before administration and it is not practicable to include the particulars in 1(a), (d), and (e) these may omitted too. On strips of 'bubbles' the particulars in 1(a), (d), (e), and 12 may be displayed at frequent intervals (regulation 5(4),(5),(7)).

If the package immediately enclosing the container is itself a bubble pack, then 1(a), (d), (e) and 12 may be displayed at intervals along the strip and complete particulars must be shown on the package which immediately encloses the bubble pack (regulation 5(6)).

Ingredients

The container and package immediately enclosing it must carry the particulars 1(a), (b), (c), (d), (e), 2, 6, 7, 9, 10, 11, and 12, unless is a 'small' container as above, i.e. ampoules, wrappers and sealed units. Substances specified in the Control of Substances for Manufacture Order are 'ingredients' for this purpose (regulation 8).

Surgical Materials

The container and package immediately enclosing it must be labelled with 1(a), (b), (d), (e) 3, 4 and 6–12. The label must also state the origin and nature of the product and its quantity in terms of weight, volume or length (regulation 10).

Products Exempt from Product Licences

There are three such groups of products and modified labelling provisions apply to them except when they are dispensed or packed in 'small' containers

(a) *Foods and Cosmetics* – when they are exempt from licensing. Cosmetics are exempt from the labelling provisions (except those imposed under the Consumer Protection Act). Foods may be subject to the Labelling of Food Regulations. Foods which are medicinal products must be labelled with 1(a),(d),(e), 2 and 6 and the name and address of the manufacturer on both the container and the enclosing package. Containers must also bear 1(c) and 7, and packages 1(b) (regulation 11(1)a.)

(b) *'Specials'* – These are products exempt from licensing under the Special and Transitional Cases Order 1971 or the Special and Miscellaneous Cases Order 1972 as amended. Some manufacturers are licensed to manufacture products to a formula provided by a pharmacist or a practitioner. Such products do not require product licences and are called 'specials'. The container and immediate package must be labelled with 1(a), (c), (d), (e), 2,6,7,10, and 11. The package must also state the pharmaceutical form and the name and address of the manufacturer or of the person responsible for he composition of the product or who first sold or supplied it as a medicinal product (regulation 11(1b)).

(iii) *Pharmacists 'Own-Remedies'* – Many general practice pharmacists have formulae which they make and sell (sometimes under a proprietary name). When these are not advertised and are only sold from the premises on which they were prepared they are exempt from product licensing under the Act (section 10(5)). The container and immediate package must be labelled with 1(a), (c), (d), (e), 2, 3, 6, 7, and the name and address of the seller. The package must also be labelled with the pharmaceutical form (regulation 11(1c). Since such products will be [P] medicines regardless of their composition, those for internal use must be labelled 'Warning. Do not exceed the stated dose', unless one of the other warning labels (for asthma preparations or those containing antihistamines) are appropriate. Furthermore, they must be marked [P]. Great care should be taken in identifying recommendations for use and particularly to avoid the use of the following terms –

Amenorrhoea; Angina; Atherosclerosis; Erysipelas; Gallstones; Multiple sclerosis; Osteoarthritis; Phlebitis; Thrombosis; Ulcer (except when used in the phrase Aphthous ulcer or Mouth ulcer.

Products for Use in Clinical Trials

Products intended for administration during clinical trials are subject to special labelling requirements contained in regulation 6 and schedule 2. Special requirements are necessary so as to permit 'double blind' trials to take place. The requirements apply to containers and to the package immediately enclosing the container. These, except for ampoules, must be labelled with any special storage or handling requirements. In addition, all must bear the following details –

(a) The name and address of the place at which the trial is to be carried out or the name and address of the holder of the licence or certificate authorising the trial;

(b) A designation to identify the trial;

(c) A designation to identify the person to whom the product is to be administered;

(d) If more than one product is to be supplied, a designation that will identify each product; this enables the placebo to be differentiated from the active product when assessing the results of the trial;

(e) Any other information required by the licence or certificate.

Products for Use in Animal Tests

As for products for use in clinical trials and for the same reasons, these are subject to special provisions which are laid down in regulation 7 and Schedule 3.

All containers and all packages immediately enclosing them must bear the words 'For Animal Test Use Only' and the following information –

(a) A designation to identify the test;

(b) Where more than one product is supplied in the test, the container must bear a designation to identify the product;

(c) The quantity of product (number of dosage units, or weight, or volume) in the container;

(d) The purposes for which it is to be used, the dose, the directions for use, route of administration, contra- indications, warnings and any restrictions on its use;

(e) Where it is for incorporation into an animal feeding stuff, directions as to incorporation, the species and categories of species to which it is to be administered and a statement that the incorporation must be in accordance with the terms of the licence or certificate;

(f) Any special handling or storage requirements;

(g) Expiry date;

(h) Any other information required by the licence or certificate.

If the product to be tested is a medicated feeding stuff or a medicinal product for incorporation into a feeding stuff, then in addition to the requirements stated above it must be labelled with any statements required by the licence or certificate and with instructions as to use.

Medicinal Products for Incorporation into Animal Feeding Stuffs or which are Medicated Animal Feeding Stuffs

These provisions are intended to provide manufacturers of medicated animal feeding stuffs with the information they need in order to label their products in accordance with the Labelling of Medicated Feeding Stuffs Regulations 1973. The detail is contained in regulation 14 and Schedule 4 to the Labelling Regulations. It is worth noting that somewhat different requirements apply to the labelling of medicated feeding stuffs *per se* and these are described in detail in Chapter 15.

Where the product is licensed for incorporation into a feeding stuff, or is itself a feeding stuff, the container and the package must be labelled wwith the following particulars –

1. Its proprietary name (if any);

2. The quantity of each active ingredient, conspicuously displayed and identified by its non-proprietary name;

3. If any of the names above are monograph names or abbreviations of such names, the name or letters identifying the publication and, unless in the current edition, figures identifying the edition;

4. If the product or ingredient has an INN different from the monograph name used, then the INN followed by the letters INN must also be given;

5. The quantity of the product in the container stated in terms of weight, volume, capacity or number of dosage units;

6. The purposes for which it may be used and the directions for use, including the daily permissible level of administration (where this is specified in the licence) and the species and categories within species, of animals to which it may be administered;

7. Where the product is to be incorporated into a feeding stuff, the directions for incorporation including the amount of active ingredient to be present in

the complete feeding stuff, and a statement that the incorporation must be in accordance with either the product licence or a prescription given by a veterinarian;

8. Any contra-indications, warnings, and precautions required by the licence to be given to the user of the product;
9. Any restrictions on the use of the product imposed by the licence;
10. Any special handling or storage requirements;
11. The expiry date;
12. The name and address of the product licence holder, or in certain circumstances the person who made or assembled it;
13. The product licence number preceded by PL, or the number of the direction under which it was assembled;
14. Batch number;
15. Manufacturer's licence number preceded by ML, or the name and address of the person who manufactured it;
16. Any statements required by the licence or by the direction;
17. If the product is a medicated feeding stuff and either a protein concentrate or a feed supplement, and is sold otherwise than to a manufacturer, a statement that it is a medicated feed supplement or a medicated protein concentrate;

Where the container is too small to carry all of these particulars, the label should show 1 to 4, 6 to 10 and 13 and 14, and a leaflet giving all of them should also be supplied.

Where the feed is not packed in a container, e.g. when delivered in bulk, a leaflet giving all of the particulars must be supplied to the purchaser.

Products for Importation or Exportation

The labelling requirements applicable to such medicinal products (including those for incorporation into feeding stuffs or which are medicated feeding stuffs) are specified in regulation 12. The box or crate or other package enclosing packages immediately enclosing containers of the same product must be labelled with –

(a) Any special requirements for handling or storage of the product;

(b) The batch number; and

(c) either –

(i) Its product licence number, preceded by the letters PL;

or (ii) The name and address of the product licence holder;

or (iii) The manufacturer's licence number preceded by the letters ML;

or (iv) The name and address of the manufacturer;

or (v) The name and address of the person responsible for its composition.

The above requirements apply to all biological veterinary products and any other medicinal products if the particulars specified above are not shown on the container or on the package immediately enclosing it and the outer package contains only one medicinal product.

Contact Lens Substances

The following provisions of the Contact Lens Fluids and Other Substances (Labelling) Regulations 1979 have begun to take effect. The products affected are solutions intended to be used for sterilising, cleaning, lubricating, or storing contact lenses or blanks, or for use as 'artificial tears' between the lens and the eyeball. Also included are solid products such as powders or tablets which are to be dissolved to make such a solution.

The requirements imposed by these regulations apply to the labels and leaflets used in connection with any contact lens substance which a person sells, supplies, or possesses for sale or supply in the course of his business.

Normally, the container of the substance should be labelled with the following particulars (regulation 5) –

(a) Its product licence number;

(b) Its batch number;

(c) Its name or an appropriate description thereof;

(d) For which of the following purpose(s) it is to be used i.e. cleaning, disinfecting, irrigating, lubricating, wetting, soaking or rinsing a contact lens or blank or as a barrier between such lens or blank and the human eyeball;

(e) The name and address of the product licence holder;

(f) Where it is recommended that the substance should not be applied directly to the eye, a warning, printed in capital letters, to that effect; and

(g) The name and percentage strength of any antimicrobial agent present (the percentage to be calculated in terms of weight in weight (w/w), weight in volume (w/v), or volume in volume (v/v) as appropriate).

Where the warning required by (f) above is necessary on the label of a solid preparation, it should be so expressed (in capital letters) as to relate to the substance in the liquid form in which it is to be administered.

In the event that the container is too small for it to carry a label containing all of the above particulars, the label shall carry as many as is reasonably practicable, precedence being given to them in the order in which they appear above. The remaining particulars shall be shown on a label on the package in which the container is immediately enclosed or in a leaflet which is supplied or intended to be supplied with the product. If the size or nature of the container is such that it is not reasonably practicable to show any of the particulars specified above on a label thereon, they shall be shown on a label on the package in which the container is immediately enclosed or in a leaflet which is supplied with it (regulation 4).

The following particulars must be shown either on a label on the container in which any contact lens substance is contained or on a label on the package in which the container is immediately enclosed or in a leaflet which is supplied with it (regulation 6) –

(a) An expiry date;

(b) A period within which it should be used after the container has first been opened;

(c) Directions for use;

(d) A warning in capital letters, 'DO NOT MIX WITH OTHER FLUIDS EXCEPT AS DIRECTED'; and

(e) A warning that the substance should not be administered to the eye concurrently with any eye medicament except on the advice of a doctor.

Where any contact lens substance is or is to be sold or supplied in solid form as a powder or tablets –

(i) Instructions as to how it is to be prepared for use, including a warning that only recommended fluids should be used for dissolving the substance for administration;

(ii) The particulars specified in paragraph (c) and (e) should be so expressed as to relate to the substance in the liquid form in which it is to be administered; and

(iii) An explanation must accompany the warning set out in paragraph (d) that the warning relates to the substance in the liquid form in which it is to be administered.

Veterinary Drugs

The following requirements apply to veterinary drugs except when they are dispensed products (regulation 14D).

(a) A product which is licensed for sale in Great Britain only or in Northern Ireland only, must be labelled to that effect on both the container and immediate package.

(b) Where the product is included in schedules 1,2 or 3 to the Exemptions from Restrictions on Retail Sale or Supply of Veterinary Drugs Order, is sold or supplied by retail it should be labelled –

   (i) PML if included in schedule 1 or 2 to the above Order and must also bear this when sold by wholesale unless the product is GSL.

   (ii) POM if the product is included in Schedule 3.

Products which are not GSL must be labelled as above when sold by wholesale.

The product, must of, course bear the appropriate warning labels if it contains aspirin, aloxiprin, salicylamide or hexachlorophane.

Contract Manufacture and Assembly

Special labelling requirements apply to products sold or supplied by one company to another before final assembly. Such a situation may arise when Company A manufactures tablets for Company B and the latter company assembles the tablets into their final containers. Alternatively, one company may pay another company to pack the first company's products. The immediate package must be labelled with the name of the product, the name and address of the supplier, the product licence number if any, and the batch number (regulation 15).

Delivery

Where containers and /or packages of a single medicinal product (including a medicated feeding stuff) are packed in a crate, packing case or the like for the purposes of storage or transport, the crate must bear details of the storage and handling requirements, the expiry date and batch number (regulation 13).

WARNINGS AND OTHER SPECIAL REQUIREMENTS

These are contained in regulations 14A, 14B, 14C, 14D, and in Schedules 5 and 6. The requirements specified below must be stated on the container and on the package immediately enclosing it. However, the particulars need not appear on small containers (10 ml or smaller) or unit packs or wrappers (regulation 14E).

Certain phrases and symbols are required to be enclosed within a rectangle in which no other material is included. These are so enclosed below. Where a product contains more than one ingredient requiring more than one warning, it is permissible sometimes to include them all (in modified form) within one rectangle. An example is given below.

The requirements apply to products sold or supplied by retail or offered or exposed for sale by retail. They also apply to those products which can lawfully be sold from automatic machines. They do not apply, unless otherwise stated, to dispensed medicines.

In order to clear existing stocks following a change in the legal status of a product, a period of six months grace is permitted during which products labelled to comply with the 'old' labels may be sold (1981/1791).

General Sale List Products

(a) Products for human use (except when for external use) containing aspirin, aloxiprin or paracetamol must state –

(i) The recommended dosage; and

(ii) 'If the symptoms persist, consult your doctor.'

Such products must also be prominently labelled –

| Contains an aspirin derivative | if aloxiprin is present,

| Contains aspirin | if aspirin is present (unless the name of the product includes 'aspirin') or

| Contains paracetamol | if paracetamol is present, unless the name of the product includes 'paracetamol.'

Paracetamol products must also be labelled –

'Do not exceed the stated dose'

adjacent to the directions or recommended dosage.

A product which contained both aspirin and paracetamol, neither word being used in the name of the product, could be labelled –

| Contains aspirin and paracetamol |

(b) Veterinary drugs containing aloxiprin, aspirin or salicylamide must be prominently labelled –

Unsuitable for cats

If aloxiprin is present | Contains an aspirin derivative |

or if aspirin is present | Contains aspirin |

unless the word(s) is (are) included in the name.

Where a product would be GSL but for the provisions of regulation 8 of the Miscellaneous Provisions Regulations (restrictions as to pack size), it must be labelled [P]. This applies to sales at wholesale and retail.

Pharmacy Medicines

(a) If they contain aspirin, aloxiprin or paracetamol, they must be labelled as above.

(b) If for human use and containing a POM substance which is exempt from POM control because of strength or dosage they must be labelled –

Warning. Do not exceed the stated dose

unless the product is for external use or contains any of the substances specified in (c) below.

(c) If for internal use in humans and the product contains any of the following substances or their salts or molecular compounds –

antazoline, bamipine, bromodiphenhydramine, brompheniramine, buclizine, carbinoxamine, chlorcyclizine, chlorpheniramine, cinnarizine, clemastine, clemizole, cyclizine, cyproheptadine, dimenhydrinate, dimethindene, diphenhydramine, diphenylpyraline, doxylamine, embramine, hyoscine, isothipendyl, mebhydrolin, meclozine, mepyramine, methapyrilene, phenindamine, pheniramine, phenyltoloxamine, promethazine, pyrrobutamine, thenyldiamine, tripelennamine, and triprolidine,

must be labelled –

Warning. May cause drowsiness. If affected do not drive or operate machinery. Avoid alcoholic drink.

(d) Products for human use (other than for external use) in treating asthma or other conditions associated with bronchial spasm or containing ephedrine or any of its salts must be labelled –

Warning. Asthmatics should consult their doctor before using this product.

(e) The products must be labelled [P] (unless they are POM) and must be so labelled when sold by wholesale.

(f) Embrocations, liniments, lotions, liquids antiseptics and other liquid preparations and gels for external use must be labelled –

For external use only

This applies to dispensed medicines as well as those sold by retail.

(g) Products for human use containing hexachlorophane must be labelled –

Not to be used for babies

or with a warning that it should not be used, except on medical advice, in the treatment of a child under 2 years of age. This is also required on dispensed products.

(h) Veterinary products for oral use in treating or preventing liver fluke disease in cattle and containing hexachlorophane should bear a warning that the product should not be used in lactating cattle.

(i) Veterinary products containing hexachlorophane for oral use in treating or preventing liver fluke disease in cattle or sheep should bear a warning that protective clothing should be worn by the operator when administering the product.

The warnings in (h) and (i) should be enclosed in a rectangle, and are also required on dispensed products.

It is permissible to combine warnings when appropriate, e.g. if a product contained an antihistamine and ephedrine, it could be labelled

Warning. May cause drowsiness. If affected do not drive or operate machinery. Avoid alcoholic drink. Asthmatics should consult their doctor before using this product.

Prescription Only Medicines

These must be labelled [POM]. They must also bear any of the appropriate warnings in (f), (g), (h) or (i) above.

Herbal, Homoeopathic and Certain Other Remedies

When a product is labelled to show its use in any of the diseases or complaints for which advertisements are normally prohibited by schedule 2 to the Labelling and Advertising to the Public Regulations 1978, two other warning labels must also be attached to the container and package. These are –

(1) If a herbal remedy, 'A herbal remedy for . ...',

if a homoeopathic remedy, 'A homoeopathic remedy for.....................',

if a biochemic remedy, 'A biochemic remedy for ....',

if an anthroposophic product, 'An anthroposophic remedy for...'.

(2) 'Warning: If you think you have . consult a registered medical practitioner before taking this product. If you are already receiving medical treatment, tell your doctor that you are also taking this product.'

In both cases the name of the disease or complaint must be stated in the space provided (schedule 5 to the Labelling and Advertising to the Public Regulations).

As is the case for pharmacist's 'own remedies', the words Amenorrhoea, Angina etc may not be used except as part of a warning regarding contra-indications or precautions.

Spermicidal Contraceptives

The Labelling and Advertising to the Public Regulations 1978 require every container and every package containing a spermicidal contraceptive to bear the following –

> 'Warning. A higher degree of protection against pregnancy will be afforded by using another method of contraception in addition to a spermicidal contraceptive.'
>
> 'Where avoidance of pregnancy is essential, the choice of contraceptive should be made in consulation with a doctor or a family planning clinic.'

LEAFLETS

Some manufacturers enclose a leaflet with the container of their products. Such leaflets may promote the sale of others of the company's products, and, as advertisements, are subject to control under the advertising regulations. Other leaflets are used to amplify the instructions given to patients so as to enhance the effect of the product or to improve patient compliance with the dosage regimen. These leaflets are called 'package inserts' or 'patient package inserts' (PPI's) and can be viewed as ancilliary labels. It therefore makes sense to impose the same sorts of control over them as apply to labels. This control is applied by menas of the Leaflets Regulations. As is the case with labels, excessive amounts of information on the leaflet reduces the effectiveness of the leaflet. Leaflets which merely describe the method for using an appliance for administering a dose of the product are not subject to control because the appliance is not a medicinal product.

Whereas a manufacturer must pack his product in a container and label it with the particulars described above, there is no obligation upon him to include a leaflet with the product. However, when a leaflet is supplied with a proprietary medicinal product (i.e. a ready-made product on the market in the UK under a special name and in a special pack) it must contain the following particulars –

(a) The proprietary name and the appropriate non-proprietary name;

(b) The appropriate quantitative particulars as for labels;

(c) Where an ingredient has an INN which is different from the monograph name, the INN;

(d) Directions for use but these may be omitted on POM's and where the product licence permits;

(e) Therapeutic indications, but these are not required on products which are POM or supplied only to appropriate practitioners or where the product licence directs that they must not be included;

(f) Contra-indications, warnings and precautions;

(g) Any special handling or storage requirements;

(h) Name and address of the person who either holds the product licence or who sells it by retail;

(i) Name and address of the manufacturer and, if different, of the person who assembled it.

All particulars shall be in English and shall be consistent with the relevant product licence. Such a leaflet may only refer to another product if –

(i) The leaflet contains instructions for using an appliance for administering the proprietary product, and that appliance can be used for administering other products having the same pharmaceutical form, or

(ii) Contains the particulars (d) to (h) above and exactly the same particulars would apply to other products of a different description, or

(iii) The other product is mentioned in connection with contra- indications or precautions or action to be taken in the event of over-dosage of the proprietary product.

The required particulars shall be clearly separate from the remainder of the contents of the leaflet.

The product licence holder shall supply the licensing authority with a copy of the particulars at least 6 weeks before the first leaflet is issued. The authority will immediately acknowledge its receipt, and may within 21 days of receiving the particulars, notify the licence holder that the leaflet should not be issued or should be modified. In the absence of such notification, the licence holder can assume that the leaflet has been approved for issue.

LABELLING OF DISPENSED PRODUCTS

Regulation 9 contains the detail, and in the context of labelling, 'dispensed' means supply by or on the prescription of, a practitioner, and also includes 'counter-prescribed' products and those made to a formula provided by the purchaser. When a pharmacist 'counter-prescribes' a medicinal product or when he makes one to the formula of the customer, he may either label it as described below or with the full details required when products are sold.

The container (or the package immediately enclosing the container) of a dispensed product must be labelled with –

(a) The name of the patient, if for human use;

(b) The name and address of the owner or the person having charge of the animal, if for animal use;

(c) Directions for use (unless the purchaser provided the formula);

(d) Name and address of the seller;

(e) Date of dispensing;

(f) Where a product has been prescribed by a practitioner, such of the following as he requests –

  (i) The name of the product,

  (ii) Directions for use, and

  (iii) Precautions relating to the use of the product, where a pharmacist is of the opinion that any of the prescribed particulars is inappropriate and is unable to contact the prescriber he may substitute other particulars of the same kind. The pharmacist may add further information if he considers it necessary.

Dispensed medicines must of course comply with the general provisions in 'Keep out of the reach of children' and, if appropriate, 'for animal treatment only'.

Where the product is dispensed on the prescription of a veterinarian and consists of a medicated animal feeding stuff or a product to be incorporated into a feeding stuff, it must be labelled with (b) to (f) above. In addition, the label must state the name of the product, its active ingredients (using official names where possible), the amount of the product, its contra-indications etc, special handling requirements and any other information required by the licence.

Dispensed products which are embrocations, liniments, lotions, liquid antiseptics or other liquid preparations for external use must be labelled 'for external use only.' No definition of 'external use' is given in the Labelling Regulations nor in the Act (though it is in the Fluted Bottles Regulations and in several other statutory instruments). Presumably this was a deliberate omission intended to permit pharmacists and others involved in in labelling products to use their discretion in particular cases. Whilst embrocations, lotions and liniments are always used externally, and would need to be labelled as such, products such as gargles, mouthwashes, pessaries and some suppositories can give rise to difficulty. It is suggested that the advice contained in the Pharmaceutical Handbook is normally more appropriate viz –

> 'Not to be taken' for eye lotions, eye drops, ear drops, nasal drops, pessaries and suppositories.
>
> 'Not to be swallowed' for mouthwashes and gargles.
>
> 'Not to be taken by mouth' for enemas.

Furthermore, products containing hexachlorophane shall bear the appropriate warnings (see above) on the CONTAINER and PACKAGE.

Where a package encloses a number of containers of the same product, it is only necessary to label the package with the required particulars, there is no need to label each individual container. Thus the particulars specified above would appear on an ampoule box but not necessarily on each ampoule. Similarly, 'blister' and 'bubble packs' are containers so again the information required above could be written on the box in which the bubble strips were packed.

Modern medicines are carefully designed and made, and in order to achieve the optimal therapeutic effect with the minimum of side-effects, they should be taken or used at the correct times and in the correct manner. The doctor normally informs the patient as to the amount and frequency of dosage, but many patients fail to assimilate the information completely and some even forget it. The pharmacist reinforces the doctor's instructions by writing them on the label. In addition, it is now a professional requirement for the pharmacist to include the appropriate supplementary labels so as to enhance the efficacy and safety of the product. Such information may be regarded as 'further information' as mentioned in (f) above. These supplementary labels are of two types, one is advisory and aims at improving the effect of the product. The other is cautionary and is chiefly concerned with safety. The labels and the circumstances in which they should be used are reprinted in Appendix 2. They are also listed in Appendix 4 of the BNF No.9, and the relevant numbers are stated against each product in the Formulary.

The Council of the Pharmaceutical Society of Great Britain directed that from January 1st 1984, all labels on dispensed products should be mechanically produced. Some pharmacists have responded by purchasing typewriters for the purpose. Others have chosen to use computers which, in addition to printing the label, can sometimes be programmed to print the appropriate warning labels. Several coputer systems automatically adjust stock levels to take account of quantities of drugs dispensed.

OFFENCES

The offences that can be committed in relation to packaging and labelling medicinal products, and in relation to leaflets supplied with such products are as follows –

(a) Selling or supplying a product not in a container (section 85(4));

(b) Issuing a false or misleading label (or leaflet) with a medicinal product (sections 85(1), and 86(3));

(c) Packing a product in a container which does not comply with the requirements of the regulations (section 87(2));

(d) Selling or supplying (or possessing for sale etc.) a product which is not of the colour or not marked in the manner required by the regulations (section 88(3));

(e) Selling products from an automatic machine which is not marked in the manner required by the regulations (section 89(2));

(f) To fail to submit a leaflet to the authority, or to ignore a direction that it should not be issued or that it should be modified before issue (Leaflets Regulations, regulation 5).

Contraventions of Part V of the Act or of regulations made under it are triable either summarily or on indictment.

DEFENCES

It is possible that a wholesaler or a retailer could be prosecuted for selling or possessing a product which had been incorrectly labelled by the manufacturer. In such a case, the seller may be able to avail himself of one of the defences specified in sections 121 or 122 of the Act, though it is probable that proceedings would be taken directly against the manufacturer. However, a retailer would be liable if some important piece of information had been obscured by, for example, an adhesive price ticket.

ENFORCEMENT

Under arrangements made by the Ministers, the Pharmaceutical Society have powers to enforce the provisions made under sections 85 and 87(2) both generally and in respect of registered pharmacies. The maximum penalties for such offences are –

(i) On summary conviction £1000 fine, or

(ii) On conviction on indictment, an unlimited fine and/or 2 years imprisonment.

References

Pharm. J., 1982, i, 107

Medicines Commission Report for 1980, paragraph 4.6

Pharm. J., 1985, i, 366-7

Chapter 17
The Quality of Medicinal Products Reaching the Consumer

INTRODUCTION

There are three aspects to the provision of quality with respect to medicinal products, namely the quality as manufactured, the maintenance of this quality during storage by the wholesaler and retailer, and the prevention of adulteration by retailers.

The quality of any product has to be built into it during manufacture. Compliance by the manufacturer with the specifications laid down in the product licence should ensure the quality of medicinal products at the completion of manufacture. Similarly, the aim of the wholesale dealer's licence is to ensure that only persons having the knowledge and facilities to store medicines correctly are allowed to carry on this activity. Furthermore, the wholesaler sells original packs of products (unless he also holds an 'assembler's' licence) and therefore adulteration is unlikely to occur. Thus, products reaching the retailer, pharmacist, or practitioner should be of the appropriate quality. Although all products reach the basic requirements of the product licence, the standards of some manufacturers are higher than others so it is not necessarily true to say that all products that meet the official specifications are of the same quality.

All that now needs to be done is to ensure that deterioration or adulteration does not occur at this last link in the distributive chain. We shall see that there are random checks on retailers, including general practice pharmacists, to detect the sale or supply of products which are sub-standard either due to faulty or prolonged storage, or because they have become adulterated either deliberately or accidently. There are no such checks on hospitals, dispensing doctors, dentists or veterinarians.

For over a century, the responsibility for ensuring that drugs (and foods) were of suitable quality when offered for sale by retail has been with a number of local 'Food and Drugs Authorities,' set up under the Food and Drugs Acts. The system worked reasonably well but there were some problems. The Food and Drugs Acts laid down no standards for drugs. This was not an oversight because the Select Committees which studied the Bills that became the Food and Drugs Act 1879 and that of 1894–6, both rejected the proposal that the British Pharmacopoeial standards should apply to drugs. Consequently, it was left to the court in each case to decide upon the appropriate standard. Another disadvantage was that while some Authorities provided their analyst with excellent staff, facilities and equipment, others were less generous so that the effectiveness of the Act varied from place to place. A third problem arose when it was decided that the supply of a defective drug on an NHS prescription was not an offence under the Act. This occurred in 1967 when a pharmacist supplied a proprietary medicinal product containing a sliver of glass to a patient on a NHS prescription. The local Food and Drug authority prosecuted the pharmacist under section 2 of the Food and Drugs Act for 'selling to the prejudice of the purchaser a drug not of the quality demanded'. The magistrates held that the pharmacist did not sell the product to the executive council, he provided 'services'. The case went to the High Court by way of a 'case stated'. Here the Lord Chief Justice and their Lordships upheld the magistrates' decision (Pharm. J., 1968, p.430).

The Medicines Act has remedied these defects in so far as medicinal products are concerned, but it has retained the basic mechanism of enforcement laid down in the Food and Drugs Act. The retail pharmacist does, of course, sell various products which are foods, and consequently is also subject to inspection under the Foods Act 1983.

The provisions described below therefore complement the licensing provisions to ensure that medicinal products sold or supplied to the public comply with the highest standards. The provisions are to found in sections 63–65 in Part III of the Act, and in sections 98–103 in Part VII. Schedule 3 contains the details as to the carrying out of sampling procedures and related matters, and the form of certificates of analysis are specified in the Certificates of Analysis Regulations 1977. The powers of Ministers in relation to the enforcement of the Act, and their ability to delegate some of these to the Pharmaceutical Society of Great Britain and to Food and Drug authorities are to be found in sections 108–110. Similarly the rights and responsibilities of inspectors appointed to enforce the provisions are contained in sections 111–116.

In order to avoid any possible infringement of the Act, the prudent retailer will purchase medicinal products only from reputable companies. He will also ensure that the products are stored correctly, sold in rotation and that old stock is destroyed. Similarly, a product which has an abnormal appearance is immediately removed from stock and either destroyed or returned to the manufacturer for examination. Products likely to be affected by heat or sunlight should not be displayed in shop windows. These points are now contained in the Guide to Good Dispensing Practice (Part IV).

Sometimes a substance or product is used for non-medicinal purposes and 'commercial' or 'technical' grades are available which are suitable for the purpose and frequently cheaper, e.g. turpentine oil. When selling such a product, the pharmacist should ensure that it is clearly labelled –

COMMERCIAL TURPENTINE
NOT FOR MEDICINAL USE

together with any other necessary information or warnings.

STANDARDS FOR MEDICINAL PRODUCTS

Pharmacopoeias

The Medicines Act requires medicinal products and certain other substances and articles used in medicine, surgery, midwifery, dentistry or in veterinary practice and surgery to comply with official standards (section 65). The British Pharmacopoeia (BP) contains 'relevant information' (i.e. descriptions of, standards for, or notes or other information) relating to such substances and articles or used in the manufacture of such products (section 99(7)).

Part VII of the Act enabled the copyright in the British Pharmacopoeia to be transferred to Her Majesty from the General Medical Council who had held it since the Medical Act 1858. This permitted the British Pharmacopoeia Commission to assume responsibility for future editions. The Commission is also authorised to produce other compendia containing relevant information about medicinal products and substances and articles used in medicine. To date, it has published the list of British Approved Names, and the Infra-Red Reference Spectra which contains the spectra of almost 400 substances in the main volume and three supplements. The British Pharmacopoeia (Veterinary) contains relevant information about substances and articles used in or in the manufacture of veterinary products and animal feeding stuffs.

A pharmacopoeia typically contains an entry (called a 'monograph') for each drug substance in common use. It also contains a monograph for each officially recognised pharmaceutical preparation of the substance. The name used at the head of the monograph is regarded as the official name, and other names (called 'synonyms') may also be given. Many substances also have an abbreviated name. A 'monograph name' means any of these names. The word 'monograph' means a monograph in the European Pharmacopoeia, the British Pharmacopoeia, any compendium published under section 99 of the Act, the British Pharmaceutical Codex (1971/973; 1972/2076; 1981/164). If the substance is a pure chemical its structural formula, empirical formula, molecular weight and other chemical properties are described and usually a brief description of its appearance. Some tests which can be used to identify the substance are given and usually a detailed procedure is laid down for its assay. This is very important, because different assay procedures often give different results.It is therefore imperative that all analysts use the same method.

Even when the same method is used, different analysts obtain slightly different results when analysing different portions of the same sample, especially when analysing pharmaceutical preparations so to take account of this variation, the limits are drawn slightly wider than they really need to be. This also allows for some deterioration due to storage and also to variations in sample due to manufacturing procedures. Unfortunately, some manufacturers take advantage of the wide limits and aim to make their product in such a way as to comply with the specifications but towards the lower end of the range. The product can truthfully be labelled 'BP' but if the substance is not very stable, or if the sample is tested by an analyst who 'reads low', then it may fail to comply with the specifications and cause problems for the seller. It must therefore be realised that the official standards are the minimum permissible for products when sold to the public. Reputable manufacturers have far higher 'in house' standards which are designed to ensure that the product will retain its quality until the end of its stated shelf life if correctly stored.

In addition to monographs on the various substances, a pharmacopoeia typically contains a number of tests of more general application. For example, the BP contains tests which measure the rate of disintegration of tablets, and tests for the uniformity of weight of tablets. It also contains details of procedures used to sterilise injection solutions and other products which are required to be sterile and standard methods for the performance of sterilty tests on such products.

Over the years, countries have developed different tests and standards for many of these purposes and these have been incorporated into the national pharmacopoeia. While there is usually very little practical difference in the effects of these tests and procedures, they cause difficulties for companies wishing to market a product in different countries. Two attempts have been made to overcome this problem, the first involved the publication by the World Health Organisation of the International Pharmacopoeia or to give it its official name 'Specifications for the Quality Control of Pharmaceutical Preparations'. More recently, the European Pharmacopoeia has been published under the direction of the Council of Europe. Section 65(7) of the Medicines Act authorised the Ministers to notify a date in the Gazette from which the European Pharmacopoeia (Eur.P.) would take precedence over the standards published in the BP.

The Medicines Act also recognised the standards published in other books (section 103). The British Pharmaceutical Codex published by the Pharmaceutical Society of Great Britain has for over 70 years contained legally recognised standards for numerous drugs, preparations and surgical dressings. Many of these products are still used either in the UK or abroad but are less popular than formerly. The Codex was also useful in that it provided standards and methods for the preparation of obsolescent 'galenical' products such as tinctures and extracts, which no longer appear in the BP. It also contained the formulae for numerous mixtures, creams, ointments, pastes and other dosage forms. The last BPC to contain this information was published in 1973 and continues to be 'current' for the purposes of the Act. The Pharmaceutical Codex published in 1979 contains the formulae but not the standards for many products and, in addition, a considerable amount of information of value in a clinical setting.

Similarly, the British Veterinary Codex contains standards for drugs used in veterinary practice. Both sets of standards will continue to be recognised until such time as they are replaced by standards of the Eur.P, BP, or BP(Vet).

The BP is published by the Health Ministers on the advice of the Medicines Commission, while the BP(V) is published by the Agriculture Ministers on similar advice (section 99).

Since 1st July 1973, the standards of the European Pharmacopoeia (Eur.P) together with any amendments or alterations published in the London Gazette, have taken precedence over those of the BP. The Medicines Commission may approve a name as a synonym for the name at the head of a monograph in the European Pharmacopoeia, and when such a name is published in the Gazette it becomes an 'approved synonym' (section 65(7),(8)).

There are, therefore, several sets of standards, and the Act ranks them in order of precedence. Documents, for example labels and specifications in applications for licences, often refer to one or other of the books of standards, and the Act calls these books 'specified publications'.

Formularies

There are also two formularies published jointly by the British Medical Association and the Pharmaceutical Society, namely the British National Formulary (BNF) and the Dental Practitioners'Formulary (DPF). These have a different purpose from the pharmacopoeias. A pharmacopoeia is a book of standards, a formulary on the other hand is designed to provide prescribers, nurses, and pharmacists with the information they require for the effective treatment of patients.

The British National Formulary contains the formulae for a number of standard preparations and notes as to the actions, strengths, dosages and routes of administration of most of the drugs in current use. There is also an indication of their price. A valuable feature of the book is the inclusion of an introductory section which gives information on prescribing for children, for the elderly, for pregnant women and for nursing mothers as well as for those suffering from liver or renal diseases. There are also sections on adverse reactions to drugs, drug dependence, and the emergency treatment of poisoning. The remainder of the book is divided into 15 sections each of which deals with a particular body system (e.g. gastro-intestinal system) or other major topic (e.g. infections). Each section starts with a classification of the drugs described therein, and each class begins with a comparison of the properties of the members of every group of drugs involved. It is published biannually, and is designed to provide doctors and pharmacists with an authoritative summary of the current status of the drugs. The Dental Practitioners' Formulary contains the formulae of a few preparations used in dental practice. Both formularies are recognised by the National Health Service, and in fact, dentists are limited by their terms of service with the NHS to prescribing only preparations mentioned in the DPF.

Specified Publications

This means any of the following –

(a) the European Pharmacopoeia (Eur.P);

(b) the British Pharmacopoeia (BP);

(c) the British Pharmaceutical Codex (BPC);

(d) the British Veterinary Codex (BVetC);

(e) the British National Formulary (BNF);

(f) the Dental Practitioners' Formulary (DPF);

(g) any compendium prepared and published under section 99;

(h) the list of British Approved Names (BANs).

Current

Where a label, licence or certificate refers to any of the above publications, but not to a particular edition, then, unless the licence or certificate expressly states otherwise, the reference is to the edition current at the time of the alleged offence (not that current at the time of issue of the licence etc.). The current edition at any time is the edition in force at that time and includes any amendments, additions and deletions made to it up to that time (section 65(4), section 103). In relation to an obsolete edition, it means the specification in force immediately before it was superseded by a subsequent edition.

Appropriate Current Monograph

Where a product is the subject of a monograph in more than one publication, the 'appropriate current monograph' in relation to a particular name means the monograph (if any) headed by that name, or by a name for which it is an approved synonym, in the current edition of –

(a) the European Pharmacopoeia, or, if there is no such monograph,

(b) the British Pharmacopoeia, or if there is no such monograph,

(c) of a compendium published under Part VII of the Act, or if there is no such monograph,

(d) of the British Pharmaceutical Codex or British Veterinary Codex (section 65(5) as amended).

Relevant Monograph

The phrase 'relevant monograph' is often used in relation to the sale or supply of products. Where the purchaser or a prescriber uses a name which is a monograph name and also specifies an edition of a particular publication, the phrase means that edition of that monograph. If there is no such monograph, it means the appropriate current monograph (if any) as above. If, however, the name and the publication were specified but not the edition, then the phrase means the monograph in the current edition, or if there is no such monograph, the appropriate current monograph (if any) or if there is no such, then the monograph which appeared in the last edition of the publication which did contain that monograph. If no publication is specified, it means the appropriate current monograph.

The phrase is similarly interpreted in the case of products offered or exposed for sale in containers labelled in any of those ways.

OFFENCES

Compliance with Standards

Where a purchaser or a prescriber requests a product by means of a name which is used at the head of a 'relevant monograph' or is an approved synonym of such a name, then it is an offence to sell or supply a product which does not comply with the monograph standards (section 65(1)). It is not necessary for a conviction that the purchaser or prescriber specify the publication, it is sufficient for them to use the name or synonym. Thus a request for 'Soluble Aspirin Tablets' must be filled by supplying Dispersible Aspirin Tablets BP.

It is also an offence to offer or expose for sale or supply a product by reference to a monograph name if that product does not meet the specified standards (section 65(2)).

Where in any of the above cases the name is that of the active ingredient but not of the product itself, then the product must comply with the standards for the active ingredient (section 65(3)).

Adulteration

This means the addition of a substance to, or the removal of a substance from, a product. An example of the former is the addition of water to milk or to glycerol. The removal of an ingredient is more difficult to achieve but was not uncommon when crude drugs such as senna pods were sold, the pods could be soaked in water to extract the active ingredients and then removed and carefully dried before being sold.

Section 63 makes it an offence to adulterate medicinal products 'so as to affect injuriously the composition of the product with intent that the product be sold in that state.' It is also an offence to sell, offer or expose for sale or to possess such a product for sale. Clearly, if the product is not 'injuriously affected' by an addition or removal no offence has been committed. Likewise, if the addition or removal was carried out to enhance the stability of the product, as for example, the addition of antioxidants to oils, no offence is committed but it would be wise to label the product with details of the addition. It should be noted that a retailer may be convicted of this offence (selling or possessing for sale) a product that was adulterated by someone else, e.g. a supplier or even a dishonest employee.

Products Not of the Nature or Quality Demanded

A related but separate offence is to sell to the prejudice of the purchaser any medicinal product not of the nature or quality demanded (section 64(1)). Such an offence could arise by selling an adulterated product. However, it might be easier to prove than adulteration. It is also an offence to supply such a product on a prescription.

It is NOT a defence to plead that a person who purchased a medicinal product for analysis had not been prejudiced (section 64(2)). This provision has been included in all Food and Drugs Acts since a magistrate dismissed a summons against the seller of watered milk. An inspector (Hoyle) purchased a sample of milk from Hitchman and told him that it would be analysed. The milk contained 24% additional water. In cross examination, Hoyle admitted that he personally had not been 'prejudiced' because the money he had paid for the milk was provided by the local authority, nor had he been injured. The magistrate dismissed the case because the sale had not been 'to the prejudice of the purchaser'. Hoyle appealed and the Divisional Court directed the magistrate to convict because the Act was intended to protect the public from fraud, it was not necessary to show that Hoyle had personally been 'prejudiced'. The phrase 'to the prejudice..' had been inserted to prevent someone being prosecuted for selling a *superior* product (Hoyle v. Hitchman 1879).

If the purchaser is told before the sale takes place that a drug is not of the usual nature or quality, then presumably, no offence has been committed. Thus, in an emergency, one could sell to a practitioner a product that had passed its expiry date provided that this had been drawn to the purchaser's attention. Similarly, the presence of extraneous matter in a product does not constitute an offence if it is proved to be an inevitable consequence of the process of manufacture or preparation of the product (section 64(3)).

DEFENCES

Most of the offences relating to quality are 'absolute' offences, i.e. the prosecutor does not have to prove that the defendant knew of the offence or that he actually committed it, it is sufficient that the product sold did not meet the necessary specifications. Nevertheless, two defences are available.

Where a Third Party is Responsible

If the person charged (e.g. a retailer) can prove that the contravention was due to the act or default of another person (e.g. a manufacturer or a wholesaler or an employee), this other person may be convicted of the offence. Furthermore, if the retailer can also prove that he used all due diligence to ensure compliance with the provisions then he is entitled to be acquitted. In order to take advantage of this defence, the original defendant must give 7 days notice to the prosecutor that he believes the offence to be due to the conduct of X and that he intends to use this defence. X is then notified so that he can prepare his defence (section 121).

This defence may be used for offences arising out of sections 63, 64, 65, 85, 86, 87, 88, 89, 90, 93, 94, 95, and 96 and any regulations made under them.

Warranty Defence

This defence can only be used in cases involving the sale, offer or exposure or advertisement for sale, or possession for sale of any article or substance. The offences in relation to which the defence can be used are sections 63(b), 64, 65, 85, 86, 87, 88, and 90 and of any regulations made under them.

If the defendant can prove that –

(1) he purchased the article or substance as being one which could lawfully be sold or dealt with in the manner in which he in fact dealt with it, and with a written warranty to that effect; and

(2) at the time of the offence he had no reason to believe that it was otherwise; and

(3) that is was then in the same state as when he purchased it, then he may plead the warranty defence.

The written warranty may take the form of a name or description entered on a delivery note or invoice or label or a statement in a price list or catalogue. It is sometimes quite easy to prove each of the three items specified above, particularly when the product is sold in sealed containers. However, when products are sold from stock which has been opened previously it might be very difficult to prove that the product was sold in the same state as when it was purchased. It is even more difficult when a product has been stored in a container different from that in which it was received from the supplier. For this reason the use of 'shop rounds' etc. is not recommended. It is also useful and prudent to stamp the labels of incoming products with the date of receipt, and possibly the name of the supplier (e.g. wholesaler).

A defendant who intends to rely on the warranty defence, must send to the prosecutor a copy of the warranty and a statement of the name and address of the person from whom he received it. He must also notify that person. These notices must be sent at least 3 clear days before the date set for the court hearing (section 122).

ENFORCEMENT

The enforcement of those provisions of the Act relating to the purity and quality of medicines and the protection of the public rests with th appropriate Ministers (sections 108(1), 109(1) and 110(1)). For the sake of simplicity the arrangements made for England and Wales will be described in full, it being understood that analogous provision is made for Scotland and for Northern Ireland.

Section 108(2) permits the Minister to make arrangements with or give directions to either Food and Drugs Authorities or to the Pharmaceutical Society of Great Britain, or both, to enforce (concurrently with him) certain provisions in so far as they apply to the retail sale, possession, offer or exposure for sale or supply in circumstances corresponding to retail sale. The provisions concerned are found in sections 62(1), 63(b), 64, and 65. The Minister has used his powers in this respect by making arrangements with the Pharmaceutical Society to enforce the provisions of sections 63(b), 64 and 65 in all retail shops and pharmacies. The Ministers do not appear to have used their powers to delegate the enforcement of section 62(1)(a).

Section 108(4) permits the making, jointly by the Minister of Health and the Minister of Agriculture, of regulations specifying a body (i.e. the Pharmaceutical Society, a Food and Drugs Authority, a council of a county district which is not a Food and Drugs Authority, or the overseers of the Inner Temple and the Middle Temple) to enforce regulations made under section 66. Likewise, regulations made jointly may require the Pharmaceutical Society or a Food and Drugs Authority or both, to have a power concurrently with the appropriate Minister to enforce the provisions of sections 53 and 54 (section 108(7)). These have been made in regulation 2 of the Sale or Supply (Miscellaneous Provisions) Regulations 1980, and the Pharmaceutical Society are responsible for enforcement in pharmacies and the premises of sellers of products in Articles 3, 4 and 5 of the Veterinary Drugs Exemption Order, while food and drug authorities are responsible for enforcing the law in other retail shops.

The Pharmaceutical Society has a concurrent duty to enforce the provisions of sections 52 and 58, and regulations made under sections 60 or 61 in their application to premises where medicines are sold by retail or supplied in circumstances corresponding to retail sale (section 108(6)).

The council of every county or county borough and of every London borough and the Common Council of the City of London have a duty, concurrently with the appropriate Minister, to enforce in their area any order made under section 62(1)b of the Act, i.e. prohibitions relating to animal feeding stuffs, and section 90 (provisions relating to the labelling and packaging of medicated animal feeding stuffs) and any regulations made under it (section 108(8)). Standards for medicated animal feeding stuffs are imposed under the Act together with provisions for their enforcement. These are dealt with in Chapter 15.

Only the Ministers may enforce the provisions of the Act in relation to –

(1) any hospital;

(2) premises used by a practitioner in carrying on his practice;

(3) any other premises used for veterinary medicine or veterinary surgery for the purposes of an institution (section 108(9)).

Furthermore, if a Minister feels that any of the bodies is failing in respect of any provisions to perform its duty he may decide to enforce those provisions himself (section 108(10)).

The 'appropriate Minister' means where the matter concerns exclusively veterinary drugs or section 90 or regulations made thereunder, the Minister of Agriculture. In any other case it means the Minister of Health.

Thus, the Ministers have a duty to enforce all of these provisions. They may delegate enforcement duties to various other bodies, and can do this in one or more of several ways, e.g. by direction, by making 'arrangements', and by making regulations.

The enforcement in Scotland is dealt with in section 109. Basically, the Secretary of State has the same powers and duties as the Ministers have in section 108 and has used them in an identical way. However, in Scotland, only a Procurator Fiscal can institute criminal proceedings, so the enforcement authorities cannot themselves institute proceedings (section 109(4)).

In Northern Ireland, the duty of enforcement lies with the Minister of Health and Social Services (or for veterinary drugs and medicated animal feeding stuffs, jointly with the Minister of Agriculture). The Minister of Health may arrange or direct that health authorities enforce the relevant provisions in their area (section 110).

Inspection

Every inspector employed by an enforcement authority is provided with a written authority, which must be produced on demand. An inspector is entitled to enter any premises at any reasonable time to ascertain whether any contravention of the Act or of its subordinate legislation has taken place. Similarly, he may enter and inspect any ship, aircraft, hover vehicle, or any other vehicle or any stall for the same purpose. If the premises is used only as a private dwelling house the inspector must give 24 hours notice of his intended entry, but, a justice of the peace may, on sworn information given in writing, issue a warrant authorising entry, by force if necessary. Such a warrant will only be issued when the justice is satisfied that either admission has been refused or a refusal is likely and notice of the intention to apply for a warrant was given to the occupier. He may also issue a warrant when an application for admission or the giving of such notice would defeat the object of the entry. Warrants may also be issued when the case is urgent, or the premises are unoccupied or the occupier is temporarily absent. A warrant shall continue in force for 1 month (section 111).

The inspector may buy any substance or article appearing to him to be a medicinal product, or to be a package, container, label or leaflet intended to be used in connection with such a product, or any equipment which may be used in the preparation or assembly or testing of medicinal products. In addition, he may take a sample, or may purchase a sample. He can inspect any book or other document relating to the business of manufacturing, assembling, selling or supplying medicinal products and may take copies of any entry in such a document. Furthermore, he may require a person having authority to do so, to open any container, package, automatic vending machine or to permit him to do so. Any sample obtained shall be dealt with as specified in Schedule 3 to the Act. Where an inspector reasonably believes that a substance or article to be connected with an offence, he may seize or detain it. He may similarly seize any document as evidence. He must notify the owner of the seizure. The owner of the seized substance may, within 21 days of notification, request that a sample of the material be set aside or the seized substance be treated as a sample, whichever the inspector considers the most appropriate. However, the inspector need not comply with the request if it is not reasonably practicable. The seized material shall be divided into three parts, each of which is sealed and marked, and one part shall be supplied to the person who requested it. The provisions of Schedule 3 then apply (section 113). Where an inspector enters a building, vehicle, ship, aircraft, or stall in the absence of the owner he shall leave it as effectively secured against trespass as he found it. It is an offence to wilfully obstruct an inspector, wilfully fail to comply with any requirement made by him, or without reasonable cause fail to give him any other assistance or information. The giving of false information is a more serious offence.

The enforcing authority authorises persons to act as 'sampling officers'. A sampling officer has the right to purchase any drug, including POMs and Controlled Drugs for subsequent analysis. Normally, the purchase is completed before the officer identifies himself, but when restricted substances are to be purchased, the seller is entitled to satisfy himself that the purchaser is a bona fide sampling officer. In the case of POMs (including of course Controlled Drugs) the officer must present an order signed by a public analyst, sampling officer, agricultural analyst or other person authorised by an enforcement authority, stating his status and the amount of POM required (see Schedule 4 to POM Order).

As before, the sample is divided into three parts and each part is packed and sealed. The seller retains one part and may send it privately to an analyst. The sampling officer keeps the other two. Where a sample consists of substances or articles enclosed in unopened containers and the officer feels that it is not reasonably practicable to open the containers or that to do so would impede the analysis or affect the composition of the product, he may purchase several containers and divide them into three lots. Where the sample is obtained from an automatic machine, one part of the sample is supplied either to the person whose name and address are stated thereon as the owner of the machine, or, if there is no such name and address, the person who is the occupier of the premises on which it stands or to which it is fixed. Where the sample was manufactured or assembled by a person whose name and address in the UK are stated on the container (not being the person to whom one part of the sample was supplied) the sampling officer shall notify that person that a sample has been obtained and specify the person from whom it was obtained. This must be done within 3 days of obtaining the sample.

The sampling officer then submits one part of the sample for analysis or examination by a public analyst or some other laboratory with which arrangements have been made and approved by the appropriate Minister. The analyst shall analyse or examine the sample as soon as practicable and send the sampling officer a certificate specifying the result. The person to whom a part of the sample was supplied may obtain a copy of the certificate on payment of a fee to the enforcement authority. The certificate may be used as evidence in any proceedings for an offence under the Act but the person giving the certificate may be called as a witness.

If the defendant intends to produce a certificate of analysis or to call as a witness a person who issued a certificate he must notify the other party at least 3 clear days before the hearing and supply a copy of the certificate with that notice.

The third part of the sample shall be produced in court and may be sent to the Government Chemist for analysis either at the court's request or at the request of either party.

Any member of the public who pays the prescribed fee in advance may submit a sample of a product he has purchased to a public analyst. He must also send a part of the sample to the seller and keep the third part for production in court if necessary.

MEDICATED ANIMAL FEEDING STUFFS

These too are required to meet certain specifications. Similar powers exist to inspect these. The enforcement (including assay procedures) are discussed in Chapter 15.

References

Hoyle v. Hitchman, 1879, 4 QB 232

Pharm. J., 1968, i, 430

Chapter 18
Promotion of Sales of Medicinal Products

INTRODUCTION

The aims of advertising are –

(a) to draw the attention of the public, or a section of the public, to the availability and utility of a product or service, thus creating a demand for it, and

(b) to keep the product or service in the public eye so as to maintain or increase its market share.

All industries and the majority of companies advertise their products or services, even state-owned monopolies, so there must be a commercial advantage in spending the large sums involved. Recently, some professions have changed their rules to permit members to advertise their services, which perhaps indicates that advertising is becoming 'respectable' or possibly that the public interest is better served when the client can 'shop around'.

The advertising of medicines has long been the subject of comment and criticism. Formerly, the concern was directed against the 'patent medicine maker', and the 'cancer curer', etc. Early in the century, when patent medicines were becoming popular, really disgraceful claims were made for some of them. Not only did swindlers like Macaura make a rich living from deceiving the ignorant and gullible, they also cruelly raised the hopes of those unfortunate enough to be suffering from such serious complaints as cancer, tuberculosis, deafness and blindness.

Another serious criticism made against the makers of patent medicines (including those which did not claim the impossible) was that inordinately large amounts of money were spent on advertising these medicines. It was often, in fact, the major cost in their production. We have seen (Chapter 1) that a Select Committee was set up to study the matter and reported that the chief source of expenditure by the patent medicine makers was advertising. Wincarnis spent £50,000 a year on advertising, while 'Daisy' powders spent £3,000. The Proprietary Articles section of the London Chamber of Trade estimated that about £2,000,000 was spent on advertising patent medicines. It is interesting to note that the Price Commission in 1979 found '... that for a number of well-established products advertising expenditure is as much as 25% of sales revenue.' [Price Commission Report, paragraph 9.2]

When the Select Committee were studying patent medicines the most popular advertising medium was the newspaper, and the revenue generated by advertisements was the major source of income for many papers. Some papers exercised some form of censorship over advertisements relating to medicines but only the Spectator wholly excluded them. Apparently, the 'religious' press were particularly keen on accepting such advertisements and many very objectionable examples (including some for abortifacients) were to be found in its columns. The Committee pointed out that the revenue the papers received from advertisements for patent medicines precluded them from publishing articles critical of the trade. It said that few papers reported a trial in Edinburgh in the course of which the judge described the business of the makers of Bile Beans as 'based on unblushing falsehood for the purpose of defrauding the public'.

In 1931 a Bill was introduced into Parliament to deal with the situation, but it fell, so it was not until the Pharmacy and Medicines Act 1941 that the worst of the excesses were overcome. The 1941 Act prohibited the advertisement of products 'in terms calculated to lead to the use of the product in the treatment of tuberculosis, Bright's disease, glaucoma, diabetes, epilepsy, cataract, locomotor ataxy, paralysis'. The Act also prohibited advertisements likely to lead to the use of a product as an abortifacient. Advertisements relating to products for the prevention or treatment of venereal diseases, and indeed, offering any advice in connection with the prevention or treatment of these diseases had been prohibited by the Venereal Diseases Act 1917, and the Cancer Act 1939 imposed comparable restrictions on advertisements relating to cancer. The Food and Drugs Act prohibited advertisements which falsely described a product or were calculated to mislead as to its quality.

Despite these legal controls, some of the advertisements published in newspapers, on hoardings or television have been criticised as being misleading. In a debate in the House of Lords in 1961, Lord Taylor gave several examples of such advertisements and described one as 'plainly dishonest'. While many people agreed with much of what he said, none of the companies responsible were prosecuted under the Food and Drugs Act. There are at least two possible reasons for the lack of enthusiasm to prosecute. Perhaps local authorities were reluctant to bear the expense of the prosecution, or it was due to the difficulty of finding witnesses to give evidence. Again, it may be significant that despite the fact that a government department is now responsible for bringing prosecutions against advertisers, no cases have been brought. It may well be that except in the most blatant cases, prosecution is less certain and less effective than the persuasive powers of the licensing authority or of the Codes.

The Council of the Pharmaceutical Society have long deprecated the use of promotional schemes aimed at encouraging the public to buy large quantities of medicines.

All of these provisions have now been repealed and replaced by the Medicines Act and its subordinate legislation.

Since the NHS was created in 1948, the concern of many people (particularly politicians) has been concentrated on advertisements directed at practitioners, especially doctors. Such people believe that pharmaceutical companies spend an excessive amount on advertising to doctors and that this needlessly increases the NHS drug bill. In 1965, the Minister of Health and the Secretary of State for Scotland set up a Committee of Enquiry into the Relationship of the Pharmaceutical Industry with the NHS under the chairmanship of Lord Sainsbury. Chapter 7 of the Report of the Committee [Cmnd 3410, 1967] reported on sales promotion and marketing practices. It seemed that the cost of sales promotion of products used in the NHS was approximately 14% of the value of UK sales of those products. When the expenditure on sales promotion was expressed as a percentage of the total UK sales, it was shown that American companies spent the most and that the expenditure amounted to about 15% of sales. The British companies' expenditure was about 12% of sales, Swiss companies about 12.7% of sales and other European companies spent 17.5% of sales. The Report also commented on the forms of promotion and its effect on the prescribing habits of doctors. It found (not surprisingly), that some advertisements and promotional literature were good and provided a balanced review of the product, while other examples were poor and even misleading. Many of the recommendations in the Report were subsequently given statutory force in the Medicines Act.

Like many other things, advertising can be taken too far, and in the past some companies have made unsubstantiated claims, used bogus 'facts', misleading graphs and histograms, both in advertisements aimed at practitioners and those aimed at the general public. It is easy to fool the ignorant and controls are therefore essential to protect the public from the less scrupulous advertisers. There is a moral dilemma too, is it right to make money out of misfortune and ill-health? The questions arise –

1. Should medicines be advertised?
2. If so, what sort of controls should be imposed over advertisements?
3. Who should monitor the controls?
4. What sort of penalties should be inflicted on transgressors?

It seems that in the United Kingdom we have decided to permit the advertising of medicines, and two separate systems of controls have been set up. Firstly, there are the voluntary codes of practice drawn up various interested organisations, e.g. the Proprietary Association of Great Britain, the Association of the British Pharmaceutical Industry, the British Herbal Medicine Association, that of the Health Food Manufacturer's Association, and the code set up by the advertising industry itself. Over and above these are the legal controls now contained in the Medicines Act and also in the Trade Descriptions Acts.

The sources of legal controls over advertising are Part VI of theAct, various sets of regulations, and standard provisions attached to product licences.

STANDARD PROVISIONS

The standard provisions for product licences (including licences of right) are particularly useful in that they permit the advertising of a product to be controlled in the most appropriate way. Furthermore, they only operate when the Authority invokes them by writing to the licence holder explaining what is required. Thus, this form of control is specific to a particular product or to a class of products. Three paragraphs (numbers 9, 10 and 11) are involved. Paragraphs 9 and 11 can only be used by the authority for one or more of the following purposes –

(a) to ensure that adequate information is given,

(b) to prevent the giving of misleading information,

(c) to promote safety.

Paragraph 9 of the Standard Provisions requires the licence holder not to issue or consent to the issue of an advertisement which contains particulars as to the uses, nature or effects of a product or warnings concerning it, unless they correspond with those specified in the licence, in the application for the licence or in a written notice sent to the authority at least 42 days before the issue of the advertisement. Where the terms of the advertisement were included in the application or sent in writing, the authority may within 21 days inform the licence holder that the advertisement should not be issued without the written consent of the authority.

Paragraph 10 enables the authority to request details as to contents and form, the means, media or medium by which it is to be issued and time of issue of planned advertisements prior to their issue. In effect, it allows the authority to 'pre-vet' advertisements for a product.

Paragraph 11 enables the authority to give a written direction that advertisements of a particular kind should be not be issued, or issued again or should be modified or contain particular warnings or precautions. Such a direction can be used to prevent the issue of an advertisement which had been examined under the paragraph 10 procedure.

CODES FOR ADVERTISING PRACTICE

There are several of these relating to the advertising of medicines. All of them are voluntary but persons or companies who fail to observe their provisions are subject to sanctions, including expulsion from the organisation and possible boycott by the rest of the advertising industry.

British Code of Advertising Practice

This is enforced by the Advertising Standards Authority (ASA), an independent body created by the advertising business. It has an independent chairman, who appoints 12 council members, eight of whom have no links with the business. The members act as individuals, not as representatives of business, pressure groups, etc. The function of the ASA is to investigate complaints made in relation to advertisements (the results are published as Case Reports), and also to monitor advertisements to ensure compliance with the rules. Where necessary, it obtains expert advice from scientific and technical consultants.

The Code has the support of about 20 organisations, including the Advertising Association, Newspaper Publishers Association, Incorporated Society of British Advertisers, Institute of Practitioners in Advertising, and the Proprietary Association of Great Britain. Representatives of the organisations constitute the Code of Advertising Practice (CAP) Committee. The Code applies to all advertisements except broadcast commercials on radio and television (which are subject to a similar code enforced by the Independent Broadcasting Authority), those published abroad, and those relating to medicines advertised to the medical and allied professions (these are controlled by the codes of the Association of the British Pharmaceutical Industry).

The British Code of Advertising Practice (the CAP Code) requires advertisements to be 'legal, decent, honest and truthful'. The Code contains a number of general rules relating to these matters and to price comparisons, worth and value claims. There is a special section (IV) on health claims and several appendices on various related areas. Appendix D specifies a number of unacceptable claims relating to medical matters, Appendix G deals with the hair and scalp, Appendix C with slimming, and Appendix K with vitamins and minerals.

Appendix D enumerates illnesses and conditions for which advertisements should not make recommendations or offer products, treatments or advice, unless the recommendation is in accord with a FULL PRODUCT LICENCE issued under the Medicines Act.

In the event that an advertiser or agency refuses to amend or withdraw an advertisement, the following sanctions may be applied –

(1) Adverse publicity in ASA's Case Reports.

(2) Advertising space or time may be withheld.

(3) The agency's trading privileges may be withdrawn.

(4) Other consumer protection agencies may be notified.

Proprietary Association of Great Britain (PAGB)

This is the trade association which represents the views of manufacturers of non-prescription medicines, i.e. medicines which can be sold to the public without prescription. The PAGB devised its first self-regulatory Code of Advertising Practice in 1936 and has revised it regularly ever since. Strict compliance with the Code is a condition of membership of the Association. Companies must submit all advertising copy to the PAGB before the advertisement is issued. This applies to radio and television commercials, posters, leaflets, newspaper advertisements, labels, booklets and any other promotional material. The copy is examined by a specialist staff of pharmacists and consultant physicians to ensure compliance with the Code and approval lasts for 2 years. Hence, advertisements are kept in line with current developments in medical and public opinion. Furthermore, companies must lodge a copy of the relevant parts of the product licence with the PAGB and all advertisements are compared with this to ensure that unauthorised claims are not made. Moreover, the impression created by careful study of the advertisement is considered as well as that created by a more casual or brief exposure to the document.

The Code does not apply to advertisements issued in the trade or professional press.

The pre-vetting procedures used by the PAGB Code are obviously preferable to a procedure under which advertisements are only scrutinised after they have been issued, if only because they prevent the unscrupulous advertiser obtaining an advantage over his more conscientious rivals. There are many people in all walks of life who would risk a rebuke to obtain a short term advantage and this is precluded by the PAGB scheme. Perhaps the best evidence of its effectiveness was contained in the Price Commission Report, p. 33, para. 5.16, 'The number of complaints about proprietary medicines is about 0.2% of all complaints (presumably complaints made to the ASA) and the number upheld is less than 0.1%. The conclusion is therefore that the system of control is effective.'

The Association regularly monitors publications in which the advertisements are published to ensure compliance with its requirements.

The PAGB Code also applies other restrictions on promotional activities such as the giving of samples, the organising of competitions and schemes which aim at encouraging the sale of medicines.

The sanctions which could be used against those who fail to comply with the Code are those stated for the ASA since the PAGB is one of the sponsoring organisations of the ASA.

Independent Broadcasting Authority Code (IBA Code)

The IBA is required by the Broadcasting Act 1981 to formulate a code relating to advertising practice and methods, to keep it up to date, and to enforce it. The 1981 Act also requires the IBA to set up a Medical Advisory Panel to advise the

Authority on advertisements relating to medicines, medical and surgical treatments and appliances, as well as those relating to toilet articles which contain therapeutic or prophylactic claims. The Panel also advises on corresponding veterinary products.

Such a code has been produced and contains a number of matters of general application to advertisements. In Appendix 3 it contains a set of guidelines applicable to the advertising of medicines and treatments. Most of the guidelines follow the general requirements of the CAP Code and the PAGB Code, but some are applicable only to broadcasting or television. A more detailed consideration of the principles laid down in the IBA Code is contained in the Independent Television Companies Association (ITCA) booklet No.6, 'Medicines, Treatments and Health Claims'.

Advertisers must submit a copy of all material to the IBA for the approval of the Panel before the advertisement is issued.

Association of Britain Pharmaceutical Industry Codes (ABPI)

The Association have drawn up two Codes, one applicable to human medicines and the other for veterinary products. The codes do not merely control advertisements, they seek to control all methods of sales promotion including such matters as frequency of calls by representatives, hospitality and gifts. The appropriate Code is now printed in the ABPI Data Sheet Compendium, so as to enable the doctor, dentist or veterinarian to read it and complain if he considers that the Code is not being obeyed.

Each Code is administered by a committee having a legally qualified chairman. The committee for human medicines also consists of two medical practitioners (one a general practitioner, the other a consultant) from outside the industry, and 12 members from the industry (including at least four having medical qualifications). The committee meets regularly to examine complaints, discuss amendments to the Code and deal with related matters. Complaints may originate in the Medicines Division, in other companies, or from practitioners, pharmacists, consumer bodies (especially those with an interest in a disease or group of diseases), and even from members of the lay public. The corresponding veterinary committee consists of a veterinarian and a livestock farmer both from outside the industry and 11 members (including some veterinarians) from the industry.

The ABPI does not operate a mandatory 'pre-vetting' scheme. However, it does routinely scrutinise advertisements for human medicines appearing in professional journals and the effectiveness of this is soon to be improved by employing a doctor to scrutinise the medical claims made in the advertisements. When an advertisement is suspected of infringing the Code, the ABPI write to the offending company requesting changes and if these are made the matter ends. If the company disagrees with the ABPI's view, or refuses to comply with the request, the matter is referred to the Code of Practice Committee for investigation. This Committee meets every 6 weeks and deals with about 6–10 complaints at each meeting. The Committee gives its ruling, and if the company is found 'guilty' it is asked to sign a document agreeing to stop the offending advertisement (or other behaviour) at once. Companies that renege on this agreement may be expelled from the Association.

Critics of the industry argue that the Ministers should prosecute companies that mislead doctors as to the value or use of their products. They suggest that the present system of relying mainly on the Codes and persuasion is ineffective (Herxheimer, 1984). It must be stated that the present system is much quicker than prosecution (it can take between 6 and 12 months to bring a case to a magistrates court and even longer to a Crown court) and can be much more expensive (in a magistrates court the maximum fine is £2,000, whereas the cancellation of a promotional campaign can cost several times more). Furthermore, if the case were put to a jury, it might be difficult to obtain a conviction because of the probable conflict of evidence. The present scheme does have the advantage that doctors (or veterinarians) are involved in the 'judgment'. In addition, the case reports are published and are usually reprinted in the professional press and often by the lay press too, and companies do their utmost to avoid such publicity.

One disadvantage of the scheme is that not all companies are members of the ABPI and cannot therefore be expelled for non-compliance with decisions of the Committee. In such cases the ABPI notify the Medicines Division of the facts.

Compliance with the Codes

As with so many other human activities, it is one thing to lay down controls, whether statutory or in the form of voluntary codes, it is less easy to enforce them. The major difficulty is with the interpretation of the controls; there are no rigid, objective criteria that can be applied and we are left with matters of opinion. While most people will agree that a particular advertisement is 'legal, decent...' and that another is not, there is a considerable area in between where opinions may be strongly held either way. The question is, will the settlement of the dispute be managed better by a judge and jury (possibly after prolonged legal argument in which all manner of 'red herrings' may be introduced) or by a collection of people having expert knowledge of the problems and devices of the industry? Again, the answer is a matter of opinion!

All of the Codes mentioned above recognise the existence of the various statutory restrictions on the promotion of medicines, and are obviously compatible with these restrictions. It is usually the case that the law imposes the minimum acceptable standards, and that professional and similar bodies impose higher standards on their members.

STATUTORY CONTROLS

The present law relating to the promotion of sales of medicines is contained in Part VI of the Act. As always, the aim is to promote safety, quality and efficacy. Safety is promoted by the prevention of –

(1) self-medication for certain diseases;

(2) the promotion of certain classes of medicines;

(3) the use of certain words and phrases likely to mislead the public:

(4) the issue of misleading advertisements to practitioners.

Quality is protected by ensuring that advertisements do not contain misleading or false information as to the nature of the remedy.

Efficacy is protected by ensuring that products are only promoted to practitioners or to the public for indications which were specified in the product licence. In relation to products advertised to the public, the advertisements are also limited to the less serious conditions.

Section 95 permits regulations to be made by the Ministers to prohibit the issue of advertisements or the making of the representations –

(a) relating to products of a specified class;

(b) likely to lead to use of an article (including articles which are NOT medicinal products) in the treatment, diagnosis or prevention of specified diseases or physiological conditions;

(c) containing words or specified phrases which are likely to mislead the public as to the nature or effects of the products.

Such regulations may also control labels and leaflets.

The licensing authority may require any person to supply up to 12 copies of any advertisement (including data sheets) which he has issued or caused to be issued in the past 12 months. It is an offence to fail to comply with the requirement without reasonable excuse (section 97).

To ensure that adequate information is given with respect to medicinal products, or to promote safety or prevent the giving of misleading information in relation to them, regulations may be made to impose such requirements as are considered necessary. All of these powers have been used and six sets of regulations have been made, namely –

(a) Data Sheet Regulations 1972/2076 as amended by 1979/1760 and 1981/1633;

(b) Advertising of Medicines Regulations 1975/298;

(c) Advertising of Medicines (No.2) Regulations 1975/1326 as amended by 1979/1760;

(d) Labelling and Advertising to the Public Regulations 1978/41;

(e) Advertising to Medical and Dental Practitioners Regulations 1978/1020;

(f) Contact Lens Fluids and Other Substances (Advertising and Miscellaneous Amendments) Regulations 1979/1760.

MEANING OF 'ADVERTISEMENT' AND 'REPRESENTATION'

'Advertisement includes every form of advertising, whether in a publication, or by the display of any notice, or by means of any catalogue, price list, letter (whether circular or addressed to a particular person) or other document, or by words inscribed on any article, or by exhibition of any photograph or a cinematograph film or by way of sound recording, sound broadcasting or television, or in any other way' (section 92(1)).

The Act specifically *excludes* from the above definition, spoken words except those forming part of a sound recording, broadcast, etc., or forming part of a sound track (section 92(2)) but these constitute a 'representation' and are controlled as such.

Furthermore, for most of the purposes of Part VI, neither of the following constitute the issue of an advertisement –

(a) the sale, supply, offer or exposure for sale or supply of a medicinal product in a labelled container or package,

(b) the supply with a medicinal product of any description, of a leaflet, relating solely to medicinal products of that description (section 92(3)).

It must be remembered, however, that both labels and leaflets given with the product are now controlled under Part V of the Act. If a leaflet also contains a reference to another product, or is distributed other than with the product, it does constitute an 'advertisement'.

This definition is very wide and includes almost anything that brings the availability of the product to the notice of the public or to the professions. Moreover, it need not necessarily by an inducement to buy or prescribe the product so that the trade announcements about pack changes or price alterations or even entries in reference books would be advertisements within the meaning of the Act. Perhaps the scope of the definition is best illustrated by the fact that it has been necessary in one set of regulations to exempt from control company reports and circulars to shareholders giving details of the company's products.

While the definition of 'advertisement' is broad and all-embracing, many of the restrictions over advertisements apply only to a 'commercially interested party', i.e. the holder of the product licence of the product or someone who manufactures, sells, supplies, imports or exports the product in the course of his business (section 92(4)). In other words, a commercially interested party is anyone whose business will or might gain financially from the sale of the product. Consequently, authors of medical books are free to discuss the uses of products without restriction despite the fact that what was written would constitute an 'advertisement'. Some regulations have been made which impose fewer restrictions on 'reference advertisements' and 'trade advertisements' and these are defined and described in Chapter 19.

According to section 92(5) 'representation' means 'any statement or undertaking (whether constituting a condition or a warranty or not) which consists of spoken words other than words falling within paragraph (a) or paragraph (b) of subsection (2) of this section, and any reference to making a representation shall be construed accordingly.' In other words, 'representation' means spoken words except those on records, films, broadcasts, etc. (which are advertisements). Again, this definition is broad enough to cover ordinary conversations between members of the public. The legal restrictions on representations therefore only apply to those made in the course of a 'relevant business', which means any business which consists of or includes the sale or supply of medicinal products (section 92(4)).

Many of the prohibitions relate to false or misleading statements, but others apply to the use of an 'unauthorised recommendation' which is defined 'as a recommendation whereby a product of a description to which the licence is applicable is recommended to be used for purposes other than those specified in the licence' (section 93(10)).

OFFENCES RELATING TO ADVERTISEMENTS

Part VI of the Act creates a number of offences relating to advertisements and representations. Most of them are punishable on summary conviction by a fine of up to £2,000, or on indictment by an unlimited fine and/or 2 years imprisonment. The exception ((c) below) is £200 fine on summary conviction only.

It is an offence for any commercially interested party or any person acting at his request or with his consent to issue –

(a) a false or misleading advertisement relating to medicinal products of ANY description (section 93(1));

(b) in relation to a licensed medicinal product, an advertisement which contains an unauthorised recommendation (section 93(2));

(c) for anyone other than the product licence holder or someone acting with his consent, to issue an advertisement relating to that product (section 94).

OFFENCES RELATING TO REPRESENTATIONS

It is an offence for anyone in the course of a relevant business carried on by him or while acting on behalf of a person carrying on such a business –

(a) to make a false or misleading representation relating to a medicinal product of any description in connection with the sale or offer for sale of the product (section 93(3)).

(b) to make a false or misleading representation relating to a medicinal product or any description in order to induce –

(i) a practitioner to prescribe or supply it, or

(ii) a patient to request a practitioner to prescribe it, or

(iii) a person to purchase it from a retailer (section 93(3));

(c) to use an unauthorised recommendation in a representation relating to a licensed product in connection either with a sale or for any of the purposes mentioned in (b) above (section 93(4)).

For the purposes of the offences specified above, an advertisement or representation (whether it contains an accurate statement of the composition of medicinal products of the description in question or not) shall be taken to be false or misleading if (but only if) –

(a) it falsely describes the description of medicinal products to which it relates;

(b) it is likely to mislead as to the nature or quality of medicinal products of that description or as to their uses or effects (section 93(7)).

The word 'description' is open to several interpretations but is defined in section 130(8) as follows –

'(8) For the purposes of this Act medicinal products are of the same description if (but only if) –

(a) they are manufactured to the same specification, and

(b) they are, or are to be, sold, supplied, imported or exported in the same pharmaceutical form,

and in this Act 'description', in relation to medicinal products, shall be construed accordingly.'

There is a possible ambiguity here. All aspirin tablets of a particular strength which comply with the BP specifications could be described as being of the 'same description'. However, different manufacturers may have used different disintegrating agents in their formulation, so to this extent the specifications are different. On the other hand, the word 'specification' might refer only to the specification of each of the ingredients of the product (as laid down in the product licence application for example), the performance 'specification' of the product being referred to as the 'standard'. In this case, 'description' applies to an individual product. This ambiguity can only be resolved by a decision of the court.

Whatever the true meaning of 'description', an advertisement is false if it describes a product as BP when it does not comply with the relevant specifications (or standards), or if it describes a hypnotic drug as an analgesic.

Similarly, a product labelled as 'Aspirin Tablets 300 mg' would be falsely described as 'Aspirin Tablets Paediatric'.

If any of the offences relating either to advertisements or to representations are committed by a person due to the act or default of another person, then whether proceedings are taken against the first mentioned person or not, the other person may be charged and convicted (section 121 (1)). If the person charged satisfies the court that he exercised all due diligence to secure that the provision in question would not be contravened and that the contravention was due to the act or default of another party, then the first mentioned person shall be acquitted. In order to take advantage of this defence it is necessary for the person charged to notify the prosecutor at least 7 days before the hearing and give such information as he possesses as will identify the true culprit (section 121(2),(3)).

DEFENCES

It shall be a defence to anyone charged with any of the above offences to prove that he did not know and could not with reasonable diligence have discovered that the advertisement or representation was false or misleading or that it contained unauthorised recommendations. The position of a person whose business comprises the issue of advertisements and who acts in good faith is also protected (section 94(6)).

When a contravention of the provisions of sections 90, 93, 94, 95, or 96 or of a regulation made under one of these is an offence, the person charged may be able to use the defence described in section 121. This would require him to satisfy the court that he exercised due diligence to secure compliance with the provision but that the offence was due to the act or default of another person. He must notify the prosecutor of his intention to use this defence and identify if possible the true culprit. For further details please see Chapter 2.

ENFORCEMENT

The Pharmaceutical Society of Great Britain has concurrent responsibility with the Ministers for enforcing the provisions of sections 93, 94 and 95. In relation to advertisements and to representations made in connection with medicines the Society's powers are limited to those issued or made on or in premises or any other place (e.g. any ship, aircraft, stall) where medicines are sold or supplied and to advertisements on or near any automatic machine used for selling medicines (section 108(3)).

It follows therefore that only the Ministers may prosecute in respect of advertisements sent, or representations made, to practitioners, or shown on television or published in newspapers and the like. This is no doubt a consequence of the intention of the Ministers to rely mainly on persuasion to enforce these provisions. The Ministers recognise the difficulties that might be encountered in securing a conviction in the Courts. They also recognise that both the pharmaceutical and the advertising industries have a powerful incentive in ensuring the success of the various codes of advertising practice. Therefore, the aim is to rely mainly on the committees that devise and enforce the various codes and reserve the courts for use as a last resort.

References

Prices, Costs and Margins in the Production and Distribution of Proprietary Non-ethical Medicines, HC469, HMSO 1978, paragraph 9.2

Report of the Committee of Enquiry into the Relationship of the Pharmaceutical Industry with the National Health Service. Cmnd 3410, 1967

Chapter 19
Advertisements and Representations Directed to Practitioners

INTRODUCTION

Although the Act permits advertisements directed to all practitioners to be controlled, to date the emphasis seems to be on controlling only those directed to doctors and dentists. The only controls over advertisements directed at veterinarians are those mentioned in the Act and those applying to data sheets. This is undoubtedly due to the fact that most medicinal products prescribed for human beings in the UK are paid for by the NHS and therefore there is a public interest in keeping the cost of this to a minimum. This is shown by the fact that some advertisements are required to state the basic NHS cost of one day's treatment or of a course of treatment. One way of achieving this reduction in the drug billis to persuade doctors to prescribe drugs by reference to their generic names rather than their proprietary names. The innovative companies, whose investment in research results in new drugs, obviously want doctors to use the brand names, and therefore advertise to keep these names in front of the doctor. In 1975, the government told the ABPI of its intention to reduce the cost of promotion of drugs by 25% (Pharm.J., 17/5/75, p.441). Apparently, in 1973 M£32 had been spent on home sales promotion by companies with sales exceeding M£1, and this amounted to about 13.8% of sales. The DHSS proposed that 10% was more suitable and had prepared a formula to calculate how much should be spent bearing in mind a company's size and expenses. The Medicines Act contains no provisions which enable advertising expenditure to be controlled by the authority, but it is achieved by the Pharmaceutical Price Regulation Scheme (PPRS).

The provisions of the various sets of regulations discussed below attempt to curb the more unethical practices of certain advertisers, e.g. making unwarranted claims for safety or efficacy, the use of misleading graphs or tables. They also aim to ensure that sufficient emphasis is placed on relevant information to enable the practitioner to obtain a balanced view of the product's usefulness, hazards, etc. At the centre of these controls is the 'Data Sheet', a document which is intended to provide an objective statement of the basic information about the product. This information must correspond with that contained in the product licence.

Types of Advertisements

For the purposes of this chapter there are several types of advertisements that may be directed to practitioners, namely –

(a) Data sheets;

(b) Trade advertisements, notifying pack changes, price changes and similar matters;

(c) Reference advertisements, entries in books such as MIMS;

(d) Postal advertisements, e.g. 'reminders';

(e) Advertisements published in professional journals, these may be quite large, i.e. multi-page advertisements, or quite small, so-called 'abbreviated' advertisements;

(f) Audio-visual advertisements, films, slide–tape presentations, video tapes, etc.;

(g) Promotional aids, these are gifts given to doctors or dentists to remind them of a product, e.g. pens, diaries.

Different provisions apply to the several types of advertisements.

SPECIFIC LIMITATIONS ON ADVERTISEMENTS

No advertisement of any type may be sent to a doctor or dentist if it contains claims or suggestions that it is safer, more efficacious, or has fewer side-effects than another product unless there is clear evidence for the claim. Nor may the word 'safe' be used without qualification. The product cannot be advertised as 'new' more than a year after it became generally available in the United Kingdom. Similarly, claims for a new indication cannot be made after 1 year from the date of the first advertisement which mentioned that indication. Moreover, no reference to the Commission, an expert committee or to the licensing authority may be made unless specifically required by the authority (1978/1020, regulation 8).

Graphs and tables included in advertisements must be relevant to any claim made and give a fair and true view of the data (1978/1020, regulation 9).

DATA SHEETS

Importance of Data Sheets and the Intention Behind Them

A data sheet is a document relating to a particular product prepared by the holder of the product licence. It complies with the requirements as to size, form and content and does not contain any information about the product other than that required by law.

The purpose of the data sheet is to provide the reader with a synopsis of the most important and relevant facts about the product. These facts must be consistent with the information given in the application for a product licence. It can be viewed therefore as that part of the product licence that is available to the health professions generally and can thus be used as a 'yard-stick' against which the accuracy and truth of all subsequent advertisements can be measured and assessed.

It is an offence for a commercially interested party to give or send an advertisement to a practitioner or for anyone carrying on a relevant business to make any representation to a practitioner, relating to a medicinal product unless –

(1) A data sheet relating to the product has been sent to the practitioner within the previous 15 months, or is given at the time, and

(2) The advertisement or representation is consistent with the particulars contained in the data sheet (section 96 (1), (2), (3)).

A commercially interested party is someone (including a legal person, e.g. a company) with a financial interest in selling a product. It includes the manufacturer, the holder of any licence applicable to the product or anyone who can sell it, and employees of such people. A relevant business means any business which consists of or includes the sale or supply of medicines.

Thus a data sheet is only necessary when a licence holder intends to advertise or make a representation to a practitioner about a particular product. Conversely, if a company markets a product but does not wish to advertise or make representations about it, no data sheet is required for that product. The Departments take the view that the issue to practitioners of a price list or catalogue containing no recommendations as to the use of particular products or assertions as to their quality (e.g. a trade advertisement) would not in itself necessitate the issue of a data sheet. Many pharmaceutical companies ensure that practitioners receive data sheets annually by participating in the production of the relevant ABPI Data Sheet Compendium. Users of the ABPI compendium for human products may find that certain companies do not include entries for all of their products, presumably omitting those which are not to be promoted during the next year.

At the suggestion of the Medicines Commission, the ABPI Compendium now contains an index of non-proprietary names.

Structure and Provisions Relating to Data Sheets

The Data Sheet Regulations (1972/2076 as amended) specify in detail the form of data sheets, their size, colour and typesetting, as well as the information to be included in each data sheet. The Regulations also permit the publication of compendia of data sheets (for example the compendia published annually by the ABPI (one of the human medicines and the other for veterinary products)) and lay down certain specifications for these. A company may produce a compendium of data sheets relating to its products but if the company markets both human and veterinary products, a separate compendium is required for sheets of each type. In any event, a compendium must indicate on its cover that it contains data sheets. The compendium may also include certain other information of use to the practitioner.

A data sheet which is in the form of a loose sheet must be prominently marked 'Data Sheet' at the top, and may contain a trade mark, printer's mark and the device for the Queen's Award to Industry (if applicable). The sheet may refer to a substance or article other than the medicinal product to which it relates ONLY in so far as is necessary to explain contra-indications, precautions or the treatment of overdosage, or to assist the practitioner in the proper understanding, recognition, administration or use of the product to which the sheet relates. The particulars required to be included shall be given in English and include (for products for human use) –

1. Name of product	i.e. its name and approved name (if any).
2. Presentation	Description of its appearance, pharmaceutical form and details of its composition the ingredients being identified where possible by their 'official' names.
3. Uses	The chief action and purposes for which it is recommended to be used.
4. Dosage and administration	The dosage (if any) recommended for adults and for children unless the product is only recommended for one of these groups; also methods and routes of administration and, where appropriate, recommendations as to diluents.
5. Contra-indications, warnings, etc.	Contra-indications, warnings, precautions and action to be taken in the event of over-dosage, the main side effects and adverse reactions likely to be associated with the product *and* where there are no such particulars to be given, a statement to that effect. Where required in the interests of safety, the antidote or action to be taken in the event of over-dosage.
6. Pharmaceutical precautions	Storage requirements, special precautions and advice as to diluents, excipients or other additives, and as to suitable containers or, if none state 'none'.
7. Legal category	Reference to statutory provisions relating to sale or supply.
8. Package quantities	Details as to retail pack size.
9. Further information	Such other information as is necessary to help the practitioner in the proper understanding, recognition, administration and use of the product.
10. Product licence number, etc.	The P.L. number of the product and the name and address of the P.L.holder.
11. Date of preparation or last review.	Date on which it was prepared, reviewed or revised.

The data sheet shall contain all the headings specified above and where it is not appropriate to give such particulars the heading shall be followed by the word 'Nil'.

The information required to be given in relation to veterinary products is very similar to that specified above but contra-indications, warnings, etc. shall also include measures to be taken to protect operatives, consumers and other livestock and wild life.

CONTROLS OVER ADVERTISEMENTS IN PROFESSIONAL PUBLICATIONS

In this context 'professional publication' means a publication sent only (or mainly) to doctors or dentists (1978/1020). It may also include a publication containing an advertisement for a POM, or one containing an advertisement for a product which is the subject of a data sheet (1975/1326).

The restrictions imposed upon advertisements in professional publications apply only to the commercially interested party; the editor and owners of the publication cannot be prosecuted for any infringement of the regulations (regulation 12).

Two sets of regulations apply to such advertisements, namely –

Advertising of Medicines (No.2) Regulations 1975/1326, and

Advertising to Medical and Dental Practitioners Regulations 1978/1020

Both sets of regulations apply only to advertisements relating to medicinal products for human use including in the case of 1975/1326, substances and articles specified in the Surgical Materials Order, the Dental Filling Substances Order or the Specified Articles and Substances Order (except for contact lens fluids and substances). The provisions, however, do not apply to data sheets, trade advertisements or to certain reference advertisements.

The Advertising of Medicines (No.2) Regulations require that an advertisement published in professional publications shall –

(i) In so far as it contains particulars included in the data sheet be 'not inconsistent' with those in the data sheet and

(ii) State prominently that a data sheet will be sent to a practitioner on request (unless all reasonable steps had previously been taken to ensure that all practitioners had received a data sheet).

These provisions do not apply to advertisements relating to products exempt from licensing under the Foods and Cosmetics Order, nor to advertisements in publications which are sold generally to persons who are not practitioners.

A licensee who fails to comply with a request for a data sheet or has not, within the preceding 15 months sent three copies of the data sheet to the licensing authority, shall not be regarded as having complied with the provisions,

Under 1978/1020, every such advertisement (or every page of an advertisement) must contain –

(1) The relevant product licence number;

(2) The name and address of the product licence holder;

(3) A list of the active ingredients of the product (placed immediately below the most prominent display of the name and in a type size which occupies a total area at least as large as that occupied by the name or in 10 point bold);

(4) One or more of the indications for the product consistent with the terms of product licence;

(5) Where relevant, a succinct statement of the data sheet entries relating to the side-effects, precautions and contra-indications;

(6) Dosage and method of use relevant to the indications shown;

(7) Any warnings required by the Commission etc. to be included in advertisements;

(8) The cost (excluding VAT) of either a specified package or of a specified quantity or of the recommended daily dose;

(9) The particulars in (5), (6) and (7) shall be clearly and legibly printed and so placed that their relationship to the claims and indications for the product can be readily appreciated by the reader.

In relation to (3) above,

(a) Where the product is described in a monograph in a specified publication, the name at the head of the monograph (or an approved synonym of Eur.P. name), or

(b) Where (a) is not applicable, but the active ingredients are described in monographs in a specified publication, the names at the head of those monographs (or an approved synonym of a Eur.P. name), or

(c) Where neither (a) nor (b) apply, but the active ingredients have approved names, such names or if there are no approved names the approved INN, or

(d) Where none of the above apply but the product or its active ingredients are described in a foreign or international compendium of standards, the name at the head of the monograph together with letters and figures identifying the publication and edition, or

(e) In any other case, the accepted scientific name or other name descriptive of the true nature of the product or its active ingredients.

The requirement relating to the price of the product need not be published in a professional publication whose circulation outside the UK exceeds 15% of its total circulation. The authority may require proof of circulation data.

ABBREVIATED ADVERTISEMENTS

These are advertisements printed in a professional publication (not one enclosed in such a publication or sent by post) which do not exceed 420 square centimetres in area. They are exempt from the requirements specified above for full advertisements but must contain the following information about the product –

1. The name of the product (either non-proprietary or proprietary);
2. List of active ingredients as stated above;
3. Name and address of the licence holder or the address of his business;
4. A statement that additional information is available on request or in a data sheet.

The advertisement may also specify one indication for the use of the product or two or more related indications together with a concise statement of the reasons for the recommendation.

The advertisement must not contain any additional information about the product but may give information about the company or other matters.

The authority may issue a direction that abbreviated advertisements should not be issued for a product if the Commission, an expert committee or the authority have required a warning to be included in all advertisements relating to the product (regulation 5(d)). This will only be done when a serious warning is involved. The licence holder will be notified of the fact that abbreviated advertisements cannot be issued for that product.

Where the abbreviated advertisement does not exceed 200 square centimetres in area and is contained in the same therapeutic section of a publication consisting mainly of reference advertisements as a reference advertisement for that product, the requirements as to type size do not apply (Schedule 2).

MULTI-PAGE ADVERTISEMENTS

These must contain the particulars specified in 'professional publications' above on at least one of the pages. In addition, every page except that on which, or facing which, the particulars are printed, must on its outer edge specify the page on which the particulars are to be found. This must be in type in at least 8 point.

Furthermore, in a double page spread, the information given on the first or last page must not be false or misleading if read in isolation.

PROMOTIONAL AIDS

These are non-monetary gifts given to a prescriber and intended to keep the name of the product (or products) in the prescriber's mind particularly at the time of writing the prescription. Objects which would naturally be kept on his desk are the most popular, e.g. calendars, desk-tidies, diaries, paper weights, and pens. Some companies seek to be 'different' and give coat-hangers, golf balls or other useful items.

If the advertisement consists only of one or more of the following –

(a) Name of the product,

(b) Name and/or address of the product licence holder,

(c) Where the name of the product is a trade mark, an indication that such a name is a trade mark, there is no need to comply with any of the other requirements of these regulations. Consequently, provided that no indications are
specified the regulations do not apply either to the aid or to the advertisement (regulation 6).

AUDIO-VISUAL ADVERTISEMENTS

These comprise sound recordings, films, radio or television broadcasts and words shown or spoken as part of them. These advertisements must refer to the folllowing particulars –

(1) Where relevant, a succinct statement of the data sheet entries relating to the side-effects, precautions and contra- indications;

(2) Dosage and method of use relevant to the indications shown;

(3) Any warnings required by the Commission etc. to be included in advertisements;

Alternatively, written material giving such particulars may be handed to an audience.

DIRECT MAIL ADVERTISEMENTS

The full requirements as set out under 'professional publications' above, apply to an advertisement (or to a page of an advertisement) relating to a medicinal product for human use sent by post or otherwise addressed to a doctor or dentist. These particulars must be given on at least one or more continuous pages and, where the advertisement is more than four pages long, a clear statement of its location is given (regulation 7).

TRADE ADVERTISEMENTS

These are entries in catalogues, price lists and similar documents sent to persons who sell or administer medicines to human beings in the course of their business. Such an entry must not contain any recommendation as to the use of the product, but the document may divide the products into therapeutic classes.

Trade advertisements do not need to contain the particulars specified under 'professional publications'.

REFERENCE ADVERTISEMENTS

These are exempt from the need to contain the specified particulars provided that the following conditions are met. The publication carrying the advertisement must contain an alphabetical index listing all the non-proprietary names of all the active ingredients of the products for which reference advertisements are shown. The product must be the subject of a data sheet and three copies of it had been sent to the authority. The publication in which the advertisement appears contains a notice stating that data sheets are available on request and a list of the names and addresses of the product licence holders.

Where a direction has been issued under the Standard Provisions requiring the inclusion in all advertisements of a specifically worded warning, and it is proposed that the reference advertisement should not carry the warning or should modify it, the licence holder must formally object to the issue of the advertisement and notify the authority of this (regulation 5 (c)).

EXCEPTIONS

The prohibitions and requirements described above do not apply to –

(a) Written notices of changes of packaging, warnings of adverse reactions, etc. if no medical claims are made in the notice or,

(b) Any advertisement *the receipt of a copy of which has been acknowledged by the licensing authority* but which the authority have not within 6 weeks notified the holder should not be issued, or

(c) Any letter to a practitioner written in reply to a specific enquiry or comment relating to the product.

ENFORCEMENT

These provisions are enforced by the authority. As explained in Chapter 18, the authority endeavours to ensure compliance with the requirements by persuasion and the use of the codes of advertising practice.

OFFENCES AND DEFENCES

These are described and discussed in Chapter 18.

Chapter 20
Advertisements Directed to the Public

INTRODUCTION

The danger that can be caused to the public by unscrupulous advertisers has already been described and so have some of the problems associated with attempts to remedy the situation by law. The industry, and particularly the PAGB, has done much to improve standards of advertising relating to medicines sold to the public. Legal force has recently been applied to the problem by the Labelling and Advertising to the Public Regulations 1978/41. This set of regulations is extremely detailed and at first sight seems to prevent the advertising of almost every medicinal product. The list of ailments, diseases and the like for which medicines cannot be advertised is very long but is similar to that drawn up by the PAGB some years earlier. There is little that is controversial about the restrictions as regards the complaints and ailments and the result is that the advertising of medicines to the public is confined to more or less trivial complaints.

All of the restrictions contained in the regulations apply to medicinal products but the restrictions contained in regulation 2 apply also to articles and substances, e.g. any non-medicinal substance or any device. Furthermore, in regulations 2 and 4 the word 'advertisement' has the extended meaning and applies to labels and leaflets too. In addition, many of the restrictions apply to representations made by commercially interested parties including retailers (regulation 5). Thus, a retailer would be making an unauthorised representation if he told a customer that a licensed product was useful for a complaint not specified in the product licence. Retailers therefore would be well advised to confine their recommendations to those mentioned in the data sheet (if any) or to those mentioned on the label or a leaflet produced by the manufacturer. Since it is also possible for such an offence to be committed by a sales assistant, pharmacists must take care to train their staff thoroughly, and especially to insist that all such questions be referred to the pharmacist for answer.

Furthermore, an offence would be committed when representation was made by a commercially interested party (e.g. a retail pharmacist) which is likely to lead to the use of the product for any of the stated purposes and is made –

(a) In connection with the sale, supply or offer or exposure for sale of a product to which the restriction applies; or

(b) To induce a person to purchase such a product; or

(c) To induce a person to request a doctor or dentist to prescribe it.

However, a pharmacist may make such a representation when dispensing a product on a prescription or where the patient has asked the pharmacist to counter-prescribe for one of the specified diseases. Chiropodists, nurses and midwives may also make representations under certain circumstances (regulation 5).

It should be noted that in many cases an offence is committed not only when a disease, disorder, etc. is mentioned by name, but also when the advertisement (including labels and leaflets) 'is likely to lead to the use' of the product in treating or preventing the disease. Great care is therefore necessary in framing such documents etc. Similarly, it is important to avoid representations which can give rise to an offence. Retailers must also bear in mind that the display or exposure for sale of containers labelled with particulars for the treatment or prevention of any of the complaints mentioned in Tables 1, 2 or 3 below constitute the issue of an advertisement.

The regulations are framed so as to create a series of offences, but it is easier to consider the requirements in a more positive way. Diseases, complaints, body systems and various 'purposes' are all mentioned in the restrictions and sometimes the prohibition is total while on other occasions it is subject to exemptions. The details of most of the diseases are contained in Schedule 2, of which there are five parts. For the sake of brevity, the location of the detail is shown as 2(I), 2(II), 2(III), 2(IV), or 2(V) respectively.

Table 1 Total Prohibition on Advertisements

(1) Serious diseases

Advertisements phrased in terms likely to lead to the use of a product or any other substance or article in the treatment or the diagnosis (except under medical supervision) of the following serious diseases are completely prohibited –

Cancer
Cataract
Diabetes
Epilepsy or fits
Glaucoma
Kidney disease
Paralysis
Tuberculosis
Venereal disease (i.e. syphilis, gonorrhoea or soft chancre)

Also prohibited are advertisements relating to the procuring of the miscarriage of women (regulation 2 and Schedule 1).

However, advertisements relating to products sold as a food or dietary supplement suitable for consumption by diabetics are permitted (regulation 2(2)).

(2) Likely to lead to the use of a product for any of these purposes –

(a) Treatment or prevention of any clinical psychiatric or psychotic condition

(b) Restoration or enhancement of sexual potency or libido

(c) Alleviation of fatigue or tiredness of a chronic or persistent nature

(d) Rejuvenation or the prevention of ageing

(e) Contraception except by means of spermicidal contraceptives

(f) Increasing or decreasing fertility

(g) Treatment of addiction to any substance, except for the purpose of reducing the desire to smoke tobacco by the administration of a product sold or supplied for that purpose

(h) Treatment of sleeplessness or insomnia other than by the secondary effect of the relief of pain or other symptoms

(i) Sedation or tranquillising

(j) General anaesthesia

(k) Regulation of menstrual flow

(l) Diagnosing any disease or physiological condition specified in 1 above or any disease of any system specified in 6 below (regulation 4 and Schedule 2(V)).

(3) Diseases or adverse conditions of the following types or body systems –

(a) Senility or degenerative conditions associated with ageing (Schedule 2(1))

(b) Liver, biliary system and pancreas (Schedule 2(II))

(c) Kidneys and ureters (Schedule 2(II))

(d) Cardiovascular system –

All diseases of the myocardium and heart valves, including rheumatic heart disease and coronary artery disease

Hypertension

Thrombosis

Oedema

Retinal vascular change (Schedule 2(III))

(e) Blood and lymphatic system –

Bleeding disorders

Leukaemia or other lymphoproliferative diseases (Schedule 2(III))

Table 2 Partial Prohibition on Advertisements

There are a number of diseases, adverse conditions and purposes for which advertising to the public is subject to a partial prohibition. The diseases affected are those of the type or of the body systems specified below, but any exemptions and the conditions applicable to exemptions, are detailed in Table 3 'Permitted advertisements'.

(a) Bacterial, fungal or viral infections (Schedule 2(I))

(b) Parasitic diseases (Schedule 2 (I))

(c) Treatment of diseases of malnutrition (including vitamin and mineral deficiency states) but dietary supplements are excluded (Schedule 2(I))

(d) Gastro-intestinal system (Schedule 2(II))

(e) Nervous system (Schedule 2(II))

(f) Genito-urinary system and mammary glands (Schedule 2(II))

(g) Skin, hair and scalp (Schedule 2(II))

(h) The following conditions of the cardiovascular system –

Peripheral artery disease

Peripheral venous disease (Schedule 2(III))

(i) Anaemia (Schedule 2(III))

(j) Any organic or functional condition related to under or over activity of any part of the endocrine system (Schedule 2(III))

(k) Any organic condition affecting sight, hearing or balance (Schedule 2(III))

(l) Any condition of the musculo-skeletal system referred to as slipped disc, arthritis, osteoarthritis, rheumatoid arthritis or gout (Schedule 2(III))

(m) Diseases of the lungs, pleura and bronchial tree (Schedule 2(III))

(n) Teeth and gums (Schedule 2(III))

(o) Skeletal fractures, and extensive burns, scalds or injuries (Schedule 2(IV))

Table 3 Permitted Advertisements

Many of the permitted advertisements are subject to conditions. Sometimes the permitted advertisement is limited to the display of a container labelled to show a particular indication. At other times the relaxation of the prohibition applies only to products for external use, or only for the treatment of a complaint or perhaps only for the symptomatic relief of some condition. Clearly, it is necessary to read the requirements with care.

(a) The following bacterial, fungal or viral infections –

(i) Products for external use in the treatment or prevention of –

minor skin infections,

athlete's foot,

boils,

for the relief of pruritus or exanthematous rashes of childhood infection, e.g. measles;

(ii) Aphthous ulcers;

(iii) Relief of symptoms of the common cold, coughs, influenza, and similar upper respiratory tract infections;

(iv) Treatment of minor acute inflammatory conditions of the buccal cavity and pharynx (Schedule 2(I)).

(b) The treatment of the following parasitic diseases –

scabies,

infestation by lice, threadworms or roundworms.

The advertisements may consist only of labelled containers or packages or leaflets given with the product (Schedule 2(I)).

(c) Malnutrition including vitamin and mineral deficiency states –

dietary supplements may be advertised for such purposes.

(d) The gastro-intestinal system for the following purposes –

(i) Relief of indigestion, heartburn, hyperacidity, dyspepsia, halitosis or flatulence;

(ii) Symptomatic relief of colicky pain, stomach-ache or nausea;

(iii) Relief of occasional or non-persistent diarrhoea or constipation;

(iv) Prevention of travel-sickness or related symptoms (Schedule 2(II)).

(e) The nervous system for the following purposes –

(i) Symptomatic relief of headache including migrainous headache;

(ii) Prevention of migraine;

(iii) Treatment of neuralgia.
Advertisements for (ii) and (iii) may consist only of labelled containers or packages or leaflets given with the product (Schedule 2(II)).

(f) The genito-urinary system and mammary glands for the following purposes –

(i) Symptomatic relief of dysmenorrhoea;

(ii) Relief of sore nipples during lactation by means of local applications;

(iii) Contraception by means of spermicidal contraceptives BUT the containers, packages and leaflets must be labelled –

'Warning. A higher degree of protection against pregnancy will be afforded by using another method of contraception in addition to a spermicidal contraceptive.'

Advertisements must also carry the same warning. In addition, advertisements must not state or suggest that the spermicidal contraceptive used alone is a highly reliable means of contraception. The advertisement etc. may recommend another contraceptive substance or device but not a diaphragm or cap made of a substance likely to be deleteriously affected by that spermicidal contraceptive.

The container, package and any leaflet must also bear the words (in bold face) –

'Where avoidance of pregnancy is essential, the choice of contraception should be made in consultation with a doctor or family planning clinic.' (regulation 6 and Schedules 2(11) and 3).

(g) The skin, hair and scalp –

(i) External preparations for –

treating acne

treating eczema

treating skin allergies

preventing or treating dandruff

temporarily relieving psoriasis

treating hard skin or corns with solvents or plasters

preventing or treating contact dermatitis by protective applications.

(ii) Products for the prevention or relief of –

dry or chapped skin

cold sores

nettle rash

pruritus

insect bites

napkin rash

other minor skin conditions (Schedule 2(II)).

(h) Peripheral artery disease, but only the treatment of chilblains (Schedule 2(III))

(i) Peripheral venous disease, but only the treatment of haemorrhoids by relief of symptoms by locally effective preparations or by stool softening agents and lubricants (Schedule 2(III)).

(j) Anaemia but only for the prophylactic administration of iron and folic acid to avoid deficiency states in persons with inadequate diet or with increased dietary requirements (Schedule 2(III)).

(k) The endocrine system but only for weight reduction by means of a reduced calorie or joule intake (Schedule 2(III)).

(l) The optical or auditory systems but only for relief of symptoms by local application of –

eye preparations or

solvents for ear wax (Schedule 2(III))

(m) Musculo-skeletal system but only the symptomatic relief of muscular pain and stiffness including backache, sciatica, lumbago, fibrositis, rheumatic pain and cramp (Schedule 2(III)).

(n) Respiratory system but only for –

(i) Temporary relief of symptoms of hay-fever, rhinitis or catarrh

(ii) Relief of blocked-up sinuses

(iii) Alleviation of an attack of bronchial asthma (Schedule 2(III))

(o) Teeth and gums but only for the prevention and treatment of pyorrheoa or the prevention of gingivitis by means of oral hygiene (Schedule 2(III)).

(p) Skeletal fractures, extensive burns, scalds or injuries but advertisements only for dressings, plasters, etc. applied to the surface of the body for alleviating discomfort or protecting the injured part (including the prevention of infection and sunburn) (Schedule 2(IV))

OTHER PROHIBITED ADVERTISEMENTS

The advertising to the public of POM medicines for human use is prohibited. Similarly, products which are the subject of a prohibition order such as phenacetin and chloroform, cannot be advertised to the public (regulation 3).

Advertisements which contain a reference to the Commission, an appropriate committee or the licensing authority are also prohibited unless the authority specifically require that reference (regulation 7).

EXCEPTIONS

None of the prohibitions, requirements or restrictions above apply (regulation 8) –

(a) Where the product licence holder has sent a copy of the advertisement to the licensing authority and the authority has not within 6 weeks of receiving it, notified him that the advertisement should not be issued;

(b) A letter written to a person in reply to an inquiry about a product;

(c) A letter addressed to a member of either House of Parliament or of the Northern Ireland Assembly;

(d) Representations made by a commercially interested party or advertisements sent exclusively or included in a journal of other publication sent to or films or sound recordings played to –

  (i) Persons who in the course of their business or profession prescribe, sell, supply, manufacture, assemble or administer the product, or

  (ii) Persons who instruct students being trained for a qualification in such a business or profession, or

  (iii) Persons engaged in preparing the printed matter, film or recording, or

  (iv) A Minister of the Crown, Government Department, local authority, or a charitable, educational or scientific body interested in the treatment, diagnosis or prevention of any of the diseases specified above;

(e) Any reference to a product which is either POM or the subject of a prohibition order, contained in a company report or other circular sent to shareholders etc. giving information about the company's affairs;

(f) Any printed matter, photographs, film, recording or any material broadcast on sound or television provided that the material was not prepared or issued by or on behalf or at the request of a commercially interested party and was not intended to induce a person to purchase it or request its prescription;

(g) A notice intended to encourage employees to participate in a health care programme.

The scope of the above exceptions indicates the extent of the definition of the word 'advertisement'.

LABELS AND LEAFLETS EXEMPTED FROM CONTROLS

Regulation 9 exempts from the prohibitions, restrictions and requirements of these regulations, those labelled containers or packages or leaflets supplied with products supplied on the prescription of a doctor or dentist.

With the exception of those diseases listed as 'serious diseases' in Table 1, the prohibition on advertisements relating to diseases or body systems specified above does not apply to a labelled container or package (or to a leaflet supplied therewith) of a product which has been 'counter-prescribed' by a pharmacist. However, none of the following words or phrases may be used except where necessary to explain the contra-indications, precautions or action to be taken in the event of over-dosage of the product –

Amenorrhoea, Angina, Atherosclerosis, Erysipelas, Gallstones,
Multiple Sclerosis, Osteoarthritis, Phlebitis, Thrombosis,
Ulcer (except as Mouth Ulcer or Aphthous Ulcer)

Similar exceptions apply to herbal remedies and homoeopathic and similar preparations recommended for any of the same diseases but the container must be labelled –

'A herbal remedy for ....', or
'A homoeopathic remedy for ....', or
'A biochemic remedy for ....', or
'An anthroposophic remedy for ....'

together with this warning, properly completed –

'Warning. If you think you have .... consult a registered medical practitioner before taking this product. If you are already receiving medical treatment, tell your doctor that you are also taking this product'

The name of the disease must be entered in the space.

Chapter 21
Pharmacies

INTRODUCTION

The legal controls over those who practise pharmacy originated in the last century, but controls over their premises (pharmacies) are more recent. Since the two topics are interlinked, a brief account of the development and scope of these controls may be helpful.

In 1843 the newly formed Pharmaceutical Society of Great Britain was granted a Royal Charter and this restricted membership to those in business on their own account as chemists and druggists. Thereafter, only those who satisfied the examiners as to their knowledge would be admitted to membership. The Pharmacy Act 1852 confirmed the Charter and gave protection to the Society by requiring it to keep a register of those entitled to use the titles 'Pharmaceutical Chemist' , 'Pharmaceutist' or 'Member of the Pharmaceutical Society'. The Society were empowered to sue for a penalty of £5 any unauthorised person who used any of these titles. Registers of associates and of students were also kept. Thus, the Society became a statutory body. However, anyone could sell poisons. The Pharmacy Act 1868 remedied this by restricting the sale, compounding and dispensing of poisons to persons registered either as chemists and druggists or as pharmaceutical chemists under the Act. It also made the Society responsible for proposing changes to the list of poisons and for the drafting of regulations for controlling the keeping, dispensing and selling of poisons. For the next eight decades, enactments linked pharmacy with poisons and the Acts were called 'Pharmacy and Poisons Acts'.

The Poisons and Pharmacy Act 1908 brought bodies corporate, and in Scotland, firms or partnerships who carried on the business of chemists and druggists under the control of the Society. Such bodies and firms had to employ a pharmacist as superintendent to be responsible for the business in so far as the poisons were concerned. In addition, a pharmacist had to be in control of each premises where poisons were kept, sold, or dispensed and he was responsible for supervising these activities. The pharmacist's certificate of qualification had to be prominently displayed at the premises. The 1908 Act also empowered local authorities to licence persons, bodies corporate and firms to sell agricultural and horticultural poisons, e.g. weed-killers, sheep dips, which contained arsenic or the alkaloids of tobacco where the existing facilities for their sale were inadequate.

The Pharmacy and Poisons Act 1933 made several important changes both to the profession and to the control of poisons. In respect of the former, membership of the Society ceased to be voluntary, so that a person registered as a pharmacist also became a member of the Society. This was an important change because up until then the criterion for practising as a pharmacist was knowledge, and this was separate from membership; in future, membership was to be the criterion for practise. Furthermore, it required the creation of an internal disciplinary body (called the 'Statutory Committee') with powers over pharmacists, those applying for registration as pharmacists, bodies corporate carrying on the business of retail pharmacy, and representatives of retail pharmacists who had died, become bankrupt or insane. Such persons could lose their authority to practise pharmacy if their names were removed from the register. In regard to poisons, the responsibility for updating the poisons list and for changes to the Poisons Rules, was transferred to the Home Secretary acting on the advice of the Poisons Board. The class of licensed seller was changed to 'listed seller of Part II poisons' and the range of poisons such persons could sell was increased. Furthermore, there was no need for such people to show that the existing facilities were inadequate.

The Pharmacy Act 1954 repealed the older Pharmacy Acts and also those sections of the 1933 Act which dealt with membership of the Society, certificates of registration, restrictions on the use of personal titles (pharmaceutical chemist etc.), and the powers of the Statutory Committee over pharmacists. It left unchanged, those sections dealing with the Committee's powers over bodies corporate and representatives of pharmacists who are deceased, bankrupt or insane. When the Medicines Act was drafted, it was realised that the 1933 Act would be repealed and replaced by a Poisons Act dealing mainly with non-medicinal poisons. It was therefore necessary to include in the Medicines Act, the provisions relating to bodies corporate and representatives and certain other matters such as titles, registration of pharmacies and the like. Consequently, the law relating to pharmacists and pharmacies is to be found partly in the Pharmacy Act 1954 and partly in the Medicines Act. For convenience, relevant sections of the 1954 Act have been reproduced at the end of this volumetogether with a reprint of the Statutory Committee Regulations.

PHARMACISTS

Since 1852 it has been necessary to pass the examinations of the Pharmaceutical Society in order to become a pharmacist. In 1962 the rules were changed so as to require that in future only graduates in pharmacy would be eligible for membership of the Pharmaceutical Society of Great Britain, though persons qualified as pharmacists in certain other countries could be registered under reciprocal arrangements. It is also possible for a person qualified in another country to satisfy an adjudicating panel of the Society that his knowledge of the English language and of the practice of pharmacy in Great Britain is sufficient to permit him to be registered as a pharmacist. The Society however, retain some control of the pharmacy courses held at universities and polytechnics because they have the right to recognise or not, the degrees awarded by these bodies. Only persons holding a 'recognised' degree in pharmacy are eligible for registration as a pharmacist. The Society sends a 'visitation panel' to each school of pharmacy every 5 years, and the panel reports on the syllabus, staff, and facilities available to students. A school which was the subject of an adverse report at one visitation and failed to remedy the position before the next, might find that its degree was not recognised by the Society as being of a suitable standard, and consequently, its future graduates would not be eligible for membership of the Society. This is not a mere theoretical possibility, one university school lost its 'recognition' about a quarter of a century ago. After graduation, the intending pharmacist must undergo 1 year's pre-registration training in a pharmacy, or hospital or 6 months in industry plus 6 months in a hospital or pharmacy. Provided that the supervising pharmacist does not submit an adverse report on him, the young person then becomes eligible for registration.

The person applies for registration by completing a special form and paying the appropriate fee. A registration certificate is issued. As in many other professions, one can only practise if one is registered, and, in fact, the definition of a pharmacist is '..a person registered in the register of pharmaceutical chemists . .. ' (section 132). Thus registration is all-important and may be lost by failing to pay the annual retention fee, or by direction of the Statutory Committee for being convicted of an offence or being guilty of misconduct. Every pharmacist is subject to the Code of Ethics which the Committee uses as a guide, but only as a guide, to professional conduct.

RETAIL PHARMACY BUSINESS

The person who owned or conducted a retail pharmacy business was called an 'authorised seller of poisons' by the Pharmacy and Poisons Act 1933. This expression has been replaced in the Medicines Act by the phrase 'persons lawfully conducting a retail pharmacy business'. A 'retail pharmacy business' means a business (not being a professional practice carried on by a practitioner) which consists of or includes the retail sale of medicinal products other than medicinal products on the general sale list (GSL) (whether medicinal products on such a list are sold in the course of that business or not) (section 132). Such a business may be carried on from a number of premises. It has been suggested that at each premises, medicines should be sold to the public as well as being supplied on prescription, and this would clearly be desirable and the norm. However, it does not seem to preclude the possibility that at a given premises only dispensing is undertaken, provided that the business elsewhere involves the sale of medicines. The Code of Ethics, however, requires that services to the public should be efficient and meet the reasonable needs of those whom the pharmacist serves (see Guidance Note ID(i)).

Under section 69 of the Act only the following classes of persons are eligible to conduct a retail pharmacy business –

(a) Pharmacists (or a partnership consisting solely of pharmacists or in Scotland a partnership in which at least one of the partners is a pharmacist),

(b) Bodies corporate,

(c) The representative of a pharmacist who was 'lawfully conducting..' but has died, become bankrupt or is mentally ill.

In order to be 'lawfully conducting' such a business the person must comply with the following conditions –

(1) In all cases, at each premises where the business is carried on and medicinal products (other than those on the GSL) are sold by retail –

  (a) The business so far as concerns the retail sale of medicinal products (including those on the GSL) must be under the personal control of a pharmacist, and

  (b) The name and registration certificate of the pharmacist must be conspicuously displayed, (sections 70(1), 71(1), 72(2)).

In other words, at a pharmacy, the distribution of ALL medicines must be under the personal control of a pharmacist. Where the owner of a pharmacy also owns another shop at which only GSL medicines are sold (often called a 'B' shop), it is not necessary for that shop to be under the control of a pharmacist but the owner must notify the Society of its existence.

(2) A body corporate must employ a pharmacist as superintendent with the duty of managing the business so far as concerns the keeping, preparing and dispensing of medicinal products and of directing the activities of those pharmacists who are managing the various sets of premises which together comprise the business as a whole. He may personally control a particular premises. He may not act as superintendent for more than one company. He must send to the Registrar a written statement, signed by himself, and on behalf of the body corporate specifying his name and stating whether he is, or is not, a member of the board of the company (section 71). If he is a member of the board, the company may use certain restricted titles.

(3) When a pharmacist who has been carrying on a retail pharmacy business –

(a) Dies,

(b) Becomes bankrupt or enters into a scheme or deed of arrangement with his creditors or the analogous situation in Scotland, or

(c) Suffers from a mental disorder and a receiver is appointed for him (or the corresponding arrangements are made in Scotland or Northern Ireland),

a representative is appointed to carry on the business on his behalf. The representative must comply with the following conditions –

(i) He must notify the Registrar of his name and address and those of the pharmacist he represents,

(ii) He must employ a pharmacist to take personal control of each set of pharmacy premises at which the business is carried on.

The representative is only permitted to carry on the business for a limited period. This period is 5 years in the case of the death of a pharmacist, and 3 years in other cases. Should the period be insufficient, the representative may apply to the Statutory Committee for an extension. The word 'representative' includes an executor or administrator or any of the other persons specified in section 72(4).

If the business is carried on one or more separate or distinct parts of a building, then each part is to be regarded as a separate premises and each will need a pharmacist in personal control of it (section 69(2)).

It must be emphasised that all of the appropriate conditions must be fulfilled in order to be 'lawfully conducting'. Two points seem to give rise to particular difficulty, the personal control requirement and the duties and responsibilities of the superintendent of a body corporate.

'Personal control' has not been defined in the statutes but its meaning has been considered in the courts and also by the Statutory Committee. Ideally, personal control means that a pharmacist should always be available on the premises for consultation with his staff and customers during the hours when the shop is open for business. The occasional brief absence from the premises might be permissible but to be absent for an hour every day would not (Pharm. J., 1966). The reason for this is that the profession believes that medicines should not be sold by persons having inadequate knowledge of their properties. It follows therefore, that there should always be a pharmacist available to give advice to intending customers.

The duties and responsibilities of the superintendent pharmacist of a body corporate are clearly laid down in the Code of Ethics of the Society. Briefly, the superintendent should regard himself as the owner of the business in so far as the control over medicines and the professional conduct of the pharmacy is concerned.

The Health Ministers have powers to amend the conditions under which pharmacies may lawfully be conducted (section 73).

REGISTRATION OF PHARMACIES

It has long been necessary for pharmacy premises to be registered with the Society and for the Registrar to keep and publish the register of premises. In Northern Ireland similar powers and duties reside in the Pharmaceutical Society of Northern Ireland. Under the previous Acts neither the Registrar nor the Society had power to refuse to register a premises provided that application was made in the proper manner and the appropriate fee paid, though premises could in certain circumstances be removed from the register by the Statutory Committee. Those premises which were registered on the 31st December 1973 were transferred to new registers kept under the Medicines Act during 1974 and since the 1st January 1974 a different procedure for registering new premises has been in operation, section 75 and S.I.1973/1822 as amended by 1980/1806, 1981/1713 and 1984/1886.

The person who carries on, or intends to carry on, a retail pharmacy business at a premises must apply in writing to the Registrar giving the following particulars –

(a) His name and residential address (or, if a partnership the names and residential addresses of all of the partners, or if a body corporate, the address of its registered office). A representative must send the name and number of the registration certificate of the pharmacist in personal control of the premises.

(b) The business name of the business if different from those given in (a).

(c) The names of the pharmacist(s) in personal control of the premises and, for a body corporate, the name of the superintendent.

(d) The full postal address of the premises.

(e) If the application is due to a change of ownership, the name and address of the former owner and the date of change of ownership.

(f) The date or intended date of the commencement of the business at those premises.

(g) A brief description of the layout of the premises as regards the areas where medicines are to be sold, stored, dispensed, etc. and a scale plan showing these areas. In addition, a statement showing whether or not it is possible for a pharmacist to simultaneously supervise dispensing and the sale of products.

On receipt of the application, the Registrar will notify the appropriate Health Minister of the premises and the date of application. Registration will not occur until 2 months have elapsed unless the Minister consents to it. The premises may only be registered if the Registrar is satisfied that the applicant is, or will be on the date of commencement of the business, a person lawfully conducting a retail pharmacy business. A registration fee is payable in respect of each premises. For 1985 the fees are £75 (£38.50 in Northern Ireland).

The Ministers have powers under section 66 to lay down various requirements as to the facilities available at a premises. This power has not yet been exercised but it could be used to prevent the registration of unsuitable premises though the Act does permit an appeal, section 75.

Every year a retention fee must be paid in order to keep the premises on the register. For 1985 this fee is £45 (£33 in Northern Ireland). Failure to pay the fee within 2 months may result in a Council direction to the Registrar to remove the premises from the Register. The premises can be restored to the Register if the fee together with a penalty fee of £50 (£36 in Northern Ireland) is paid during that year. The fee accompanies the annual return of premises which everyone carrying on a pharmacy business must send to the Registrar every January. The return lists all of the premises occupied by the person at which medicines are sold, including B shops, and the names of the pharmacists in control of the pharmacies.

When the ownership of a registered pharmacy changes hands, the registration becomes void after 28 days,(or if due to the death of the owner or a partner 3 months). The new owner must apply for the premises to be restored to the Register but there is no need for a description etc. of the premises and the application is processed by the Registrar without reference to the Minister.

The Society receives and may use all the money collected as registration, penalty and retention fees.

RESTRICTED TITLES

It is an offence to take or use any of the following titles otherwise than in accordance with the specified conditions.

(a) 'Chemist and druggist', 'druggist', 'dispensing druggist', 'dispensing chemist'

These titles may only be used in connection with a registered pharmacy, and then only when the user is either –

(i) An individual lawfully conducting a retail pharmacy business either alone or as a member of a partnership, or

(ii) Is a body corporate lawfully conducting..., and its superintendent is a member of the board.

The use of the word 'chemist' in connection with the retail sale or supply of any goods is also restricted to the conditions specified above, (section 78(2), (3) and section 84(2)).

(b) 'Pharmacy'

This description may only be used in connection with a business which includes the retail sale of goods in respect of a registered pharmacy or the pharmaceutical department of a hospital or health centre, section 78(4). The use of the word in connection with a business shall be taken to be likely to suggest that the owner of the business (where that owner is not a body corporate) is a pharmacist and that the person in control of the premises is also a pharmacist (section 78(7)).

(c) Only a pharmacist, i.e. someone whose name is registered as a pharmaceutical chemist, may use the following titles –

'pharmaceutical chemist', 'pharmaceutist', 'pharmacist', 'member of the Pharmaceutical Society', 'Fellow of the Pharmaceutical Society'. The titles cannot be used in connection with a business unless the premises is a registered pharmacy or a health centre or hospital (section 78(5)).

(d) A representative of a pharmacist may use any of the titles which the pharmacist could have used (section 78(8)).

(e) No one may use in connection with any business any emblem or description likely to suggest that he or any of his employees possess any qualification with respect to the sale, manufacture or assembly of medicinal products which he does not in fact possess (section 78(7)).

DISQUALIFICATION AND REMOVAL FROM THE REGISTER

Sections 80–83 re-enact certain provisions of the Pharmacy and Poisons Act 1933. They deal with the powers of the Statutory Committee over bodies corporate which carry on retail pharmacy businesses and are described in detail under the Statutory Committee (see below).

A court may order the disqualification for up to two years of any premises used as a pharmay (section 68(1)). Such action can only be taken if –

(1) The person is convicted of an offence which consists of the contravention of regulations made under section 66;

(2) The enforcing authority (the Pharmaceutical Society of Great Britain in Great Britain or the Department of Health and Social Services for Northern Ireland) so request the court;

(3) The court thinks it expedient to do so in view of the gravity of the offence or the unsatisfactory condition of the premises or that the person had previously been convicted of similar offences;

(4) The enforcing authority had given the person at least fourteen days notice of the intention to seek such an order.

As yet (July 1985) only one set of regulations has been made under section 66, namely the Medicines (Sale or Supply) (Miscellaneous Provisions) Regulations 1980/1923.

STATUTORY COMMITTEE

In the United Kingdom, one of the hall-marks of a profession is the existence of an internal disciplinary body. The purpose of such a body is two-fold, firstly it protects the public by ensuring that members of the profession who lack the required competence or integrity or who behave in an unprofessional manner are removed from the profession. Secondly, of course, it protects the reputation of the profession itself.

The Pharmacy Act 1868 empowered the Privy Council to order the removal from the Register of the names of those who had been convicted of offences under the Pharmacy Acts. In fact this power was never used possibly because there was no means of subsequently reinstating the person to the Register. The Pharmacy and Poisons Act 1933 really established pharmacy as a profession by creating the Statutory Committee to act as the disciplinary body for pharmacy. It is an example of an English legal custom dating back to 1215 that a man should be judged by his peers. Although the Committee consists mainly of pharmacists, the link with the Privy Council remains because it appoints as chairman of the

Committee a person 'having practical legal experience'. During the last 50 years, some very eminent judges have been appointed including some former Lords Justices of Appeal. The presence of a lawyer on the Committee is beneficial to the profession because not only does he ensure that its proceedings are conducted in a fair and impartial way by following the dictates of natural justice, but also, being in a pharmaceutical sense a layman, he is free from any pharmaceutical bias. It is surely noteworthy that although the Committee has heard hundreds of cases since its first meeting in 1936, only 12 persons have appealed to the High Court and only three of these were successful.

The Committee is a committee of the Pharmaceutical Society NOT of its Council. The distinction is important because in the majority of cases of alleged misconduct the complaint is brought to the notice of the Committee by the Council, a proceeding which would tend to make the Council both prosecutor and judge if a closer bond existed between the two. There are links between the Council and the Committee, e.g. the Council appoints the five members of the Committee. The Council is also involved in the formulation of the Code of Ethics which replaced 'The Statement upon Matters of Professional Conduct' in 1984. This is used as a guide (but only as a guide) to the profession's views of desirable and undesirable conduct.

The current sources of law relating to the Committee are –

(a) Pharmacy Act 1954, (P.A.) sections 7–11 inclusive which specify its powers over pharmacists, persons applying for registration as pharmacists, and persons whose names have been removed from the Register for non-payment of fees, and certain employees. Schedule 1 to the Act specifies the constitution of the Committee.

(b) Medicines Act 1968,(M.A.) sections 80–83 inclusive, which specify its powers over bodies corporate and representatives who are carrying on a retail pharmacy business.

(c) The Pharmaceutical Society (Statutory Committee) Order in Council 1978 (S.I.1978/20) which contains the regulations governing the Committee's proceedings.

Constitution

The Committee consists of –

(a) A chairman, being a person 'having practical legal experience' appointed by the Privy Council, and

(b) Five members appointed by the Council of the Society, one of whom must be a pharmacist resident in Scotland. Although the Act permits the Council to appoint non-pharmacists to the Committee, its appointees are invariably experienced pharmacists.

The chairman and members serve for 5 years and are eligible for re-appointment. They may resign by giving written notice to the Clerk to the Privy Council or to the Registrar of the Society. A person may be removed from the Committee for misbehaviour or for inability to perform his duties.

The quorum of the Committee is three, of which the chairman shall be one. The Committee acts by a majority and the chairman has a casting vote. Some of the directions of the Committee (e.g. removal of a name or disqualification of a body corporate) may only be made with the assent of the chairman. The Committee may make regulations as to its procedure but these must be approved by the Privy Council before they become operative.

Procedure

When the secretary of the Committee (a member of the Society's staff) receives information which indicates that a person or a body corporate within the jurisdiction of the Committee has been allegedly guilty of misconduct or has been convicted of an offence, the chairman is notified. After examining the information and any evidence or explanation received from the 'accused', the chairman after consultation with the members will deal with the matter in one of the following ways –

(1) If he considers that the case is outside the Committee's jurisdiction, or frivolous, or due to lapse of time or other circumstance the complaint should be disregarded, he shall decide that the case shall not proceed further;

(2) If he is of the opinion that the offence or misconduct is not serious and that an inquiry is unnecessary, he may after consulting the Committee direct the secretary to send a reprimand to the affected person and caution him as to his future conduct;

(3) In any other case, he must direct the holding of an inquiry.

When an inquiry is to be held a solicitor is instructed to investigate the facts and present the case to the Committee. Alternatively, the complainant may present his own case. If the solicitor reports that there is insufficient evidence to prove the case the Committee may decide not to proceed with the inquiry.

At least 28 days before the date of the inquiry, the person affected must be notified of the date, time and place of the inquiry and given details of the matters into which it will be held. He is entitled to copies of any information or summary sent to the chairman and is entitled to be legally represented. The case is heard in public though the Committee may decide to hear parts of it in private. If the person affected does not appear at the inquiry, the Committee may adjourn the hearing or proceed in his absence.

At the inquiry, the case against the person is stated and evidence produced to support it. The person affected then states his case and produces evidence in its support. Witnesses may be examined and cross-examined at the hearing and evidence may be given orally or by written and signed statement or by statutory declaration. The Committee shall disregard oral evidence given by a person who refuses to submit to cross-examination, and have discretion to decline to admit the written statement or statutory declaration of a person who is not present and must disregard it if he is present but refuses to submit to cross-examination.

After hearing all the evidence, the Committee deliberates in private. The chairman then announces the decision in public. The Committee may postpone the decision or a part of it, in which case the chairman must announce this together any terms on which it is made. The secretary subsequently notifies the person affected of the Committee's decision in writing.

Jurisdiction

The Committee is informed whenever any of the persons specified below is alleged to have been guilty of misconduct or has been convicted of any criminal offence –

(a) A person applying for registration as a pharmacist (e.g. a student, a person qualified abroad, P.A section 8(1)a)

(b) A pharmacist or anyone employed in his business (P.A section 8(1)b)

(c) A person whose name has been removed from the Register for non-payment of fees, or anyone employed in his business (P.A. section 8(1)c)

(d) Any member of the board or officer or employee of a body corporate carrying on a retail pharmacy business (M.A. section 80(1))

(e) A representative of a deceased, bankrupt or mentally ill pharmacist or any employee in the business (M.A. section 80 (4)).

The Committee is also informed whenever a body corporate carrying on a retail pharmacy business is convicted of an offence under the Pharmacy Acts (including the Poisons Act 1972), the Medicines Act or the Misuse of Drugs Act.

The only sanction available to the Committee under the Acts is to prevent the person (or the body corporate) from practising pharmacy, though one or more of the premises of the body corporate may be removed from the Register of Premises. These sanctions may only be applied with the assent of the chairman.

Where the offence or misconduct was committed by an employee, the Committee may only apply the sanction to the employer when it is satisfied that one or more of the following facts has been proved and that the employer should be regarded as responsible –

(1) That the offence or misconduct was instigated or connived at by the employer or by the board or a member of the board ;

(2) That within the previous 12 months, the employer or an employee in the business had been guilty of a similar act or omission and the employer had, or reasonably ought to have had knowledge of the act or omission ;

(3) If the act or omission was a continuing one, the employer had, or reasonably ought to have had, knowledge of its continuance ;

(4) Where the offence was under the Pharmacy Acts etc., the employer, or board, had not used reasonable care to ensure that the law was complied with (P.A. section 9(2); M.A. section 81).

In practice,these sanctions are used only in serious cases and the Committee usually adopt one of the following courses –

(a) Direct that no further action be taken, or

(b) Admonish or reprimand the person or body corporate, or

(c) Adjourn the case, usually for a year; this is a type of 'probation'.

When the Committee directs that a name should be removed from, or not entered in, the Register, or that a body corporate be disqualified or some of its premises removed from the Register,the decision does not take effect for 3 months. This is to allow time for an appeal to be made to the High Court. If an appeal is made, the direction does not take effect until it has been withdrawn or determined (P.A. section 10; M.A. section 82(2)). Furthermore, where the appeal relates to the removal of a pharmacist's name, or the refusal to register or restore to the Register the name of a person, if the High Court dismiss the appeal, then the name cannot be registered except with the approval of the Privy Council (P.A. section 11(1)). Apart from this, the Committee may subsequently, either of its own volition or at the request of the affected party revoke its decision (P.A. section 8(1)(2); M.A. section 83). If the Committee refuses a request to revoke its previous decision, the person affected may appeal to the High Court. A person who is reprimanded or admonished by the Committee cannot appeal to the High Court but can apply for a 'judicial review' and one such was successful (*Pharm. J.*, 1983a).

Since its first meeting in August 1936, the Committee has heard over a thousand cases. The majority involved pharmacists, but bodies corporate have also been involved. Between 1936 and the end of 1983, about 160 cases resulted in a pharmacist's name being removed from the Register (or being refused restoration to the Register). About ten bodies corporate have been disqualified usually because they had been convicted of selling poisons or medicines otherwise than under the supervision of a pharmacist. It is interesting to study these figures in a little more detail.

Convictions

Of the 170 cases which ended in persons being removed from the register or disqualified, 125 were in respect of convictions. These can be divided into four main groups, namely –

(1) Those involving pharmacy, e.g. Misuse of Drugs Act, medicines, poisons –

There have been 39 removals for these offences, 14 involved dangerous (controlled) drugs, 24 involved poisons (medicines) and one involved the Food and Drugs Act.

(2) Abortion, use of instruments , indecency –

There have been 18 of these, most of them before 1959.

(3) Dishonesty, theft –

There have been 58 removals for various species of theft.

(4) Miscellaneous offences –

There were 7 of these.

Misconduct

Whereas everyone knows what constitutes a conviction for a criminal offence, the meaning of 'misconduct' is more nebulous. It can be described as unprofessional conduct and may arise –

(a) As a result of a breach of professional rules or ethics, i.e. doing something which, though legal, is contrary to accepted ethical rules, such as advertising, or otherwise bringing the profession into disrepute, or

(b) Committing a crime which, for some reason, is not brought to a prosecution and consequently cannot give rise to a conviction, or

(c) Where the person was convicted of an offence but was discharged (either absolutely or conditionally) and therefore under the Powers of Criminal Courts Act 1973, the conviction cannot be used for the purposes of the Statutory Committee, or

(d) As a combination of the above.

An important point to be borne in mind with regard to misconduct is that the professional conscience is constantly developing and public opinion also changes. Consequently, what was acceptable as professional behaviour in the past might become unacceptable in the future and vice versa. In order to obtain an idea as to what constitutes misconduct it is useful to consider some of the cases which have been brought before the Committee.

Cases of misconduct can be classified into –

(1) Those which put the safety of the public at risk

These include dirty or untidy premises, out of date stock, lack of proper facilities and equipment, carelessness in dispensing, faulty or illegible labels. In all, there have been ten such cases. There are four recent cases which come within this class, and in each case the pharmacist having been given time to remedy the situation had failed to do so. These cases tend to occur in areas where redevelopment is taking place and the population has been dramatically reduced. Like the neighbourhood, the premises is old and needs modernising but, because of reduced income, the owner is unable to maintain it properly. This creates a real dilemma both for the pharmacist and for the Committee because if the man is struck off the local residents are usually deprived of their only neighbourhood pharmacy (*Pharm. J.,* 1980; *Pharm. J.*, 1982; *Pharm. J.*, 1983a).

One pharmacist who had been the subject of numerous complaints about his professional conduct, particularly in regard to dispensing errors was stuck off (*Pharm. J.*, 1971).

(2) Those which reflect badly on the profession

These include drunkenness and addiction. These may also put the patient's safety at risk and may also involve criminal offences. There have been 14 such cases since 1936.

(3) Contraventions of the Code involving the supply of medicines

Six pharmacists have been removed from the register for selling drugs to addicts. Some of these sales were perfectly lawful in themselves, the misconduct arose out of the quantities sold, or the frequency of the sales. In one case the Committee found misconduct in the regular sale of Phensedyl to an addict (*Pharm. J.*, 1982b).

A more complicated case involved two retail pharmacy companies, the two pharmacists who owned them and the two managers of two sets of premises. The managers were exonerated because they had only recently been employed at the shops. It seems that between them, the two companies had sold 185,700 amyl nitrite vitrellae in 1 year. At the time amyl nitrite was a Part I poison and could be sold without a prescription so there was no criminal offence. The Council of the Society believed that the sale of such huge amounts of a drug the medical use of which was almost obsolete constituted misconduct especially when it is realised that it can be abused. The Committee decided to strike the names of the two pharmacist owners from the Register. This case was also of interest because the pharmacists appealed successfully to the High Court. The High Court had no doubt that they deserved to be removed from the Register but felt that they should have had an opportunity to refute the evidence that amyl nitrite had harmful effects though the Court did not believe that it was necessary to rely on the existence of harmful effects. Consequently, the pharmacists' names were not removed from the register (*Pharm. J.*, 1976).

(4) Advertising professional services.

The only case of this occurred in the 1960s.

The other removals due to misconduct involved a variety of criminal activities which for one reason or another were not brought to prosecution.

Cases Involving Bodies Corporate

In ten cases resulting in disqualification, the body corporate had been convicted of selling medicines (or poisons) illegally. Almost invariably this arose because the unqualified owner of the business sold medicines after the pharmacist manager or superintendent had gone home. Sometimes, the business was being run without a pharmacist in personal control. In another case, the company was disqualified, and the name of its pharmacist owner removed from the Register, for conducting a pharmacy in a manner likely to be a hazard to the safety of the public and also likely to bring the profession into disrepute.

Appeals

Eleven appeals against removal of names or disqualification have been made to the High Court, and one application for a judicial review. Only two appeals were successful, one was the amyl nitrite case stated above, and the other concerned a body corporate (Zygmunt Chemists Ltd) in 1966.

References

Pharm. J., 1966, i, 311

Pharm. J., 1983a, i, 13

Pharm. J., 1980, ii, 254

Pharm. J., 1982a, ii, 699

Pharm. J., 1983b, ii, 450

Pharm. J., 1971, i, 72

Pharm. J., 1982b, i, 1

Pharm. J., 1976, ii, 430

Appendix 1

Definitions of Words and Phrases Used in the Act and Subordinate Legislation

The persons responsible for drafting a piece of legislation aim to achieve clarity and avoid ambiguity in the document. However, most words have shades of meaning and the interpretation of the statute or instrument becomes difficult for those who have to obey or enforce it, especially when such persons are not lawyers. In the last analysis, it is a judge who has to decide whether a particular set of circumstances fall within or outside a given set of words, but this may be too late for the citizen who may have done utmost to keep within the law. It should, however, be pointed out that government departments and others who have a duty to enforce a piece of legislation are usually willing to advise members of the public as to its meaning and effects.

In order to help those who have to obey or enforce the law an 'interpretation' section, regulation or rule containing a number of technical terms used in the document is often included. In the Medicines Act, sections 13O, 131 and 132 are devoted to this purpose. However, many other terms are defined in other sections and are sometimes less easy to locate. Furthermore, numerous statutory instruments also define various words and phrases and these definitions are not always identical with those used in the Act. To facilitate reference to these definitions, they have been collected together and printed alphabetically with the exception of 'medicinal product' and 'wholesale' and 'retail' sale which, in view of their importance, are treated separately.

Where a definition has been taken from a statutory instrument, the reference number of the instrument is stated.

'ABBREVIATED ADVERTISEMENT' means an advertisement, other than a loose insert, in a professional publication which complies with the requirements imposed by regulation 5d of, and Schedule 2 to, these Regulations. (1978/1020)

The requirements relate to size, specifically, the advertisement must not exceed 420 square centimetres in area.

'ACTIVE INGREDIENT' means any chemical or other substance specified in a product licence or animal test certificate and included in a medicated feeding stuff for a medicinal purpose; (1973/1530)

'ADMINISTER' means administer to a human being or an animal, whether orally, by injection or by introduction into the body in any other way, or by external application, whether by direct contact with the body or not; and any reference in this Act to administering a substance or article is a reference to administering it either in its existing state or after it has been dissolved or dispersed in or diluted or mixed with, some other substance used as a vehicle. (section 130(9))

'ADMINISTER' has the same meaning as in section 130(9) of the Act as modified by Article 2 of and paragraph 9 of Part II of Schedule 2 to, the Specified Articles and Substances Order; (1979/1759)

Thus, administer may be construed as extending to include the application of such substances to contact lenses or blanks.

'ADVERTISEMENT' includes every form of advertising, whether in a publication, or by the display of any notice, or by means of any catalogue, price list, letter (whether circular or addressed to a particular person) or other document, or by words inscribed on any article, or by the exhibition of a photograph or by a cinematograph film, or by way of sound recording, sound broadcasting or television, or in any other way, and any reference to the issue of an advertisement shall be construed accordingly; (section 92(1))

However, 'ADVERTISEMENT', does not include spoken words except:

(1) words forming part of a sound recording or embodied in a soundtrack associated with a cinematograph film, and

(2) words broadcast by way of sound broadcasting or television or transmitted to subscribers to a diffusion service. (section 92(2))

Furthermore, except as provided by section 95 of this Act,for the purposes of this Part of this Act neither of the following shall be taken to constitute the issue of an advertisement, that is to say –

(a) the sale or supply, or offer or exposure for sale or supply of a medicinal product in a labelled container or package;

(b) the supply, with a medicinal product of any description of a leaflet relating solely to medicinal products of that description. (section 92(3))

'ADVERTISEMENT' has the same meaning as in section 92(1) and (2) of the Act; (1978/41)

'ADVERTISEMENT' has the same meaning as in section 92(1) and (2) of the Act but these Regulations shall only apply to advertisements which are issued for the purpose of inducing a doctor or dentist to prescribe, supply, administer, or procure the administration of medicinal products of a particular description; (1978/1020)

This very restricted meaning of advertisement is intended to limit the application of the regulations to doctors and dentists and what they may prescribe on the NHS.

'AEROSOL' means a product which is dispersed from its container by a propellent gas or liquid; (1983/1212)

'AGRICULTURAL ANALYST' means an agricultural analyst appointed under section 67 of the Agriculture Act 1970 and includes a deputy agricultural analyst appointed for the same area; (1985/273)

'AGRICULTURAL REQUISITES' means things used in the cultivation of the soil or in the keeping of animals for the production of food or as game and equipment used in or for the collection of produce from animals kept for the production of food and things used for the maintenance of such equipment, and includes any protective clothing but does not include any other kind of human apparel;(1984/1861)

'AGRICULTURE MINISTERS' means the Minister of Agriculture, Fisheries and Food, the Secretaries of State concerned with Agriculture in Scotland and in Wales and the Department of Agriculture for Northern Ireland; (section 1(1) as amended by 1975/1349; 1976/31 and 1978/272)

'AMPHOTERICIN B' is any antimicrobial substance or mixture of such substances produced by *Streptomyces nodosus*. The expression includes any salt or derivative, or salt of a derivative, of amphotericin B and any substance the chemical and biological properties of which are identical with or similar to those of amphotericin B but which is produced by other means; (1971/1200)

'AMPHOTERICINS' are antimicrobial substances or mixtures of such substances produced by *Streptomyces nodosus*; (1977/2131)

'ANALYSIS' includes microbiological assay but no other forms of biological assay, and 'analyse' has a corresponding meaning; (section 132)

'ANIMAL' includes any bird, fish or reptile; (section 132)

In fact, it is intended to include insects and all other members of the animal kingdom.

'ANIMAL FEEDING STUFF' means any substance which is intended for use either by being fed to one or more animals or as an ingredient in the preparation of such a substance, not being in either case a medicinal product; (section 132)

'ANIMAL FEEDING STUFF' includes a complete feeding stuff, a feed supplement and a protein concentrate. (1973/1530, 1976/1726 and 1985/273)

'ANIMALS' means domestic animals of the bovine species, swine, sheep, goats, solipeds and poultry, and wild animals of these species and wild ruminants which have been raised on a holding; (1982/626)

'ANIMAL TEST CERTIFICATE' means a certificate issued certifying that, subject to the provisions of the certificate, the licensing authority have consented to the test in question and that certificate is for the time being in force and the test is to be carried out in accordance with that certificate; (section 32(2)b)

'ANTIGENS' are substances which on administration to a human being or an animal are capable of eliciting a specific immunological response; (1971/1198, 1971/1200, 1971/1309, and 1971/1326)

'ANTIMICROBIAL PROPERTIES' means the capacity to inhibit the growth of, or to destroy bacteria and other micro-organisms whether in-vitro or in-vivo; (1973/367)

'ANTISERA' are substances which consist wholly or partly of sera derived from animals which have been immunised against one or more micro-organisms, viruses or other antigens; (1971/1198; 1971/1200; 1971/1309; 1971/1326)

'ANTITOXINS' are substances which consist wholly or partly of immunoglobulins of antisera derived from animals which have been immunised against one or more toxins whether detoxified or not;(1971/1198; 1971/1200; 1971/1309; 1971/1326)

'APPLICATION' means the request for the grant of a licence together with the particulars required by these regulations, but does not include a request to renew a licence; (1971/974)

'APPLICATION' means a request for the grant of a product licence (other than a product licence of right) or the issue of a clinical trial certificate or animal test certificate (other than a clinical trial certificate or animal test certificate issued under section 37(4) of the Act) but does not include a request to renew a product licence or a clinical trial certificate or animal test certificate; (1971/973)

'APPROPRIATE COMMITTEE' in this Act 'the appropriate committee', for the purposes of any provision of this Act under which a function falls to be performed, means such committee established under this section for purposes which consist of or include any of those specified in subsection (3) of this section as the authority performing that function considers appropriate in the circumstances; (section 4(6))

'APPROPRIATE CURRENT MONOGRAPH' in relation to a particular name, means –

(a) the monograph (if any) headed by that name, or by a name for which it is an approved synonym, in the current edition of the European Pharmacopoeia, or

(aa) if there is no such monograph, then the monograph (if any) headed by that name in the current edition of the British Pharmacopoeia, or

(b) if there is no such monograph, then the monograph (if any) headed by that name in the current edition of a compendium published under Part VII of this Act, or

(c) if there is no such monograph, then the monograph (if any) headed by that name in the current edition of the British Pharmaceutical Codex or the British Veterinary Codex; (section 65(5))

'APPROPRIATE MINISTERS' In this Act, except where the contrary is expressly provided, 'the appropriate Ministers' –

(a) for the purpose of performing any function under this Act (whether by the making of any regulations or order or otherwise) where the function is performed exclusively in relation to matters other than veterinary drugs and the treatment of diseases of animals means the Health Ministers; and

(b) in any other case, means the Ministers; (section 1(2))

'APPROPRIATE NON-PROPRIETARY NAME' in relation to a medicinal product or ingredient means –

(i) where the medicinal product or ingredient is described in a monograph in a specified publication any name, or abbreviation of such name, at the head of that monograph or, in the case of the European Pharmacopoeia, an approved synonym, or where such name consists of two or more words, any name derived from a suitable inversion of such words which is permitted by that specified publication, or

(ii) where the medicinal product or ingredient is not described in a monograph in a specified publication but has an approved name, such approved name, or

(iii) where the medicinal product or ingredient is not described in a monograph in a specified publication and does not have an approved name, but has an international non-proprietary name, such international non-proprietary name, or

(iv) where the medicinal product is not described in a monograph in a specified publication and does not have an approved name or an international non-proprietary name, the accepted scientific name or any other name descriptive of the true nature of the medicinal product or ingredient; (1976/1726; 1983/1727)

'APPROPRIATE QUANTITATIVE PARTICULARS' means

(i) the quantity of each active ingredient, or that part of the active molecule responsible for the therapeutic or pharmacological activity, identified by its appropriate non-proprietary name, in each dosage unit of the medicinal product expressed in terms of weight, volume, capacity, or units of activity, or, where the medicinal product consists of confectionery in the form of a pastille or lozenge, expressed as aforesaid or in terms of a percentage by weight or volume of such pastille or lozenge, or, where the medicinal product is a homoeopathic product expressed in terms of the dilution of the unit preparation of that active ingredient, or

(ii) where there is no dosage unit, the quantity of each active ingredient or that part of the active molecule responsible for the therapeutic or pharmacological activity identified by its appropriate non-proprietary name, in the container of the medicinal product expressed in terms of weight, volume, capacity, or units of activity, or percentage by weight or volume of the total quantity, or, where the medicinal product is a homoeopathic product, expressed in terms of the dilution of the unit preparation of that active ingredient, or

(iii) where the medicinal product contains any active ingredient that cannot be definitively characterised, the quantity of each ingredient or that part of the active molecule responsible for the therapeutic or pharmacological activity, identified by its appropriate non-proprietary name, expressed in terms of weight, volume, capacity, or units of activity or percentage by weight or volume, from which each dosage unit of the medicinal product, or, where there is no dosage unit, the quantity of the medicinal product in the container has been prepared or, where the medicinal product is a herbal remedy in solution in liquid form, the total quantity of the active ingredient which is in solid form in the container, or, where the medicinal product is a homoeopathic product, expressed in terms of the dilution of the unit preparation of that active ingredient, or

(iv) where there are no active ingredients in the medicinal products the quantity of the ingredient which is present in the highest proportion whether in weight, volume or capacity identified by its appropriate non-proprietary name, expressed in terms of weight, volume, capacity, or percentage by weight or volume of the total quantity from which the medicinal product in the container has been prepared, except where such ingredient is a diluent, excipient, preservative, stabiliser or bulking agent, or where the medicinal product is a homoeopathic product, expressed in terms of the dilution of the unit preparation of that ingredient, or

(v) where the medicinal product includes a biological substance to which an antimicrobial preservative has been added in addition to an active ingredient, the quantity of such antimicrobial preservative in the container of the medicinal product, expressed in terms of weight, volume, capacity or percentage by weight or volume of the total quantity; (1976/1726 as amended; 1983/1727)

'APPROVED NAME' in relation to a constituent is the name of the substance or article which appears in the current edition of the list prepared by the appropriate body in accordance with section 100 of the Act and published by the Ministers on the recommendation of the Medicines Commission; (1971/973)

'APPROVED NAME' means the name which appears in the current edition (as defined in section 103(5) of the Act) of the list prepared and published under section 100 of the Act as in force at the date of preparation or last review or revision of the data sheet; (1972/2076).(A similar definition is given in 1978/1020 and, as respects labels, in 1976/1726 and 1983/1727)

'APPROVED NAME' in relation to a constituent is either the name of the substance or article which appears in the current edition of the list prepared by the appropriate body in accordance with section 100 of the Act and published by the Ministers on the recommendation of Medicines Commission or the international non-proprietary name recommended by WHO; (1981/164)

'APPROVED SYNONYM' means a name declared to be approved by the Medicines Commission (and published in the Gazette) as a synonym for a name at the head of a monograph in the European Pharmacopoeia; (section 65(8); 1976/1726; 1978/1020)

'ASPIRIN EQUIVALENT' means, in relation to a quantity of aloxiprin, the quantity of asprin which is equal in weight to 81·25 per cent of that quantity of aloxiprin; (1985/1540).

'ASSEMBLE' in relation to a medicinal product, means enclosing the product (with or without other medicinal products of the same description) in a container which is labelled before the product is sold or supplied, or, where the product (with or without other medicinal products of the same description) is already enclosed in the container before the product is sold or supplied, labelling the container before the product is sold or supplied in it, and 'assembly' has a corresponding meaning; (section 132)

Examples of assembly are 'breaking bulk' i.e. repacking 1 gallon of liquid paraffin into 100 ml bottles and labelling them, or repacking 5000 tablets in 50 bottles each containing 100 tablets. It also includes filling one bottle from another or even simply removing a manufacturer's label and replacing it with another.

'ASSEMBLE' means to label the container in which a medicinal product is already enclosed and in which it is to be sold or supplied before the product is sold or supplied in it, and 'assembly' has a corresponding meaning; (1979/1114)

'BACITRACIN' is any antimicrobial polypeptide produced by strains of *Bacillus licheniformis* and of *Bacillus subtilis (var. Tracey)*, which yields on hydrolysis with mineral acids the amino acids L-cysteine, D-glutamic acid,

L-histidine, L-isoleucine, L-leucine, L-lysine, D-ornithine, D-phenylalanine and DL-aspartic acid. The expression includes any salt or derivative or salt of a derivative of bacitracin and any substance the chemical and biological properties of which are identical with or similar to those of bacitracin but which is produced by other means; (1971/1200)

'BATCH' means a homogeneous collection of sealed containers prepared in such a manner that the risk of contamination is the same for each of the units in the collection; (1971/972, Schedule 4, Part 2)

'B.C.G.' means the bacillus of Calmette and Guérin; (1977/675)

'B.C.G. VACCINE' means a vaccine that is a preparation of the bacteria in a living pure culture of a strain of the bacillus of Calmette and Guérin; (1977/675)

'BENZESTROL' means 4,4′-(1,2-diethyl-3-methyltrimethylene) diphenol and salts and esters thereof; (1982/425; 1982/518; 1982/626)

'BIOLOGICAL SUBSTANCE' includes an antigen, toxin, antitoxin, serum, antiserum, or vaccine; (1976/1726)

'THE BOARD' in relation to a body corporate, means the body of persons controlling the body corporate, by whatever name called: (insofar as Part IV of the Act is concerned); (section 69)

'BRITISH APPROVED NAME' means the name which appears in the current edition of the list prepared by the appropriate body in accordance with section 100 of the Act and published by the Ministers on the recommendation of the Medicines Commission; (1984/673)

'BUSINESS' includes a professional practice and includes any activity carried on by a body of persons, whether corporate or unincorporate; (section 132)

'BUSINESS NAME' means the name or style under which any business is being carried on, being a name or style required to be registered under the Registration of Business Names Act 1916; (1972/2076; 1976/1726)

'CAPREOMYCIN' is any antimicrobial polypeptide or mixture of such polypeptides produced by the strain of *Streptomyces capreolus* which on lst September 1967 was number NRRL 2773 in the culture collection of the Northern Utilisation Research and Development Branch of the United States Department of Agriculture, and which yields on hydrolysis with mineral acids the amino acids α,β-diaminopropionic acids and α-(-2-iminohexahydro-4-pyrimidyl) glycine together with serine, alanine and β-lysine. The expression includes any salt or derivative, or salt of a derivative of capreomycin and any substance the chemical and biological properties of which are identical with or similar to capreomycin but which is produced by other means; (1971/1200)

'CEPHALOSPORINS' means antimicrobial substances containing in their chemical structure a fused dihydrothiazine β-lactam nucleus; (1977/2131)

'CERTIFICATE' means a clinical trial certificate or an animal test certificate; (1974/832)

'CHORIONIC GONADOTROPHIN' is a dry, sterile preparation of the gonad stimulating substance obtained from the urine of pregnant women; (1971/1200)

'CLINICAL TRIAL' means an investigation or series of investigations consisting of the administration of one or more medicinal products of a particular description –

(a) by, or under the direction of, a doctor or dentist to one or more patients of his, or

(b) by, or under the direction of, two or more doctors or dentists, each product being administered by, or under the direction of, one or other of those doctors or dentists to one or more patients of his,

where (in any such case) there is evidence that medicinal products of that description have effects which may be beneficial to the patient or patients in question and the administration of the product or products is for the purpose of ascertaining whether, or to what extent, the product has, or the products have, those or any other effects, whether beneficial or harmful; (section 31(1))

'CLINICAL TRIAL CERTIFICATE' means a certificate certifying that, subject to the provisions of the certificate, the licensing authority have consented to the clinical trial in question and that the certificate is for the time being in force and the trial is to be carried out in accordance with that certificate; (section 31(3)b)

'CLINICAL TRIAL CERTIFICATE' and 'ANIMAL TEST CERTIFICATE' do not include certificates to which an applicant is entitled who satisfies the requirements of section 37(4) of the Act; (1971/973)

'COASTAL VOYAGE' means a voyage which starts and ends in the United Kingdom and does not involve calling at any place outside the United Kingdom; (section 111(8))

'COLISTIN' is any antimicrobial polypeptide or mixture of such polypeptides produced by strains of *Bacillus polymyxa (var. colistinus)* which yields on hydrolysis with mineral acids only the amino acids leucine, threonine and, α,γ-di-aminobutyric acid together with 6-methylheptanoic acid and 6-methyloctanoic acid. The expression includes any salt or derivative, or any salt of a derivative, of colistin and or substance the chemical and biological properties of which are identical with or similar to those of colistin but which is produced by other means; (1971/1200)

'COMMERCIALLY INTERESTED PARTY' In Part VI of the Act 'commercially interested party' in relation to medicinal products of any description, means any person who:-

(a) is the holder of a licence under Part II of this Act which is applicable to medicinal products of that description, or

(b) not being the holder of such a licence, is a person who in the course of a business carried on by him, is engaged, in relation to medicinal products of that description in any such activities as are mentioned in subsection (2) or subsection (3) of section 7 or in subsection (2) or subsection (3) of section 8 of this Act, or

(c) sells by retail any medicinal products of that description in the course of a business carried on by him,

and any reference to the request or consent of a commercially interested party includes a reference to any request made or consent given by a person acting on behalf of a commercially interested party; and 'relevant business' means any business which consists of or includes the sale or supply of medicinal products; (section 92(4); 1972/2076; 1978/41; 1978/1020)

'COMMISSION' means the Medicines Commission established under this Act; (section 132; 1970/746)

'COMPLETE FEEDING STUFF' means a substance or a mixture of substances designed for feeding to animals without further mixing with other feeding stuffs; (1973/1530; 1976/1726 and 1985/273)

'COMPOSITION' in relation to a medicinal product, means the ingredients of which it consists and the proportions and the degrees of strength, quality and purity in which those ingredients are contained in it respectively; (section 132)

'CONTACT LENS' refers only to a contact lens which consists of a thin curved shell of glass, plastic or other hard or soft material intended for use by being applied to the human eyeball; (1979/1759); (1979/1585 as amended by 1979/1745, and this definition applies for use in the phrase 'contact lens substance')

'CONTACT LENS SUBSTANCE' means any substance for use in cleaning, disinfecting, irrigating, lubricating, wetting or storing any contact lens or blank from which the contact lens is to be prepared or any fluid in which such lens or blank is soaked or rinsed or any fluid used as a barrier between such lens or blank and the human eyeball or any other substance used in connection with the use of such lens or blank; (1979/1585; 1979/1760)

'CONTACT LENS SUBSTANCE' means any substance or fluid described in paragraph 2 of Schedule 1 to the Specified Articles and Substances Order 1976; (1979/1759)

'CONTAINER' in relation to a medicinal product, means the bottle, jar, box, packet or other receptacle which contains or is to contain it, not being a capsule, cachet or other article in which the product is or is to be administered and where any such receptacle is or is to be contained in another such receptacle includes the former but does not include the latter receptacle; (section 132)

'CONTRAVENTION' includes a failure to comply and 'contravene' has a corresponding means; (section 132)

'CONTROL PRODUCTS' in relation to a clinical trial the primary object of which is to assess what, if any, are the effects of medicinal products of a particular description, means substances or articles that are administered by way of such a trial, in order that the effects, if any, of those substances or articles may be compared with effects, if any, of those medicinal products; (1974/498)

'CONTROLLED DRUG' has the meaning assigned to it by section 2 of the Misuse of Drugs Act 1971; (1980/1923; 1980/1924; 1983/1212; 1985/1288)

'CORTICOTROPHIN' is a substance obtained from the anterior lobe of the pituitary gland and which contains the peptide hormone that increases the rate at which corticoid hormones are secreted by the adrenal gland; (1971/1200; 1971/1309; 1971/1326)

'COSMETIC' means any substance or preparation intended to be applied to the various surfaces of the human body including epidermis, pilary system and hair, nails, lips and external genital organs, or the teeth and buccal mucosa wholly or mainly for the purpose of perfuming them, cleansing them, protecting them, caring for them or keeping them in condition, modifying their appearance (whether for aesthetic purposes or otherwise) or combating body odours or normal body perspiration; (1971/1410; 1980/1924; 1984/749)

'THE COUNCIL' in Part IV of the Act means the Council of the Pharmaceutical Society of Great Britain; (section 69(3))

'THE COUNCIL DIRECTIVE' means the Council Directive 81/851/EEC of the 28th September 1981 (OJ No. L. 317, 6.11.81 p1); (1971/972; 1983/1730)

'CURRENT' means current at the time when the medicinal product in question is demanded, described in a prescription or offered or exposed for sale, as mentioned in subsection (1) or subsection (2) of this section; (section 65(4))

'CYANOGENETIC SUBSTANCES' means preparations which –

(a) are presented for sale or supply under the name of, or as containing, amygdalin, laetrile or vitamin B17 or

(b) contain more than 0.1 per cent by weight of any substance having the formula either α-Cyanobenzyl-6-O-β-D-glucopyranosyl-β-D-glucopyranoside or α-Cyano- benzyl-β-D-glucopyranosiduronic acid; (1984/187; 1984/746)

'DATA SHEET' means a document relating to medicinal products of a particular description which is prepared by or on behalf of the holder of a product licence which is applicable to medicinal products of that description and which –

(a) complies with such requirements as to dimensions and form, as to the particulars be contained in it, and as to the manner (whether in respect of type size, colour, disposition or lettering or otherwise) in which any such particulars are to be so contained, as may be prescribed for the purposes of this subsection, and

(b) does not contain any information relating to medicinal products of that description except the particulars so prescribed; (section 96(6); 1972/2076; 1975/1326; 1976/1726; 1978/1020; 1979/1760)

'DATA SHEET COMPENDIUM' has the meaning assigned to it by regulation 2(1)(b) of these regulations; (1972/2076)

'DENTIST' means a person registered in the dentists register under the Dentists Act 1984 or entered in the list of visiting EEC practitioners under Schedule 4 to that Act; (section 132)

'DESCRIPTION' – see 'MEDICINAL PRODUCTS OF THE SAME DESCRIPTION' below

'DEXTRANS' are the substances produced by the fermentation of sucrose by means of strains of *Leuconostoc mesenteroides*, or by means of purified enzymes derived from such strains being polymers of glucose in which the linkages between the glucose units are almost entirely of the α 1,6 type; (1971/1200)

'DEXTRAN INJECTIONS' are preparations of solutions of dextrans in physiological saline or other vehicle suitable for intravenous injection of dextrans; (1971/1200)

'DIENOESTROL' means 4,4′-(diethylideneethylene) diphenol and salts and esters thereof; (1982/425; 1982/518; 1982/626)

'DISEASE' includes any injury, ailment or adverse condition, whether of body or mind; (section 132(1))

'DISPENSED MEDICINAL PRODUCT' means –

(i) a medicinal product prepared or dispensed by a practitioner or prepared or dispensed in accordance with a prescription given by a practitioner, or

(ii) a medicinal product for use by being administered to human beings where that medicinal product has been sold or supplied by a doctor or dentist for administration to a particular patient of his and that doctor or dentist sells or supplies that medicinal product to that patient or to a person under whose care that patient is, or

(iii) a medicinal product for use by being administered to animals where that medicinal product has been sold or supplied by a veterinary surgeon or veterinary practitioner for administration to a particular animal or herd which is under the care of that veterinary surgeon or veterinary practitioner, to a person having the possession or control of that animal or herd, or

(iv) a medicinal product prepared or dispensed in a registered pharmacy by or under the supervision of a pharmacist in the circumstances set out in sections 10(3) or 10(4)(a) of the Act, or

(v) a medicinal product where the person selling or supplying the medicinal product sells or supplies it for administration to a particular person after being requested by or on behalf of that person and in that person's presence to use his own judgment as to the treatment required; (1976/1726)

'DOCTOR', means a fully registered medical practitioner within the meaning of Schedule 1 to the Interpretation Act 1978; (section 132(1))

'DOSAGE UNIT' means –

(i) where the medicinal product is in the form of a tablet or capsule or is an article in some other similar pharmaceutical form, that tablet, capsule or other article, or

(ii) where the medicinal product is not in any such form, that quantity of the product which is used as the unit by reference to which the dose is measured: (1983/1212;). 1976/1726 is very similar. 1985/1288; 1984/768 and 1984/1861 are similar but refer only to veterinary drugs.

'ENEMA' means a preparation to be administered into the rectum as an aqueous or oily solution or suspension; (1985/1540)

'EFFERVESCENT' in relation to a tablet means containing not less than 75% by weight of the tablet, of ingredients included wholly or mainly for the purpose of releasing carbon dioxide when the tablet is dissolved or dispersed in water; (1980/1923)

'ENFORCEMENT AUTHORITY' means any Minister or body on whom a duty or power to enforce any provisions of this Act or of any regulations or order made thereunder is imposed or conferred by or under sections 108 to 110 of this Act; (section 132)

'ENROLLED NURSE' means a person for the time being enrolled as a nurse:

(i) in relation to England and Wales, under the Nurses Act 1957;

(ii) in relation to Scotland, under the Nurses (Scotland) Act 1951;

(iii) in relation to Northern Ireland under section 17 of the Nurses and Midwives Act (Northern Ireland) 1970; (1980/1924)

'ERYTHROMYCIN' is any antimicrobial weakly basic substance or mixture of such substances produced by *Streptomyces erythreus* (Waksman) which has the following characteristics –

(a) it forms a dihydrate which has a melting point of about 135°C;

(b) on mild acid hydrolysis it yields the base erythralosamine with a melting point of about 206°C.

The expression includes any salt or derivative, or salt of a derivative, of erythromycin and any substance the chemical and biological properties of which are identical with or similar to those of erythromycin but which is produced by other means; (1971/1200)

'EXCIPIENT' means a substance which does not contribute to the pharmacological action of the medicinal product or which so contributes only by regulating the release of the active ingredients; (1984/769). 1984/768 is similar but refers only to veterinary drugs.

'EXEMPTION' means an exemption under Article 2 of this Order from the restriction on assembly imposed by section 8(2) of the Act; (1979/1585) 79/1114 is slightly different.

'EXPIRY DATE' means the date after which, or the month and year after the end of which, the medicinal product should not be used or the date before which, or the month and year before the beginning of which, the medicinal product should be used; (1976/1726 as amended by 1977/996)

'EXPORT' means export from the United Kingdom, whether by land, sea or air, and 'import' has a corresponding meaning; (section 132)
The Channel Islands and the Isle of Man are outside the United Kingdom.

'EXTERNAL USE' means –

(a) in relation to medicinal products for use by being administered to human beings, application to the skin, teeth, mucosa of the mouth, throat, nose, ear, eye, vagina, or anal canal;

(b) in relation to veterinary drugs, application to the skin, hair, fur, feathers, scales, hoof, horn, ear, eye, mouth or mucosa of the throat or prepuce,

in either case when a local action only is necessary and extensive systemic absorption is unlikely to occur and references to 'medicinal products for external use' shall be read accordingly except that in paragraph (a) above the references shall not include throat sprays, throat pastilles, throat lozenges, throat tablets, nasal drops, nasal sprays, nasal inhalations or teething preparations; (1977/2130)

'EXTERNAL USE' means –

(i) in relation to medicinal products for use by being administered to human beings, application to the skin, hair, teeth, mucosa of the mouth, throat, nose,ear, eye, vagina, or anal canal

(ii) in relation to veterinary drugs, application to the skin, hair, fur, feathers, scales, hoof, horn, ear, eye, mouth or mucosa of the throat or prepuce, in either case when a local action only is intended and extensive systemic absorption is unlikely to occur; and references to 'medicinal products for external use' shall be read accordingly except that in relation to paragraph (i) in this definition such references shall not include throat sprays, throat pastilles, throat lozenges, throat tablets, nasal drops, nasal sprays, nasal inhalations or teething preparations; (1980/1924)

'EXTERNAL USE' means –

(a) in relation to medicinal products for use by being administered to human beings, application to the skin, teeth, mucosa of the mouth, throat, nose, ear, eye, vagina or anal canal but does not include the use of throat sprays, nasal drops, nasal sprays, nasal inhalations, teething preparations or dental gels;

(b) in relation to medicinal products for use by being administered to animals, application to the skin, hair, fur, feathers, scales, hoof, horn, ear, eye, mouth, mucosa of the throat, or prepuce; (1978/40)

'EXTERNAL USE' means application to the skin, hair, fur, feathers, scales, hoof, horn, ear, eye, mouth or mucosa of throat or prepuce, when local action only is necessary and extensive systemic absorption is unlikely to occur; (1985/1288; 1984/1861); 1984/768 is similar

'EXTERNAL USE' means –

(a) in relation to the medicinal products for use by being administered to human beings, application to the skin, hair, teeth, mucosa of the mouth, throat, nose, ear, eye, vagina or anal canal,

(b) in relation to veterinary drugs application to the skin, hair, fur, feathers, scales, hoof, horn, ear, eye, mouth, mucosa or the throat or prepuce; (1979/1181).

'EXTERNAL USE' means application to the skin, hair, teeth, mucosa of the mouth, throat, nose, ear, eye, vagina or anal canal when a local action only is intended and extensive systemic absorption is unlikely to occur; and references to medicinal products for external use shall be read accordingly except that such references shall not include throat sprays, throat pastilles, throat lozenges, throat tablets, nasal drops, nasal sprays, nasal inhalations or teething preparations; (1983/1212; 1984/769)

'FALSE OR MISLEADING' (insofar as section 93 is concerned) an advertisement (whether it contains an accurate statement of the composition of medicinal products of the description in question or not) shall be taken to be false or misleading if (but only if) –

(a) it falsely describes the description of medicinal products to which it relates, or

(b) it is likely to mislead as to the nature or quality of medicinal products of that description or as to their uses or effects; (section 93(7), 1978/1020)

'FEED SUPPLEMENT' means a substance or a mixture of substances designed for further mixing before feeding to animals at an inclusion rate of less than 5% with other animal feeding stuffs; (1973/1530; 1976/1726 and 1985/273)

'FINALLY DISPOSED OF' has the same meaning as in section 27(7) of the Act; (1972/2076)

'THE FIRST APPOINTED DAY' has the meaning assigned to it by section 16(1) of this Act (Sect.132).

It was the 1st September 1971.

'FOLLICLE-STIMULATING HORMONE' is an extract of post-menopausal urine containing that hormone which has the property of stimulating growth and maturation of germinal follicles in the ovary. Such extract may contain substances with interstitial cell stimulating hormone activity; (1971/1200)

'FOOD' includes beverages, confectionery and articles and substances used as ingredients in the preparation of food and includes any manufactured substance to which there has been added any vitamin and which is advertised (within the meaning of section 92 of the Act) as available and for sale to the general public as a dietary supplement; (1971/1410; 1980/1924; 1984/769)

'FOOD' includes articles and substances used as ingredients in the preparation of food and includes any manufactured substance to which there has been added any vitamin and which is advertised (within the meaning of section 92 of the Act) as available and for sale to the general public for consumption by animals; (1984/768)

'FOOD AND DRUGS AUTHORITY' has the meaning assigned to it for the purposes of the Food Act 1984 by section 71 of that Act; (section 132)

'FOREIGN OR INTERNATIONAL COMPENDIUM OF STANDARDS' means the national pharmacopoeia or similar compendium of a foreign country or the Specifications for the Quality Control of Pharmaceutical Preparations published by the World Health Organisation; (1976/1726)

'THE GAZETTE' means the London, Edinburgh and Belfast Gazettes; (section 132)

'GENTAMICIN' is any antimicrobial basic substance or mixture of such substances produced by the strain of *Micromonospora purpurea* which on 1st September 1967 was numbered NRRL 2953 in the culture collection of the Northern Utilisation Research and Development Branch of the United States Department of Agriculture. The expression includes any salt or derivative, or salt of a derivative, of gentamicin and any substance the chemical and biological properties of which are identical with or similar to those of gentamicin but which is produced by other means; (1971/1200)

'GENTAMICINS' is any antimicrobial basic substance or mixture of such substances produced by the strain of *Micromonospora purpurea* which on 1st September 1967 was numbered NRRL 2953 in the culture collection of the Northern Utilisation Research and Development Branch of the United States Department of Agriculture; (1977/2131)

'HEALTH AUTHORITY' –

(i) in relation to England and Wales, has the same meaning as in the National Health Service Act 1977,

(ii) in relation to Scotland means a Health Board constituted under Section 2 of the National Health Service (Scotland) Act 1978, and

(iii) in relation to Northern Ireland means a Health and Social Services Board established under Article 16 of the Health and Personal Social Services (Northern Ireland) Order 1972; (1978/988; 1980/1924)

'HEALTH CENTRE' means a health centre maintained under section 2 or 3 of the NHS Act 1977, section 36 of the NHS (Scotland) Act 1978, or Article 5 of the Health and Personal Social Services (Northern Ireland) Order 1972; (section 132)

'HEALTH MINISTERS' means the following Ministers, that is to say, the Secretaries of State respectively concerned with health in England, in Wales and in Scotland and the Minister of Health and Social Services for Northern Ireland, and in the case of anything falling to be done by the Health Ministers, means those Ministers acting jointly; (section 1)

'HEALTH PRESCRIPTION' means a prescription issued by a doctor or dentist under or by virtue of –

(i) in England and Wales, the National Health Service Act 1977;

(ii) in Scotland, the National Health Service (Scotland) Act 1978; and

(iii) in Northern Ireland, the Health and Personal Social Services (Northern Ireland) Order 1972; (1983/1212). (1977/2132 and 1980/1923 are similar.)

'HEPARIN' is a substance containing the sodium salt of a sulphated polysaccharide obtained from mammalian tissues which has the property of prolonging the clotting time of blood in human beings or animals; (1971/1200; 1971/1309; 1971/1326)

'HERBAL REMEDY' means a medicinal product consisting of a substance produced by subjecting a plant or plants to drying, crushing or any other process, or of a mixture whose sole ingredients are two or more substances so produced, or of a mixture whose sole ingredients are one or more substances so produced and water or some other inert substance; (section 132)

'HERD' includes a flock; (section 132)

'HEXOESTROL' means 4,4′-(1,2 diethylethylene)diphenol and salts and esters thereof; (1982/425; 1982/518; 1982/626)

'HOME-GOING SHIP' means a ship plying exclusively in inland waters or engaged exclusively in coastal voyages; and for the purposes of this subsection 'inland waters' means any canal, river, lake, loch, navigation or estuary and 'coastal voyage' means a voyage which starts and ends in the United Kingdom and does not involve calling at any place outside the United Kingdom; (section 111(8))

'HOMOEOPATHIC PRODUCT' means a medicinal product prepared in accordance with the methods of homoeopathic medicine or similar system which is sold or supplied as a homoeopathic product and is so described by the person who sells or supplies that medicinal product; (1976/1726)

'HOSPITAL' includes a clinic, nursing home or similar institution; (section 132)

'HOVER VEHICLE' means a vehicle designed to be supported on a cushion of air; (section 132)

'HYALURONIDASE' is a substance prepared from mammalian testicles or sperm or from other sources of the enzymes which diminish the viscosity of the hyaluronic acid present in mammalian tissues; (1971/1200; 1971/1309; 1971/1326)

'IMPORTED PROPRIETARY PRODUCT' means a proprietary medicinal product imported other than from a member State of the European Communities; (1971/974; 1977/1052; 1977/1053; 1977/1056)

'IMPORTED READY-MADE VETERINARY DRUG' means a ready-made veterinary drug imported other than from a member State of the European Communities; (1971/974; 1977/1052; 1983/1725; 1983/1731)

'INFORMATION SHEET' means an advertisement, other than a data sheet, in the form of a leaflet relating to a contact lens substance; (1979/1760)

'INGREDIENT' in relation to the manufacture or preparation of a substance, includes anything which is the sole active ingredient of that substance as manufactured or prepared; (section 132)

'INHALER' does not include an aerosol; (1983/1212;1983/1213)

'INLAND WATERS' means any canal, river, lake, loch, navigation or estuary; (section 111(8))

'INSPECTOR' means a person authorised by an enforcement authority for the purposes of the enforcement of the Act; (1985/273)

'INSULIN' is a preparation of the specific antidiabetic principle of the pancreas; (1971/1200; 1971/1309; 1971/1326)

'INTERNATIONAL NON-PROPRIETARY NAME' means a name which has been selected by the WHO as a recommended international non- proprietary name and in respect of which the Director-General of the WHO has given notice to that effect in the WHO CHRONICLE; (1976/1726; 1983/1727; 1984/673)

'INTRA-UTERINE CONTRACEPTIVE DEVICE' means any instrument, apparatus or appliance for use by being inserted in the uterus of a human being for the purpose of contraception; (1978/1138;1980/1467)

'IRRIGATION' means to bathe by means of the application of a fluid in a continuous stream; (1985/1540)

'KANAMYCIN' is any antimicrobial substance or mixture of such substances produced by *Streptomyces kanamyceticus*. The expression includes any salt or derivative, or salt of a derivative of kanamycin and any substance the chemical and biological properties of which are identical with or similar to those of kanamycin but which is produced by other means; (1971/1200)

'KANAMYCINS' is any antimicrobial substance or mixture of such substances produced by *Streptomyces kanamyceticus*; (1977/2131)

'LABELLING' in relation to a container or package of medicinal products means affixing to or otherwise displaying on it a notice describing or otherwise relating to the contents, and 'label' has a corresponding meaning; (section 132)

'LEAFLET' includes any written information; (section 132)

'LICENCE' (except where that word occurs as part of the expression 'product licence', 'manufacturer's licence' or 'wholesale dealer's licence') means a licence under Part II of the Act; (1974/832)

'LICENCE OF RIGHT' means a licence to which a person is entitled by virtue of this section, including such a licence which has been renewed (with or without modifications) but not a licence granted instead of the renewal of such a licence; (section 25(4))

'LICENSING AUTHORITY' means –

(i) For the purposes of Part II of this Act the authority responsible for the grant, renewal, variation, suspension and revocation of licences and certificates shall be a body of Ministers consisting of all the Ministers specified in paragraphs (a) and (b) of section 1(1) of this Act.

(ii) Any function conferred on the licensing authority by or under this Act may be performed by any one of those Ministers acting alone or by any two or more of them acting jointly.

(iii) In accordance with the preceding provisions of this section, in this Act 'the licensing authority' means any one or more of those Ministers, and, in the case of anything falling to be done by the licensing authority, means any one or more of those Ministers acting as mentioned in subsection (ii) of this section; (section 6)

'THE LINCOMYCINS' are the antimicrobial substances produced by *Streptomyces lincolnensis (var. lincolnensis)*. These substances are the basic amides of hygric acid or of a substituted hygric acid with 6-amino-6,8-dideoxy-1-thiogalacto-octopyranose or with substituted 6-amino-6,8-di-deoxy-1-thiogalacto-octopyranose. The expression includes any salt, or derivative, or salt of a derivative of any lincomycin and any substance the chemical and biological properties of which are identical with or similar to those of any lincomycin but which is produced by other means; (1971/1200)

'THE LINCOMYCINS' are the antimicrobial substances produced by *Streptomyces lincolnensis (var. lincolnensis)*. These substances are the basic amides of hygric acid or of a substituted hygric acid with 6-amino-6,8-dideoxy-1-thiogalacto-octopyranose or with substituted 6-amino-6,8-di-deoxy-1-thiogalacto-octopyranose; (1977/2131)

'LINCOMYCIN' is one of the lincomycins which incorporates *trans*- L-4-propylhygric acid and a methylthio group in the pyranose ring; (1971/1200)

'LOCAL AUTHORITY' means –

(a) in relation to England and Wales, the Greater London Council, a county council, a London borough council, a district council or the Common Council of the City of London,

(b) in relation to Scotland, a regional, islands or district council,

(c) in relation to Northern Ireland, a district council; (1978/41)

'MANUFACTURE' in relation to a medicinal product, includes any process carried out in the course of making the product, but does not include dissolving or dispersing the product in, or diluting or mixing it with, some other substance used as a vehicle for the purpose of administering it and does not include the incorporation of the product in any animal feeding stuff; (section 132)

'MANUFACTURER'S LICENCE' does not include a manufacturer's licence of right; (1971/974)

'MARK' includes a device, brand, name, signature, word, letter, numeral, or any combination thereof; (1972/2076)

'MASTER' includes any person (except a pilot) having command or charge of a ship; (Merchant Shipping Act 1894 section 742).

This is the definition referred to in 1980/1924 and 1983/1212.

'MAXIMUM DAILY DOSE' or 'MDD' means the maximum quantity of a substance contained in the amount of the medicinal product for internal use which it is recommended should be taken or administered in any period of twenty-four hours; (1977/2130; 1983/1212; 1984/769). 1979/45, 1983/1213 and 1984/768 are similar but refer to veterinary drugs.

'MAXIMUM DOSE' or 'MD' means the maximum quantity of a substance contained in the amount of the medicinal product for internal use which it is recommended should be taken or administered at any one time; (1977/2130; 1983/1212; 1984/769). 1983/1213 is similar but refers to veterinary drugs.

'MAXIMUM STRENGTH' means such of the following as may be specified –

(i) the maximum quantity of a substance by weight or volume contained in a dosage unit of a medicinal product,

(ii) the maximum percentage of a substance contained in a medicinal product calculated in terms of weight in weight, weight in volume, volume in weight, or volume in volume, as appropriate; (1985/1288)

'MAXIMUM STRENGTH' means such of the following as may be specified –

(i) the maximum quantity of a substance by weight or volume contained in a dosage unit of a veterinary drug,

(ii) the maximum percentage of a substance contained in a veterinary drug calculated in terms of weight in weight (w/w), weight in volume (w/v), volume in weight (v/w) or volume in volume (v/v), as appropriate, and

(iii) the maximum amount of a substance contained in a stated weight of a veterinary drug calculated in terms of international units (iu) of biologically determined potency; (1985/1288)

'MAXIMUM STRENGTH' means either the maximum quantity of the substance by weight or volume contained in a dosage unit of the veterinary drug or the maximum percentage of the substance contained in a veterinary drug calculated in terms of weight in weight (w/w), weight in volume (w/v), volume in weight (v/w) or volume in volume (v/v), as appropriate; (1984/768; 1984/1861). 1984/769 is similar but refers to medicinal products.

'MEDICATED' when used in relation to an animal feeding stuff, feed supplement or protein concentrate, means having a medicinal product incorporated therein; (1976/1726).

'MEDICATED' when used in relation to an animal feeding stuff, feed supplement or protein concentrate, means having a medicinal product or a substance incorporated for a medicinal purpose, incorporated therein; (1973/1530)

'MEDICATED FEEDING STUFF' means any substance which is manufactured, sold, supplied, imported or exported for use wholly or mainly in either or both of the following ways, that is to say –

(a) use by being fed to one or more animals for a medicinal purpose or for purposes that include that purpose, or

(b) use as an ingredient in the preparation of a substance which is to be fed to one or more for a medicinal purpose or for purposes that include that purpose; (section 130(3B)).

'MEDICINAL PRODUCTS OF THE SAME DESCRIPTION' – for the purposes of this Act medicinal products are of the same description if (but only if) –

(a) they are manufactured to the same specification, and

(b) they are, or are to be, sold, supplied, imported or exported in the same pharmaceutical form,

and in this Act 'description', in relation to medicinal products, shall be construed accordingly; (section 130(8))

'MEDICINAL TEST ON ANIMALS' means an investigation or series of investigations consisting of any of the following, that is to say –

(a) the administration of a medicinal product of a particular description to one or more animals, where there is evidence that medicinal products of that description have effects which may be beneficial to, or otherwise advantageous in relation to, that animal or those animals, and the product is administered for the purpose of as ascertaining whether, or to what extent, it has those or any other effects, whether advantageous or otherwise;

(b) the administration of a medical product to one or more animals in circumstances where there is no such evidence as is mentioned in the preceding paragraph, and the product is administered for the purpose of ascertaining whether or to what extent, it has any effects relevant to a medicinal purpose;

(c) the administration of any substance or article other than a medicinal product, to one or more animals for the purpose of ascertaining whether it has any effects relevant to a medicinal purpose, whether there is evidence that it has effects which may be beneficial to, or otherwise advantageous in relation to, that animal or those animals or not; (section 32(6))

'MEMBER' in the expression 'member State' refers to membership of the European Communities; (1971/972; 1977/1053; 1983/1730)

'MINERAL SALTS' means salts of any one or more of the following, iron, iodine, calcium, phosphorus, fluorine, copper, potassium, manganese, magnesium or zinc; (1971/1410)

'the MINISTERS' has the same meaning as in the Act; (1970/746)

'the MINISTERS' means all the Ministers specified in paragraphs (a) and (b) of this subsection and in the case of anything falling to be done by the Ministers means all those Ministers acting jointly; (section 1(1)b)

The Ministers concerned are the Secretary of State for Social Services, for Scotland, for Wales, the Minister of Agriculture, Fisheries and Food, the Department of Health and Personal Social Services for Northern Ireland and the Department of Agriculture for Northern Ireland.

'THE MISUSE OF DRUGS REGULATIONS' means in relation to England Wales and Scotland, the Misuse of Drugs Regulations 1973 and in relation to Northern Ireland, the Misuse of Drugs (Northern Ireland) Regulations 1974; (1983/1212; 1985/1288)

'MONOGRAPH' means a monograph in the current edition of the European Pharmacopoeia, any compendium published by the Ministers under Section 99 of the Act, the British Pharmacopoeia, the British Pharmaceutical Codex or the British Veterinary Codex, and 'monograph name' means, in relation to a constituent, the name which appears at the head of the relevant monograph; (1971/973) Similar for 1972/2076 and that used in 1981/164 is similar but excludes reference to the British Veterinary Codex

'MONOGRAPH NAME' means the name or approved synonym which appears at the head of a monograph in the British Pharmacopoeia, the British Pharmaceutical Codex, the European Pharmacopoeia or a foreign or international compendium of standards; (1984/673)

'MULTIPAGE ADVERTISEMENT' means an advertisement inserted on two or more consecutive pages of a professional publication; (1978/1020)

'NEOMYCIN' is any antimicrobial substance or mixture of such substances produced by *Streptomyces fradiae* which are complex organic bases and which yield on hydrolysis with mineral acids the base neamine. The expression includes any salt or derivative, or salt of a derivative, of neomycin and any substance the chemical and biological properties of which are identical with or similar to those of neomycin but which is produced by other means; (1971/1200)

'NEOMYCINS' is any antimicrobial substance or mixture of such substances produced by *Streptomyces fradiae* which are complex organic bases and which yield on hydrolysis with mineral acids the base neamine; (1977/2131)

'THE NORTHERN IRELAND ENFORCEMENT AUTHORITY' means any Northern Ireland Departmant having a duty to enforce any provision of this section or of regulations under it; (section 40)

'NOTICE' means notice in writing; (1981/164)

'OCCUPATIONAL HEALTH SCHEME' means a scheme in which a person, in the course of a business carried on by him, provides facilities for his employees for the treatment or prevention of disease; (1980/1924; 1983/1212)

'OFFENCE UNDER THIS ACT' includes any offence under any regulation or order made under this Act; (section 132)

'OPERATOR' in relation to an aircraft, means the person for the time being having the management of the aircraft;(1980/1924; 1983/1212)

'OPTICIAN' means a person who is registered in either of the registers of ophthalmic opticians established and maintained under section 2(a) of the Opticians Act 1958; (1979/1585)

'OPTICIAN' means a person who is registered in any register established and maintained under section 2 of the Opticians Act 1958 either as an ophthalmic optician or as a dispensing optician; (1979/1760)

'OXYTETRACYCLINE' is a 4-dimethylamino-1,4,4a,5,5a,6,11,12a-octahydro-3,5,6,10,12,12a,hexahydroxy-6-methyl-1-11-dioxo-naphthacene-2-carboxamide. The expression includes any salt of oxytetracycline; (1971/1200)

'PACKAGE' in relation to any medicinal product, means any box, packet or other article in which one or more containers of the products are or are to be enclosed, and, where any such box, packet or other article is or is to be itself enclosed in one or more other boxes, packets or other articles, includes each of the boxes, packets or articles in question; (section 132)

'PARENTERAL ADMINISTRATION' means administration by breach of the skin or mucous membrane; (1977/675; 1980/1923; 1980/1924; 1983/1212; 1984/768; 1984/769). 1985/1288 is very similar.

'PARENTERAL INJECTION' in relation to any substance includes any administration of the substance by insertion into the body by any route other than that of the gastro-intestinal tract but does not include any application of the substance to the skin; (1971/1200)

'PENICILLIN' is any antimicrobial acid, any salt thereof, or any derivative which is obtained therefrom which contains in its structure a fused thiazolidine β-lactam nucleus; (1971/1200)

'PENICILLINS' is any antimicrobial acid which contains in its structure a fused thiazolidine β-lactam nucleus; (1977/2131)

'PERSON RESPONSIBLE FOR THE COMPOSITION OF A MEDICINAL PRODUCT' means a person who, in the course of a business carried on by him –

(a) procures the manufacture of the product to his order by another person, where the order specifies, or incorporates by reference to some other document, particulars of the composition of the product ordered, whether those particulars amount to a complete specification or not, or

(b) he manufactures the product otherwise than in pursuance of an order which fulfils the conditions specified in the preceding paragraph. (section 7(6); 1976/1726; 1976/1972)

'PHARMACEUTICAL SOCIETY' in relation to Great Britain means the Pharmaceutical Society of Great Britain, and in relation to Northern Ireland means the Pharmaceutical Society of Northern Ireland; (section 132)

'PHARMACIST' in relation to Great Britain means a person registered in the register of pharmaceutical chemists established in pursuance of the Pharmacy Act 1852, and maintained in pursuance of section 2(1) of the Pharmacy Act 1954, and in relation to Northern Ireland (subject to any order made under paragraph 1 of Schedule 4 to this Act) means a person registered in the register of pharmaceutical chemists for Northern Ireland made out and maintained under Articles 6 and 9 of the Pharmacy (Northern Ireland) Order 1976; (section 132 as amended)

'PHARMACY MEDICINE' means a medicinal product which is not a prescription only medicine or a medicinal product on the general sale list; (1980/1924)

'PHARMACY MEDICINE' means a medicinal product which is not a prescription only medicine and which either –

(i) is not a medicinal product on a general sale list, or

(ii) is a product referred to in regulation 8 and is not presented for sale in the manner described in relation to that product in that regulation; (1980/1923)

'PHENACETIN-ONLY PRODUCT' means a medicinal product of which phenacetin is the sole active ingredient; (1979/1181)

'PLANT' includes any part of a plant; (section 132)

'PLASMA' means the fluid element of uncoagulated blood; (1971/1200; 1971/1309; 1971/1326)

'POLYMIXIN B' is any antimicrobial polypeptide or mixture of such polypeptides produced by strains of *Bacillus polymyxa* which yields on hydrolysis with mineral acids only the amino acids leucine, phenylalanine,threonine, and α,γ -diamino-butyric acid together with 6-methylheptanoic acid and 6-methyloctanoic acid. The expression includes any salt or derivative, or salt of a derivative, of polymixin B and any substance the chemical and biological properties of which are identical with or similar to those of polymixin B but which is produced by other means; (1971/1200)

'POLYMIXINS' is any antimicrobial substance produced by any strain of *Bacillus polymyxa*; (1977/2131)

'POULTRY' means domestic fowls, turkeys, geese, ducks, guinea- fowls, pigeons, pheasants, and partridges; (section 132)

'PRACTITIONER' (except where that word occurs as part of the expression 'veterinary practitioner') means a doctor, dentist, veterinary surgeon or veterinary practitioner; (section 132)

'PREMISES' includes a stall of a permanent nature situated at a market or an agricultural showground; (1984/1861, articles 3(16) and 5(16))

'PREPARATIONS OF BLOOD' include whole blood from human beings or animals, serum or plasma made from such blood, any protein or other substance separated from such blood and any dried product prepared from any such serum, plasma, protein or other substance; (1971/1200)

'PREPARATIONS OF THE PITUITARY (POSTERIOR LOBE)' include the active principles thereof (whether obtained by fractionation of the gland or by synthesis) and derivatives of those principles with the same specific biological action; (1971/1200;1971/1309;1971/1326)

'PRE-SCHOOL DENTAL SCHEME' means a scheme supervised by a doctor or dentist in which medicinal products are supplied to parents or guardians of children under five, for use by such children for the purpose of preventing dental caries; (1980/1924)

'PRESCRIBED' means prescribed by regulations under this Act; (section 132)

'PRESCRIPTION ONLY MEDICINE' means a medicinal product of a description or falling within a class specified in Article 3 of the Medicines (Prescription Only) Order 1980; (1980/1923; 1980/1924)

'PRESCRIPTION ONLY MEDICINE' means a medicinal product of a description or falling within a class specified in Article 3; (1983/1212; 1985/1288)

'PRODUCT LICENCE OF RIGHT' means a product licence to which an applicant is entitled by virtue of section 25 of the Act;

'PROFESSIONAL PUBLICATION' means a publication sent or delivered wholly or mainly to doctors or dentists, a publication containing an advertisement relating to a medicinal product which may only lawfully be sold by retail or supplied in circumstances corresponding to retail sale in accordance with a prescription given by a practitioner, or a publication containing an advertisement relating to a medicinal product in respect of which a data sheet has been issued; (1975/1326)

'PROFESSIONAL PUBLICATION' means a publication sent or delivered wholly or mainly to doctors or dentists containing an advertisement to which these regulations apply; (1978/1020)

'PROMOTIONAL AID' means a non-monetary gift made to a doctor or dentist for promotional purposes by or on behalf of a holder of a licence under Part II of the Act; (1978/1020)

'PROPRIETARY DESIGNATION' means a word or words used or proposed to be used in connection with the sale of a medicinal product, substance or article or constituent for the purpose of indicating that they are the goods of a particular person by virtue of manufacture,selection, certification, dealing with or offering for sale; (1971/973, 1976/1726; 1983/1727)

'PROPRIETARY MEDICINAL PRODUCT' means a ready-prepared medicinal product placed on the market in the United Kingdom under a special name and in a special pack; and for the purposes of this definition medicinal product does NOT include –

(i) vaccines, toxins, or serums,

(ii) medicinal products based on human blood or blood constituents or radioactive isotopes,

(iii) homoeopathic medicinal products or,

(iv) additives for animal feeding stuff to which the provisions of Council Directive 70/524/EEC apply;

(section 7(7), 1971/972; 1971/973; 1977/1052; 1977/1053; 1982/1729; 1983/1725; 1983/1726; 1983/1727; 1983/1728; 1983/1729; 1983/1931). 1977/1055; and 1977/1056 are similar but apply to veterinary drugs.

'PROPRIETARY VETERINARY DRUG' means a veterinary drug which is a proprietary medicinal product; (1983/1727)

'PROTEIN CONCENTRATE' means a substance or a mixture of substances designed for further mixing before feeding to animals at an inclusion rate of 5% or more with other animal feeding stuffs; (1973/1530; 1976/1726 and 1985/273)

'PURPOSE' in relation to the administration of a radioactive medicinal product means the purpose of diagnosis, treatment or research; (1978/1006)

'QUALIFIED PERSON' is a person who as respects qualifications and experience satisfies the provisions of Articles 23 and 24 of the Second Council Directive; A licence holder may regard a person as satisfying the provisions of the said Article 24 as respects formal qualifications if he produces evidence that he is a member of the Pharmaceutical Society or of the Royal Institute of Chemistry or of such other body as may appear to the licensing authority to be an appropriate body for the purpose, and that he is regarded by the body of which he is a member as so satisfying those provisions; (1971/972 as amended)

'QUALIFYING BUSINESS' means a business in respect of which more than one half of the total sales for its last accounting period was derived from the retail sale of agricultural requisites;(1984/1861)

'QUANTITY' means, where the quantity is not the exact quantity, the quantity which is as near to the exact quantity as is reasonably practicable or which differs from the exact quantity only to such an extent as is reasonably necessary in the circumstances having regard to the nature of the medicinal product in question; (1976/1726)

'RADIOACTIVE MEDICINAL PRODUCT' means a medicinal product which is, which contains or which generates a radioactive substance and which is, contains or generates that substance in order, when administered, to utilise the radiation emitted therefrom; (1978/1006)

'RADIOACTIVE SUBSTANCE' means any substance that contains one or more radionuclides of which the activity or the concentration cannot be disregarded as far as radiation protection is concerned; (1978/1004; 1978/1006)

'READY-MADE VETERINARY DRUG' means a ready-prepared veterinary drug placed on the market in the United Kingdom in a pharmaceutical form in which it may be used without further processing, not being a drug placed on the market under a special name and in a special pack; and for the purposes of this definition 'veterinary drug' does not include –

(i) vaccines, toxins or serums,

(ii) veterinary drugs based on radioactive isotopes,

(iii) veterinary drugs specially prepared for administration by a veterinary surgeon or veterinary practitioner to a particular animal or herd which is under his care,

(iv) homoeopathic veterinary drugs, or

(v) additives for animal feeding stuffs to which the provisions of Council Directive 70/524/EEC apply;

(section 7(7); 1971/974; 1977/1052; 1983/1725; 1983/1726; 1983/1727; 1983/1728; 1983/1729; 1983/1931)

'REFERENCE ADVERTISEMENT' means an advertisement which is in the form of, and limited to, a brief description of a medicinal product, its uses and any contra-indications and warnings relating thereto appearing without charge in a publication consisting wholly or mainly of such advertisements where the publication is sent or delivered to practitioners or pharmacists by a person who is not a commercially interested party; (1975/298; 1975/1326; 1978/1020)

'REGISTER' means a bound book and does not include any form of loose leaf register or card index; (1977/2132; 1980/1923)

'REGISTERED OPHTHALMIC OPTICIAN' means a person who is registered in either of the registers of ophthalmic opticians established and maintained under section 2(a) of the Opticians Act 1958; (1977/2133; 1980/1923; 1980/1924; 1983/1212)

'REGISTERED PHARMACY' means premises for the time being entered in the register required to be kept under section 75 of this Act; (section 74(1))

'REGISTERING BODY' means any professional body whose members customarily administer medicinal products to human beings in the course of their profession and which is required by law to maintain a register of its members; (1979/1114)

'THE REGISTRAR' in relation to Great Britain means the person appointed under section 1 of the Pharmacy Act 1954, as registrar for the purposes of that Act, and in relation to Northern Ireland means the person appointed under Article 9(1) of the Pharmacy (Northern Ireland) Order 1976 as registrar for the purpose of that Act; (section 69(3))

'RELEVANT BUSINESS' means any business which consists of or includes the sale or supply of medicimal products; (section 92(4))

'RELEVANT MONOGRAPH' means in relation to the sale or supply of a medicinal product which has been demanded, described in a prescription, offered or exposed for sale, by or by express reference to a particular name –

(a) if, together with that name, there was specified a particular edition of a particular publication, means the monograph (if any) headed by that name in that edition of that publication, or, if there is no such monograph in that edition, means the appropriate current monograph (if any) headed by that name;

(b) if, together with that name, there was specified a particular publication, but not a particular edition of that publication, means the monograph (if any) headed by that name in the current edition of that publication, or, if there is no such monograph in that edition, means the appropriate current monograph (if any) headed by that name, or in default of such a monograph, means the monograph headed by that name in the latest edition of the specified publication which contained a monograph so headed;

(c) if no publication was specified together with that name, means the appropriate current monograph (if any); (section 65(4))

'RELEVANT PRACTITIONER' means a doctor, where the medicinal product is for use exclusively by or under the direction of a doctor, or a dentist where the medicinal product is for use exclusively by or under the direction of a dentist, or a doctor or dentist, where the medicinal product is not for either exclusive use as aforesaid; (1975/1326)

'RENEWAL APPLICATION' means an application for the renewal of a licence or certificate under section 24 or, as the case may be, under section 38 of the Act; (1974/832)

'REPEATABLE PRESCRIPTION' means a prescription which contains a direction that it may be dispensed more than once;(1980/1923; 1983/1212; 1985/1288)

'REPRESENTATION' means any statement or undertaking (whether constituting a condition or a warranty or not) which consists of spoken words other than words falling within paragraph (a) or paragraph (b) of subsection (2) of this section, and any reference to making a representation shall be construed accordingly; (section 92(5); 1978/41)

'RETAIL PHARMACY BUSINESS' means a business (not being a professional practice carried on by a practitioner) which consists of or includes the retail sale of medicinal products other than medicinal products on a general sale list (whether medicinal products on such a list are sold in the course of that business or not); (section 132)

'THE RIFAMYCINS' are a group of related antimicrobial macrolactams produced by the growth of *Streptomyces mediterranei* and containing the chemical structure of 11-acetoxy-7,9,15-trihydroxy-13-methoxy-2,6,8,10,12,-penta-methylpentadeca-2,4,14-trienoic acid amide attached by the nitrogen atom and by the oxygen atom in the 15-position respectively to the 7- and 2-positions of a 5,6,9- trioxygenated 2, 4-dimethyl-1 oxonaphtho (2,1-b) furan. The expression includes any salt or derivative, or salt of a derivative, of any rifamycin and any substance the chemical and biological properties of which are identical with or similar to those of any rifamycin but which is produced by other means; (1971/1200). (1977/2131 is very similar)

'RIFAMIDE' is an antimicrobial base produced from a rifamycin known as rifamycin B and has the chemical structure of 11-acetoxy-7,9,15-trihydroxy-13-methoxy-2, 6, 8, 10, 12-penta- methy-pentadeca-2, 4,14-trienoic acid amide, attached by the nitrogen atom and by the oxygen atom in the 15 position respectively to the 7- and 2- positions of 5,6 dihydroxy-2,4-dimethyl-1-oxonaphtho [2,1-b] furan-9-oxyacetic acid diethylamide; (1971/1200)

'RISTOCETINS' means antimicrobial substances produced by a strain of *Nocardia* species referred to as *Nocardia lurida*; (1977/2131)

'SADDLERY BUSINESS' means a business in respect of which more than half of the total sales for its last accounting period was derived from the retail sale of saddlery requisites; (1984/1861)

'SADDLERY REQUISITES' means equipment used in the keeping or horses or ponies and things used for the maintenance of such equipment and includes any human apparel used in the keeping of horses or ponies; (1984/1861)

'SAMPLED PORTION' in relation to any animal feeding stuff means an amount of that feeding stuff (as prescribed under the provisions of Part I of Schedule 2 to these regulations) constituting a unit and having characteristics presumed to be uniform from which a sample has been taken or set aside by an inspector in the manner prescribed in Parts II and III of the said Schedule, being an amount –

(a) consisting either-

  (i) entirely of feeding stuffs packed in one or more containers; or

  (ii) entirely of feeding stuffs not so packed; and

(b) not exceeding, in the case of an amount consisting of feeding stuffs so packed, the requisite quantity, that is to say, five tonnes or 5,000 litres, except where –

  (i) it consists of feeding stuffs packed in a single container; or

  (ii) it consists of feeding stuffs packed in two or more containers each of which holds less than the requisite quantity, in which case the prescribed amount may be the contents of the lowest number of those containers which together hold the requisite quantity; (1985/273)

'SCHOOL DENTAL SCHEME' means a scheme supervised by a doctor or dentist in which medicinal products are supplied at a school to pupils of that school for the purpose of preventing dental caries; (1980/1924)

'SECOND COUNCIL DIRECTIVE' means the Second Council Directive 75/319/EEC of the 20th May 1975, (OJ No.L147 9/6/75 p.13); (1977/1053)

'SELF-SERVICE METHODS' means any method of sale which allows a purchaser to help himself on or before payment; (1984/1861)

'SELL' means sell by retail as defined in section 131 of the Act and 'sale' has a corresponding meaning; (1980/1923; 1980/1924; 1983/1212; 1985/1288)

'SELL BY RETAIL' includes offer or expose for sale by retail and supply in circumstances corresponding to retail sale, and cognate expressions shall be construed accordingly; (1984/1861)

'SERA' means the fluid element of coagulated blood; (1971/1198;1971/1200; 1971/1309; 1971/1326)

'SERUM' means a fluid fraction of coagulated blood; (1977/675)

'SMALLPOX VACCINE' means a vaccine that is a preparation of an infective vaccinia virus; (1977/675)

'SOAP' means any compound of a fatty acid with an an alkali or amine; (1983/1212; 1985/1288)

'SOUND RECORDING' has the meaning assigned to it by section 12 of the Copyright Act 1956 and section 48(3) of that Act shall have effect for the purposes of this section as it has for the purposes of that Act; (section 92(6))

'THE SPECIAL CASES ORDER' means the Medicines (Exemption from Licences) (Special and Transitional Cases) Order 1971; (1972/1200)

'A SPECIALLY AUTHORISED PERSON' means in relation to a veterinary drug either –

(a) a person specially authorised by virtue of a direction of the licensing authority under Article 3(1) of the Medicines (Exemptions from Licences)(Special and Transitional Cases) Order 1971, to assemble that drug otherwise than in accordance with a manufacturer's licence, or

(b) a person specially authorised by the product licence in respect of that drug to sell the drug under an alternative product name specified in the licence; (1984/1861)

'THE SPECIFIED PARTICULARS' means the particulars required by regulations 2(1) and 3(1) of, and Schedule 1 to, these regulations; (1978/1020)

'SPECIFIED PUBLICATION' means any of the following, that is to say –

(a) the European Pharmacopoeia;

(b) the British Pharmacopoeia;

(c) the British Pharmaceutical Codex;

(d) the British Veterinary Codex;

(e) the British National Formulary;

(f) the Dental Practitioners' Formulary;

(g) any compendium prepared under subsection (3) and published under subsection (6) of section 99 of this Act; and

(h) any list of names prepared and published under section 100 of this Act; (section 103(1); (1976/1726; 1978/1020)

'SPERMICIDAL CONTRACEPTIVE' means a contraceptive substance or article (not being a veterinary drug) which acts wholly or mainly by chemical spermicidal means, but does not include –

(a) a contraceptive substance or article which is administered orally,

(b) an intra-uterine contraceptive device, or

(c) a spermicidal lubricant which is or is to be applied to a condom, cap or diaphragm; (1978/41)

'STANDARD PROVISIONS FOR LICENCES OR CERTIFICATES' means those provisions prescribed by the Medicines (Standard Provisions for Licences and Certificates) Regulations; (1971/973)

'STANDARD PROVISIONS FOR LICENCES' means those standard provisions prescribed by the Medicines (Standard Provisions for Licences and Certificates) Regulations 1971; (1971/974)

'STANDARD PROVISIONS' means those conditions prescribed by regulation made under section 47(1) of the Act which are for the time being in force;

'STATE REGISTERED CHIROPODIST' means a person who is registered in the register established and maintained under section 2(1) of the Professions Supplementary to Medicine Act 1960 by the Chiropodists Board; (1980/1924; 1983/1212)

'STATE REGISTERED PHYSIOTHERAPIST' means a person who is registered in the register established and maintained under section 2(1) of the Professions Supplementary to Medicine Act 1960 by the Physiotherapists Board; (1977/2132)

'STATUTORY COMMITTEE' in relation to Great Britain means the committee appointed under section 7 of the Pharmacy Act 1954, and in relation to Northern Ireland means the committee appointed under Article 19 of the Pharmacy (Northern Ireland) Order 1976; (section 69(3))

'STILBENES' means substances which consist wholly of any of the following (a) Benzestrol, (b) Dienoestrol (c) Hexoestrol or (d) Stilboestrol; (1982/425; 1982/518; 1982/626)

'STILBOESTROL' means (E)α,β diethylstilbene 4,4′diol and salts and esters thereof: (1982/425; 1982/518; 1982/626)

'STREPTODORNASE' is the substance produced by strains of streptococcus which catalyses the depolymerisation of deoxyribonucleic acid; (1971/1200)

'STREPTOKINASE' is the substance produced by strains of streptococcus which activates an inactive precursor of a fibrinolytic enzyme present in plasma; (1971/1200)

'STREPTOMYCIN' is any antimicrobial complex organic base or mixture of such bases produced by *Streptomyces griseus* which –

(a) yields on hydrolysis which mineral acids the base streptidine (*meso*-1:3 diguanidocyclohexane-2,4,5,6- tetraol); and

(b) yields on hydrolysis by a 4 per cent solution of sodium hydroxide the substance maltol (3-hydroxy-2-methyl-γ- pyrone).

The expression includes any salt or derivative, or salt of a derivative, of streptomycin and any substance the chemical and biological properties of which are identical with or similar to those of streptomycin but which are identical with or similar to those of streptomycin but which is produced by other means; (1971/1200)

'STREPTOMYCINS' means any antimicrobial complex organic base or mixture of such bases produced by *Streptomyces griseus* which

(a) yields on hydrolysis which mineral acids the base streptidine (*meso*-1:3 diguanidocyclohexane-2,4,5,6- tetraol); and

(b) yields on hydrolysis by a 4 per cent solution of sodium hydroxide the substance maltol (3-hydroxy-2-methyl-γ-pyrone); (1977/2131)

'SUBSTANCE' means any natural or artificial substance, whether in solid or liquid form or in the form of a gas or vapour; (section 132)

It has a chemical meaning which is probably intended for most purposes of the Act.

'SULPHANILAMIDE' means *p*-aminobenzenesulphonamide, having any of the hydrogen atoms of either or both nitrogen atoms substituted by an equal number of univalent atoms or radicals; (1977/2131)

'SUPPLIER' means a person selling or supplying, or procuring the sale, supply, manufacture or assembly of, a medicinal product for the purposes of a clinical trial; (1981/164)

'SUPPLY' means supply in circumstances corresponding to retail sale as defined in section 131 of the Act; (1979/1759; 1980/1924; 1983/1212; 1985/1288)

'SURGICAL MATERIALS' means

(1) A surgical ligature and surgical suture prepared from the gut or any tissue of an animal, or any form of binding material prepared form the gut or any tissue of an animal, which is manufactured, sold, supplied, imported or exported wholly or partly for use in surgical operation upon the human body.

(2) Any other surgical ligature or surgical suture prepared from any source, which is manufactured, sold, supplied, imported or exported wholly or partly for use in surgical operations upon the human body and is capable of being absorbed by body tissues.

(3) Any absorbent or protective material manufactured, sold, supplied, imported or exported wholly or partly for use in surgical operations upon the human body and capable of being absorbed by body tissues; (1971/1267)

'TESTS FOR STERILITY' means a test for bacterial sterility and a test for fungal sterility and 'sterility' has a corresponding meaning; (1971/972, Schedule 4, Part II)

'TETRACYCLINE' is 4-dimethylamino-1,4,4a,5,5a,6,11,12a-octahydro-3,6,10,12, 12a,pentahydroxy-6-methyl-1,11,dioxonaphthacene-2-carboxamide. The expression includes any salt of tetracycline; (1971/1200)

'THE TETRACYCLINES' are the antimicrobial bases which contain the chemical structure naphthacene-2-carboxamide, hydrogenated to any extent, and having each of the positions, 1,3,10,11,12 and 12a substituted by an hydroxyl or an oxo group; (1971/1200; 1977/2131)

'THE TIME ALLOWED' in Part II of, and Schedule 2 to, this Act has the meaning assigned to it by section 21(8) of this Act; (section 132)

'THYROSTATIC SUBSTANCES' means anti-thyroid substances with a depressant effect on thyroid activity and thyroid hormone production for use by administration to animals to increase their bodyweight; (1982/425; 1982/518; 1982/626)

'TOXINS' are substances used in the diagnosis, prevention or treatment of disease consisting wholly or partly of poisonous substances derived from specific micro-organisms, plants or animals; (1971/1198; 1971/1200; 1971/1309; 1971/1326; 1977/675)

'TRADE ADVERTISEMENT' means an advertisement relating to a medicinal product issued by means of a catalogue, price list or other document for the purpose of the sale (whether by the person who manufactures it or otherwise) of that medicinal product to persons who buy such product for one or more of the purposes specified in section 131(2) of the Act (wholesale) where such catalogue, price list or document does not contain any recommendation relating to the use of the medicinal product other than as part of the name of the medicinal product or as part of any heading or sub-heading indicating a therapeutic classification; (1975/298; 1975/1326; 1978/1020)

'TRADE MARK' means a mark used or proposed to be used in relation to the medicinal product to which the data sheet relates for the purpose of indicating, or so as to indicate, a connection in the course of trade between that medicinal product and some person having the right either as a proprietor or as a person authorised by a proprietor to use the mark; (1972/2076)

'TREATMENT' in relation to disease, includes anything done or provided for alleviating the effects of the disease, whether it is done or provided by way of cure or not; (section 132)

'UNIT' means an animal feeding stuff identifiable as such by reason of its manufacturer, packer, uniform manner of packaging or labelling; (1985/273)

'UNIT PREPARATION' means a preparation, including a mother tincture, prepared by a process of solution, extraction or trituration with a view to being diluted tenfold or one hundredfold, either once or repeatedly, in an inert diluent, and then used either in this diluted form or, where applicable, by impregnating tablets, granules, powders or other inert substances for the purpose of being administered to human beings; (1983/1212; 1980/1924). 1976/1726 is similar. (1985/1288 is similar but for administration to animals)

'VACCINES' are substances which consist wholly or partly of –

(a) any micro-organisms, viruses or other organisms in any state,

(b) any toxins of microbial origin which have been detoxified, or

(c) any extracts or derivatives of any micro-organisms or of any viruses,

being substances which, when administered to human beings or animals, are used for the prevention or treatment of specific diseases; (1971/1198; 1971/1200; 1971/1309; 1971/1326.) 1976/675 is similar.

'VANCOMYCIN' is any mixture of antimicrobial substances produced by *Streptomyces orientalis*. The expression includes any salt or derivative, or salt of a derivative of vancomycin and any substance the chemical and biological properties of which are identical with or similar to those of vancomycin but which is produced by other means; (1971/1200)

'VENEREAL DISEASE' means syphilis, gonorrhoea, or soft chancre; (1978/41)

'VETERINARY DRUG' means a medicinal product which is manufactured, sold, supplied, imported or exported for the purpose of being administered to animals, but not for the purpose of being administered to human beings; (section 132)

'VETERINARY DRUGS EXEMPTION ORDER' means the Medicines (Exemptions from Restrictions on the Retail Sale or Supply of Veterinary Drugs) Order 1984; (1983/1212; 1980/1923; 1985/1288)

'VETERINARY MEDICINAL PRODUCT' means any medicinal product intended for animals but does not include –

(a) vaccines, toxins or serums;

(b) veterinary medicinal products based on radio-active isotopes;

(c) veterinary medicinal products not prepared in advance and intended for one particular animal or small number of animals;

(d) homoeopathic veterinary medicinal products;

(e) additives for feeding stuffs to which the provisions of Council Directive 70/524/EEC apply;

(f) medicated feedingstuffs. (1983/1732)

'VETERINARY PRACTITIONER' means a person registered in the supplementary veterinary register kept under section 8 of the Veterinary Surgeons Act 1966; (section 132)

'VETERINARY PRESCRIPTION' means a written prescription given by a veterinary surgeon or a veterinary practitioner; (1973/1530)

'VETERINARY SURGEON' means a person registered in the register of veterinary surgeons kept under section 2 of the Veterinary Surgeons Act 1966; (section 132)

'VIOMYCIN' is any antimicrobial organic base produced by the growth of *Streptomyces griseus (var. purpureus)*, which yields on hydrolysis with mineral acids urea, L-serine, α,β-diaminopropionic acid, and 3,6,-diaminohexanoic acid. The expression includes any salt or derivative or salt of a derivative, of viomycin and any substance the chemical and biological properties of which are identical with or similar to those of viomycin but which is produced by other means; (1971/1200)

'VITAMIN PREPARATION' means any medicinal product the active ingredients of which consist only of vitamins or vitamins and mineral salts; (1971/1410)

'VITAMINS' means any one or more of the following, vitamins A, B1, B2, B6, C, D and E, biotin, nicotinamide, nicotinic acid, pantothenic acid and its salts, biflavonoids, inositol, choline, para-aminobenzoic acid, cyanocobalamin or folic acid; (1971/1410)

'A WHOLESALE DEALER'S LICENCE' does not include a wholesale dealer's licence of right; (1971/974)

'WRITING' includes any form of notation, whether by hand or by printing, type-writing or any similar process, and 'written' has a corresponding meaning; (section 132)

Appendix 2

Recommended Warning and Advisory Labels for Dispensed Medicines

(as revised in March 1985)

---

1. 'WARNING. MAY CAUSE DROWSINESS'

   To be used on children's preparations containing antihistamines, e.g. paediatric elixirs and linctuses, or other preparations given to children where the warnings of label 2 on driving or alcohol would not be appropriate.

2. 'WARNING. MAY CAUSE DROWSINESS. IF AFFECTED DO NOT DRIVE OR OPERATE MACHINERY. AVOID ALCOHOLIC DRINK'

   To be used on preparations that can cause drowsiness, thereby affecting the ability to drive and operate hazardous machinery. The main preparations are most antihistamines; sedatives and hypnotics used as sedatives during the day; central nervous system depressants such as anxiolytics, antipsychotics and tricyclic antidepressants; some antihypertensives; some analgesics; some antiepileptics; some antiemetics; and some muscle relaxants. Label 2 may not be appropriate for hypnotics, but the patient should be counselled about the possible persistence of effects the next day. *It is an offence to drive while under the influence of drink or drugs.*

   Label 1 is more appropriate for children.

   Some of these preparations only cause drowsiness in the first few days of treatment and the patient then becomes tolerant; some only cause drowsiness in higher doses.

   In such cases the patient should be told that the advice to avoid driving, etc. applies until the effects have worn off. Many of these preparations can produce a slowing of reaction time and a loss of mental concentration that can have the same effects as drowsiness on activities that require alertness to avoid hazard.

   The avoidance of alcoholic drink is recommended, since the effects of CNS depressants are enhanced by alcohol, but it must be realised that a strict prohibition could lead to certain patients not taking the medicine at all.

Pharmacists should explain the risks and encourage compliance, particularly in patients who may think they already tolerate the effects of alcohol (see also label 3).

Queries from patients with epilepsy regarding fitness to drive should be referred back to the patient's doctor.

There are other side-effects unrelated to drowsiness that may affect a patient's ability to drive or operate machinery safely, for example, blurred vision, dizziness, or nausea.

In general, no label has been recommended to cover these cases, but the patient should be suitably counselled.

The narcotic analgesics have not been included under label 2 because of the special circumstances in which they may be prescribed. Label 2 may, however, be added at the prescriber's request.

3. 'WARNING. MAY CAUSE DROWSINESS. IF AFFECTED DO NOT DRIVE OR OPERATE MACHINERY'

To be used on monoamine-oxidase inhibitors (because alcohol is covered by label 10 and the MAO1 treatment card).

Some patients given CNS depressants may have been advised how much alcohol they may drink by their doctor and in such cases label 3 may be more appropriate than label 2.

4. 'WARNING. AVOID ALCOHOLIC DRINK'

To be used on preparations where a reaction such as flushing may occur if alcohol is taken, e.g. metronidazole, chlorpropamide. Alcohol may also enhance the hypoglycaemia produced by oral antidiabetic drugs.

For most interactions with alcohol label 2 is more appropriate.

5. 'DO NOT TAKE INDIGESTION REMEDIES AT THE SAME TIME OF DAY AS THIS MEDICINE'

To be used in conjunction with label 25 on preparations coated to resist gastric acid, such as enteric-coated tablets, capsules and granules.

The coating may be ruptured prematurely in the presence of alkalis present in antacids.

6. 'DO NOT TAKE IRON PREPARATIONS OR INDIGESTION REMEDIES AT THE SAME TIME OF DAY AS THIS MEDICINE'

To be used on preparations of doxycycline, minocycline and penicillamine. These drugs chelate iron and calcium ions and are less well absorbed when given with iron or calcium- containing antacids. If necessary these incompatible preparations may be given about 2 hours apart.

7. 'DO NOT TAKE MILK, IRON PREPARATIONS OR INDIGESTION REMEDIES AT THE SAME TIME OF DAY AS THIS MEDICINE'

To be used on preparations of tetracyclines (except doxycycline and minocycline). These drugs chelate iron, calcium and magnesium ions and are then less well absorbed. If necessary these incompatible preparations may be given about 2 hours apart.

8. 'DO NOT STOP TAKING THIS MEDICINE EXCEPT ON YOUR DOCTOR'S ADVICE'

To be used on preparations of beta-adrenoceptor blocking drugs, certain antihypertensive drugs, drugs used in the treatment and prophylasis of asthma, antituberculous drugs, and allopurinol.

This label is used to encourage compliance where the drug is to be taken over long periods without the patient necessarily perceiving any benefit. Patients should be told that this label does not override the need to consult the prescriber if side-effects occur.

For certain medicines the patient should be advised to ensure that the supply does not run out.

9. 'TAKE AT REGULAR INTERVALS. COMPLETE THE PRESCRIBED COURSE UNLESS OTHERWISE DIRECTED'

To be used on preparations where a course of treatment should be completed to reduce the incidence of relapse, the development of resistance or failure of treatment. The preparations are antibiotics, antibacterial drugs, and antifungals given by mouth.

Very occasionally, some of these antimicrobial agents may have severe side-effects and in such cases the patient may need to be advised of reasons for stopping treatment quickly and returning to the doctor. Examples are the development of diarrhoea in patients receiving clindamycin or lincomycin (see BNF), or sensitivity reactions with penicillins.

10. 'WARNING. FOLLOW THE PRINTED INSTRUCTIONS YOU HAVE BEEN GIVEN WITH THIS MEDICINE'

To be used particularly on anticoagulants, monoamine-oxidase inhibitors, and oral corticosteroids. The appropriate treat- ment card should be given to the patient and any necessary explanations given.

The label may also be used on other preparations to remind the patient of the instructions that have been given.

11. 'AVOID EXPOSURE OF SKIN TO DIRECT SUNLIGHT OR SUN LAMP'

To be used on preparations that may cause phototoxic or photo-allergic reactions if the patient is exposed to ultraviolet radiation. Many drugs other than those listed (e.g. phenothiazines and sulphonamides) may on rare occasions cause reactions in susceptible patients. Reactions have also been caused by external preparations (e.g. coal tar) and by various ingredients or perfumes and cosmetics. Exposure to high intensity ultraviolet radiation from sunray lamps and sunbeds is particularly likely to cause reactions and in advising patients this should be mentioned.

The drugs involved are amiodarone, azapropazone, demeclocycline, nalidixic acid and protriptyline.

12. 'DO NOT TAKE REMEDIES CONTAINING ASPIRIN WHILE TAKING THIS MEDICINE'

To be used on preparations containing salicylate derivatives, where it may not be known to the patient that the medicine has a similar action to aspirin, and on preparations containing the uricosuric drugs probenecid and sulphinpyrazone whose activity is reduced by aspirin.

Label 12 should not be used for anticoagulants: label 10 is more appropriate.

13. 'DISSOLVE OR MIX WITH WATER BEFORE TAKING'

To be used on preparations that are intended to be dissolved in water (e.g. soluble tablets) or mixed with water (e.g. powders, granules) before use. In a few cases the manufacturer's literature indicates that other liquids such as fruit juice or milk may be used.

14. 'THIS MEDICINE MAY COLOUR THE URINE OR STOOLS'

To be used on preparations that may cause the patient's urine to turn unusual colours. These include anthraquinones (alkaline urine red), phenolphthalein (alkaline urine pink), triamterene (blue), levodopa (reddish/dark colour), phenazopyridine (reddish orange) and rifampicin (red). Iron preparations may colour the urine and stools black.

15. 'CAUTION FLAMMABLE: KEEP AWAY FROM NAKED FLAMES'

To be applied to preparations containing sufficient alcohol, acetone, ether or other flammable solvent to render them flammable if exposed to a naked flame. The term 'flammable' is now used by the British Pharmacopoeia and in legislation in preference to 'inflammable'. Since both terms are now liable to cause confusion, the pharmacist should make sure that the patient understands what is meant.

16. 'ALLOW TO DISSOLVE UNDER THE TONGUE. DO NOT TRANSFER FROM THIS CONTAINER. KEEP TIGHTLY CLOSED. DISCARD EIGHT WEEKS AFTER OPENING.'

To be used on glyceryl trinitrate tablets to remind the patient not to transfer the tablets to plastic or less suitable containers. The manufacturer's original pack normally carries most of this wording and it may only be necessary to add 'Discard eight weeks after opening'.

17. 'NOT MORE THAN .... IN 24 HOURS'

To be used on preparations for the treatment of acute migraine except those containing ergotamine, for which label 18 is used.

It may also be used on preparations for which no dose has been specified by the prescriber.

18. 'NOT MORE THAN ... IN 24 HOURS OR ... IN ANY ONE WEEK'

To be used on preparations of ergotamine tartrate. The number of tablets should correspond to 6–8 mg in a day and 10–12 mg in a week.

21. '... WITH OR AFTER FOOD'

To be used on preparations liable to cause gastric irritation with nausea and vomiting or those that are better absorbed with food.

The incidence of gastric irritation may be reduced when some preparations are given during or immediately after a meal. The presence of food in the upper gastro-intestinal tract may reduce the rate of absorption of certain drugs. Nausea and vomiting are liable to decrease compliance and possibly lead to loss of the drug from vomiting.

Patients may on occasions be advised to take their medicine with or after food in the interest of compliance when normally it should be taken before meals. There is a wide variation in the instructions given for iron salts and their preparations. They are usually best absorbed when given on an empty stomach and may then cause irritation. They are therefore often taken with a meal.

The prescriber's instructions should be followed.

The word 'food' is used in preference to 'meal' in the label. Patients differ in their interpretation of the words and many decide not to take a dose if it has to be taken with a meal that they normally omit.

Patients should be advised when to take their doses, according to their particular circumstances, and that a small amount of food is sufficient.

22. '...................................... HALF TO ONE HOUR BEFORE FOOD'

To be used on some anticholinergic or antacid preparations; some pancreatin and other enzyme preparations; most appetite suppressants, and certain other drugs whose absorption or local effect is thereby improved.

23. '.......... AN HOUR BEFORE FOOD OR ON AN EMPTY STOMACH'

To be used on some oral antibiotics whose absorption may be reduced by the presence of food and acid in the stomach.

Many of the antibiotics introduced in recent years are less affected by acid and/or food in the stomach and may be given at any time relative to meals.

24. '.. SUCKED OR CHEWED'

To be used on preparations that may be sucked or chewed. Certain preparations must be chewed before swallowing to improve their absorption or because of their size; others have been specially formulated to be chewed. All pastilles and lozenges should be sucked slowly to aid their local effect on the oropharynx. The pharmacist should use his discretion as to which of these words is appropriate.

25. '.................................... SWALLOWED WHOLE, NOT CHEWED'

To be used on preparations designed for sustained release; certain preparations that are very unpleasant or may damage the mouth or oesophagus if not swallowed whole; and with label 5 for enteric-coated preparations which rely on the coating of pellets, granules, tablets, or capsules or compression in a matrix material to achieve their effect. Chewing can cause premature release of active ingredient.

26. '.. DISSOLVED UNDER THE TONGUE'

To be used on preparations intended for sublingual use. Several drugs are absorbed into the circulation more effectively from the mucosa of the mouth, thereby avoiding the portal circulation into the liver. Patients should be advised to hold the tablet still under the tongue and avoid swallowing until the tablet has dissolved. The buccal mucosa between the gum and cheek is occasionally specified by the prescriber and specific directions should then be used.

27. '.. WITH PLENTY OF WATER'

To be used on preparations that should be well diluted (e.g. chloral hydrate), where a high fluid intake is required (e.g. sulphonamides), or where water is required to aid the action of the preparation (e.g. methylcellulose). The patient should be advised that 'plenty' means at least 150 ml (about a tumblerful). In most cases a beverage such as fruit juice, tea or coffee could be used. There have been reports of solid-dose preparations sticking in the oesophagus, particularly in the elderly and all patients should be reminded of the necessity of taking capsules and tablets with water or other liquid. As much as 100 ml may be required and the patient should stand or sit while taking the dose.

28. 'TO BE APPLIED SPARINGLY...'

To be used with external corticosteroid preparations and dithranol preparations.

The application of excessive quantities to the skin can increase the incidence of local side-effects and give rise to undesirable systemic effects.

Appendix 3

Code of Ethics of the Pharmacutical Society of Great Britain

Preamble

The Code of Ethics is intended to set the standard of professional conduct for all pharmacists and 'persons lawfully conducting a retail pharmacy business' within the meaning of the Medicines Act 1968. It shall be regarded as governing the conduct of all pharmacists both within and outside the practice of pharmacy.

In the case of persons lawfully conducting a retail pharmacy business, the Code shall be regarded as extending to the department or departments in which the preparation, dispensing, sale or supply of medicinal products is carried on or where surgical appliances or allied products of a kind commonly associated with pharmacy are sold or supplied.

Not all matters which should be subject to a standard of professional conduct are included in the Code; the matters mentioned are those upon which it is thought that guidance may be needed. The Council, in considering whether or not action should be taken, do not regard themselves as being limited to those matters which are mentioned in this Code.

By law the arbiter of what constitutes misconduct is the Statutory Committee from whose decisions appeal lies to the High Court. (See Medicines Act 1968.)

I. A pharmacist's prime concern shall be for the welfare of both patients and public.

II. A pharmacist shall uphold the honour and dignity of the profession and not engage in any activity which may bring the profession into disrepute.

III. A pharmacist shall at all times have regard to the laws and regulations applicable to pharmaceutical practice and maintain a high standard of professional conduct. A pharmacist shall avoid any act or omission which would impair confidence in the pharmaceutical profession. When a pharmaceutical service is provided a pharmacist shall ensure that it is efficient.

IV. A pharmacist shall respect the confidentiality of information relating to patients and their families. Such information shall not be disclosed to anyone without the patient's or appropriate guardian's consent except where it is in the best interest of the patient so to do.

V. A pharmacist shall keep abreast of the progress of pharmaceutical knowledge in order to maintain a high standard of professional competence relative to his sphere of activity.

VI. A pharmacist shall neither agree to practise under any conditions of service which prevent his professional independence nor impose such conditions on other pharmacists.

VII. Publicity for professional services is permitted provided that such publicity does not create an invidious distinction between pharmacists or pharmacies, is dignified and does not bring the profession into disrepute.

VIII. A pharmacist offering services directly to the public shall do so in premises which reflect the professional character of pharmacy.

IX. A pharmacist shall at all times endeavour to co-operate with professional colleagues and members of other health professions so that patients and the public may benefit.

Guidance Notes

Introduction

These notes are intended to explain the Code of Ethics and apply it to certain circumstances which have occurred. Like the Code of Ethics they do not pretend to be comprehensive because from time to time new circumstances arise which will be held to be professional misconduct. By law the arbiter of what constitutes misconduct is the Statutory Committee for whose decision appeal lies to the High Court.

Note: In these Guidance Notes the term 'medicinal product' applies to those products used for a medicinal purpose as defined below or as an ingredient in such a product.

A 'medicinal purpose' means any one or more of the following purposes:

(a) treating or preventing disease;
(b) diagnosing disease or ascertaining the existence, degree or extent of a physiological condition;
(c) contraception;
(d) inducing anaethesia;
(e) otherwise preventing or interfering with the normal operation of physiological function, whether permanently or temporarily, and whether by way of terminating, reducing or postponing, or increasing or accelerating the operation of that function or in any other way.

I. A pharmacist's prime concern shall be for the welfare of both patients and public.

(A) Safety

(i) A pharmacist should take all reasonable steps to ensure that working conditions are so arranged that the safety of the public and people working on the premises is protected. All working practices should be kept under review and the new information applied where appropriate. Checks should be carried out to ensure that working practices which have been laid down are in fact carried out.

(ii) Dispensing procedures should be adopted which aim to prevent dispensing errors and checking procedure should be used. (See Appendix: Guide to the Self-Assessment of Professional Practice Activities).

(iii) A pharmacist should not purchase, sell or supply any medicinal product where there is any reason to doubt the safety or quality. In assessing safety and quality, the pharmacist should have regard to the source, storage conditions, labels, appearance and any other available information regarding the product. As each product becomes available it is the pharmacist's responsibility to satisfy himself as to the safety and quality of the product either by direct means or by checking that the relevant testing has been carried out by a responsible organisation. Further, a pharmacist should keep abreast of developments and re-evaluate each product when doubts are raised about safety or quality. In assessing safety during use the pharmacist should have regard to the capabilites of the proposed user or customer and should take steps to protect user or customer and should take steps to protect and/or give appropriate advice to vulnerable people (e.g. blind and other disabled people). Where a pharmacist has information about the purpose for which a medicinal product will be used with or without concurrent treatment, he should take this into account when assessing its safety during use.

(iv) A pharmacist should exercise his professional judgment in controlling the purchase of unnecessary and excessive quantities of medicines.

(Safety and quality are as defined in the Medicines Act 1968.)

(B) Environment

The pharmacist should comply with the guidelines which are appropriate to his field of work, i.e. in the manufacturing industry and hospitals, the Guide to Good Manufacturing Practice available from the Department of Health; in retail pharmacy, the Guide to Good Dispensing Practice (see Appendix); and, when appropriate, the Guide to Small-Scale Manufacturing in the Retail Pharmacy (see the Pharmaceutical Codex).

All premises where medicinal products are manufactured, assembled, stored, sold or supplied should be maintained in a good state of repair and precautions should be taken to protect against the entrance and harbouring of animals (including pets), birds and insects. The premises should be maintained in a clean and tidy condition. There should be sufficient space in all work areas to allow an efficient and safe system of work. The environment (e.g. temperature, lighting, humidity and noise levels) should be controlled so as to avoid any adverse effects on the medicinal products either directly or indirectly through an effect on the staff.

(C) Efficacy of medicinal products

A pharmacist should not give an impression to a purchaser that a medicinal product is efficacious when he has reason to believe it is not.

(D) Efficient service to the community

(i) When providing a service to the community, a pharmacist should ensure that the service is efficient and meets the reasonable needs of those whom he serves.

(ii) A pharmacist should not substitute (except with approval of the prescriber or a hospital drug and therapeutics committee or in an emergency) any other product for a specifically named product even if he believes that the therapeutic effect and quality of the other product is identical. There will be situations of emergency when a pharmacist finds it necessary to substitute another product for a specifically named product prescribed by a practitioner: in such cases reasonable steps should be taken to ensure that the effect and quality of the substitute so far as can be ascertained is identical to that prescribed.

(iii) A pharmacist should do everything reasonably within his power to assist a person in need of emergency medical treatment (see also paragraph III (A) and Guidelines for Emergency Supplies [*PJ*, March 17, 1979, p. 223]).

(iv) A pharmacist should not deviate from the prescriber's instructions when dispensing a prescription, except when necessary to protect the patient. If a pharmacist is uncertain about the content of a prescription or believes that the prescribed medicinal product could harm the patient, he should make every effort to contact the prescriber. Even if the prescriber confirms that the product which the pharmacist believes could harm the patient should be dispensed, the pharmacist may refuse to dispense the prescription. However, before refusing to dispense, the pharmacist must carefully weigh up the consequences for the patient of refusing to dispense the prescription against the harm which may arise if the prescription is dispensed.

If it is impossible to contact the prescriber, the pharmacist should use his professional judgment and decide, in all the circumstances, what course of action would be in the best interest of the patient.

(v) A pharmacist who may be called upon in the course of his duties to supply Controlled Drugs should maintain sufficient stocks of such drugs for the purpose of dealing with all likely requests for urgent supplies.

(E) The sale of medicinal products liable to abuse

Among the medicinal products that can be sold only under the supervision of a pharmacist, there are those which present special problems. If abused, they can give rise to dependence or serious side-effects. Abuse, in this context, usually means the consumption over a lengthy period of doses substantially higher than those recommended. A pharmacist should apply additional control over sales of medicinal products known to be likely to cause such difficulties. It is recommended that the products concerned should be sold personally by the pharmacist.

Medicinal products becoming the subject of abuse will change as new products become available and it is important to take local circumstances into account. A pharmacist should remain vigilant and detect such changes.

(F) Medicinal products used for slimming

The use of medicinal products which depress appetite, prevent absorption of food or reduce body fluid involve risks which make it advisable for extra caution to be exercised in their supply. Excessive quantities of emetics and/or laxatives may be used by people attempting to reduce body weight and pharmacists should give suitable advice and, where appropriate, refuse sales if there is reason to believe such products are being misused.

(G) The supply of medicinal products to children

A pharmacist should not supply medicinal products to children, whether they are receiving the medicinal product for their own use or as messengers for others, unless he has satisfied himself that the product will be used correctly and will be delivered safely to an adult.

(H) Methods of sale of medicinal products

Methods by which medicinal products are sold to the public should reflect the pharmacist's professional responsibility, the need to maintain the confidence of the public in his knowledge, ability and judgment and his position as guardian of public interest in the safety, quality and efficacy of medicines.

The following methods are inconsistent with the above view and a pharmacist should neither take part in such activities nor display nor buy on terms which involve their acceptance. A pharmacist should not give any encouragement to the sale of medicinal products which are promoted by such methods (see also paragraph I.(I)).

Promotion to the public by means of:

(a) free samples, prizes, gifts, competitions, circulars (door-to-door or direct mail), vouchers; temporary price reductions, bonus, 'money off' or other special offers;

(b) advertisements or display material which contravene the principle that the quantity supplied should be limited to the reasonable need of the customer;

(c) display of medicinal products in a manner inconsistent with paragraph 5.4 of the Guide to Self-Assessment of Professional Practice which states:

> 'Medicines for sale should normally be displayed. Those restricted to sale from pharmacies should not be accessible to the public as this could constitute a danger to health. Other medicines should not be displayed on self-selection where there is a possibility that they might be obtained without the intervention of a pharmacist or suitably trained person.'

(I) Distribution of medicinal products

A pharmacist should not normally distribute or encourage the distribution of medicinal products by post in response to advertisements (mail order).

Where it is in the patient's interest to dispatch medicinal products or appliances by post, carrier or other means, a pharmacist should ensure that the patient receives the same standard of advice and instruction which he would have received if he had been present in the pharmacy, and should wrap the product securely.

(J) The sale of preparations other than medicinal products

(i) There is a number of preparations other than medicinal products sold or supplied in pharmacies which require control by pharmacists to ensure that the health and safety of customers are not put at risk. Such products include herbal remedies, food supplements and other products associated with the maintenance of health. A pharmacist should not sell any of those products where there is any reason to doubt their safety or quality. A pharmacist should not give an impression to a purchaser that those products are efficacious when he has reason to believe they are not so.

(ii) A pharmacist should not stock, sell or advise people to buy any preparations (whether classified as medicinal products or not) which are claimed to counteract the undesirable effects of alcoholic beverages because of the possibility of misuse and consequent danger to the public.

(iii) Products other than medicinal products can be misused and pharmacists should be vigilant in order to detect local patterns of misuse and should apply appropriate additional controls on sales when necessary.

(K) Sale of chemicals to children

A pharmacist should take steps to ensure that all chemicals supplied to children or to adults for use by children, whether in chemistry sets or otherwise, will be used in appropriate circumstances. In particular, the following chemicals which can be used for making fireworks should not be sold to young persons:

Chlorates, nitrates, magnesium, potassium permanganate, sulphur, powdered aluminium, phosphorus.

If any request from anyone irrespective of age for the above substances or similar reducing or oxidising agents is received reasonable steps should be taken to ensure that they are required for a proper purpose and will not be used for making explosives or fireworks.

(L) Sale of industrial chemicals or chemicals for use in hobbies

A pharmacist should take reasonable steps to satisfy himself that the purchaser of chemicals, including solvents, for industrial purposes or for a hobby has sufficient knowledge to handle the chemicals safely and will use the chemicals for a bona fide purpose. (A pharmacist should be aware not only of the poisons legislation but the requirements of the Health and Safety at Work etc. Act 1974.)

(M) Disposal of medicinal products and chemicals

In disposing of medicinal products and chemicals a pharmacist should take all reasonable care to ensure that the substances are disposed of correctly and safely. In carrying out his duties in this respect he should use his pharmaceutical knowledge and skill and where necessary seek expert advice and help.

II. *A pharmacist shall uphold the honour and dignity of the profession and not engage in any activity which may bring the profession into disrepute.*

(A) Honour and dignity of the profession

A pharmacist should not bring the profession into disrepute by acting unlawfully or disregarding the reasonably accepted standards of behaviour both within and outside his professional practice.

(B) Use of name, title or qualifications

pharmacist should not use or permit the use of his qualifications or his position as a pharmacist to mislead or defraud. He should not allow others to use his name, qualifications, address or photograph in connection with the distribution to the public of any medicinal product or the provision of his professional services.

While there is no objection to the use by pharmacists of higher degree qualifications, a pharmacist should not deliberately use a doctorate degree in such a way as to lead the public to believe that he is a medical practitioner. In this connection the use of 'Doctor' or 'Dr' on the fascia of a retail pharmacy business or on dispensing labels will be regarded as misleading. The use of awards, civil decorations, qualifications or descriptions of membership of organisations may create an invidious distinction between pharmacists and bring the primary professional qualifications into disrepute. A pharmacist should exercise restraint in the use of such designatory letters but may use such letters where they are relevant in the context of his practice.

III. *A pharmacist shall at all times have regard to the laws and regulations applicable to pharmaceutical practice and maintain a high standard of professional conduct. A pharmacist shall avoid any act or omissions which would impair confidence in the pharmaceutical profession. When a pharmaceutical service is provided, a pharmacist shall ensure that it is efficient.*

(A) Legislation

A pharmacist should familiarise himself with and keep abreast of changes in the Medicines Act 1968, the Misuse of Drugs Act 1971, the Poisons Act 1972, the National Health Service Acts and the Regulations made under those statutes. A pharmacist should equally be aware of the requirements of the additional legislation relating to his particular field of practice.

A pharmacist should at all times comply with such laws and regulations but at the same time he should do all in his power to assist a person in need of emergency medical treatment (see also paragraph I. (D) (ii) and (iii)).

(B) Codes of practice

A pharmacist should be aware of and comply with accepted codes of practice relevant to his field of practice (see also paragraph I. (B)).

(C) Self-assessment

A pharmacist should review frequently the service he provides in accordance with the Guide to Self-Assessment of Professional Practice. A pharmacist should apply up-to-date knowledge and expertise in carrying out his professional activities (see also paragraph I. (A) and (D)).

(D) Professional responsibilty

As an independent practitioner a pharmacist should act within his professional competence and be personally responsible for his decisions. A pharmacist who accepts a post as superintendent pharmacist of a body corporate is responsible for the observance of all legal and professional requirements of the body corporate in relation to the pharmaceutical aspects of the business (see also paragraph VI.(B)).

(E) Efficient service – availability of a pharmacist

In retail pharmacy premises, a pharmacist should normally be readily available for consultation on pharmaceutical matters and other aspects of health care (see also paragraph I. (D)).

IV. *A pharmacist shall respect the confidentiality of information relating to patients and their families. Such information shall not be disclosed to anyone without the patient's or appropriate guardian's consent except where it is in the patient's interest so to do.*

(A) Information

(i) Information concerning patients and their families may be made available to pharmacists and their staff in many ways and is retained through memory and/or held in records which can be manually, mechanically or electronically maintained. Access to the records should be restricted to those staff who have need to use the information. A pharmacist should instruct staff who have access to any patient records or other information that those are confidential and that they must not be disclosed to anyone without reference to him. Furthermore, he should take reasonable measures to ensure that staff respect the confidential nature of the information.

(ii) If a pharmacist believes that it is in the best interest of the patient to reveal any information concerning that patient to a third party he must normally seek the consent of the patient or, of the patient is a child, the parent or guardian. When such consent is sought the patient should be made aware of all relevant facts. In very rare instances a pharmacist may believe that it is in the patient's best interest to disclose confidential information without the patient's consent. In such instances, the pharmacist must evaluate carefully the consequences of disclosure and weigh the benefits of disclosure against any detriment which the patient may incur. If the pharmacist is still convinced of the need to disclose the information he should do so in confidence to those who act only in the patient's interest.

Otherwise patient records should be disclosed only to those whom the pharmacist has ascertained have legal authority to examine them.

A pharmacist should make every effort not to impair the patient's confidence in his practitioner. A practitioner's prescribing, advice and instructions to the patient should be questioned with discretion and only when it is necessary to do so to protect the patient's health or welfare.

V. *A pharmacist shall keep abreast of the progress of pharmaceutical knowledge in order to maintain a high standard of professional competence relative to his sphere of activity.*

(A) Continuing education

A pharmacist should continually review his level of professional knowledge and expertise by self-assessment in accordance with the Guide to Self-Assessment of Professional Practice (Appendix I), and by regular updating through professional journals, attending meetings and frequent participation in continuing education programmes (see also paragraph III. (C)).

(B) Records

A pharmacist should ensure that appropriate records are made of dispensed prescriptions, of extemporaneous preparations made on his advice, and of all other parts of his professional activities to which it is probable that future reference might be made.

Patient medication records either collated by the pharmacist in a retail pharmacy business or made available within the hospital service, are particularly helpful if the pharmacist is to play his part in ensuring that the correct medication regimen is followed by the patient.

(C) Information

A pharmacist has a general responsibility to provide information and advice, and he should take reasonable precautions to see that it is both accurate and appropriate. He should ensure that appropriate information sources are available at all times, and ensure that information is held in a manner which facilitates retrieval and is kept up-to-date.

VI. *A pharmacist shall neither agree to practise under any conditions of service which prevent his professional independence nor impose such conditions on other pharmacists.*

(A) Employment as a pharmacist

(i) A pharmacist must be free to exercise his professional judgment when carrying out his duties as a pharmacist and his employer must recognise that he has such professional responsibility.

(ii) Although in the case of bodies corporate the duties of a superintendent pharmacist are established by law (see paragraph VI. (B)) every pharmacist in personal control of retail pharmacy premises should ensure additionally the observance of a proper standard in the premises that he controls.

Any obstruction of a pharmacist in personal control of a retail pharmacy business by anyone in managerial control of the business which results in failure to maintain a proper standard of conduct within that business will be regarded as failure on the part of the owner of the business to observe a proper standard as well as on the part of the pharmacist.

(iii) Employment as the sole pharmacist in a retail or hospital pharmacy or other organisation should not be accepted by a pharmacist who is not able to exercise the full duties of a pharmacist in charge of that pharmacy, or the pharmaceutical requirements of the organisation. Likewise, employment as a sole pharmacist should not be offered to a pharmacist who is not required to exercise the full duties of a pharmacist within that organisation.

(B) Duties of a superintendent pharmacist

A superintendent of a company which is a 'person lawfully conducting a retail pharmacy business' is appointed in accordance with the terms of Section 71 of the Medicines Act 1968. He is required to be responsible for the management of the business so far as it concerns the keeping, preparing and dispensing of medicinal products. The business is required to be carried on under his 'personal control' or, if not under his personal control, subject to his direction under the personal control of a manager or assistant who is a pharmacist.

In addition to his legal responsibilities, a superintendent should ensure compliance with the professional standards currently accepted in pharmacy. The superintendent who permits his directors to exercise functions which are his own responsibility, can only blame himself if, as a result of his neglect or inactivity, he is accused of failing to carry out his duties as superintendent of a company for which he acts in that capacity.

The superintendent has responsibility for the following matters:

1. The nature, quality and adequacy of amount of goods and services of all kinds reasonably necessary to enable an adequate pharmaceutical service to be provided, and choice of the suppliers of such goods and services.

2. In relation to the pharmaceutical service:

(a) the control of staff and the allocation of duties to individual members;
(b) the observance of all legal and professional requirements;
(c) the condition of the pharmacy.

3. The settlement of all questions concerning the nature and extent of the pharmaceutical service or which involve in any way pharmaceutical knowledge or professional conduct.

VII. *Publicity for professional services is permitted provided that such publicity does not create an invidious distinction between pharmacists or pharmacies, is dignified and does not bring the profession into disrepute.*

(i) For the purpose of the correct interpretation of the reference to professional services in this paragraph of the Code of Ethics, the professional services which may be provided by pharmacists include:

1. Dispensing of prescriptions.
2. Sale or supply of medicinal products.
3. Sale or supply of surgical dressings and appliances.
4. Sale or supply of poisons and chemicals.
5. Sale or supply of aids to mobility.
6. Response to symptoms described in pharmacies – 'counter prescribing'.
7. Facilities for sale or supply of hearing aids.
8. Pregnancy testing.
9. Sale of goods, supply of services or the provision of advice where the pharmacist uses his scientific and pharmaceutical knowledge.

(ii) It is in the public interest for pharmacists to make available information about the professional services which they are able to provide. Information, announcements, advertisements or any other form of publicity should not be of a character which could reasonably be regarded as likely to bring the profession into disrepute. Additionally, publicity for professional services must be discreet and dignified so as to impress upon the public that medicines are not ordinary articles of commerce and that pharmacists are professional people providing in addition to the supply of medicines, skilled and informed advice on pharmaceutical matters and health care.

(iii) Publicity must be factual, accurate and not misleading.

(iv) In order to avoid the creation of an invidious distinction between pharmacists or pharmacies there should be no criticism of the services of other pharmacists or pharmacies and there should be no claim of superiority over any other pharmacist or pharmacy either expressed or implied.

(v) Publicity by bodies representing pharmacists and/or pharmacies and seeking to promote the profession as a whole is to be encouraged.

(vi) Publicity informing the public of the availability of professional services should comply with the guidelines in (ii), (iii) and (iv) above. In addition it should contain no matter other than:

(a) the name, address and telephone number of the pharmacy;

(b) the hours of service;

(c) the words 'pharmacy', 'chemist', 'pharmacist', and 'MPS' or 'FPS' (see also paragraph II.(B)) of which one word only may be used in an advertisement in a discreet manner and then only once in an advertisement whether or not the word appears in the company or business name;

(d) an indication of the availability of specific products and/or a general indication of the professional services available including any specialised services.

In addition, publicity referring to 'dispensing services' shall be permitted only in the following:

(a) press when the size of the publicity shall be no larger than 7.5 cm x double column;

(b) Teletext or similar information service;

(c) telephone directories (standard entry only).

Except that the phrase 'dispensing chemist' may appear on fascias and business stationery which includes labels and bags.

Notes

(1) The hours of service given should be those hours when a pharmacist is available to give a professional service.

(2) A specialised professional service should only be referred to in any publication if a comprehensive service in that specialisation is provided, e.g. the stocking of a limited number of prepacked homoeopathic remedies is insufficient for description as a homoeopathic pharmacy.

(3) Publicity in practitioners' surgeries, health centres, clinics, hospitals or similar institutions should not be undertaken unless it contains information on the total professional services available in the area.

(vii) The use of any restricted title, e.g., 'pharmacy', 'pharmacist', 'chemist', 'chemists', 'MPS', or 'FPS' in an advertisement for non-professional goods or services causes the advertisement to be regarded as an indirect means of advertising the professional services of the pharmacist or pharmacy. It, therefore, becomes necessary to exercise restraint not only in the use of those titles but also in the general context of the publication. Only the title 'chemist(s)' may be used and then once only in such an advertisement for non-professional goods or services. No more prominence should be given whether by position, size, type or any other feature, than is reasonably necessary to establish the nature of the business of the advertiser.

This guideline shall apply to all forms of advertising, whether in newspapers, on television, on vehicles, on counter bags, or elsewhere. When the restricted title 'chemist(s)' is used orally, such as in a radio announcement, no particular emphasis should be placed upon it.

Advertisements for non-professsional goods or services using the restricted title 'chemists' should not be displayed in a practitioner's surgery, health centre, clinic, hospital or similar institution.

(viii) Interviews with the press related to advertising raise particular difficulties; many newspapers wish to carry photographs with editorial matter and advertisements relating to products sold by the business. The occasion for those announcements may be the rebuilding or modernisation of the premises and claims are sometimes made that the firm is of long standing and reliable. Almost invariably such announcements carry the implication that the pharmacy is superior to other pharmacies in the neighbourhood and, for this reason, are unacceptable.

Pharmacists have expressed surprise at such matter appearing in the newspaper and claim that they are not responsible for it. The method of obtaining indirect advertising by taking part in an 'advertising feature' of the kind in question has been strongly criticised. A pharmacist should exercise great care and do everything reasonably possible when speaking to the press to ensure that he does not directly or indirectly contravene the Code of Ethics. Before a pharmacist speaks to a reporter he should obtain an undertaking from the reporter that, if there is an article, the pharmacist will see it before publication and, if there is any objection to the article, he will have the opportunity to alter or strike it out or do whatever is necessary to make the article acceptable.

VIII. *A pharmacist offering services directly to the public shall do so in premises which reflect the professional character of pharmacy.*

(A) Layout of pharmacies

Even when environmental standards are satisfactory (see also paragraph I.(B)), the visual impact of a pharmacy, externally and internally, is a major feature in influencing the public opinion of the profession.

It is therefore vital that the external appearance of retail pharmacy premises and hospital pharmacies should not only give clear indication that professional services are available within, but also inspire confidence in the nature of health care that can be expected.

Inside retail pharmacy premises, no matter to what extent commercial activities may be conducted, the public should be able to recognise clearly that part of the premises in which professional services are provided.

(B) Signs and notices on the exterior of retail pharmacy premises

The wording on fascias and the exhibition of signs and notices featured in the windows and on the doors of retail pharmacy premises should be restrained. The size, content and position should be related to the size of the premises themselves and the wording used should be dignified and professional in character. The general appearance should reflect the professional nature of pharmacy.

(C) Displays outside and/or proximate to the premises

Exhibition of merchandise and dumper bins outside pharmacy premises is unprofessional. Anyone seeking to use trestle boards outside premises should recognise the need for the environs of the premises to reflect the professional nature of pharmacy.

Signs displayed other than on the premises themselves which direct the public to a pharmacy should be used only in exceptional circumstances; they should in every respect follow the guidance given in paragraph VIII. (B) and the Pharmaceutical Society should be consulted for prior approval.

IX. *A pharmacist shall at all times endeavour to co-operate with professional colleagues and members of other health professions so that patients and the public may benefit.*

(A) Business associations with medical practitioners

While the closest professional co-operation between pharmacist and medical practitioner is to be welcomed, a pharmacist should not have an undesirable business association with a medical practitioner.

There is no objection to a pharmacist being employed by a medical practitioner providing a dispensing service.

(B) Recommendation of a medical practitioner

A pharmacist should not recommend a medical practitioner or medical practice unless so requested by a member of the public seeking medical advice.

Appendix 3B

Guide to Good Dispensing Practice

The community pharmacist is the last link in the chain which is designed to ensure the quality, safety and efficacy of all medicines delivered to the patient. It is important, therefore, that premises should be so designed, equipped and organised that they can fulfil their essential role in the protection of public health. N.B.: Premises means registered pharmacy premises and hospital pharmacy departments.

Part 1: Suitability of premises

(i) The premises should be maintained in a good state of repair and precautions should be taken to protect against the entrance and harbouring of animals and birds (including pets), rodents, insects and other pests. In particular no animal should be kept in the dispensary.

(ii) All parts of the premises, particularly the dispensary, should be maintained in a clean and tidy condition.

(iii) All parts of the premises should have suitable and effective means of heating, lighting and ventilation.

(iv) There should be sufficient space in the dispensary to allow an efficient flow of work and effective communication and supervision.

(v) All working surfaces, cupboards and shelves in the dispensary should be finished with a smooth, impervious and washable material, and maintained in a good state of repair. Walls, floors and ceilings should be kept clean. A regular cleaning schedule is recommended.

(vi) Toilet facilities should be appropriately located, designed and equipped and should have hand washing facilities. They should be kept clean and in efficient order and so designed that no offensive odours penetrate into the dispensary. A clearly legible notice requesting users to wash their hands after using the toilet should be placed in, or near, the toilet. Disposable towels or hot-air hand driers are advised. Toilet areas should not be used for the purpose of storing stock or as a source of water for the preparation of medicinal products.

(vii) The environment (e.g. temperature, lighting, humidity, noise levels, etc.) should be such that there is no adverse effect on the dispensed product either directly or indirectly via dispenser.

(viii) Waste material should not be allowed to accumulate and should be collected in suitable covered receptacles for removal to collection points preferably outside the building, for disposal at regular and frequent intervals.

(ix) The processing of substances for non-medicinal use should be effectively segregated from the dispensing of medicinal products.

Part 2: Equipment

A pharmacist should satisfy himself that the equipment in the premises is adequate and suitable for all the operations to be carried out. All equipment should be kept clean and checked for cleanliness prior to each use. With the exception of non-returnable containers, equipment must be of such material and be kept in such good repair and condition as to enable it to be thoroughly cleaned to prevent any risk of contamination. Use of stainless steel and glass is recommended, not enamelled iron or plastics.

Equipment should include:

(i) A dispensing bench of adequate size, having a smooth, impervious working top, e.g. stainless steel, melamine or Formica. Such bench should be used solely for the purposes of compounding and dispensing and allied operations.

(ii) A sink should be fitted in the dispensary, together with an adequate supply of hot and cold running water. Cold water should be obtained directly from a mains water supply.

(iii) A suitable means for counting tablets and capsules. Steps should be taken to avoid cross contamination, particularly when using mechanical counters.

(iv) An accurate dispensing balance with a comprehensive range of weights, e.g. class B.

(v) An accurate weighing scale balance with an adequate range of weights (where applicable).

(vi) A suitable range of graduated, stamped, glass measures.

(vii) A suitable range of pestles and mortars both glass and earthenware.

(viii) A refrigerator unit capable of storing products within a selected temperature range from 0° to 10°C. Its efficiency should be regularly checked.

(ix) Suitable means for the sterilisation of medicinal products, if prepared on the premises.

(x) A suitable range of tablet and capsule containers.

(xi) A suitable range of plain liquid containers and poison containers.

(xii) A suitable range of containers for the dispensing of creams and ointments.

N.B.: All containers specified under the foregoing sections (x) –(xii) should comply with the appropriate specifications laid down in any current British

Standard for containers together with any others which from time to time may be recommended in the British Pharmacopoeia and/or the Pharmaceutical Codex.

(xiii) A suitable range of labels should be available with the foregoing containers.

(xiv) An adequate supply of spatulae should be available.

Part 3: Cleanliness and hygiene

(i) All persons engaged in dispensing should observe high standards of personal cleanliness. Protective clothing should be regularly and frequently laundered.

(ii) No person with open lesions or skin infections should be engaged in dispensing processes. Staff should be encouraged to report infections and skin lesions.

(iii) All persons should keep any cut or abrasion on any exposed part of their persons covered with a suitable waterproof dressing.

(iv) Smoking is forbidden in any area where medicines are dispensed, sold or supplied. No meals should be prepared or consumed in those areas.

(v) Direct contact should be avoided between the operator's hands and the dispensed products.

Part 4: Control of materials

(i) The compounding and dispensing of medicinal products should be carried out by a pharmacist, or by other suitably trained personnel or those undergoing training under the personal supervision of a pharmacist.

(ii) The compounding and dispensing of medicinal products should be subject to an adequate check system.

(iii) All raw materials used in compounding and dispensing should be obtained, where possible, from licensed suppliers, and be of such quality suitable for medicinal use.

(iv) All containers of raw materials should be kept in a good, clean condition, clearly labelled and should have indentifying reference marks, manufacturer's name and, if appropriate, batch numbers and expiry dates clearly marked on them.

(v) All material should be stored under suitable conditions, bearing in mind the nature of the material concerned. Particular attention should be paid to protection from sunlight, atmospheric moisture and adverse temperature. Where stock is transferred from one container to another, the particulars specified in (iv) above should be attached, and risk of contamination minimised. A pharmacist should exercise in full his knowledge of stability of materials and be prepared to destroy any substances which have been in stock for unduly long periods, which have deteriorated, or which have passed their expiry dates.

N.B.: Materials, or raw materials, in this context includes all prescription ingredients, finished products, proprietary preparations and any other medicinal substances purchased for the purpose of dispensing, whether as received or as component in a preparation to be dispensed.

Part 5: Miscellaneous

(i) Due regard should be given to the ratio of unqualified to qualified personnel.

(ii) Containers used in dispensing should be appropriate to the particular product being dispensed, bearing in mind particularly the need to protect the contents from atmospheric moisture and sunlight as well as mechanical stresses encountered in the course of normal transport and use by the patient.

(iii) Labels of medicinal products should be legible and clear. Lettering on labels should be mechanically printed.

(iv) Except in an emergency, substitution of articles or ingredients should not be made without the prior consent of the prescriber.

(v) An appropriate system should be introduced for the orderly retention in chronological sequence of all those documents required to be kept under various enactments.

(vi) A bound book with numbered pages should be used for the purpose of recording the dispensing of non-NHS prescriptions and counter-prescribed items.

(vii) An adequately stocked library should be available, containing such current reference books as are considered appropriate to the practice of pharmacy.

(viii) A pharmacist should keep adequate records, particularly in reference to small scale manufacturing processes, e.g. the preparation of own nostrums, stock mixtures, etc.

Appendix 3C

Guide to the Self-assessment of Professional Practice Activities

This guidance is designed to help pharmacists to undertake a self-assessment of whether they are providing a sufficient and satisfactory service. It is also intended to be of use to those who are responsible for designing undergraduate courses, preregistration experience programmes, and relevant continuing education programmes.

Part 1: Introduction

1. STRUCTURE AND AIMS OF THE GUIDE

1.1 The Guide has been prepared in three parts. Following the Introduction, Part 2 covers the general professional activities of pharmacists in different aspects of practice. In Part 3 the main specialised aspects of pharmacy practice are described.

1.2 Pharmacists should apply up-to-date knowledge and expertise in carrying out their professional activities.

1.3 The Guide will help pharmacists to undertake a self-assessment of whether they are providing a sufficient and satisfactory service.

1.4 It will also be a helpful indication of the content of certain aspects of pharmacy practice for those who are responsible for designing undergraduate courses, preregistration experience and relevant continuing education programmes. They should also take account of the several Council Statements, e.g. the Statement upon Matters of Professional Conduct and the Guide of Good Dispensing Practice.

1.5 It is intended that the Guide will be reviewed periodically to take account of changes in pharmaceutical knowledge and practice, and of available data.

1.6 The principle upon which all of the pharmacist's professional practice activities are based is that, while co-operation and collaboration with members of other health professions is an important factor to be taken into consideration, the pharmacist is an independent practitioner who should act within his professional competence and is fully responsible for his decisions.

1.7 The definitions which have been applied to certain terms used in the Guide appear at the end.

Part 2: General Activities

2. ADMINISTRATION

2.1 (i) Security and safety

(a) The pharmacist should ensure that the security of the premises is satisfactory in general and, particularly, in relation to the medicines kept on the premises.

(b) The pharmacist should ensure the implementation of the Health and Safety etc. Act and other regulatory requirements which apply to the professional activities carried out in the premises concerned.

(ii) Staff

The pharmacist, and also the superintendent pharmacist in the case of a body corporate, should ensure:

(a) that there are sufficient pharmacists and members of supporting staff to provide the pharmaceutical services required by the institution or community concerned;

(b) that all members of staff are of appropriate capability;

(c) that suitable training is given to support staff.

(iii) Information sources

(a) The pharmacist has a general responsibility for the provision of information and advice, and should take reasonable precautions to see that it is both accurate and appropriate.

(b) The pharmacist should: communicate effectively, and ensure that appropriate information sources are available at all times, and be aware of their relative merits and limitations; ensure that information is stored in a manner which facilitates retrieval and is kept up-to-date; be aware of additional sources of information; interpret questions so that the actual needs of the inquirer are ascertained, obtain all relevant information and assess the urgency of the request; document those inquiries relating to information which could be useful for future reference; contribute information to local liaison and similar committees dealing with drugs and therapeutics; in appropriate situations in which information has not been requested, provide it to the patient; in some circumstances, particularly in pharmaceutical practice associated with specialised medical practice, circulate printed information to appropriate colleagues or members of other professions; know how to proceed when unable to provide information from the resources immediately available; and appreciate the difference between providing factual information and providing an opinion based on an evaluation of data in relation to patient information.

(iv) Patient and other records

The pharmacist has a general obligation to ensure that appropriate records are made of dispensed prescriptions, of sales made on his advice, and of all other parts of his professional activities to which it is probable that future reference might be made.

Patient medication records, stored in the general practice pharmacy and maintained under the supervision of the pharmacist, can be beneficial and are particularly helpful as a basis for the advice that can be given to the prescriber and to the patient.

In the hospital service, the pharmacist should have access to the patient's medical record to enable the pharmaceutical services to be provided satisfactorily. Information about patients is an important basis for many of the pharmaceutical services, e.g. patient counselling, monitoring drug treatment. Any relevant information arising from those services should be added to the record.

(v) Indemnity

The pharmacist should ensure that:

(a) Personal professional liability is adequately covered by indemnity insurance to meet legal representation as well as other costs or damages;

(b) Other insurance risks for persons, equipment and premises in his charge are properly covered.

3. PROCUREMENT OF MEDICINES, INGREDIENTS AND RELATED PRODUCTS

3.1 The pharmacist has a responsibility to the patient to supply medicines of acceptable quality with reasonable promptness.

3.2 It is the responsibility of the pharmacist to have confidence in the sources from which he obtains pharmaceutical supplies. The pharmacist should be satisfied that any regulatory requirements have been met in relation to the item concerned.

3.3 All containers of raw materials should be kept in a good clean condition, clearly labelled and should have identifying reference marks, manufacturer's name and, if appropriate, batch numbers and expiry dates clearly marked on them.

3.4 All materials should be stored under suitable conditions bearing in mind the nature of the material concerned. Particular attention should be paid to protection from sunlight, atmospheric moisture and adverse temperature. Where stock is transferred from one container to another, the particulars specified in 3.3 above should be attached and the risk of contamination minimised. A pharmacist should exercise in full his knowledge of stability of materials and should destroy any substances which have been in stock for unduly long periods, or which have deteriorated, or which have passed their expiry dates.

N.B. Materials, or raw materials, in this context includes all prescription ingredients, finished products, proprietary preparations and any other medicinal substances purchased for the purpose of dispensing, whether as received or as a component in a preparation to be dispensed.

3.5 The pharmacist should comply immediately with any hazard warning or drug recall; wherever possible, he should inform persons who could be adversely affected by the circumstance; he should actively participate in any arrangements made for warning the profession of those or other problems, and should inform appropriate bodies of hazards which come to his attention.

4. DISPENSING PROCEDURES

4.1 Dispensing, which should be undetaken by or under the direct supervision of a pharmacist, includes all of the activities which occur from the pharmacist's initial scrutiny of a prescription to the collection of the dispensed medicine by the patient or agent.

4.2 If the information *on the prescription* is incomplete or indicates a potential hazard, the pharmacist should only dispense the prescription when he is completely satisfied that it represents the prescriber's wishes and that the medicine and the amount prescribed will not harm the patient. The final professional responsibility for dispensing the prescription or not lies with the pharmacist.

4.3 The pharmacist should be aware of the probable methods of prescription forgery and should be satisfied that the prescription is genuine, taking particular care in the case of medicines which are suspected of being misused currently.

4.4 Even when the prescription is genuine, in that it contains the order made by the medical practitioner for the patient in question, the pharmacist must also ensure that it is valid.

4.5 It is the pharmacist's responsibility to ensure that the medicine is accurately and properly dispensed, and that an appropriate container and correct label are used.

4.6 In general practice, the pharmacist should by the arrangement of the dispensary and medicines sales counter, be in a position to undertake or supervise the dispensing and sale of medicines.

4.7 When the pharmacist is assured that the correct medicine has been properly dispensed he should be in a position to give, or supervise staff giving any necessary advice or cautions, printed or oral, to the patient or the patient's agent when the medicine is collected.

5. THE SALE OF SUPPLY OF MEDICINE, POISONS AND CHEMICALS , OTHER THAN BY DISPENSING

5.1 With regard to medicines which can only be sold or supplied from pharmacies and which are not restricted to supply on prescription, arrangements should be introduced which result in a personal communication between the pharmacist and any member of staff selling or supplying such a medicine. The public should be aware of the pharmacist's close involvement in such sales or supplies and it is therefore unsatisfactory for the extent of supervision to be merely an acknowledgement of the sale or supply from some distance. Whenever appropriate the pharmacist should personally be involved in the sale or supply of these medicines and should discreetly ascertain whether it is appropriate for the person concerned.

5.2 All medicines, sold or supplied in general practice, should be located where the pharmacist can intervene in a sale or supply where there is a possibility of the provision of regular large quantities, the provision of more than one medicine with the same ingredient, the provision of medicines which might interact with medicines which the pharmacist knows have been prescribed for the patient, and whenever there is any other doubt about the sale or supply to be made.

5.3 In hospitals when medicines, including general sale list medicines, are supplied to departments, clinics or wards, in which other health professionals will be concerned with the supply to individual patients, the supply from the pharmacy should be under the control of the pharmacist.

5.4 Medicines for sale should normally be displayed. Those restricted to sale from pharmacies should not be accessible to the public as this could constitute a danger to health. Other medicines should not be displayed on self selection where there is a possibility that they might be obtained without the intervention of a pharmacist or suitably trained person.

5.5 At all times the pharmacist must be aware of the legal requirements for the sale and supply of medicines, and must ensure that staff who are involved are also cognisant of those aspects relating to their activities.

5.6 Potentially dangerous chemicals and poisons, and medicines liable to misuse should, where appropriate, only be sold or supplied by the pharmacist.

6. PROFESSIONAL RELATIONSHIPS

6.1 The pharmacist should establish and maintain regular contacts with those health professionals, particularly practitioners, with whom he is involved in his daily practice. The pharmacist should, whenever possible, discuss prescribing procedures and any developments concerning medicines, at regular intervals with them.

6.2 The pharmacist should co-operate with all authorised inspectors and officials.

6.3 The pharmacist should co-operate with other pharmacists, with a view to providing the best possible service to patients.

7. DEALING WITH THE PUBLIC ON GENERAL HEALTH MATTERS

7.1 As well as providing advice and assistance on all matters relating to medicines, the pharmacist and his staff should be able to and be prepared at all times to give advice to the public on general health matters. This will require in the pharmacy comprehensive information on local and national health facilities.

7.2 The pharmacist should ensure that suitable provisions have been made to deal with minor first aid situations, and any emergencies which might arise.

7.3 The pharmacist should be aware of current health education activity in the area and should co-operate whenever possible in local and national campaigns.

8. DIAGNOSTIC TESTING AND ANALYSIS

8.1 Diagnostic tests, such as pregnancy tests and blood pressure measurements, and analysis of body fluids, should only be carried out in a pharmacy when the necessary trained staff are available and the facilities are satisfactory. Alternatively, such activities may be arranged through suitable laboratories.

9. CONTINUING EDUCATION

9.1 The pharmacist must continually review his level of professional knowledge and expertise, by self-assessment in relation to the procedures contained in this Guide, and by regular up-dating through professional journals, meetings and regular participation in continuing education programmes.

9.2 In addition to keeping abreast of pharmaceutical matters it is the pharmacist's duty to be aware of and implement immediately any legislative changes which affect pharmacy.

Part 3: Specialised aspects of practice

10. INTRODUCTION

10.1 The nature and extent of specialised aspects of practice undertaken by pharmacists will be dependent upon the establishments in which they practice, and upon the consequent available resources.

10.2 In Part 2 of the Guide, paragraph 2.1(ii)(c), it has already been stated that there is a general responsibility upon all pharmacists to ensure that suitable training is given to support staff. Pharmacists in specialised aspects of practice have a particular responsibility to contribute to the education and training of pharmacists and support staff in that speciality. This will include training to be given to preregistration graduates who undertake part of their experience under the pharmacist's supervision.

11. RESPONSE TO SYMPTOMS

11.1 Pharmacists, particularly those in general practice, are called upon to advise members of the public on symptoms which are described to the pharmacist.

11.2 In fulfilling this responsibility the pharmacist should:

(a) Obtain from the inquirer sufficient information about the symptoms to enable a proper assessment of the situation to be made. This information should include the extent and frequency of the symptoms, other prescribed or purchased medicines which are being taken or have recently been taken, associated symptoms, and any previous medical diagnosis of similar symptoms;

(b) Determine the symptoms which are being experienced by any person who has requested advice on a self-diagnosed condition, i.e., when the patient has made a decision on the condition being suffered because of presumed knowledge that these symptoms lead to such a conclusion. When those symptom have been determined, the procedure described in (a) should be followed;

(c) Decide whether the symptoms are those which might be strongly associated with a serious condition, and in such circumstances refer the patient for immediate medical advice;

(d) In the case of other symptoms give appropriate advice, with or without the sale of a medicine, as necessary, and

(e) When medicines are supplied make records when appropriate and advise the inquirer to consult a medical practitioner should the symptoms persist.

12. PHARMACEUTICAL SERVICE AT WARD LEVEL

General activities

12.1 In fulfilling general responsibilities the pharmacist should:

(a) Design the system of distribution to meet the needs of its recipients, taking into account the necessity for direction and control by pharmacists;

(b) be responsible for the range of items issued as stock and ensure that distribution is efficient and prompt;

(c) ensure that regulatory requirements concerned with requisition, storage and record keeping are fulfilled;

(d) co-operate with medical and nursing staff to ensure that a safe system of prescribing and administration is in operation; and where professional activities impinge on those of other professions, ensure that the standards of the professions concerned are met;

(e) make emergency supplies, on request, to any ward or department, and also ensure that supplies which would be necessary in medical emergencies are available in the wards or departments concerned;

(f) make arrangements for the emergency supply of medicines when the pharmacy is closed, and where necessary operate an out of hours service; and

(g) aid policy making and promote a cost effective use of resources by contributing to the work of drug and therapeutics, or similar, committees.

Services at ward level

12.2 A ward pharmacy service is generally recognised as providing support to medical and nursing staff, and contributing to the safety and economy with which medicines are used. Such a service should be available to all patients, although the frequency of visiting and the range of tasks to be undertaken vary according to the local situation.

12.3 In fulfilling those tasks, the ward pharmacist should:

(a) Scrutinise all prescriptions at regular, frequent intervals to ensure that:

(i) They are complete, unambiguous and valid,

(ii) items are prescribed by a name which corresponds to a name on the container,

(iii) dosage is within acceptable limits,

(iv) the items of administration are appropriate,

(v) the route of administration is appropriate,

(vi) treatment is not duplicated,

(vii) prescribed doses are being administered,

(viii) there are no therapeutic or pharmaceutical incompatibilities, and

(ix) no drug is prescribed to which the patient is known to be hypersensitive;

(b) encourage the reporting of adverse reactions and co- operate with schemes operated by the Committee on Safety of Medicines;

(c) play an important part in the interpretation of results, where facilities exist for drug level monitoring;

(d) where appropriate, be a member of the parenteral nutrition team and advise on the solutions that can be prepared within the resources of the hospital;

(e) ensure that local policies on intravenous (IV) additives are being properly implemented;

(f) wherever possible and appropriate, obtain a drug history of the patient;

(g) ensure that patients are properly counselled in relation to their drug therapy;

(h) participate in the acquisition and provision of drug related information; and

(i) in performing the above activities, maintain a good and regular contact with other staff at ward level.

13. SPECIALIST INFORMATION SERVICES

13.1 Pharmacists who have specialised in the provision of information services should:

(a) Develop and maintain an effective system for handling the range of information sources, including books, journals, microforms, papers, abstracts, manufacturers' literature, and computerised and commercially available retrieval systems;

(b) contribute to the current awareness of pharmacist colleagues and members of other professions by providing an information source to those practising in hospitals and in the community;

(c) facilitate current awareness by actively disseminating information in the form appropriate to the recipient;

(d) be skilled in the evaluation of data and commercial claims, in abstracting, and in presenting information effectively;

(e) appreciate the comparative benefits and limitations of commercially available, and sometimes sophisticated indexing, abstracting and retrieval services, and advise on their suitability;

(f) co-ordinate information resources and co-operate with other centres to avoid duplication and to provide extensive coverage of the literature.

14. QUALITY ASSURANCE AND MANUFACTURING

14.1 Because of the close integration between quality assurance and manufacturing, both activities have been included in the same section. There are however separate roles for pharmacists in quality control and manufacturing to be carried out independently but in co-operation.

14.2 Health authorities have been asked to act as if they were subject to the controls applied to commercial manufacturers for the manufacture of medicinal products. In view of the application of Crown Exemption, it is not normally necessary for formal licensing documents to be issued, but health authorities are expected to act as if they were subject to the conditions of appropriate licences. This guidance is contained in Health Service Circular HSC(IS) 128.

14.3 There should be a comprehensive system, so designed, documented and implemented and so furnished with personnel and equipment as to provide assurance that products will be of a quality appropriate to their intended use. The attainment of that quality objective requires the involvement and commitment of the pharmacists responsible for both quality control and manufacturing.

14.4 The objectives of quality assurance are achieved when processes have been defined which, when followed, will yield a product which complies with its specification, and when the finished product:

(a) Contains the correct ingredients in the correct proportions;

(b) is of the purity required;

(c) has been correctly processed, according to the defined procedures;

(d) is enclosed in its proper container;

(e) bears the correct label; and

(f) is stored and distributed so that its quality is maintained.

Quality control

14.5 The quality control pharmacist should achieve effective control of quality by ensuring that:

(a) Adequate facilities and staff are available for sampling, for the inspection and testing of raw materials, packaging materials, intermediate bulk and finished products, and for the quality of the environment;

(b) samples of raw materials, packaging materials, finished products and intermediate products are taken by personnel using methods approved by and under the direction of the quality controller;

(c) results of the inspection and testing of materials, and of intermediate bulk or finished products are formally assessed against specifications by the quality controller (or a person designated by him) before materials are released for use, or products are released for further processing, sale or supply; product assessment should include a review and evaluation of relevant manufacturing (including packaging) documentation; and

(d) sufficient reference samples of products are retained (where possible in the final pack) to permit future examination if necessary.

Manufacturing

14.6 The pharmacist responsible for manufacturing should implement the basic requirements of good manufacturing practice by ensuring that:

(a) The manufacturing process is defined before the commencement of any activity;

(b) the necessary facilities and resources are provided including:

(i) appropriately trained personnel,

(ii) adequate premises and space,

(iii) suitable equipment,

(iv) correct materials,

(v) approved procedures,

(vi) suitable storage and transport,

(vii) store for representative samples of each batch produced;

(c) procedures are written in instructional form, in clear and unambiguous language;

(d) operators are trained to carry out procedures correctly;

(e) records are made during manufacture (including packaging) to demonstrate that all the steps required by the defined procedures were, in fact, taken and the quality and quantity produced were those expected.

(f) records of manufacture and distribution which enable the complete history of a batch to be traced, are retained in legible and accessible form; and

(g) a system is available to recall any batch of product, should that be necessary.

15. RADIOPHARMACY

15.1 Radiopharmacy, which the preparation of radiopharmaceuticals for diagnostic purposes and occasional dispensing for therapeutic purposes is a team approach requiring close co-operation between the pharmacist, physicist and nuclear medicine medical staff. It is important that the radiopharmacist should be fully responsible for the radiopharmacy department.

Preparation of radiopharmaceuticals

15.2 Although the range of preparations depends upon the facilities available and the expertise of the radiopharmacist, the pharmacist should take responsibility for the preparation of non-radioactive reagents, diluents, sterile containers and kits used in the preparation of radiopharmaceuticals, and for the synthesis, manufacture and dispensing, labelling, packaging and transport of radiopharmaceuticals.

Records and labelling

15.3 The radiopharmacist should ensure that appropriate pharmaceutical and radiological records are maintained. It is particularly important that every aspect of the manufacture, control and distribution of radiopharmaceuticals should be readily traceable from these records.

15.4 In addition to the standard pharmaceutical labelling requirements, radiopharmaceuticals must be labelled in accordance with the appropriate Radiation Code of Practice.

Quality assurance

15.5 Because of the short life of these products there are particular production and quality control problems.

15.6 The radiopharmacist should be responsible for releasing the finished product for use, having ensured that all proper quality assurance procedures have been satisfactorily undertaken, including the measurement of the radiation dose, radionuclidic purity and identity, and radiochemical purity.

Radiological and other equipment

15.7 In association with the physicist, the radiopharmacist should ensure that all equipment used in the radiopharmaceutical unit for counting and measuring radiation is accurately calibrated and standardised, and is regularly maintained.

Advisory

15.8 The radiopharmacist should provide advice to officers, health authorities and other relevant persons on the pharmaceutical aspects of radiopharmacy, including premises, equipment, procedures, records and quality control.

Facilities

15.9 The radiopharmacist should ensure that appropriate facilities are provided for the preparation of radiopharmaceuticals and, in co-operation with the radiation protection officer, should ensure that the appropriate radiation codes of practice are implemented at hospital level.

15.10 The radiopharmacist should comply with guidance provided in documents issued by the British Standards Institution, the Department of Health, the European Community, and appropriate professional bodies.

Supply

15.11 The radiopharmacist should ensure that radiopharmaceuticals are only supplied to those practitioners authorised to use them, in accordance with EC regulations.

Safety

15.12 Because of the particular hazards associated with radiopharmaceuticals, the radiopharmacist should ensure that, in addition to normal safety requirements, the special requirements relating to radiopharmaceutical departments and the procedures associated with the storage, disposal and transport of radioactive materials are properly implemented.

16. ADMINISTRATION

Introduction

16.1 Administration and management are closely connected and all pharmacists have, to a greater or lesser extent, administrative responsibilities. The extent of those responsibilities and the range of skills required to carry them out varies according to the grade and type of position occupied by the pharmacist.

16.2 Therefore, while all pharmacists need to develop skills of communication and leadership early in their careers properly to fulfil their roles within the health care team, the involvement in the following activities of the pharmacist who specialises in administration will be determined by the position occupied within the employing company, authority or organisation. As well as being thoroughly familiar with the administrative and organisational structure within which he works, the pharmaceutical administrator should also be familiar with the other aspects of pharmacy.

Planning and objectives

16.3 The pharmacist should contribute to both long term and operational planning, e.g. the NHS strategic and operational plans. Objectives should be established and continuously reviewed, to reassess priorities in relation to currently available resources.

Financial control and budgeting

16.4 The pharmacist should have a thorough knowledge of the allocation of financial resources and should develop a skill in successfully competing for an adequate share of available resources to ensure the balanced development of the services for which he is responsible.

16.5 The pharmacist should also be able to manage and account for the financial resources which he administers.

Legislation

16.6 The pharmacist administrator should have a sound knowledge and understanding of legislation directly affecting his activities, to supplement his knowledge of the other legislation affecting pharmacy.

Personnel functions

16.7 The pharmacist administrator should be skilled in the wide range of activities which are involved in the management of staff, including:

(a) selection and interviewing;

(b) induction and subsequent training;

(c) deployment;

(d) counselling;

(e) leadership and motivation; and

(f) the use of disciplinary and grievance procedures.

Communication skills

16.8 The ability to communicate is central to the role of the pharmacist administrator. He should demonstrate the following skills within his own activites and in relation to related disciplines:

(a) negotiating;

(b) report writing;

(c) committee work;

(d) chairmanship; and

(e) representation.

Co-ordination and arbitration

16.9 The pharmacist administrator should have sufficient knowledge and expertise to co-ordinate the activities of specialists, and should demonstrate an ability to assess priorities and take decisions in the best interests of the activities under his jurisdiction.

DEFINITIONS

The following definitions apply when the terms concerned are used in this Guide:

Control For hospital pharmacy the definition contained in the Noel Hall report has been used, namely: 'The person controlling confirms that the working procedures laid down are being properly followed through a personal inspection of reports and of details of checks being carried out during the working procedure.'

Section 70 of the Medicines Act 1968 requires that pharmacies, from which the sale of medicines take place, must be under the personal control of a pharmacist. Relevant statements by Chairmen of the Statutory Committee can be construed to mean that normally a pharmacist should be available for consultation on professional practice matters.

Direction The person directing lays down the working system to be followed, decides who is responsible for carrying out each task, and ensures that the working system incorporates checks at appropriate stages. (Definition from the Noel Hall report on hospital pharmacy.)

Dispensing The supply of a medicine to an individual patient in accordance with a practitioner's prescription.

General sale list medicine Medicines included in descriptions or classes of medicinal products which are specified by order by the appropriate Ministers under section 51 of the Medicines Act 1968, as being products which in their opinion can with reasonable safety be sold or supplied otherwise than by or under the supervision of a pharmacist.

Good manufacturing practice Is that part of quality assurance aimed at ensuring that products are consistently manufactured to a quality appropriate to their intended use. It is thus concerned with both manufacturing and quality control procedures.

Pharmaceutical supplies Products liable to licensing under the Medicines Act 1968, including medical gases; raw materials used in the manufacture of such products; unlicensed medicines, reagents or materials used in diagnostic testing; chemicals; dressings; medical and surgical equipment and appliances; medicines delivery systems, including containers, giving sets, apparatus and equipment used in the pharmacy.

Pharmacist A person registered as a pharmaceutical chemist in Great Britain.

Pharmacy A hospital department under the control of a pharmacist and concerned with the provision of pharmaceutical services; or a pharmacy registered under Section 74 and 75 of the Medicines Act 1968.

Premises Pharmacy premises registered under the Medicines Act 1968; or a pharmacy department of a hospital, clinic, etc.

Quality assurance The sum total of the organised arrangements made with the object of ensuring that products be of the quality required by their intended use. It is good manufacturing practice plus such factors as original product design, development and stability.

Quality control Is that part of good manufacturing practice which is concerned with sampling, specification and testing and with the organisation, documentation and release procedures which ensure that the necessary and relevant tests are, in fact, carried out, and that materials are not released for use, nor products released for sale or supply, until their quality has been judged to be satisfactory.

Supervision The person supervising personally oversees the undertaking of a task, i.e. so that he is aware of what is going on and can ensure that the task is carried out in the prescribed manner. (Definition from the Neol Hall report on hospital pharmacy.)

In relation to general practice, supervision means in effect that the pharmacist must be aware of the sale or supply of medicines and be in a position to intervene.

Symptom A phenomenon of physical or mental disorder or disturbance, experienced by the patient, which might be indicative of a departure from normal functions or of a disease.

Appendix 4

NHS Limited List

Schedule 3A to the NHS General Medical and Pharmaceutical Regulations 1985/290 as Amended by 1985/540 and 1985/803

Drugs and Other Substances not to be Prescribed for Supply Under Pharmaceutical Services

---

10 Day Slimmer Tablets
10 Hour Capsules
Abidec Capsules
Acetylcysteine Granules
Acid Gentian Mixture with Nux Vomica BPC
Acid Nux Vomica Mixture BPC
Acne Aid Bar
Actal Suspension
Actal Tablets
Actifed Syrup
Actifed Compound Linctus
Actifed Expectorant
Actifed Linctus with Codeine
Actifed Tablets
Actonorm Powder
Actonorm Tablets
Actron Tablets
Adexolin Vitamin Drops
Adult Cough Balsam (Cupal)
Adult Meltus Cough & Catarrh Linctus
Adults Tonic Mixture (Thornton & Ross)
Afrazine Nasal Drops
Afrazine Nasal Spray
Afrazine Paediatric Nasal Drops
Agarol Emulsion
Agiolax Granules
Airbal Breathe Easy Vapour Inhaler
AL Tablets
Alagbin Tablets
Alcin Tablets
Aletres Cordial (Potters)
Alexitol Sodium Suspension 360 mg/5 ml
Alexitol Sodium Tablets 360 mg
Algipan Tablets
Alka-Donna Suspension
Alka-Donna Tablets
Alka-Donna P Mixture
Alka-Donna P Tablets
Alka-Mints
Alka-Seltzer Tablets
Alkaline Gentian Mixture with Nux Vomica BPC
Alkaline Nux Vomica Mixture BPC
Alket Powders
All Fours Cough Mixture (Harwood)
All Fours Mixture (Glynwed Wholesale Chemists)
All Fours Mixture (Roberts Laboratories)
Allbee with C Capsules
Allbee with C Elixir
Almasilate Suspension

500 mg/5 ml
Almasilate Tablets 500 mg
Almazine Tablets 1 mg
Almazine Tablets 2.5 mg
Aloin Tablets 40 mg
Alophen Pills
Alpine Tea
Alprazolam Tablets 0.25 mg
Alprazolam Tablets 0.5 mg
Alprazolam Tablets 1 mg
Altacaps
Altacite Suspension
Altacite Plus Suspension
Altacite Plus Tablets
Altacite Tablets
Aludrox Gel
Aludrox Suspension
Aludrox M H Suspension
Aludrox S A Suspension
Aludrox Tablets
Aluhyde Tablets
Aluminium Hydroxide & Silicone Suspension
Aluminium Phosphate Gel
Aluminium Phosphate Tablets 400 mg
Alupent Expectorant Mixture
Alupent Expectorant Tablets
Aluphos Gel
Aluphos Tablets
Alupram Tablets 2 mg
Alupram Tablets 5 mg
Alupram Tablets 10 mg
Aluzyme Tablets
Alzed Tablets
Amisyn Tablets
Ammonia and Ipecacuanha Mixture BP
Ammonium Chloride and Morphine Mixture BP
Anadin Analgesic Capsules Maximum Strength
Anadin Analgesic Tablets
Anadin Extra Analgesic Tablets
Anadin Tablets Soluble
Ancoloxin Tablets
Andrews Liver Salts Effervescent Powder
Andrews Liver Salts (Diabetic Formula) Effervescent Powder
Andursil Liquid
Andursil Tablets
Anestan Bronchial Tablets
Aneurone Mixture
Angiers Junior Aspirin Tablets
Anorvit Tablets
Antasil Liquid
Antasil Tablets
Antistin-Privine Nasal Drops
Antistin-Privine Nasal Spray
Antitussive Linctus (Cox)
Antoin Tablets
Antussin Liquid (Sterling Winthrop)
Anxon Capsules 15 mg
Anxon Capsules 30 mg
Anxon Capsules 45 mg
Aperient Tablets (Brome & Schimmer)
Aperient Tablets (Kerbina)
Apodorm Tablets 2.5 mg
Apodorm Tablets 5 mg
APP Stomach Powder
APP Stomach Tablets
Arocin Capsules
Ascorbef Tablets
Ascorbic Acid & Hesperidin Capsules (Regent Laboratories)
Asilone Gel
Asilone For Infants
Asilone Suspension
Asilone Tablets 250 mg
Asilone Orange Tablets
Askit Powders
Askit Tablets
Aspergum Chewing Gum Tablets 227 mg
Aspro Clear Tablets
Aspro Extra Strength Tablets 500 mg
Aspro Junior Tablets
Aspro Microfined Tablets
Asthma Tablets (Cathay)
Astroplast Analgesic Capsules
Atensine Tablets 2 mg
Atensine Tablets 5 mg
Atensine Tablets 10 mg
Ativan Tablets 1 mg
Ativan Tablets 2.5 mg
Atrixo
Aveeno Bar
Aveeno Bar Oilated
Ayrtons Macleans Formula Tablets

B Complex Capsules (Rodale)
B Complex Super Capsules (Rodale)
B Extra Tablets (British Chemotherapeutic Products)
Babezone Syrup
Baby Chest Rub Ointment (Cupal)
Babylix Syrup
Balm of Gilead (Robinsons)
Balm of Gilead Cough Mixture (Wicker Herbal Stores)
Balm of Gilead Liquid (Culpeper)

Balm of Gilead Mixture (Potters)
Barker's Liquid of Life Solution
Barker's Liquid of Life Tablets
Barkoff Cough Syrup
Bayer Aspirin Tablets 300 mg
BC500 Tablets
BC500 with Iron Tablets
Becosym Forte Tablets
Becosym Syrup
Becosym Tablets
Becotab Tablets
Beechams Day Nurse Capsules
Beechams Day Nurse Syrup
Beechams Catarrh Capsules
Beechams Pills
Beechams Powders
Beechams Powders Tablet Form
Beechams Powders Mentholated
Beehive Balsam
Bekovit Tablets
Belladonna and Ephedrine Mixture, Paediatric, BPC
Bellocarb Tablets
Benadon Tablets 20 mg
Benadon Tablets 50 mg
Benafed Linctus
Benerva Compound Tablets
Benerva Injection 25 mg/ml
Benerva Injection 100 mg/ml
Benerva Tablets 3 mg
Benerva Tablets 10 mg
Benerva Tablets 25 mg
Benerva Tablets 50 mg
Benerva Tablets 100 mg
Benerva Tablets 300 mg
Bengue's Balsam
Benylin Day and Night Cold Treatment
Benylin Decongestant Linctus
Benylin Expectorant
Benylin Fortified Linctus
Benylin Mentholated Cough & Decongestant Linctus
Benylin Paediatric
Benylin with Codeine
Benzedrex Inhaler
Benzoin Inhalation BP
Beogex Suppositories
Bepro Cough Syrup
Bile Beans Formula 1 Pill
Bioflavonoid C Capsules
Bio-Strath Drops
Bio-Strath Elixir
Biovital Liquid
Biovital Tablets
Birley's Antacid Powder
Bis-Mag Lozenge
Bis-Peps Tablets
Bisma-Calna Cream
Bisma-Rex Powder
Bisma-Rex Tablets
Bismag Antacid Powder
Bismag Tablets
Bismuth Compound Lozenges BPC
Bismuth Dyspepsia Lozenges
Bismuth Pepsin and Pancreatin Tablets
Bismuth, Soda and Pepsin Mixture
Bisodol Antacid Powder
Bisodol Tablets
Bisolvomycin Capsules
Bisolvon Elixir
Bisolvon Tablets
Blackcurrant Cough Elixir (Thornton & Ross)
Blackcurrant Syrup Compound (Beben)
Blandax Suspension
Blavig Tablets
Blood Tonic Mixture (Thompsons)
Boldolaxine Tablets
Bonemeal Calfos, Vit A Ester, Vit D Tablets
Bonomint Chewing Gum
Bonomint Tablets
Booths Cough and Catarrh Elixir
Boots Cold Relief Powder for Solution
Boots Compound Laxative Syrup of Figs
Boots Cough Relief for Adults
Boots Glycerin & Blackcurrant Soothing Cough Relief
Boots Health Salts
Boots Indigestion Plus Mixture
Boots Indigestion Powder
Boots Vapour Rub Ointment
Box's Balm of Gilead Cough Mixture
Bravit Capsules
Bravit Tablets
Breoprin Tablets 648 mg
Brewers Yeast Tablets (3M Health Care)
Brewers Yeast-Super B Tablets (Rodale)
Brewers Yeast Tablets (Phillips Yeast Products)
Bricanyl Compound Tablets
Bricanyl Expectorant
Brogans Cough Mixture
Brogans Cough Syrup
Bromazepam Tablets 1.5 mg
Bromazepam Tablets 3 mg
Bromazepam Tablets 6 mg

Bromhexine Hydrochloride
  Elixir 6 mg/5 ml
Bromhexine Hydrochloride
  Tablets 8 mg
Bronalin Expectorant
Bronalin Paediatric Cough
  Syrup
Bronchial & Cough Mixture
  (Worthington Walter)
Bronchial Balsam (Cox)
Bronchial Catarrh Syrup
  (Rusco)
Bronchial Cough Mixture (Evans
  Medical)
Bronchial Emulsion (Three
  Flasks) (Thornton & Ross)
Bronchial Emulsion AS Extra
  Strong (Ayrton Saunders)
Bronchial Mixture (Rusco)
Bronchial Mixture Extra Strong
  (Cox)
Bronchial Mixture Sure Shield
  Brand
Bronchial Tablets (Leoren)
Bronchialis Mist Liquid
  (Industrial Pharmaceutical
  Services)
Bronchialis Mist Nig Double
  Strength (Phillip Harris
  Medical)
Bronchisan Childrens Cough
  Syrup
Bronchisan Cough Syrup
Broncholia Mixture
Bronchotone Solution
Bronkure Cough & Bronchitis
  Mixture (Jacksons)
Brontus Syrup
Brontus Syrup for Children
Brontussin Cough Suppressant
  Mixture
Brooklax Tablets
Brotizolam Tablets 0.125 mg
Brotizolam Tablets 0.25 mg
Bufferin Tablets
Buttercup Baby Cough Linctus
Buttercup Syrup

Cabdrivers Adult Linctus
Cabdrivers Diabetic Linctus
Cabdrivers Nasal Decongestant
  Tablets
Cafadol Tablets
Caffeine & Dextrose Tablets
Calcimax Syrup
Calcinate Tablets
Calcium Syrup (Berk
  Pharmaceuticals)
California Syrup of Figs
Calpol Six Plus Suspension
Calpol Tablets
Calsalettes Sugar Coated
  Tablets
Calsalettes Uncoated Tablets
Camfortix Linctus P1
Cantaflour
Capramin Tablets
Carbellon Tablets
Carbocisteine Capsules
Carbocisteine Syrup (any
  strength)
Carbocisteine Tablets (any
  strength)
Carisoma Compound Tablets
Carnation Instant Build-Up
Carrzone Powder
Carters Little Pills
Cascara Evacuant Liquid
  Mixture
Cascara Tablets BP
Castellan No 10 Cough Mixture
Catarrh & Bronchial Syrup
  (Thornton & Ross)
Catarrh Cough Syrup
  (Boots)
Catarrh Mixture (Herbal
  Laboratories)
Catarrh Syrup for Children
  (Boots)
Catarrh Tablets (Cathay)
Ce-Cobalin Syrup
Ceeyees Tablets
Celaton Rejuvenation Tablets
Celaton CH3 Strong & Calm
  Tablets
Celaton CH3 Triplus Tablets
Celaton CH3 + Ease & Vitality
  Tablets
Celaton Whole Wheat Germ
  Capsules
Celavit 1 Powder
Celavit 2 Powder
Celavit 3 Powder
Celevac Granules
Centrax Tablets 10 mg
Cephos Powders
Cephos Tablets
Charabs Tablets
Charvita Tablets
Cheroline Cough Linctus
Cherry Bark Cough Syrup
  Childrens (Loveridge)
Cherry Bark Linctus Adults
  (Loveridge)
Cherry Cough Balsam (Herbal
  Laboratories)
Cherry Cough Linctus (Savory &
  Moore)
Cherry Cough Mixture (Rusco)
Cherry Flavoured Extract of

Malt (Distillers)
Chest & Cough Tablets (Brome & Schimmer)
Chest & Cough Tablets (Kerbina)
Chest & Throat Tablets No 8,000 (English Grains)
Chest Pills (Brome & Schimmer)
Chest Tablets (Kerbina)
Chesty Cough Syrup (Scott & Bowne)
Chilblain Tablets (Boots)
Child's Cherry Flavoured Linctus (Cupal)
Children's Blackcurrant Cough Syrup (Rusco)
Children's Cherry Cough Syrup (Thornton & Ross)
Children's Cough Linctus (Ransoms)
Children's Cough Mixture (Beecham)
Children's Cough Mixture (Loveridge)
Children's Cough Syrup (Ayrton Saunders)
Children's Cough Syrup (Cox)
Children's Cough Syrup (Evans Medical)
Children's Cough Syrup (Thornbers)
Children's Medicine Liquid (Hall's)
Children's Phensic Tablets
Children's Wild Cherry Cough Linctus (Evans Medical)
Chilvax Tablets
Chocolate Laxative Tablets (Isola)
Chocovite Tablets
Cidal
Cinnamon Essence Medicinal Mixture (Langdale)
Cinnamon Tablets Medicinal (Langdale)
Cinota Drops
Citrosan Powder
Claradin Effervescent Tablets
Clarkes Blood Mixture
Cleansing Herb Dried (Potters)
Cleansing Herbs (Brome & Schimmer)
Cleansing Herbs Powder (Dorwest)
Clorazepate Dipotassium Capsules 7.5 mg
Clorazepate Dipotassium Capsules 15 mg
Clorazepate Dipotassium Tablets 15 mg
Co-op Aspirin Tablets BP 300 mg
Co-op Bronchial Mixture
Co-op Halibut Liver Oil Capsules BP
Co-op Paracetamol Tablets BP 500 mg
Co-op Soluble Aspirin Tablets BP 300 mg
Cobalin Injection 100 mcg/ml
Cobalin H Injection 250 mcg/ml
Cobalin H Injection 1000 mcg/ml
Cobalin Injection 250 mcg/ml
Cobalin Injection 500 mcg/ml
Cobalin Injection 1000 mcg/ml
Cod Liver Oil & Creosote Capsules (5 Oval) (R P Scherer)
Cod Liver Oil & Creosote Capsules (10 Oval) (R P Scherer)
Cod Liver Oil Caps 10 Minims (Woodward)
Cod Liver Oil High Potency Capsules (R P Scherer)
Cod Liver Oil with Malt Extract & Hypophosphite Syrup (Distillers)
Cod Liver Oil 0.3 ml Capsules (R P Scherer)
Cod Liver Oil 0.6 ml Capsules (R P Scherer)
Codanin Analgesic Tablets
Codis Soluble Tablets
Codural Tablets
Cojene Tablets
Cold & Influenza Capsules (Regent Laboratories)
Cold & Influenza Mixture (Boots)
Cold & Influenza Mixture (Davidson)
Cold & Influenza Mixture (Rusco)
Cold & Influenza Mixture (Thornton & Ross)
Cold Relief (Blackcurrant Flavour) Granular Powder Boots)
Cold Relief Capsules (Scott & Bowne)
Cold Relief Tablets (Boots)
Cold Tablets (Roberts)
Coldrex Powder
Coldrex Tablets
Colgard Emergency Essence (Lane Health Products)
Collins Elixir
Colocynth & Jalap Tablets

Compound BPC 1963
Colocynth Compound Pills BPC 1963
Cologel Liquid
Complan
Comploment Continus Tablets
Compound Fig Elixir BP
Compound Rhubarb Oral Powder BP
Compound Rhubarb Tincture BP
Compound Syrup of Glycerophosphates BPC 1963
Compound Syrup of Hypophosphites BPC 1963
Comtrex Capsules
Comtrex Liquid
Comtrex Tablets
Concavit Capsules
Concavit Drops
Concavit Injection
Concavit Syrup
Congesteze Syrup
Congesteze Tablets
Congreves Balsamic Elixir
Constipation Herb Dried (Potters)
Constipation Herbs (Hall's)
Constipation Herbs (Mixed Herbs) (Brome & Schimmer)
Constipation Mixture No 105 (Potters)
Contac 400 Capsules
Copholco Cough Syrup
Corrective Tablets (Ayrton Saunders)
Correctol Tablets
Cosalgesic Tablets
Cosylan Syrup
Coterpin Syrup
Cough and Bronchitis Mixture (Davidson)
Cough and Cold Mixture (Beecham)
Cough Balsam (Abernethy's)
Cough Balsam (Thornbers)
Cough Expectorant Elixir (Regent Laboratories)
Cough Linctus (Sanderson's)
Cough Linctus Alcoholic (Thomas Guest)
Cough Linctus for Children (Boots)
Cough Medicine for Infants & Children Solution (Boots)
Cough Mixture (Tingles)
Cough Mixture Adults (Thornton & Ross)
Cough Mixture Adults (Wicker Herbal Stores)
Cough Syrup Best (Diopharm)
Cough Tablets (Kerbina)
Covermark Removing Cream
Covonia Bronchial Balsam Linctus
Cox Pain Tablets
Crampex Tablets
Cream of Magnesia Tablets 300 mg
Cremaffin Emulsion
Creosote Bronchial Mixture (Loveridge)
Crookes One-a-Day Multivitamins with Iron
Crookes One-a-Day Multivitamins without Iron
Croupline Cough Syrup (Roberts)
Cupal Health Salts
Cyanocobalamin Injection BP
Cyanocobalamin Solution (any strength)
Cyanocobalamin Tablets (any strength)
Cytacon Liquid
Cytacon Tablets
Cytamen 250 Injection
Cytamen 1000 Injection

Dakin's Golden Vitamin Malt Syrup
Dalivit Capsules
Dalivit Syrup
Dalmane Capsules 15 mg
Dalmane Capsules 30 mg
Dansac Skin Lotion
Davenol Linctus
Daxaids Tablets
Day-Vits Multivitamin & Mineral Tablets
Dayovite
De Witt's Analgesic Pills
De Witt's Antacid Powder
De Witt's Antacid Tablets
De Witt's Baby Cough Syrup
De Witt's Cough Syrup
De Witt's PL Pills
Deakin & Hughes Cough & Cold Healer Mixture
Deakin's Fever & Inflammation Remedy Mixture
Delax Emulsion
Delimon
Dentakit Toothache First Aid Kit
Derbac Soap
Dermacolor Cleansing Cream
Dermacolor Cleansing Lotion
Dermacolor Cleansing Milk
Desiccated Liver Tablets

Desiccated Liver USNF Tablets
Detox Tablets (Hursdrex)
Dextrogesic Tablets
Dextromethorphan Hydrobromide Syrup 6.6 mg/5 ml
Dextromethorphan Hydrobromide Syrup 13.5 mg/5 ml
Dextropropoxyphene and Paracetamol Soluble Tablets
Dextropropoxyphene and Paracetamol Dispersible Tablets
DF 118 Elixir
DF 118 Injection
DF 118 Tablets
DGL 1 Suspension
DGL 2 Suspension
DGT 1 Tablets
DGT 2 Tablets
Diabetic Bronal Syrup
Dialar Forte Syrup 5 mg/5 ml
Dialar Syrup 2 mg/5 ml
Dialume Capsules 500 mg
Digesprin Antacid Tablets
Digestells Lozenges
Dihydroxyaluminium Sodium Carbonate Tablets
Dijex Liquid
Dijex Tablets
Dimotane Expectorant
Dimotane Expectorant DC
Dimotane with Codeine Elixir
Dimotane with Codeine Paediatric Elixir
Dimotapp Elixir
Dimotapp Elixir Paediatric
Dimotapp LA Tablets
Dimotapp P Tablets
Dimyril Linctus
Dinnefords Gripe Mixture
Diovol Suspension
Diovol Tablets
Disprin Tablets
Disprinex Tablets
Distalgesic Soluble Tablets
Distalgesic Tablets
Do-Do Linctus
Do-Do Tablets
Dolasan Tablets
Doloxene Capsules
Doloxene Compound Pulvules
Dolvan Tablets
Dormonoct Tablets 1 mg
Dr Brandreth's Pills
Dr D E Jongh's Cod Liver Oil with Malt Extract & Vitamins Fortified Syrup
Dr William's Pink Pills
Drastin Tablets
Dristan Decongestant Tablets with Antihistamine
Dristan Nasal Spray
Droxalin Tablets
Dry Cough Linctus (Scott & Bowne)
Dual-Lax Extra Strong Tablets
Dual-Lax Tablets
Dulca Tablets
Dulcodos Tablets
Dulcolax Suppositories
Dulcolax Tablets
Duo-Gastritis Mixture (Baldwin's)
Duphalac Syrup
Duralin Capsules Extra Strength
Duralin Tablets
Duttons Cough Mixture
Dynese Aqueous Suspension
Dynese Plus Aqueous Suspension
Dynese Tablets
D001 Capsules
D002 Capsules
D004 Capsules
D006 Capsules
D007 Capsules
D009 Capsules
D010 Capsules
D011 Capsules
D012 Capsules
D013 Capsules
D014 Capsules
D017 Capsules
D018 Capsules
D019 Capsules
D020 Capsules
D021 Capsules
D024 Capsules
D029 Capsules
D030 Capsules
D031 Capsules
D032 Capsules
D033 Capsules
D034 Capsules
D036 Capsules

Ecdilyn Syrup
Educol Tablets
Efamol Capsules
Effer-C Tablets
Effico Syrup
Eldermint Cough Mixture (Herbal Laboratories)
Elkamol Tablets
Endet Powders
Energen Starch Reduced Crispbread
Engran HP Tablets
Engran Tablets

Eno Fruit Salts
EP Tablets
Equagesic Tablets
Eskornade Spansule Capsules
Eskornade Syrup
Eso-Col Cold Treatment Tablets
Euhypnos Capsules 10 mg
Euhypnos Elixir 10 mg/5 ml
Euhypnos Forte Capsules 20 mg
Evacalm Tablets 2 mg
Evacalm Tablets 5 mg
Evans Cough Balsam
Ex-Lax Chocolate Laxative Tablets
Ex-Lax Pills
Expectorant Cough Mixtures (Beecham)
Expulin Cough Linctus
Expulin Paediatric Cough Linctus
Expurhin Paediatric Decongestant
Extil Compound Linctus
Extravite Tablets
Extren Tablets
Exyphen Elixir
E001 Capsules
E015 Capsules
E018 Capsules
E021 Capsules
E031 Capsules
E032 Capsules

Fabrol Granules
Falcodyl Linctus
Fam Lax Tablets
Famel Expectorant
Famel Linctus
Famel Original Linctus
Family Cherry Flavoured Linctus (Cupal)
Family Herbal Pills
Father Pierre's Monastery Herbs
Fe-Cap C Capsules
Feac Tablets
Feen-a-Mint Tablets
Fefol-Vit Spansules
Femerital Tablets
Feminax Tablets
Fendamin Tablets
Fennings Adult Powders
Fennings Children's Cooling Powders
Fennings Little Healers Pills
Fennings Mixture
Fennings Soluble Junior Aspirin Tablets
Fenox Nasal Drops
Fenox Nasal Spray
Ferfolic SV Tablets
Ferfolic Tablets
Fergluvite Tablets
Ferraplex B Tablets
Ferrlecit Tablets/Dragees
Ferrocap Capsules
Ferrograd C Tablets
Ferrol Compound Mixture
Ferromyn B Elixir
Ferromyn B Tablets
Ferrous Gluconate Compound Tablets
Fesovit Spansules
Fesovit 2 Spansules
Fibre Biscuits
Fine Fare Aspirin Tablets 300 mg
Fine Fare Hot Lemon Powders
Flar Capsules
Flavelix Syrup
Flora Margarine
Floradix Formula Liquid
Floradix Tablets
Floral Arbour Tablets (Cathay)
Flu-Rex Tablets
Flucaps
Flunitrazepam Tablets 1 mg
Fluralar Capsules 15 mg
Fluralar Capsules 30 mg
Flurazepan Capsules 15 mg
Flurazepam Capsules 30 mg
Flurazepam Hydrochloride Capsules 15 mg
Flurazepam Hydrochloride Capsules 30 mg
Folped
Forceval Capsules
Forceval Junior Capsules
Forprin Tablets
Fortagesic Tablets
Fortimel
Fortison Low Sodium
Fortral Capsules 50 mg
Fortral Injection
Fortral Suppositories
Fortral Tablets 25 mg
Fortral Tablets 50 mg
Fortris Solution
Fosfor Syrup
Franol Expectorant
Franolyn Sed Liquid
Frisium Capsules 5 mg
Frisium Capsules 10 mg
Frisium Capsules 20 mg
Fybranta Tablets
Fynnon Calcium Aspirin Tablets
Fynnon Salt

G Brand Linctus
Galfer-Vit Capsules
Galloway's Baby Cough Linctus

Galloway's Bronchial Expectorant
Galloway's Cough Syrup
Gamophen
Gastalar Tablets
Gastric Ulcer Tablets no 1001
Gastrils Pastilles
Gastritabs
Gastrovite Tablets
Gatinar Syrup
Gaviscon Granules
Gelusil Lac Powder
Gelusil Tablets
Genasprin Tablets
Genatosan
Gentian & Rhubarb Mixture BPC
Georges Vapour Rub Ointment
Geriplex Capsules
Gevral Capsules
GF Brand Gluten-Free Maize Biscuits with Chocolate
GF Brand Gluten-Free Maize Biscuits with Hazel-Nut
GF Brand Gluten-Free Thin Wafer Bread
Givitol Capsules
Gladlax Tablets
Glemony Balsam (Baldwin's)
Glenco Elixir
Gluca-Seltzer Effervescent Powder
Glucodin
Glycerin Honey & Lemon Cough Mixture (Isola)
Glycerin Honey & Lemon Linctus (Boots)
Glycerin Honey & Lemon Linctus with Ipecacuanha (Boots)
Glycerin Lemon & Honey and Ipecac (Thomas Guest)
Glycerin Lemon & Honey Linctus (Rusco)
Glycerin Lemon & Honey Syrup (Cupal)
Glycerin Lemon & Honey Syrup (Thomas Guest)
Glycerin Lemon & Honey Syrup (Waterhouse)
Glycerin Lemon & Ipecac Cough Mixture (Isola)
Glykola Elixir
Glykola Infants Elixir
Golden Age Vitamin & Mineral Capsules
Golden Health Tablet (Kerbina)
Golden Health Tablets (Brome & Schimmer)
Gon Tablets
Gonfalcon Tablets
Grangewood Insomnia Tablets
Granogen
Granoton Emulsion
Gregovite C Tablets
GS Tablets
Guaiphenesin Syrup (any strength)
Guanor Expectorant

H-Pantoten Tablets
Hactos Chest & Cough Mixture (Thomas Hubert)
Halaurant Syrup
Halcion Tablets 0.125 mg
Halcion Tablets 0.25 mg
Haliborange Syrup
Halibut Liver Oil A & D Capsules (Rodale)
Halin Tablets
Halocaps Inhalant Capsules
Halycitrol Emulsion
Haymine Tablets
Hayphryn Nasal Spray
Health Salts (Wicker Herbal Stores)
Health Tonic Mixture (Hall's)
Heart Shape Indigestion Tablets
Hedex Plus Capsules
Hedex Seltzer Granules
Hedex Soluble Granules
Hedex Tablets
Hemingways Catarrh Syrup
Hemoplex Injection
Hepacon B12 Injection
Hepacon Liver Extract Injection
Hepacon-Plex
Hepacon-B-Forte Injection
Hepanorm Tablets
Herbal Aperient Tablets (Cathay)
Herbal Aperient Tablets (Kerbina)
Herbal Bronchial Cough Tablets (English Grains)
Herbal Laxative Naturtabs
Herbal Pile Tablets
Herbal Quiet Nite Sleep Naturtabs
Herbal Syrup (Baldwin's)
Herbalene Herbs
Hi-g-ah Tea
Hi-pro Liver Tablets
Hill's Bronchial Balsam
Hill's Junior Balsam
Hip C Rose Hip Syrup
Histalix Expectorant
Honey & Molasses Cough Mixture (Lane Health Products)
Hot Lemon Cold Treatment (Scott & Bowne)
Hot Measure Solution (Reckitt & Colman)
Hydrotalcite Suspension 500 mg/5 ml
Hydrotalcite Tablets 500 mg
Hypon Tablets

Iberet 500 Tablets
Iberol Tablets
ICC Analgesic Tablets
Iliadin Mini Nasal Drops
Iliadin Mini Paediatric Nasal Drops
Imarale Agba Suspension
Imarale Omode Suspension
Inabrin Tablets 200 mg
Indian Brandy Solution
Indigestion Mixture (Boots)
Indigestion Mixture (Thornton & Ross)
Indigestion Mixture (William Ransom)
Indigo Indigestion Lozenges
Influenza and Cold Mixture 2315 (Wright Layman & Umney)
Inhalit Liquid Inhalation
Iodinated Glycerol Elixir 60 mg/5 ml
Iodo-Ephedrine Mixture
Iodised Vitamin Capsules
Ipecacuanha Pills 20 mg
Ipecacuanha & Morphine Mixture BP
Ipecacuanha & Squill Linctus Paediatric BPC
Ipsel Hygienic Babysalve
Irofol C
Iron & Brewers Yeast Tablets (3M Health Care)
Iron & Vitamin Tablets (Davidson)
Iron Formula Tablets (Rodale)
Iron Jelloids Tablets
Iron Tonic Tablets (Boots)
Ironorm Capsules
Ironorm Tonic
Ironplan Capsules
Ivy Tablets (Ayrton Saunders)

Jaap's Health Salts
Jacksons All Fours Cough Mixture
Jacksons Febrifuge
Jambomins Tablets
Jenners Suspension
Jenners Tablets
Junamac
Jung Junipah Tablets
Junior Cabdrivers Linctus
Junior Disprin Tablets
Junior Ex-Lax Chocolate Tablets
Junior Lemsip Powder
Junior Meltus Cough & Catarrh Linctus
Junior Mucron Liquid
Junior Tablets (Rodale)
Juno-Junipah Mineral Salts
Juvel Elixir
Juvel Tablets

Karvol Capsules
Kendales Adult Cough Syrup
Kendales Cherry Linctus
Kest Tablets
Ketazolam Capsules 15 mg
Ketazolam Capsules 30 mg
Ketazolam Capsules 45 mg
Keybells Linctus of Glycerine, Lemon & Ipecac
Kingo Cough Syrup
Koladex Tablets
Kolanticon Gel
Kolanticon Tablets
Kolanticon Wafers
Kolantyl Gel
Krauses Cough Linctus
Kruschen Salts
Kuralax Herbs

Labiton Kola Tonic
Laboprin Tablets
Lac Bismuth Mixture
Lacto Calamine
Laevoral
Lance B & C Tablets
Lane's Cut-a-Cough
Lane's Laxative Herb Tablets
Lane's Sage & Garlic Catarrh Remedy
Lantigen B
Laxaliver Pills
Laxatabs Leoren
Laxipurg Tablets
Laxoberal Elixir
Lederplex Capsules
Lederplex Liquid
Lejfibre Biscuit
Lem-Plus Hot Lemon Drink
Lemeze Cough Syrup
Lemon Eno Powder
Lemon Flu-Cold Concentrated Syrup
Lemon Glycerine & Honey Cough Syrup Compound (Carter Bond)
Lemon Glycerine & Honey Lung Mixture (Whitehall Laboratories)
Lemon Glycerine & Ipecac Cough Syrup Compound (Carter Bond)
Lemon Juice, Glycerine & Honey A S Syrup (Ayrton Saunders)
Lemon Linctus 1-472
Lemsip Powder
Lendormin Tablets 0.125 mg
Lendormin Tablets 0.25 mg
Leoren Tonic Tablets
Levius Controlled Release Tablets 500 mg
Lexotan Tablets 1.5 mg
Lexotan Tablets 3 mg
Lexotan Tablets 6 mg
Libraxin Tablets

Librium Capsules 5 mg
Librium Capsules 10 mg
Librium Tablets 5 mg
Librium Tablets 10 mg
Librium Tablets 25 mg
Lightning Cough Remedy Solution (Potters)
Limbitrol Capsules '5'
Limbitrol Capsules '10'
Linctifed Expectorant
Linctifed Expectorant Paediatric
Linctoid C
Linituss
Linoleic Acid Naudicelle, Efamol, Evening Primrose Oil
Linus Vitamin C Powder
Lipoflavonoid Capsules
Lipotriad Capsules
Lipotriad Liquid
Liqufruta Blackcurrant Cough Medicine
Liqufruta Honey & Lemon Cough Medicine
Liqufruta Medica
Liqufruta Medica Garlic Flavoured Cough Medicine
Liquid Formula (Food Concentrate) (Rodale)
Liquid Paraffin & Phenolphthalein Emulsion BP
Liquid Paraffin Emulsion with Cascara BPC
Liver Herbs (Hall's)
Livibron Mixture
Loasid Tablets
Lobak Tablets
Lofthouse's Original Fisherman's Friend Honey Cough Syrup
Loprazolam Tablets 1 mg
Loramet Capsules 1 mg
Loramet Tablets 0.5 mg
Loramet Tablets 1 mg
Lormetazepam Capsules 1 mg
Lormetazepam Tablets 0.5 mg
Lormetazepam Tablets 1 mg
Lotussin Cough Syrup
Lung Balsam (Rusco)
Lysaldin

M & B Children's Cough Linctus
Maalox Concentrate Suspension
Maalox Plus Suspension
Maalox Plus Tablets
Maalox Tablets
Maalox TC Tablets
Mackenzies Smelling Salts
Maclean Indigestion Powder
Maclean Indigestion Tablets
Magaldrate Tablets
Mainstay Pure Cod Liver Oil
Male Gland Double Strength Supplement Tablets
Male Sex Hormone Tablets (Diopharm)
Malinal Suspension 500 mg/5 ml
Malinal Tablets 500 mg
Malt Extract with Cod Liver Oil & Chemical Food (Distillers)
Malt Extract with Cod Liver Oil BPC & Hypophosphite (Distillers)
Malt Extract with Cod Liver Oil BPC Soft Extract (Jeffreys Miller)
Malt Extract with Haemoglobin & Vitamins Syrup (Distillers)
Malt Extract with Halibut Liver-Oil Syrup (Distillers)
Mandarin Tablets
Manna Herbal Rheumapainaway Tablets
Matthew Cough Mixture
Maturaplus Tablets
Maxivits Tablets
Medathlon Aspirin Tablets 300 mg
Medazepam Capsules 5 mg
Medazepam Capsules 10 mg
Medex Elixir
Medilax Tablets
Medipain Tablets
Medised Suspension
Medised Tablets
Meditus Syrup
Medocodene Tablets
Meggeson Dyspepsia Tablets
Melissin Syrup
Melo Brand Glycerin Lemon & Honey with Ipecac
Meloids Lozenges
Menthacol Liquid
Menthells Pellet/Pill
Menthol & Benzoin Inhalation BP
Menthol & Eucalyptus (M in P) Pastilles (Thomas Guest)
Menthol Inhalation
Mentholated Balsam (Loveridge)
Mentholated Balsam (Savory & Moore)
Mentholated Balsam (Wright Layman & Umney)
Mentholated Balsam Mixture (Pilsworth Manufacturing)
Mentholatum Balm
Metatone
Methylcisteine Tablets 100 mg
Midro-Tea Powder
Milk of Magnesia Tablets
Mil-Par Suspension
Minadex Syrup
Minamino Syrup
Minivits Tablets
Modifast Nutritionally Complete

Supplemented Fasting Formula
Mogadon Capsules 5 mg
Mogadon Tablets 5 mg
Moorland Indigestion Tablets
Morning Glory Tablets
Mrs Cullen's Lemsoothe Powder
Mrs Cullen's Powders
Mu-Cron Tablets
Mucodyne Capsules
Mucodyne Syrup
Mucodyne Forte Syrup
Mucodyne Forte Tablets
Mucodyne Paediatric Syrup
Mucofalk Sachets
Mucogel Tablets
Mucolex Syrup
Mucolex Tablets
Mucron Liquid
Muflin Linctus
Multi-Vitamin Tablets (English Grains)
Multivitamin Capsules (Regent Laboratories)
Multivitamin Tablets (Approved Prescription Services)
Multivitamin Tablets (Chemipharm)
Multivitamin Tablets (Evans Medical)
Multivitamin Tablets (UAC International)
Multivitamin with Mineral Capsules (Potters)
Multivitamin with Minerals Tablets (Chemipharm)
Multivite Pellets
Multone Tablets
My Baby Cough Syrup
Mycolactine Tablets
Mylanta Liquid
Mylanta Tablets
Myolgin Tablets

N Tonic Syrup (Cupal)
N-300 Capsules
Napoloids Tablets
Napsalgesic Tablets
Natex 12A Tablets
Natural Bran
Natural Herb Laxative Tablet (Kerbina)
Natural Herb Laxative Tablet (Brome & Schimmer)
Natural Herb Tablets (Dorwest)
Natural Herb Tablets (Kerbina)
Natural Herb Tablets (Lane)
Naturavite Tablets
Neo-Cytamen Injection 250 mcg/ml
Neo-Cytamen Injection 1000 mcg/ml
Neoklenz Powder
Neophyrn Nasal Drops
Neophyrn Nasal Spray
Nethaprin Expectorant
Neuro Phosphates
Neurodyne Capsules
Neutradonna Powder
Neutradonna Sed Powder
Neutradonna Sed Tablets
Neutradonna Tablets
Neutragena Soap
Neutrolactis Tablets
New Formula Beechams Powders Capsules
New Life Herbs
New Life Tablets
Newton's Children's Cough Treatment
Newton's Cough Mixture for Adults
Nezcaam Syrup
Nicobrevin
Nicorette
Night Nurse Cold Remedy
Nirolex Expectorant Linctus
Nitrados Tablets 5 mg
Nitrazepam Capsules 5 mg
Nivea
No 177 Tablets (Leoren)
Nobrium Capsules 5 mg
Nobrium Capsules 10 mg
Nocold Tablets
Noctamid Tablets 0.5 mg
Noctamid Tablets 1 mg
Noctesed Tablets 5 mg
Noradran Bronchial Syrup
Norgesic Tablets
Normacol Antispasmodic
Normacol Standard Granules
Normacol Standard Sugar Free Formula Granules
Normison Capsules 10 mg
Normison Capsules 20 mg
Norvits Syrup
Noscapine Linctus BP
Novasil Antacid Tablets
Novasil Antacid Viscous Suspension
Nulacin Tablets
Nurodol Tablets
Nurofen Tablets 200 mg
Nurse Sykes Powders
Nurse Sykes Bronchial Balsam
Nux Vomica Elixir BPC
Nylax Tablets

Oilatum Bar
Olbas Oil
Omeiri Iron Tonic Tablets
Omilcaf Suspension
Onadox 118 Tablets
One Gram C Capsules
Opas Powder
Opas Tablets
Opobyl Bailly Pills

Orange & Halibut Vitamins (Kirby Warrick Pharmaceuticals)
Organadin Elixir
Organidin Solution
Organidin Tablets
Original Indigestion Tablets (Boots)
Orovite Elixir
Orovite Tablets
Orovite 7
Orthoxicol Syrup
Otrivine Nasal Drops 0.05%
Otrivine Nasal Drops 0.1%
Otrivine Nasal Spray 0.1%
Otrivine-Antistin Nasal Drops
Otrivine-Antistin Nasal Spray
Overnight Bedtime Cold Medicine
Owbridge's Cough Mixture
Oxanid Tablets 10 mg
Oxanid Tablets 15 mg
Oxanid Tablets 30 mg
Oxymetazoline Hydrochloride Nasal Drops 0.025%
Oxymetazoline Hydrochloride Nasal Drops 0.05%
Oxymetazoline Hydrochloride Nasal Spray 0.05%

Pacidal Tablets
Paedo-Sed Syrup
Pain Relief Tablets (Cox)
Pain Relief Tablets (Davidson)
Panacron Tablets
Panadeine Co. Tablets
Panadeine Forte Tablets
Panadeine Soluble Effervescent Tablets
Panadeine Tablets
Panadol Caplets
Panadol Soluble Tablets
Panadol Tablets
Panasorb Tablets
Panets Tablets
Pango Pain Paracetamol Codeine Tablets (Cupal)
Papain Compound Tablets
Paprika Tablets (Kerbina)
Para-Seltzer Effervescent Tablets
Paracetamol & Caffeine Capsules
Paracetamol & Caffeine Tablets
Paracetamol DC Tablets
Paracetamol Dispersible Tablets
Paracetamol Soluble Tablets
Paracetamol Tablets Soluble (Boots)
Paracets Tablets 500 mg
Paracodol Tablets
Paradeine R Tablets
Paragesic Effervescent Tablets
Parahypon Tablets
Parake Tablets
Paralgin Tablets
Paramol Tablets
Paranorm Cough Syrup
Pardale Tablets
Parenamps Intramuscular Injection
Pastilaids Pastilles
Pavacol Cough Syrup
Paxadon Tablets
Paynocil Tablets
PEM Linctus
Penetrol Inhalant
Pentazocine-Aspirin Compound Tablets
Peplax Peppermint Flavoured Laxative Tablets
Peppermint Indigestion Tablets (Boots)
Pepto-Bismol Suspension
Pernivit Tablets
Persomnia Tablets
Petrolagar Emulsion Plain
Petrolagar Emulsion with Phenolphthalein
PF Plus Tablets
Pharmacin Capsules
Pharmacin Effervescent Plus C Tablets
Pharmacin Effervescent Tablets 325 mg
Pharmaton Capsules
Pharmidone Tablets
Phenergan Compound Expectorant Linctus
Phenolphthalein Tablets BP
Phenolphthalein Compound Tablets BPC 1963
Phenolphthalein Compound Pills BPC
Phensedyl Cough Linctus
Phensic Tablets
Phensic 2 Tablets
Phenylephrine Hydrochloride Nasal Drops 0.25%
Phenylephrine Hydrochloride Nasal Spray 0.5%
Phillips Iron Tonic Tablets
Phillips Tonic Yeast Tablets
Pholcolix Syrup
Pholcomed Diabetic Forte Linctus
Pholcomed Expectorant
Pholcomed Forte Linctus
Pholcomed Linctus
Pholtex Syrup
Pholtussa Mixture
Phosferine Liquid
Phosferine Multi-Vitamin Liquid
Phosferine Tablets
Phyllosan Tablets
Physeptone Linctus

Pile Mixture (Ayrton Saunders)
Pile Tablets (Ayrton Saunders)
Pine Catarrh Drops Lozenges
Plenamin Super
Plenivite with Iron Tablets
Plurivite M Tablets
Plurivite Tablets
Polyalk Gel
Polyalk Tablets
Polycrol Forte Gel
Polycrol Forte Tablets
Polycrol Gel
Polycrol Tablets
Polyvite Capsules
Potaba +6 Capsules
Potaba +6 Tablets
Potassium Bromide & Nux Vomica Mixture BPC 1963
Powdered Bran Tablets 2 g
Power Plus Super Multivitamin and Mineral Capsules
Powerin Tablets
PP Tablets
PR Tablets
Prazepam Tablets 10 mg
PRD 200 Tablets 600 mg
Pregnadon Tablets
Pregnavite Forte F Tablets
Pregnavite Forte Tablets
Premit Tablets 20 mg
Prenatal Dri-Kaps Capsules
Primes Premiums Tablets
Priory Cleansing Herbs Powder
Procol Capsules
Proctofibre Tablets
Prodexin Tablets
Proflex Tablets 200 mg
Progesic Tablets 200 mg
Propain Tablets
Pro-Plus He-Vite Elixir
Proteolised Liver Tablets
Pro-Vitamin A Capsules (Rodale)
Pru Sen Tablet Bar
Pulmo Bailly Liquid
Purgoids Tablets

Q-Panol Tablets
Quick Action Cough Cure (Brian C Spencer)
Quiet Life Tablets

Raspberry Tablets No B039
Rayglo Chest Rub Ointment
Rayglo Laxative Tablets
Reactivan Tablets
Red Catarrh Pastilles (Baldwin)
Redelan Effervescent Tablets
Redoxon Adult Multivitamin Tablets
Redoxon C Effervescent Tablet 1 g
Redoxon C Tablets 25 mg
Redoxon C Tablets 50 mg
Redoxon C Tablets 200 mg
Redoxon C Tablets 250 mg
Redoxon C Tablets 500 mg
Redoxon Children's Multivitamin Tablets
Redoxon Effervescent Tablets 1 g
Reg-U-Lett Tablets
Relanium Tablets 2 mg
Relanium Tablets 5 mg
Relanium Tablets 10 mg
Relcol Tablets
Remnos Tablets 5 mg
Remnos Tablets 10 mg
Rennie Tablets
Respaton
Rheumavit Tablets
Rhuaka Herbal Syrup
Rhuaka Tablets
Rhubarb & Soda Mixture Ammoniated BP
Rhubarb Compound Mixture BPC
Rhubarb Mixture Compound Paediatric BPC
Riddovydrin Liquid
Rinurel Linctus
Rinurel Tablets
Rite-Diet Gluten-Free Biscuits (chocolate chip cookies; half-coated chocolate biscuits; custard cream biscuits; sultana biscuit; soya bran; Lincoln and shortcake)
Rite-Diet Gluten-Free Canned Rich Fruit Cake
Robaxisal Forte Tablets
Roberts Aspirin & Caffeine Tablets
Robitussin AC Liquid
Robitussin Liquid
Robitussin Syrup
ROC Total Sunblock Creams (light tan; deep tan)
Rock Salmon Cough Mixture
Rohypnol Tablets 1 mg
Roscorbic Effervescent Tablets
Roscorbic Tablets 25 mg
Roscorbic Tablets 50 mg
Roscorbic Tablets 200 mg
Roscorbic Tablets 500 mg
Rose Hip C-100 Capsules
Rose Hip C-200 Capsules
Rose Hip Tablets (English Grains)
Rose Hip Tablets (Potters)
Rose Hip Tablets (Roberts)
Rosmax Syrup
Roter Tablets
Rovigon
Rubelix Syrup
Rubraton B Elixir
Ruby Tonic Tablets (Jacksons)

Rum Cough Elixir
Rutin Plus Tablets (Gerard)

Safapryn Tablets
Safapryn-Co Tablets
Safflower Seed Oil
Sainsbury's Cold Powders with Blackcurrant
Sainsbury's Hot Lemon Powders
Sainsbury's Indigestion Tablets
Sainsbury's Junior Soluble Aspirin Tablets
Sainsbury's Paracetamol Tablets 500 mg
Sainsbury's Soluble Aspirin Tablets
Sainsbury's Aspirin Tablets 300 mg
Salzone Tablets 500 mg
Sanatogen Junior Vitamins Tablets
Sanatogen Multivitamins Plus Iron (Formula One) Tablets
Sanatogen Multivitamins Tablets
Sanatogen Nerve Tonic Powder
Sanatogen Selected Multivitamins Plus Iron (Formula Two) Tablets
Sanatogen Tonic
Sancos Compound Linctus
Sancos Syrup
Savant Tablets
Saxin
SBL Junior Cough Linctus
SBL Soothing Bronchial Linctus
Scott's Cod Liver Oil Capsules
Scott's Emulsion
Scott's Husky Biscuits
Seaweed Vitamin A Ester BP & Vitamin D BP Capsules (Regent Laboratories)
Sedazin Tablets 1 mg
Sedazin Tablets 2.5 mg
Senna Laxative Tablets (Boots)
Senna Tablets (Potters)
Senokot Tablets
Senotabs Tablets
Serenid D Tablets 10 mg
Serenid D Tablets 15 mg
Serenid Forte Capsules 30 mg
Sertin Tablets
Setamol Soluble Tablets
Setlers Tablets
Seven Seas Cod Liver Oil
Seven Seas Formula 70 Multivitamin-Multimineral Capsules
Seven Seas Orange Syrup & Cod Liver Oil
Seven Seas Pure Cod Liver Oil Capsules
Seven Seas Start Right Cod Liver Oil for Babies
Sidros Tablets
Silk-Lax Tablets
Siloxyl Suspension
Siloxyl Tablets
Simple Soap
Sine-off Tablets
Sinutab Tablets
Skin Glow Capsules
SMA Gold Cap Powder and Ready-to-Feed
SMA Powder and Concentrated Liquid
Snufflebabe Vapour Rub
Solis Capsules 2 mg
Solis Capsules 5 mg
Solis Capusles 10 mg
Solmin Tablets
Solpadeine Forte Tablets
Solpadeine Tablets Effervescent
Solprin Tablets
Soluble Aspirin Tablets for Children (Boots)
Soluble Phensic Tablets
Somnite Suspension 2.5 mg/5 ml
Somnite Tablets 5 mg
Sovol Liquid
Sovol Tablets
Soya Powder & Nicotinamide Tablets
Special Stomach Powder (Halls)
SPHP Tablets
Squill Linctus Opiate BP (Gee's Linctus)
Squill Linctus Opiate, Paediatric, BP
Squire's Soonax Tablets
SR 2310 Expectorant
Staffords Mild Aperient Tablets
Staffords Strong Aperient Tablets
Sterling Health Salts Effervescent
Sterling Indigestion Tablets
Sterling Paracetamol Tablets
Sterogyl Alcoholic Solution
Stomach Aids Tablets
Stomach Mixture (Herbal Laboratories)
Stomach Mixture H138 (Southon Laboratories)
Stomach Powder (Diopharm)
Stomach Tablets (Ulter)
Street's Cough Mixture
Strenghtening Mixture (Hall's)
Stress B Supplement Tablets
Strychnine Mixture BPC 1963
Strychnine & Iron Mixture BPC 1963
Sudafed Co Tablets
Sudafed Expectorant
Sudafed SA Capsules
Sunerven Tablets

Super Plenamins Tablets
Super Yeast + C Tablets
Superdrug Health Salts
Surbex-T Tablets
Surem Capsules 5 mg
Surem Capsules 10 mg
Surlax Laxative Tablets
Sweetex
Sylopal Suspension
Sylphen Tablets
Syn-Ergel
Syndol Tablets
Syrtussar Cough Syrup

T-Zone Decongestant Tablets
Tabasan Tablets
Tablets No B006
Tablets No B011
Tablets No B015
Tablets No B024
Tablets No B025
Tablets No B029
Tablets No B034
Tablets No B035
Tablets No B036
Tablets No B037
Tablets No B038
Tablets No B040
Tablets No B041
Tablets No B045
Tablets No B048
Tablets No B070
Tablets No 268A (Potters)
Tablets to Formula A10
Tablets to Formula A11
Tablets to Formula A18
Tablets to Formula A19
Tablets to Formula A20
Tablets to Formula A22
Tablets to Formula A23
Tablets to Formula A31
Tablets to Formula A32
Tablets to Formula A33
Tablets to Formula A45
Tablets to Formula A51
Tablets to Formula A63
Tablets to Formula A67
Tablets to Formula A68
Tablets to Formula A69
Tablets to Formula A70
Tablets to Formula A71
Tablets to Formula A105
Tablets to Formula A111
Tablets to Formula A114
Tablets to Formula A120
Tablets to Formula A147
Tablets to Formula A157
Tablets to Formula A158
Tablets to Formula A161
Tablets to Formula A162
Tablets to Formula A164
Tablets to Formula A165
Tablets to Formula A166
Tablets to Formula A167
Tablets to Formula A169
Tablets to Formula A175
Tablets to Formula A183
Tablets to Formula A184
Tablets to Formula A190
Tablets to Formula A195
Tablets to Formula A202
Tablets to Formula A203
Tablets to Formula A213
Tablets to Formula A221
Tablets to Formula A244
Tablets to Formula A245
Tablets to Formula A246
Tablets to Formula A247
Tablets to Formula A248
Tablets to Formula A249
Tablets to Formula A250
Tablets to Formula A264
Tablets to Formula A266
Tablets to Formula A270
Tablets to Formula A271
Tablets to Formula A272
Tablets to Formula A273
Tablets to Formula A274
Tablets to Formula A275
Tablets to Formula A276
Tablets to Formula A277
Tablets to Formula A298
Tablets to Formula A301
Tablets to Formula A316
Tablets to Formula BA6
Tablets to Formula B10
Tablets to Formula B15
Tablets to Formula B18
Tablets to Formula B19
Tablets to Formula B20
Tablets to Formula B21
Tablets to Formula B22
Tablets to Formula B25
Tablets to Formula B26
Tablets to Formula B29
Tablets to Formula B41
Tablets to Formula B48
Tablets to Formula B51
Tablets to Formula B56
Tablets to Formula B58
Tablets to Formula B64
Tablets to Formula B65
Tablets to Formula B66
Tablets to Formula B67
Tablets to Formula B68
Tablets to Formula B70
Tablets to Formula B71
Tablets to Formula B72
Tablets to Formula B73
Tablets to Formula B74

Tablets to Formula B75
Tablets to Formula B76
Tablets to Formula B77
Tablets to Formula B78
Tablets to Formula B79
Tablets to Formula B80
Tablets to Formula B81
Tablets to Formula B82
Tablets to Formula B83
Tablets to Formula B85
Tablets to Formula B86
Tablets to Formula B87
Tablets to Formula B90
Tablets to Formula B91
Tablets to Formula B93
Tablets to Formula B94
Tablets to Formula B96
Tablets to Formula B98
Tablets to Formula B100
Tablets to Formula B102
Tablets to Formula B104
Tablets to Formula B117
Tablets to Formula B118
Tablets to Formula B120
Tablets to Formula B122
Tablets to Formula B124
Tablets to Formula B128
Tablets to Formula B141
Tablets to Formula B143
Tablets to Formula B145
Tablets to Formula B148
Tablets to Formula B156
Tablets to Formula B157
Tablets to Formula B158
Tablets to Formula B160
Tablets to Formula B163
Tablets to Formula B169
Tablets to Formula B178
Tablets to Formula B180
Tablets to Formula B181
Tablets to Formula B182
Tablets to Formula B190
Tablets to Formula B193
Tablets to Formula B207
Tablets to Formula B209
Tablets to Formula B210
Tablets to Formula B211
Tablets to Formula B212
Tablets to Formula B213
Tablets to Formula B214
Tablets to Formula B215
Tablets to Formula B216
Tablets to Formula B217
Tablets to Formula B218
Tablets to Formula B222
Tablets to Formula B223
Tablets to Formula B224
Tablets to Formula B225
Tablets to Formula B227
Tablets to Formula B228
Tablets to Formula B231
Tablets to Formula B234
Tablets to Formula B235
Tablets to Formula B236
Tablets to Formula B243
Tablets to Formula B248
Tablets to Formula B250
Tablets to Formula B251
Tablets to Formula B252
Tancolin Childrens Cough Linctus
Tedral Expectorant
Tensium Tablets 2 mg
Tensium Tablets 5 mg
Tensium Tablets 10 mg
Tercoda Elixir
Tercolix Elixir
Terpalin Elixir
Terperoin Elixir
Terpoin Antitussive
Terrabron
Three Noughts Cough Syrup
Titralac Tablets
Tixylix Cough Linctus
Tolu Solution BP
Tolu Syrup BP
Tolu Compound Linctus Paediatric BP
Tonatexa Mixture
Tonic Tablets (Thomas Guest)
Tonic Wines
Tonivitan A & D Syrup
Tonivitan B Syrup
Tonivitan Capsules
Top C Tablets
Toptabs
Totavit D R Capsules
Totolin Paediatric Cough Syrup
Tramil Capsules
Trancoprin Tablets
Tranxene Capsules 7.5 mg
Tranxene Capsules 15 mg
Tranxene Tablets 15 mg
Tritamyl Gluten-Free Bread Mix
Trifyba
Triocos Linctus
Triogesic Elixir
Triogesic Tablets
Triominic Syrup
Triominic Tablets
Triopaed Linctus
Triotussic Suspension
Triovit Tablets
Triple Action Cold Relief Tablets
Tropium Capsules 5 mg
Tropium Capsules 10 mg
Tropium Tablets 5 mg
Tropium Tablets 10 mg
Tropium Tablets 25 mg
Trufree Bread Mix
Trufree Pasta Mix
Trufree Plain Flour

Trufree Sweet Biscuit Mix
Tums Tablets
Tusana Linctus
Tussifans Syrup
Tussimed Liquid
Two-A-Day Iron Jelloids Tablets
Tysons Catarrh Syrup

Udenum Gastric Vitamin Powder
Ultracach Analgesic Capsules
Ultradal Antacid Stomach Tablets
Ultrarelief Tablets
Uncoated Tablets to Formula A323
Uncoated Tablets to Formula A325
Uniflu Tablets
Unigesic Capsules
Unigest Tablets
Unisomnia Tablets 5 mg
United Skin Care Programme (Uni-Derm; Uni-Salve; Uni-Wash)

Valium Capsules 2 mg
Valium Capsules 5 mg
Valium Syrup 2 mg/5 ml
Valium Tablets 2 mg
Valium Tablets 5 mg
Valium Tablets 10 mg
Valonorm Tonic Solution
Valrelease Capsules
Vanamil Tablets
Vapex Inhalant
Veganin Tablets
Veno's Adult Formula Cough Mixture
Veno's Cough Mixture
Veno's Honey & Lemon Cough Mixture
Veracolate Tablets
Verdiviton Elixir
Vervain Compound Tablets
Vi-Daylin Syrup
Vicks Coldcare Capsules
Vicks Cremacoat Syrup
Vick Cremacoat Syrup with Doxylamine Succinate
Vicks Cremacoat Syrup with Guaiphenesin
Vicks Cremacoat Syrup with Paracetamol & Dextromethorphan
Vicks Daymed
Vicks Formula 44 Cough Mixture
Vicks Inhaler
Vicks Medinite
Vicks Pectorex Solution
Vicks Sinex Nasal Spray
Vicks Vapo-Lem Powder Sachets
Vicks Vapour Rub
Videnal Tablets
Vigour Aids Tablets
Vigranon B Complex Tablets
Vigranon B Syrup
Vikelp Coated Tablets
Vikonon Tablets
Villescon Liquid
Villescon Tablets
Virvina Elixir
Visclair Tablets
Vita Diem Multi Vitamin Drops
Vita-Six Capsules
Vitalin Tablets
Vitamin & Iron Tonic (Epitone) Solution
Vitamin A & D Capsules BPC 1968 (Regent Laboratories)
Vitamin A Ester & Vitamin D2 Capsules (Regent Laboratories)
Vitamin A Ester Capsules (Regent Laboratories)
Vitamin A Ester Conc, Alpha Tocopherol Acetate Nat Capsules (Regent Laboratories)
Vitamin A 4500 Units & Vitamin D2 Capsules (Regent Laboratories)
Vitamin A 6000 Units & Vitamin D2 Capsules (Regent Laboratories)
Vitamin A, C & D Tablets (Approved Prescription Services)
Vitamin A, D & C Tablets (Regent Laboratories)
Vitamin B Complex Tablets (English Grains)
Vitamin B Complex with Brewer's Yeast Tablets (English Grains)
Vitamin B1 Dried Yeast Powder (Distillers)
Vitamin B1 Yeast Tablets (Distillers)
Vitamin B12 Tablets 0.01 mg
Vitamin B12 Tablets 0.025 mg
Vitamin B12 Tablets 0.05 mg
Vitamin B12 Tablets 0.10 mg
Vitamin B12 Tablets 0.25 mg
Vitamin B12 Tablets 0.5 mg
Vitamin B12 Tablets 1 mg
Vitamin C Tablets Effervescent 1 gramme
Vitamin Capsules (Regent Laboratories)
Vitamin Malt Extract with Orange Juice (Distillers)
Vitamin Mineral Capsules (Regent Laboratories)
Vitamin Tablets No B077
Vitamin Tablets No B081

Vitamin Tablets No B084
Vitaminised Iron & Yeast Tablets (Kirby Warrick Pharmaceuticals)
Vitanorm Malt Extract
Vitanorm Malt Extract Syrup
Vitasafe's CF Kaps Tablets
Vitasafe's WCF Kaps Tablets
Vitathone Chilblain Tablets
Vitatrop Tablets
Vitavel Powder for Syrup
Vitavel Solution
Vitepron Tablets
Vitorange Tablets
Vitrite Multi-Vitamin Syrup
Vykmin Fortified Capsules

W L Tablets
Wallachol Syrup
Wallachol Tablets
Wate-on Emulsion
Wate-on Emulsion Super
Wate-on Tablets
Wate-on Tablets Super
Wate-on Tonic
Waterhouse's All Fours
Wines
Woodwards Nursery Cream
Wrights Glucose with Vitamin D Powder
Wrights Vaporizing Fluid

Xanax Tablets 0.25 mg
Xanax Tablets 0.5 mg
Xanax Tablets 1.0 mg

Yeast & B12 Tablets (English Grains)
Yeast Plus Tablets (Thomas Guest)
Yeast-Vite Tablets
Yellow Phenolphthalein Tablets (any strengh)

Zactirin Tablets
Zefringe Sachets
Zubes Expectorant Cough Syrup
Zubes Original Cough Mixture
Zyriton Expectorant Linctus

Schedule 3B

Drugs to be Prescribed for Supply under Pharmaceutical Services only in Certain Circumstances

Drug 1	Patient 2	Condition 3
Clobazam	Any patient	Epilepsy

Index to Volume 1

abbreviated advertisement, meaning 257
  contents of 232
abortifacients, prohibition of advertisements 236
abuse of medicines 120
  and pharmacist's Code of Ethics 298
active ingredient, meaning 257
acupuncturists
  administration of medicines by 143
  sales of medicines to 111
addicts
  restriction on prescribing for 103
  sales by pharmacists, misconduct 254
administer, meanings 258
administration of medicinal products 95
  controls over 95
  in an emergency, list of products 95
  of veterinary drug 95
Adrenaline Injection, administration in an emergency 95
adulteration of medicinal products
  prohibition of 208-9
adverse reactions *see also* safety
  Committee on Safety of Medicines, role 23, 24
  early warning, 10
  register of, 24
  reporting, 10
  standard direction to industry 77, 78
  yellow card, 10, 23
advertising
  Acts controlling 216
  codes of practice 218-21
    compliance with 221
  to doctors 216, 227-34 see also advertisements to practitioners
  herbal remedies 151-4
  Medicines Act 14
  and quality of medicines, 221
  regulations 222
  restriction 6, 7
  and safety of medicines, 217, 221
  standard provisions of product licences, 217 - 18
Advertising Standards Authority 218
Advertising to Medical and Dental Practitioners Regulations 231
Advertising of Medicines Regulations 231
advertisement, *see also* representation
  abbreviated 232,
    meanings of, 222, 223, 257
  enforcement 225
  offences 223-5
    defences 225
advertisements directed to practitioners 226-34
  audio-visual 233
  data sheets 228-30
  direct mail 233
  professional publications, controls 230-2
    contents of 231, 232
    abbreviated 232
    exceptions 234
    multi-page 232, 257
    restrictions 231
  promotional aids 233, 279
  reference 234, 280
  specific limitations on contents of, 228
  trade 234, 280
  types 228-33
advertisements to public 235
  offences 235
  permitted 238-40
  prohibition 241
    exceptions 241
    partial 237, 238
    total 236, 237
  restrictions 235
advisory labels, recommended 289-94
aerosol
  meaning 258
  emergency supply of asthma remedy, 131
agricultural analyst,
  meaning 258
  sales of medicines to 111, 112
agricultural merchants
  de-registration and appeal 168
  personnel 168
  premises 167, 168
    inadequate 165, 168
  registration 167
  sale and supply 168, 169
  storage 169
agricultural requisites, meaning 259
Agriculture Ministers, meaning 259

aircraft operator or commander, drug
supply by 144
air–sea rescue launches, drug supply for 147
Aloxiprin
labelling 195, 196
pack size for general sale 97
veterinary drug, labelling of 196
warnings 195, 196
Aminonitrothiazole
pack size for veterinary products for
general sale 97
Amphotericin B, meaning 259
Amphotericins, meaning 259
ampoules, labelling of 188 *see also* labelling,
small containers
Amyl Nitrite, sales by pharmacists 254
analysis
certificates of 213
meaning of 259
purchase for, 111 112
sampling officers, powers of 111, 212, 213
animal,
dosage forms for 163, 164
meaning 163, 259
medicinal products 163-72 *See also*
veterinary drugs
animal feeding stuffs, *see also* medicated
animal feeding stuffs
manufacturers of 171
meanings 259
Animal Health Division of Ministry of
Agriculture, Fisheries and Food 19
licensing activities 48
Animal Health Trade Associations Group
(AHTAG) 168
Animal Health and Welfare Act,
provisions applicable to feeding stuffs
amendment 179
animals, definition 163, 259
animal test certificate, meaning 46, 81, 82,
259
exemption 81
labelling of products for 190-191
animal tests on potential drugs 72
anthroposophy 155
description of 155
remedies 156
advertising of, 157, 158
labelling of, 157, 158
antibiotics 42
emergency supply for oral use 131
illegal sales to farmers 165
licensing of 65
resistance in farm animals 15 See also
Swann Report
sales controlled 42, 98
antigens
meaning 259
licensing of, 65
antihistamines
labelling of 196
list of 196
antimicrobial properties
meaning 259
substances 42
licensing of 65
antisera
control over manufacture 84, 88
licensing of 65
meaning 259
antitoxins
controls over manufacture 84, 88
licensing of 65
meaning 260
application, meanings 260
appropriate committee, meaning 260
appropriate current monograph, meaning
207, 260
appropriate Ministers, meaning 260
appropriate non-proprietary name,
definitions 260-61
appropriate quantitative particulars,
meaning 261-62
approved name, meanings 262
approved synonym, meanings 262
Arsenic Act, 1851 2, 3
Aspirin
child resistant containers 183-4
colouring of products for administration
to children 184
labelling 195
name to be used 186
pack size for general sale 97
warnings 195, 196
veterinary drug 195
labelling 196
pack size for general sale 97
assemble, meanings 262
assembler's licence *see* manufacturer's
licence 87
Association of British Pharmaceutical
Industry
advertising practice codes 220-21
committee 220
Data Sheet Compendia 229
inadequacies 220-21
asthma remedies
containing Ephedrine, labelling of 197
emergency supply 131
Atropine Sulphate Injection, administration
in an emergency 95
automatic machines 116, 117
power to control information to be
displayed on 181
availability, biological 70-71

Bach remedies 156
advertising of 157, 158
labelling of 157, 158

Bacitracin, meaning 262
Bal Jivan Chamcho 56
  prohibition order 101
batch, meaning 263
batch working document 81
B.C.G. vaccine, meaning 263
Benzestrol, meaning 263
biochemic remedies 156
  advertising of 157
  description of 156
  labelling of 157
biological substance, meaning 263
blood, preparations of see preparations of blood
board, the meaning 263
body corporate
  carrying on a retail pharmacy business
    conditions applicable to 245-7
    jurisdiction of Statutory Committee 252-255
    titles permitted 248
borderline products 36, 129
bottles
  coloured glass, use 185
  fluted 184, 185
breathing gases, not subject to control 18
Brain Committee and Drug Addiction 8
British Approved Name, meaning 263
British Code of Advertising Practice 218, 219
  requirements 218
  sanctions 219
British National Formulary 206
British Pharmaceutical Codex 205
  standards 206
British Pharmacopoeia 18
  copyright 205
  description 21, 205-6
  tests 205
  Veterinary 205
British Pharmacopoeia Commission
  publications 25
  role 25
British Red Cross Society 145
British Standards Institution 146
British Veterinary Codex 206
Bromhexine Hydrochloride
  pack size for veterinary products for general sale 97
'bubble' packs, *see* package
business,
  definition 104, 263
  pharmacy – *see* retail pharmacy business
business name, meaning 263

cancer, prohibition of advertising to the public 236
Capreomycin, meaning 263
carcinogenicity 72
cataract, prohibition of advertising to the public 236
Cephalosporins, meaning 263
chemist, title use of 248
Chemistry of the Drug Substance 71, 72
Child Safety Regulations 183, 184
  child resistant containers 183-4
    exemptions from use 183, 184
  medicinal products 183
chiropodists
  administration of local analgesics by 140
  sale and supply of drugs by 139, 140
  sale and supply of drugs to 109
Chloroform, prohibition order and exemption 101, 102
Chlorpheniramine Injection, administration in an emergency 95
Chorionic Gonadotrophin, meaning 263
clinical trial 9, 263, 264
  arranged by practitioners 80-1
  exemption scheme 78
  meaning 263-4
  phases and studies 79
  product labelling 190
  purpose 46, 78
clinical trial certificate 46, 78-81 264
  application 79, 80
  exemptions 79
    doctors and dentists 80, 81
  licensed products 81
  meaning 264
  standard provisions 80
Clobazam in epilepsy 128, 345
coastal voyage, meaning 264
Cobalt Edetate Injection, administration in an emergency 95
Code of Ethics of Pharmaceutical Society of Great Britain 119, 245, 247, 297-307
  compliance with codes of practice 301
  confidentiality of information 301, 302
  efficacy 297
  efficient service 297, 298, 301
  environment 297
  guidance 296
  hours of service 305
  pharmacy premises
    displays near 306
    layout 306
  practitioner relationships 306, 307
  professional responsibility 301, 302
  professional services, publicity for 304
  records 302
  safety 296, 297
  sale of medicines
    liable to abuse 298
    for slimming 298
    methods of 299
    to children 298, 299
  sale of non-medicinal products 299
    to children 300
  signs and display 306

superintendent, duties of 303, 304
titles, use of 300, 301
codes of advertising practice 218-21
compliance with 221
Colistin, meaning 264
commercially interested party, meaning 264
Commission, meaning 265
Committee on Dental and Surgical Materials (CDSM) 27-8
Committee for Proprietary Medicinal Products (CPMP) (EEC) 15, 16
Committee on Radiation from Radioactive Medicinal Products (CRRMP) 28
Committee on the Review of Medicines, (CRM)
composition 25
drugs reviewed 27
pregnancy, safety of medicines during 26, 27
procedure 25, 26
product licences 14
role 25
sub-committees and roles 26
Committee on the Safety of Drugs (CSD) (Dunlop Committee) 10
adverse reaction reporting 10
sub-committee roles 9
Committee on the Safety of Medicines (CSM)
adverse reactions 23
composition 23
establishment and role 22, 23
subcommittees 23
complete feeding stuff, meaning 265
composition, meaning 265
Consumer Protection Act, 1961 36
contact lenses 41
fluids 41, 185
container labelling 193, 194
subject to licensing 65
meanings 265
types 40, 41
substances 41,
data sheets 222
labelling 193-4
leaflets 193-4
meaning 265
container, *See also* bottles
child-resistant 182, 184
types 184
drug 71
effect on medicine 71
fluted bottles, 184
functions 182
glass and alkalinity 183
meaning, 182, 265
offences 183
and package 182
small 188
contamination, microbial 21
contraceptives 198
advertising restrictions
intra-uterine
advertising restriction 41
meaning 41
licensing 41, 65
spermicidal
meaning 283-4
labelling and advertising 198
contravention, meaning 265
control products, meaning 46, 265
controlled drug (CD)
CD list, 126
CD inv list 125-6
CD lic list 127
CD no reg 127
emergency supply 131
prescriptions for 125
records of sales and supplies 134
Corticotrophin, meaning 265
cosmetic
meaning 265
curative claims, effects of 36, 65
labelling 36, 189
'the Council', meaning 266
'the Council Directive' meaning 266
counter-prescribing, pharmacist 132, 133
creams, emergency supply of, 131
Current Problems 24
cyanogenetic substances, meaning 42, 266

Dangerous Drugs Acts 3, 4
data sheet
importance 228, 229
meaning 266
particulars 290
requirements 229
structure and provisions 229, 230
Data Sheet Compendium, meaning 266
dental caries prevention schemes 143
dental filling substances 35, 40
dental practitioners see dentist
Dental Practitioners' Formulary 128, 206, 207
Dentist
administration of medicines by 138
advertisements etc. sent to 227-234
chloroform, sale and supply 201
exemptions from licensing requirements 52
meaning 266
phenacetin, sale or supply 101
prescribing, restrictions on under NHS 128
sale and supply of medicines by 137, 138
sale and supply of medicines to 110
description, meaning see medicinal products of the same description
deterioration of medicines 14
Dextran Injections, meaning 266

Dextrans, meaning 266
Dextrose Injection Strong BPC,
  administration in an emergency 95
diabetes, prohibition of advertising to the
  public, 236
Dienoestrol, meaning 266
Diphenhydramine Injection,
  administration in an emergency 95
disease, meaning 267
dispensary 130
dispensed medicinal product
  definition 123, 267
dispensing medicines 123-36
  collection and delivery 132
  containers 129, 130
  emergency supply 131, 132
  in hospitals 134-6
  labelling 130
  prescriber requirements 129
doctor
  meaning 267
  administration of medicines by 138
  advertisements etc. sent to 237-34
  chloroform, sale and supply 101
  exemption from licensing requirements 52
  phenacetin, sale and supply 101
  prescribing sale and supply of medicines
    137, 138
    restrictions on under NHS 128
    prescribing for addicts 103, 125
  sale of medicines to 110
  sale of medicines by 137-8
dosage unit, meaning 267
drugs, addictive see controlled drugs
  drugs, dangerous see controlled drugs
drug interactions, warnings 289-91
drug purity 1, 2
drug testing 7

educational laboratories
  sale of medicines to 112
effervescent, meaning 267
efficacy 221, 222
  advertising and 221
  clinical trials to show, 79
  definition, Medicines Act, 1968 13
  licensing 46
  pharmacists Code of Ethics 297
  quantification 13
emergency supply of medicines
  life-saving drugs 95
  prescription only medicines 130-2
    at doctor's request 130, 131
    at patient's request 131, 132
  pharmacy records of 133, 134
  Society's guidelines 131
employee, medical treatment 144
endocrine gland products 2
enforcement of provisions of the Act 30, 31
  inspection of premises of licence holders
    63
  inspection of ships, aircraft etc 63
  powers of inspectors 212
  provisions relating to purity and quality
    210, 211
  ....of medicated feeding stuffs 178
  ....of veterinary drugs 169
enforcement authority, meaning 267
enrolled nurse, meaning 267
enzymes, licensing of, 65
Ephedrine and its salts, labelling of oral
  dosage forms 197
epilepsy, prohibition of advertising to the
  public 236
ethanol
  denatured 101
  duty 100
  retail sale of 99
  use and control 99
ethical controls, medicine sales 119, 120
Erythromycin, meaning 268
European Economic Community, directives
  15, 16
European Pharmacopoeia 206
excipient, meaning 46, 268
exempted users, sales, supplies and
  administration 137-47
exemption, meaning 268
expiry date, meaning 268
export
  certificates 57
  meaning 268
  product labelling 192, 193
external use, meanings 268, 269
eye preparations
  eye drops – restrictions on sale 96
    sale etc. by opticians 142-3
  eye ointments – restriction for drops 96
    sales etc. by opticians 142-3

false or misleading, meaning 269
feeding stuffs 173-80 *See* medicated feeding
  stuffs
  additives 43
feed supplement, meaning 269
finally disposed of, meaning 269
first aid equipment suppliers 147
Fisher v. Bell, 1961 106
fluted bottles 184, 185
foetal effects 72
Follicle-stimulating Hormone, meaning 270
food
  labelling 189
  meanings 270
Food and Drugs Acts 1, 4, 11
Food and Drugs Authority
  duties 31, 203, 211
  meaning 270
foreign or international compendium of
  standards, meaning 270

the Gazette, meaning 270
G.S.L. see General Sale List
General Sale List 94
  classification 96, 97
  Orders, 96, 97
  pack size limits 97
  retail sale 116
Gentamicin, meaning 270
Gentamicins, meaning 270
glaucoma, prohibition of advertising to the public, 236
Government Chemist, feeding stuffs analysis 176
Greenwood v. Whelan, 1966 115
Griseofulvin,
  prohibition order 102
    exemptions from restrictions 102
Guide to Good Dispensing Practice 129, 309-12
  batch working document 89
  equipment 310, 311
  hygiene 311
  materials, control 311, 312
  premises suitability 309, 310
  records 89
Guide to Good Manufacturing Practice (Orange Guide) 19, 86, 87
  definition of terms 87
Guide to Self-Assessment of Professional Practice Activities 301, 313-26
  administration 314, 315, 323-4
  aims 313
  counter-prescribing *see* response to symptoms
  definitions 325-6
  diagnostic testing 317
  dispensing procedures 316
  education, continuing 318
  medicines and ingredient procurement 315
  public dealings 317
  quality assurance 321, 322
  radiopharmacy 323-5
  sale of medicines, poisons etc. 316, 317
  specialist information 320
  symptoms, response to 318, 319
  ward, service 319, 320

hair and scalp treatment 146
haemostatics, absorbable, licensing of 65
Health Authority, meaning 270
health centre, meaning 271
Health Ministers, meaning 271
health prescription, meaning 271
hearing by person appointed, 58
Heparin, definition 271
herbal remedy, meaning 271
herbal remedies 149-54
  advertising 151, 152
  control of sales 150, 151
  labelling 151, 152, 198, 242
  licensing 150
  meaning 149, 150, 271
  which are pharmacy products 152-4
  product licence application 74
  sellers, controls 156, 157
herbalists
  licensing 53, 151
  pharmacy medicines, and 153, 154
  sales control 150, 151
herd, meaning 271
Hexachlorophane labelling 197
Hexoestrol, meaning 271
High Court, appeal against Licensing Authority decision 58
home-going ship, meaning 271
  inspection of, 63
homoeopathic practitioners 156
  homoeopathic product
  description 155
  General Sale List 157
  labelling 157, 158, 198, 252
  licensing 156
  preparation and dilution permitted 158-61
  types of 156
homoeopathy 155-61
hormones, licensing of, 65
horsewormers 169-71
hospitals
  charitable, dispensing 136
  meaning 271
  NHS
    dispensing 134-6
    licensing exemption 53, 54
    Pharmacy and Therapeutics Committee 135
    take home medication 135
  private hospitals
    controlled drug licence 136
    licensing 54
hover vehicle, meaning 271
Hoyle v. Hitchman 1879 209
Hyaluronidase, meaning 271
Hydrocortisone Injection, adminstration in an emergency 95

imported proprietary product
  application for product licence for 74, 75
  meaning, 39, 272
  de Peipjer Judgment 55
  EEC Court of Justice 55
  licensing, and 54-6
  manufacturer's undertakings 74
  named patients 55, 57
  parallel importation 54, 55
  personal use, for 54
  product labelling 192
  product licence 74, 75
  re-exportation of 56
  veterinarians 54

imported ready-made veterinary drug,
  meaning 39, 272
Independent Broadcasting Authority Code
  of Advertising Practice 219, 220
industrial methylated spirits 100-1
information sheet, meaning 272
ingredient
  meaning 272
  labelling 189
inhaler, meaning 272
inland waters, meaning 272
inspector, meaning 272
Insulin
  meaning 272
  exempt from POM 98
international non-proprietary name,
  meaning 272
intra-uterine contraceptive device
  licensing, 65
  meaning 272

Kanamycin, meaning 272
Kanamycins, meaning 272
Kidney disease, prohibition of advertising to
  the public 236

Labelling
  advertising 252
  animal feeding stuffs 175-7, 191, 192
  animal test products 190, 191
  clinical trial products 190
  contact lens substances 193
  contract manufacture 194
  cosmetics 189
  crated for delivery 194
  dispensed products 200, 201
  general provisions 186, 187
  export and import 192
  herbal remedies 151
  ingredients 189
  meaning 272
  offences 201, 202
    defences 202
    penalties 202
  products for sale 187-94
  standard requirements 187, 188
  small containers 188
  'specials' pharmacist own remedies 189
  surgical materials 189
  unit packs 189
  veterinary drugs 194
  warnings 195-8, 289-94 *See also* warnings
Labelling of Medicated Animal Feeding
  Stuffs Regulations, 1973 176
  and Animal Test Certificate 177
Labels, requirements 185-7
laboratories, persons in charge and drug use
  112
leaflet
  as advertisements 198, 199
    information 199
    meaning 272
licence *See also* manufacturers', product,
  wholesale,
  applications, 21
  DHSS staff 114
  drug properties 46
  fees 46
    annual calculation 59-62
    capital 59
    late payment 61
    lesser 61
    overpayment and refund 61, 62
    penalty, late payment 61
    reduction 60
    waiver 60
  justices' 99
  meaning 272
  Medicines Division DHSS 19
  product 13, 14 *See also* product licence
  refusal and appeal 22
  review of products 176
  suspension and revocation 49, 50, 58
  variation 50
licence of right, meaning 70, 272
licensing 156
  enforcement 63
  exemptions 51-4
    dentists 51
    doctors 51
    herbalists 53
    midwives 52
    NHS hospitals 53
    nurses 52
    pharmacists 51
    veterinarians 52
  exportation 56, 57
  herbal remedies 150
  homoeopaths 156
  importation 54-6
  offences 62
    defences 62, 63
licensing authority
  appeal against 50, 57, 58
    hearing 58
  composition 48
  constraints upon 48
  meaning 48-50, 273
  parallel imports 56
  powers 49
  safety and efficacy 48
  section 21(1) notice 57
  section 44 letter 50
  suspension and revocation of licences 49,
    50
licensing system 45-63
  activities controlled 45
  advantages 47
  costs 47
  disadvantages 47

and safety 45, 46
limited list *See also* NHS Limited list
the Lincomycins, meaning 273
Lincomycin, meaning 273
local authority, meaning 273

Manual of Specifications for Ingredients and Analytical Methods 73
manufacture, meaning 273
manufacturer, packing for another 104
manufacturer's licence
activities covered by 83, 84
application for 83, 84
assembler's, 87
categories of 84
contamination 88
equipment and premises 86, 87
exemption for pharmacists 86, 87
inspection of premises 84
qualified person 84-6
duties 85
sales permitted 146
standard provisions 87, 88
mark, meaning 273
master (ship's)
foreign ship, supply of controlled drugs to 113
meaning 273
sale of medicines to 112
supply of controlled drug to 113
maximum daily dose or "MDD", meaning 274
maximum dose or "MD", meaning 274
maximum strength, meanings 274
medicated, meanings 274
medicated animal feeding stuff *see* medicated feeding stuffs
medicated feeding stuff 173-180
additives 43, 75, 173
analysis 178
definition 173, 259
future controls 179, 180
inspectors 178
labelling and packaging 175-7, 191, 192
manufacture 174
commercial companies 175
co-operatives 175
farmers, animal owners 174, 175
medication 174, 175
manufacturers, drug sales to 171
meaning 39, 40, 274
medicated, features 39, 40
compounders 90
controls 175
definition 174, 274
offences 178, 179
quality control 177
sales 177
sampled portion 282
standards, enforcement of 177, 178
types 174
medicinal products
administration of 35, 36
borderline 36
contact lens substances 40, 41
cyanogenetic substances 42
definitions 33, 35, 36, 275
dental filling substances 40
excluded products 34, 35
imported proprietary 38, 39
ingredients 34
interpretations 36, 37
intra-uterine contraceptive products 41
licensing 46
proprietary 38, 39
radioactive substances 41, 42
surgical materials 40
thyrostatic compounds 43
medicinal products of the same description, meaning 275
medicinal purpose, definition 33, 34
medicinal test on animals, meaning 275
medicines *See also* pharmacy medicines and prescription only
analysis 4
classes 94
classification 96-9
commerce 8
microbial contamination of 21
Medicines Act, 1968 11-15
defences 29, 30
development, influences 15, 16
enforcement 30, 31
expert committees 17-28 *See also* individual committee
labelling and packaging control 181-202
licensing system 45-63, 65-82, 83-92
medicinal products definitions of 33-9
offences 28, 29
safety, quality and efficacy 12
sale and distribution of medicines 93-7
warranty defence 30
Medicines Commission
constitution 20
functions 20-2
Medicines Division
Defect Report Centre 20
enforcement 20
inspection 20
legislation drafting 19, 20
licensing 19, 48
enforcement 63
member meaning 275
Mepyramine Injection, administration in an emergency 95
methylated spirits
industrial (IMS) 100, 101
restrictions 101
mineralized 100
Methylated Spirits Regulations, 100

midwives
administration of medicines 140
administration of Pethidine 140
assembly of products 52
licensing exemption 52
sale of medicines to 111
sale of Pethidine to 111
supply of pharmacy medicines 140
supply of prescription only medicines 140
mines, drug supply 141, 142
mineral salts, meaning 275
the Ministers meaning 275
agriculture 17
enforcement provision of Act 30, 31
powers and duties 17-19
product specification 18
the Misuse of Drugs Regulations, meaning 275
Regulation 5, 145
schedule 4, 127
monograph, meaning 276
monograph name, meaning 276
multipage advertisement, meaning 276

nature or quality demanded 209
naturopaths
administration of medicines by 143
sale of medicines to 111
Neomycin, meaning 276
Neomycins, meaning 276
NHS limited list 128, 129, 327-45
assessment 128
borderline products 129
complete list 329-47
Northern Ireland 12, 17, 31, 212
the Northern Ireland Enforcement Authority
agricultural merchants 169
meaning 276
saddlers 171
notice, meaning 276
nurses 52
administration of medicines by 141
assembly, exempt from licensing, 52
in factories 141
in mines 141, 142

occupational health scheme, meaning 276
supply of medicines in course of 145
offence under this Act
meaning 276
mens rea, 29
offshore installations managers 112, 113
drug supply 144
sale of medicines to 112
ointment, emergency supply of 131
operator meaning 276
ophthalmic opticians 110
sale of medicines to 111, 142, 143
emergency sales of medicines by 142
optician, meaning 276
oral contraceptive, emergency supply of 131
prescribing, Medicines Commission recommendation, 22
Orange Guide 19 *See also* Guide to Good Manufacturing Practice
Order of Malta Ambulance Corps 145
osteopaths
administration of medicines by 143
sales of medicines to 111
Oxytetracycline, meaning 276

package, meaning 182, 276
bubble pack 182, 189
inserts 198 *See also* leaflets
strip-pack 182, 189
unit pack 182, 189
pack size limits 97
Partridge v. Crittenden, 1968 106
Paracetamol
child resistant containers 183, 184
colouring of products for administration to children 184
labelling 186, 187, 188
name to be used 186
warning 195, 196
pack size for general sale 97
veterinary drug
pack size limitation 97
paralysis, prohibition of advertising to the public 236
parenteral administration, meaning 277
parenteral injection, meaning 277
patent medicines
law improvements 6, 7
non-secret remedies 6
revenue 5
secret remedies 6
Select Committee Report 4, 5
de Peijper judgement 55, 75
Penicillin, meaning 277
Penicillins, meaning 277
person appointed, hearing by 58
person responsible for the composition of a medicinal product, meaning 277
Pethidine, use by midwives 140
Pharmaceutical Price Regulation Scheme 227
Pharmaceutical Society of Great Britain
Code of Ethics 245, 247
enforcement role
agricultural merchants 169
saddlers 171
meaning 277
registering body
for pharmacists 244-5
for pharmacies 247-8
for agricultural merchant etc. 166
for saddlers 169
Royal Charter 245

Pharmaceutical Society of Great Britain v. Boots Cash Chemists (Southern) Ltd, 1952 106, 118
Pharmaceutical Society of Great Britain v. Harwood 29
Pharmaceutical Society of Great Britain v. Logan 29, 117
Pharmaceutical Society of Great Britain v. Piper 3
pharmacies
  changing hands 248
  definition 248
  equipment 310, 311
  facilities 248
  hygiene 311
  layout 306
  medicine storage 120, 121
  offences 251, 252
  personal control 246
  premises 309, 310
  records 133, 134
    controlled drugs 134
    emergency supplies 134
    prescription only medicines 112, 113
  refrigerator 121
  register, disqualification 249
  registered 51
  retail sales 117-119, 245-7
    conditions to comply 245, 246
    eligibility 245
    representative 246
  Statutory Committee 249-55 *see also* Statutory Committee
  Title restrictions 248
pharmacist
  Code of Ethics 245, 295-307 *See also* Code of Ethics
  counter-prescribing 132, 133
  examinations 244
  licensing exemption 51
  manufacturer's licence 88, 89
  meaning 277
  own brand medicines 51
    labelling 190
  poison sales 120
  registration 245
  self-assessment *see* Guide to Self-Assessment
  titles used 248, 249
Pharmacy Act, 1954 244
  Statutory Committee 250
Pharmacy and General Sale Exemption Orders 94
Pharmacy and Medicines Act 1941 11
  and advertising 7
pharmacy medicine [P]
  criteria 97, 98
  distribution chain 109
  meanings 277
pharmacy retail sale 118
PML *see* pharmacy and merchants list
pharmacy and merchants list 118, 119, 164, 165
  pharmacists records 119
  sales from pharmacies 118, 119
Pharmacy and Poisons Act, 1933 3, 4, 11, 243, 244
Phenacetin, prohibition order and exemption 101, 102
Phenacetin-only product, meaning 277
Phenobarbitone, phenobarbitone sodium for an epileptic emergency, supply of 131
Phenylephrine Hydrochloride
  pack size for veterinary products for general sale 97
plasma, meaning 278
plant, meaning 278
poisons
  Acts relating 2, 3
  labelling 4
Poisons and Pharmacy Act, 1908 3, 243
post-marketing surveillance 24
Polymixin B, meaning 278
Polymixins, meaning 278
POM's *see* prescription only medicines
Potassium Chlorate
  pack size for veterinary products for general sale 97
poultry, meaning 278
poultry vaccination services 171
practitioner, meaning 278
pregnancy, Safety of Drug Usage in 26, 27
premises, meaning 278
preparations of blood
  licensing of 65
  meaning 278
preparations of the pituitary (posterior lobe), meaning 278
pre-school dental scheme, meaning 278
prescribed, meaning 278
Prescription Only Medicines (POM)
  controlled drugs, additional restrictions over, 125
  definition 278
  distribution chain 109
  doses 98
  emergency supply 130-2
    circumstances 130
    doctor request 130, 131
    patient request 131, 132
  ingredients 98-99
  limits 98, 99
  medicines and veterinary products 98
  ophthalmic optician use 142, 143
  parenteral products 98
  prescription requirement 124, 125
prescriptions
  collection and delivery arrangements 132
    definitions 124
    repeat 125

requirements
for controlled drugs 125
for POM's 124, 125
Privy Council, pharmacist deregistration 249
product licence 13, 14, 65-78
advertising 217
application data required 67-74
Part I (general matters) 68, 69
Part II (pharmaceutical data) 69-71
development pharmaceutics 70, 71
formula and containers 69, 71
manufacturing process details 70
quality control 70
stability 71
Part III, experimental and biological 72, 73
studies in humans 73
abridged 73
authorisation 67
Chemistry of Drug Substance 71, 72
herbal remedies 74
holders 66
records 76, 77
sales 146
Standard Provision 76, 77
parallel importation PL(PI) 74
products affected 65, 66
renewal applications 78
responsibility for composition 66
special 66
specifications 67
standard directions 77
standard provisions 76
relating to advertising 217, 218
validity and renewal 78
veterinary products 75, 76
product licence of right, meaning, 278
professional publication, meaning, 278, 279
prohibition orders 101-3
Promethazine Hydrochloride Injection, administration in an emergency 95
promotional aid, meaning, 279
proprietary designation, meaning, 279
Proprietary Association of Great Britain, role 219
Code of Advertising Practice 219
proprietary medicinal product, meaning, 279
proprietary products
definitions and exclusions 38
imported 39
poisons 3
proprietary veterinary drug, meaning 279
protein concentrate, meaning 279
public, protection from quacks *see also* advertising to public
purpose, meaning 279
qualified person
at disposal of manufacturer 84-5
at disposal of importers 90
meaning 279
qualifying business, meaning 279
quality 203-13 *see also* standards
aspects 203
defective drugs 204
definition, 12, 13
enforcement 210-12
body 211
inspectors 212
Minister's role 211
Northern Ireland 212
sampling officers 212, 213
Scotland 211
manufacture, compliance with 203
medicated feeding stuffs 213
offences 208, 209
third party 209, 210
warranty defence 210
responsibilities 203
testing, purchases 111, 112
quality assurance 328
quality control
definition 328
manufacturing 322
pharmacists 321, 322
quality assurance 86
specifications 70
quantity, meaning 280

radioactive appliances 41, 42
radioactive medicinal product, meaning 280
human use restrictions 103
radioactive substance, meaning 280
radiopharmacy, self-assessment 322, 323
ready-made veterinary drug, meaning 280
records, controlled drugs 113, 114
emergency supply 134
pharmacy sales 119
prescriptions 133-4
reference advertisement, meaning 280
register, meaning 280
registered ophthalmic optician, meaning 280
registered pharmacy, meaning 280
registering body, meaning 280
the registrar, meaning 281
relevant business, meaning 281
relevant monograph, meaning 208, 281
relevant practitioner, meaning 281
renewal application, meaning 281
repeatable prescription, meaning 281
representation
meaning 223, 281
offences relating to 224, 225
response to symptoms described, 132-3
retail outlets 115, 116
shop and stall 115, 116
retail pharmacy business, meaning, 245, 281
retail sale
ethical controls 119, 120
General Sale List 116, 118

human use 115
meaning 103-7
offer or exposure 105, 106
pharmacists 117-19
records 119
self-service 117, 118
supervision 177
pharmacy and merchants list 118
premises 107 *see also* retail outlets
definition 115
prescription only medicines 119
and supply 105
revenue raising 2
stamp duty on medicines 5
the Rifamycins, meaning 281
Rifamide, meaning 282
Ristocetins, meaning 282
Roberts v Littlewoods Mail Order Stores Ltd 1943, 117
Royal National Lifeboat Institution, drug supply 144, 145

saddlers
horsewormer sales 169-71
personnel and qualifications 170
premises registration 169, 170
sale and supply 170
storage 170
saddlery business, meaning 282
saddlery requisities, meaning 282
safety
and advertising 221
definition, Medicines Act, 1968 12
licensing 48
pharmacists Code of Ethics 296, 297
quantification 13
Safety of Drugs, Joint Sub-Committee recommendations 8, 9
St Andrew's Ambulance Association 145
St. John's Ambulance Association 145
sale *see also* retail, wholesale
mail order 107
offer or exposure 105, 106
promotion *see* advertising
when and where 106
sale and distribution of drugs, controls
exemptions 94, 95
retail outlets 93
sales, exempted 137-47
Salicylamide
pack size for general sale 97
veterinary drug, labelling of 196
sampled portion, meaning 282
sampling officers 212, 213
school dental scheme, meaning 282
scientific laboratories, sales of medicines to 112
Scotland 12, 17, 31, 211
Second Council Directive, meaning 282
section 21(1) notice, 57
section 44(2) letter 50
Select Committee on Patent Medicines 4-6, 216, 217
self-service methods
meaning 282
not to be used for [P] medicines 299
use by retailers 117
use by pharmacists discouraged 117
sell, meaning 283
sell by retail, meaning 283
sera, meaning 283
serum, meaning 283
ship
administration of medicines on board 143
medicines supplied to 112
ships owners and masters 112, 113
drug supply 143
foreign 114
shop 115
chemists, *see* pharmacies
market stalls 115
meaning 115
smallpox vaccine, meaning 283
Snake Venom Antiserum, administration in an emergency 95
soap, meaning 283
Sodium Nitrite Injection, administration in an emergency 95
Sodium Thiosulphate Injection, administration in an emergency 95
sound recording, meaning 283
Special and Miscellaneous Cases Order 1972 189
Special and Transitional Cases Order 1971 189
Special Cases Order, the meaning 283
specially authorised person, a, meaning 283
specified particulars, the meaning 283
specified publication, meaning 283
current edition, meaning 207
spermicidal contraceptive, meaning 283
advertisements 198
labelling 198
special warnings 198
spirits, use and control 99-101
stability, drug 71
standard directions
on reporting adverse reactions 77
standards 204-8
appropriate current monograph 207, 208
compliance 208
formularies 206,207
pharmacopoeias 204-6
relevant monograph 208
specified publications 207
Statutory Committee 249-55
appeals 255
bodies corporate 255
constitution 250
convictions 253

courses of actions 252
disqualifications 254
jurisdiction 251
meaning 284
misconduct cases 253, 254
procedure 251
sources of law 250
standard provisions for licences
meaning 284
records of reports of adverse reactions, 76
relating to advertising 217-8
relating to particular types of products, 77
state registered chiropodist, meaning 284
state registered physiotherapist, meaning 284
Sterile Pralidoxime, administration in an emergency 95
Stilbenes
meaning 284
restriction on use in veterinary products 43
Stilboestrol, meaning 284
Stone v Boreham, 1958 115
storage of medicinal products 120, 121
of controlled drugs in pharmacies 120
importance of correct conditions 203, 204
streptodornase, meaning 284
streptokinase, meaning 284
Streptomycin, meaning 284
Prohibition order exemption 102-3
strip pack 182
substance, meaning 285
Sulphanilamide, prohibition order 102, 103
exemptions from 102
meaning 285
Summers v Roberts, 1943 115
superintendent pharmacist, duties of 303, 304
supervision of sale of [P] medicines 117
meaning of 326
supplier, meaning 285
supply, meaning 105, 285
surgical materials, meaning 285
Swann Report 15, 173, 174
Sweet v Parsley, 1969, 29

tests for sterility, meaning 285
Tetracycline, meaning 285
Thalidomide 8
Tetracyclines, meaning 285
time allowed, meaning 285
Therapeutic Substance Act, 1956 4, 11
thyrostatic substances 43
meaning 286
restrictions on use in veterinary products 43,
toothpastes
labelling, 186
toxins,
licensing of 65
meaning 286
toxicity 9
testing 72
trade advertisement, meaning 286
trade mark, meaning 286
treatment, meaning 286
tuberculosis, prohibition of advertising to the public 236
turnover, annual fee calculation 60, 61

unit, meaning 286
unit pack 182
unit preparation, meaning 286
universities, sales of medicines to 146

vaccines,
licensing of, 65
meaning 286
manufacturers licence 88
poultry 138, 171
preparation 51
Vancomycin, meaning 286
vending machines *see* automatic machines
venereal disease
Act 1917, 6, 11
meaning 287
prohibition of advertising to the public 236
veterinarians
importing 138
licensing exemption 52
sale and supply of medicines by 138, 139
sale of medicines to 110
'under his care', meaning, 138, 139
veterinary drug 163-71
abuses 165, 166
classes of 165, 166
definition 28
domestic and agricultural animals 75
feeding stuffs 167 see also feeding stuffs
horsewormers by saddlers 169-71
labelling 186, 194
meaning 287
Pharmacy and Merchant List Products 118, 164
product licence application 75, 76
proprietary 39
ready made 39
sales by agricultural merchant 167
sales to feeding stuffs manufacturers 171
sellers, controls 166, 167
Veterinary Drugs Exemption Order, meaning 165, 287
Veterinary Drugs (POM) Order 98
veterinary medicinal product, meaning 287
veterinary practitioner, meaning 287
veterinary prescription, meaning 287
Veterinary Products Committee (VPC)
establishment 24

pharmacist supervision 165
role 24
veterinary surgeon, meaning 287
Viomycin, meaning 287
vitamin preparation, meaning 287
vitamins, meaning 287
voluntary bodies, drug supply 145

warnings
alcohol interactions 289, 290
drowsiness 289, 290
General Sale List Products 195, 196
Pharmacy Medicines 196, 197
Prescription Only Medicines 196-8
recommended labelling 289-94
spermicides 198
warranty defence 30, 210
White Paper on Safety and Quality of Medicines, 11
wholesale dealer's licence 46, 90
application 90, 91
confectionery 92
exemptions 91
and manufacturer 92
requirement 90
standard provisions 91
wholesale sale 109-114
controls, reasons for 109
distribution chain 109
meaning 103-7
midwives 110, 111
pharmacy, POM 112, 113
practitioners 110
veterinarians 104
writing, meaning 287

yellow card
report numbers 23
veterinary 24